MW01469761

1 MONTH OF
FREE
READING

at

www.ForgottenBooks.com

By purchasing this book you are eligible for one month membership to ForgottenBooks.com, giving you unlimited access to our entire collection of over 1,000,000 titles via our web site and mobile apps.

To claim your free month visit:
www.forgottenbooks.com/free788405

ISBN 978-0-266-80077-4
PIBN 10788405

QUIT YOUR MEANNESS.

SERMONS AND SAYINGS

OF

REV. SAM P. JONES

OF GEORGIA.

WITH AN INTRODUCTION

BY W. M. LEFTWICH, D. D.

Only Authorized Subscription Edition.

CRANSTON & STOWE,

CINCINNATI, CHICAGO, ST. LOUIS.

1886.

Copyright by

CRANSTON & STOWE,

1886.

PREFACE.

I HAVE been gratified that, through stenographic reports of my sermons in the great daily newspapers at various points, I have been able to address a larger audience, by far, than could assemble in any hall or be reached by any human voice. I have always encouraged the press in giving the widest dissemination to what I believe to be truths worth uttering. But, when there came a demand for these discourses in the more permanent shape of a book, I naturally felt that the author should have the privilege of choosing his own publishers, and the right of final revision of such thoughts as were to be thus committed to the future.

Few men, I imagine, would care to go into a book as reported in extemporaneous speech. To protect myself I have been compelled to copyright my sermons. I am not working for literary honor, but whatever literary value there may be in my book is my own, and I will not consent to its being made a matter of speculation by thieves. I always did hate a thief, any way.

Messrs. Cranston & Stowe, of Cincinnati, are

the authorized publishers of my Cincinnati sermons, and of all others that may be published for several years. Of previous sermons the Southern Methodist Publishing House, of Nashville, Tenn., were the legitimate publishers. These houses will practice no extortion, but will sell the books as low as other books of corresponding quality, as to material and workmanship. As I have said before in a public card, I hope that no person will become a partaker in dishonesty by "dealing in stolen goods," and what is not stolen, if put out in my name, is counterfeit, save as above indicated.

Sam. P. Jones

⁎ The sermons preached in Music Hall, Cincinnati, were stenographically reported by Mr. Ed. F. Flynn for the *Cincinnati Commercial Gazette*. His reports were unusually accurate, and have been largely used for this edition.

INTRODUCTION.

NATURE, wearied of monotony, breaks up the surface of continents, here and there, by throwing up huge mountain ranges, ribbing them with rock and crowning them with snow. Thus climates are modified and the conditions of life are changed. So, in the history of the world, God, now and then, breaks the monotony of human life, by thrusting out extraordinary men, endued with power from on high, to modify the ordinary conditions of human life, and to influence the social sentiments and change the moral standards of generations. The rarest gems are from the deepest depths; the costliest jewels are from the roughest rocks; and so, the highest forms of genius are in the crudest specimens of humanity. True genius stands aloof from men, disdains beaten paths, scorns common methods, follows no footsteps, but lives and moves and has its being in a world created by and for itself. Extraordinary genius given, extraordinary works follow. Extraordinary crises in the Church are always met by extraordinary men; and these men have been, for the most part, taken from the common walks and conditions of life.

It is a noteworthy fact, that the men who have moved the world into higher conditions of thought and life, have come from families and tribes of whom nothing was said concerning priesthood. Height and depth are relative terms, and the height to which men sometimes rise can only be measured by the depths out of which they come. Many of the prophets were extraordinary men, and came from families of low degree.

Yet, the history of the Church is the biography of extraordinary men. When God would call the Church back from apostasy, and lift it out of corruption and superstition, he raises up extraordinary men, endows them with genius, endues them with power from on High, and sends them out as a voice crying in the wilderness, "Prepare ye the way of the Lord, make his paths straight." Besides the prophets, apostles, and early martyrs, Wycklif, Huss, Luther, Calvin, Knox, and Wesley, are conspicuous illustrations. The coming of these men was preceded by signs and tokens that stirred the people and awakened general expectation of extraordinary movements and great changes in the condition of the Church, just as the kindling glow along the horizon and the gray streaks of dawn that shoot up in the heavens, give certain prophecy of the coming day. We may well believe that the eyes of the people were holden then that they could not read the signs of the times, just as our eyes seem to be holden now that we can not see the signs of these times, and our ears are heavy that we can not hear the voice crying, "Repent ye, for the kingdom of heaven is at hand."

Do we not hear the voice crying in the wilderness? What mean the extraordinary movements in the Church of to-day? It becomes us to note with profound interest the work of lay-preachers and evangelists who are stirring the Church in the great centers, and to the farthest bounds. Who will dare say that this movement is not of God, and that the extraordinary men who are calling the Church to judgment and the world to repentance, are not called and commissioned of God for this very work.

"But they are evangelists." Granted. Will any man say that evangelists are not divinely called and sent to do the work of evangelists? "But we do not want evangelists." That is a matter of small concern to the Head of the Church, who "gave some apostles and some prophets, and some evangelists, for the perfecting of the saints, and for the work of the ministry." "But we do not recognize evangelists as a distinct order in the ministry." Suppose you do not. God has put the seal of his approval upon them, by working through them mightily to the pulling down of strongholds, and the saving of multiplied thousands that could not be reached by the stated pastors and local Churches. What are we that we should call in question God's wisdom, and repudiate God's methods? Whatever we may say, evangelists have come to stay, and to be a recognized power in the Church in these last days, upon whom the Lord has laid his hand for a mighty work among the people. Whether the Head of the Church is using them to prepare the way for great changes in the conditions of his kingdom, and to bring in a new era in the history of the Church, we may not know. But we do know that men of special gifts and extraordinary power are leading the hosts of God from conquering to conquest, and moving the multitudes in the great centers of population as they have never been moved before during the present generation. The highest wisdom suggests the prayerful study of this wonderful movement in the Church of God, not for purposes of hypercriticism, but to discover the hand of God and be led by it into whatever conditions of life and methods of work he may be opening for his people. Those who cry out against irregularity and crudeness of speech should be silenced by the fact that the history of all great religious movements is repeating itself both in the ground of objection and the character of objectors; or they should be warned by the words of the great Apostle to the Gentiles—"Beware, therefore, lest that come upon you, which is spoken of in the prophets : Behold, ye despisers, and wonder, and perish; for I work a work in your days, a work which ye shall in no wise believe, though a man declare it unto you."

The man who has passed the most rapidly to the front and become the most conspicuous figure in this religious movement, is the author of these sermons, the Rev. Sam P. Jones, of Georgia. Other men engaged in evangelistic work have talent, aptitudes, consecration, power. Mr. Jones has genius superadded to all of these, and his wonderful genius is not only the subject of deepest study in its intuitive knowledge of human nature, but, also, in its strange gift of power to move men as no other man can move men.

W. M. L.

BIOGRAPHICAL SKETCH.

THE REV. SAM P. JONES was born in Chambers County, Ala., October 16, 1847, and was reared in Cartersville, Bartow County, Ga., where he still resides. He has a good ancestry. Like Timothy, the unfeigned faith that is in him dwelt in his grandmother and in his own mother; and more, in his father and grandfather, and as far back as his ancestry can be traced, and latterly in his uncles, four of whom are ministers of the Gospel. When, therefore, the Holy Spirit quickened him into remembrance of these things, and he "stirred up the gift that was in him," the hereditary faith and fire flamed out as the voice of one crying in the wilderness—a voice that calls the Church to judgment, startles the gilded guilt of the world with the summons to repentance, and moves and melts with the tenderness and tears of a love and sympathy born of the experience of his own happy conversion from a life of youthful folly and dissipation.

His maternal grandmother was distinguished in her day, not more for her gentle, modest, lovable disposition, which made her a universal favorite, than for her strong faith and fervent piety, which consecrated both her temper and her tongue to God, so that the Holy Ghost seemed at times to take possession of both, and come down through them in mighty baptism upon penitents and congregations while she prayed in public. His mother was a woman of superior intelligence and piety, but she died when he was only eight years old. She left upon his young heart and life the tender ministries of motherly gentleness and love which are forever associated in his mind with the angels of God. His "precious mother," as he always calls her, is a ministering angel to him. His father, Captain John J. Jones, was a lawyer of note in Georgia, distinguished for his intelligence, integrity, probity, social qualities, and consistent piety. He prepared his son for the legal profession, which he entered in early manhood with the fairest prospects and promises of success. But his exuberant social temperament soon led him into social excesses, and on and on into the vortex of dissipation. Whisky-drinking, profanity, and their kindred evils swept him down into the deepest depths, and made him so reckless that all efforts for his reformation only maddened him, until his father, baffled and mortified, gave up all hope, and then lay down to die. While on his death-bed his father seized every opportunity to talk with him. As death approached the son grew more and more serious, until the closing scene—so triumphant over death that heaven and earth were brought together, and the prodigal boy fell down at the death-bed and cried out for mercy, saying: "I'll quit; I'll quit! 'God, be merciful to me, a sinner!'" Bitterly did he weep, repent, and pray. The sad occasion was sanctified to his salvation. The death of the father was life to the son. "That which thou sowest is not quickened except it die." Death for life, and life from death.

He was at once called of God to preach the Gospel, and he waited not to confer with flesh and blood, but at once applied for license to preach, and for admission into the traveling ministry. In October, 1872, in Atlanta, Ga., he was received on trial in the North Georgia Conference of the Methodist Episcopal Church, South. This step astonished his friends, who did not believe that he could ever succeed in the ministry. They saw no signs of promise in him. His wife bitterly opposed it, and said she would leave him forever if he became a preacher. But God overruled all, and opened the way for his entrance into the conference and his enlargement in the work of an evangelist. His first appointment was the Van Wert Circuit, in Bartow and Polk Counties, Ga., which he served three years, the people asking for his return each year. In 1876 he was sent to DeSoto Circuit, in Floyd County, where he remained two years. On this work he began to develop the peculiarities which have since made him famous. His plain, pointed, and personal denunciations of the popular vices of the people offended many, and made the stewards remonstrate with him, saying that his family would starve, because the people would not pay such a preacher. His only reply was: "I am preaching my convictions, and have no compromise to make." The sweeping revivals that followed were God's indorsement of his own truth and the fearless fidelity of his servant. In 1878 he was sent to Newborn Circuit, Newton County. He began, while on this work, to travel out and preach for others, and try his apprentice hand at evangelistic work. He was afterward sent to Monticello Circuit, in Jasper County, but the calls for his service in the adjoining towns and cities increased so rapidly that he was not afterward appointed to any pastoral charge. In 1880 he was appointed agent of the North Georgia Conference Orphans' Home, when the Home was under great financial embarrassment. He not only relieved the Home of debt and saved it from financial ruin, but he raised money and erected additional buildings, and put the institution upon a career of greatly enlarged usefulness and prosperity. This has afforded him the largest liberty in the work of an evangelist, and his uniform success has magnified his office until "the world is his parish." He has the calling, the spirit, the gift, the courage, the directness, the sympathy, the faith, the fervor, and the flexibility of a true evangelist.

That Mr. Jones has made full proof of his ministry, his successful revivals in Georgia, Alabama, Mississippi, Texas, Tennessee, South Carolina, and Brooklyn, N. Y., St. Louis, Cincinnati, and Chicago, are in evidence. Urgent appeals pour in upon him from every part of the country, from Washington to San Francisco, and from the Lakes to the Gulf. Wherever he goes the Churches are stirred and quickened into a better and higher life, and sinners are awakened and converted to Christ by hundreds and thousands. All classes, from the highest to the lowest, from the most learned and cultivated to the most ignorant and the roughest, are alike moved to repentance and a better life by him, or rather by the Holy Spirit through him. His power over men *as men* is marvelous, and his power over vast assemblies is phenomenal. He is "the master of assemblies." He despises the mere arts of oratory, as he does all shams; but he possesses the eloquence of earnestness and action, the fire and glow of passion, the surprises of thought, the wit, humor, ridicule, irony, sarcasm, invective, pathos, sympathy, love, humanity, and faith, which, expressed in the language of the shop and field, and illustrated by the common facts of life and the happiest allegories, make him the most sensational preacher now in the American pulpit. But he is more than sensational; he is endued with power from on high, and commissioned to carry the Gospel to the common people, who always hear him gladly.

Prior to the great work which God wrought through Mr. Jones in Nashville, Tenn., in the month of May, 1885, his reputation was provincial. He was known in the sections of the South where he had labored as an evangelist with great success, and had been invited to Brooklyn, N. Y., by Mr. Talmage, with whom he spent several weeks, preaching with power in his Tabernacle; but for some reason he did not reach the New York press to any great extent, and no man in this day can reach a national reputation without the metropolitan press. His meeting in the great Gospel tent in Nashville, Tenn., in May, 1885, when thousands of souls were converted to God and lifted to higher and purer living, with the efficient help of the city press, by which his wonderful sermons were scattered broadcast over the land, gave him a national reputation, and threw him up and out as the most remarkable man before the American public. From that time on his star has been ascending and becoming more brilliant as it hung in the moral heavens of St. Joseph, Mo., St. Louis, Cincinnati, and Chicago. In Cincinnati his success was remarkable. Even the great Music Hall could not contain the vast assemblies that pressed their way along the streets to hear him, and who seemed never to weary hanging upon his words. During his daily ministry of five weeks the public interest increased until, according to the statements in the public press of the city, forty thousand people sought to hear his last sermon. The hall was densely packed, and the streets for blocks away were also packed with a dense mass of struggling, surging humanity, all seeking to see and hear a man who had then been talking to them from the platform and through the press from two to three times a day for five weeks. The history of religious revivals in this country has never presented any thing like that. How many thousands of souls were converted to God by his ministry in Cincinnati eternity alone will reveal. The Churches of the city were quickened into higher and purer living as never before, and the harvest gathered from the meeting was truly great.

While this work is passing through the press Mr. Jones and his convert and efficient colaborer, Mr. Sam W. Small, are moving Chicago by the power of God, and the great Casino Rink is nightly crowded with people who hang in rapt attention upon the Word of life as preached by these faithful evangelists. The best evidence of the power and fame of the great evangelist is the fact that some of the leading daily papers of the country have leased telegraph lines for the daily transmission of his sermons. This is done as a business transaction, the public demand for Mr. Jones's sermons largely increasing their daily circulation, and making the heavy outlay of money a paying investment. There could be no stronger reason for the publication of these sermons in this permanent form, after careful revision and convenient arrangement. The next thing to hearing Mr. Jones is to read his sermons and sayings. They are presented in this volume in their best form and by his authority.

W. M. L.

CONTENTS.

————•————

MUSIC HALL, CINCINNATI, O.,

SERMONS AND SAYINGS.

SERMON I.

THE CITY WHOLLY GIVEN TO IDOLATRY.

"Now while Paul waited for them at Athens his spirit was stirred in him when he saw the city wholly given to idolatry."—ACTS XVII, 16.

I BELIEVE Saul of Tarsus was the greatest man in this world's history. When I measure his head I look and admire. When I measure his heart I am at a loss to know which is the greater, his head or his heart. It takes both head and heart to make a true man. If there was a leading characteristic in the life of this great man it was his sterling integrity, his downright honesty. There was never but one trouble in the mind of this great man, and that was touching the divinity of Christ. It took the biggest guns of heaven to arouse and convince him, but when once convinced he was loyal forever. I believe I am ready to say here in my place, that St. Paul being an honest man God put him straight once, and he never gave God a moment's trouble after that until God said: "It is enough; come up higher." St. Paul was such a man as I would imitate. I admire his character,

9

true, noble, courageous, honest. And now this man, waiting for his companions at Athens, sees the whole city given to idolatry.

The charge that God brought against his ancient people was this: "My people will not consider." The etymological definition of that word is "to look at a thing until you see it." If we look at a landscape a glance will take in the main features, such as the mountain scenery, the stream, and the hamlet. A consideration or careful examination will show the foliage of the mountain trees, the road leading to the mansion, the cattle grazing on the hill slopes, and so on. There is a great difference between glancing at an object and considering it. St. Paul had considered the state of affairs in Athens, and his spirit was stirred within him when he saw how the whole city was given to idolatry.

Now one of two things is true of this city to-night: either the eyes of Christian people are closed to the facts or else the facts are falsehoods; one or the other. You can take whichever horn of the dilemma you please. I can take the daily papers of this city and read your local columns and see without getting at the Bible that it is wrong, that there is something radically wrong about it; there are too many debauched characters, too many sui-cides, too many murders, too many that are drifting daily to destruction and ruin. The fact is, a man does n't need a Bible to see this world is all wrong; all you need to do is just to read your morning and afternoon papers, and then walk this street with your eyes open, and if you do that it will not be one week from to-day until you look on with horror that is indescribable.

Now, let me ask each of you: Did you ever look at your heart until you saw it? I grant you that you have glanced at it a thousand times, but did you ever kneel down and pray for light, and look and look and look until you saw your heart? My Bible teaches me that: "The heart is deceitful above all things, and desperately wicked." My Bible teaches me: "Keep thy heart with all diligence, for out of it are the issues of life." My Bible teaches me: "Blessed are the pure in heart, for they shall see God."

I once saw a pictorial representation of the human heart. It represented the sinner's heart; full of all kinds of wild beasts, reptiles and unclean birds—a hideous sight to look upon. Then there was the heart under conviction of sin, with the heads of all these animals turned outward as if they were getting ready to leave. Then I saw the heart converted, cleansed, and it was represented with a shining light and a cross. I saw also the back-slider's heart, with the heads of all the beasts and reptiles as if they had turned backward, and I saw the apostate's heart—a perfidious heart—as it was filled to overflowing with all manner of horrid things; and the last state of that man was worse than the first.

O, the heart! the heart! This world reminds me in some of its phases of the man down in the spring branch trying to clear the water, so he could get a clear drink. He was doing all he could to

filter and clear the water when some friend called
out to him: "Stranger, come up a little higher and
run that hog out of that spring, and it will clear itself." No trouble then. And I declare to you to-
night, the hardest job man ever undertook in this
world is to lift up his life while he has an unclean
heart.

There is no such thing as a clean life outside of
a clean heart. I know we have what we call moral
men, but I do n't believe you can separate morals
and Christianity. In fact, the morals of this world
are the paraphernalia of Christianity. The man who
is moral in the sense that he will pay his debts and
tell the truth, and that sort of thing, may be a villain
at heart. Our Savior looked at the most moral men
this world ever saw, and said: "You whitewashed
rascals, you!" That is our version. His version was:
"Ye whited sepulchers!" I had rather be called
the former.

And I want to say to you men that do n't profess
to be Christians, I do n't bring a railing charge
against you. In the life of Jesus Christ not a single
harsh word ever escaped his lips toward a sinner.
When Jesus would talk with a sinner, he would fetch
up the parable of the lost sheep, where the man left
the ninety and nine safe in the fold and followed the
poor, wandering sheep, and when he found it he
did n't take a club and beat it back home, but picked
up the poor, tired, hungry sheep and laid it on his
shoulder and brought it back to the fold. But I tell
you one thing. The Lord Jesus himself never lost
a chance to pour hot shot and grape and canister

into the Scribes and Pharaisees, and they are the gentlemen I am after, begging your pardon. Now, if the sinners about this town want to go to theaters, and want to dance and want to play cards and want to curse and want to live licentious lives, I say, "Go it. Go it, boys;" but if you members of the Church want to do it, I will brand you as hypocrites until you renounce your faith in Christ and have your name taken off the Church books. I 've got a right to say a few things along there, and neither this world, nor the flesh, nor the devil, will interpose any objection. Do n't any body say I interposed an objection to any man who do n't profess to be a Christian, or placed any obstacle in the way of his doing just as he pleases. We will attend to your case later, but now I want to look in the faces of men who have made their vows and their promises to God, and who have sworn eternal allegiance to Jesus Christ, whose lives are a shame to the Gospel and a disgrace to the character they profess. That 's it.

Now let us look at our hearts. I believe this incident, related of Mr. Moody, will illustrate the point I am on. On one occasion, when he had invited penitents to the altar, there came forward a great many, and he walked back two or three pews to where two Christian ladies were sitting, and he said: "My sisters, will you walk forward and talk to those penitents?" They looked up at him and said, "No, sir, Mr. Moody; we are praying for you." "Praying for me," he said. "Am I not trying to live right and get to heaven?" "Yes, Mr. Moody; but we are praying that you may have a clean heart."

And he said conviction entered his spirit in a moment, and he dismissed the services later and went home and fell down on his knees and prayed, "Lord God, show me my heart. Let me see it as it is." And he said, "When the light of heaven poured in upon my heart I saw it was full of Moody, and full of selfishness, and full of worldly pride; and then I said, 'Lord God, help me to

"'Cast every idol out
That dares to rival thee.'

"And," said he, "the Lord came and washed out all unrighteousness from my heart, and from that day until now I have never preached a sermon that did n't win souls to Christ." And I declare to you, if Jesus had in this town an army of pure blood-washed hearts we could win this whole city to Christ. And never, never, never will we accomplish the work and bring the world to Christ until we, who profess Christ, arouse ourselves and wake up and shake the devil's fleas off ourselves and get to be decent.

I can stand any thing better than I can stand a hypocrite. I always did have a hatred for shams and humbugs and cheats, and of all the humbugs that ever cursed the universe, I reckon the religious humbug is the humbuggest. And I tell you when a fellow gets a little Methodism in him, and a little of theaters, and a little card playing, and a little of almost every thing, and is made up out of a hundred different sorts of things, then he is a first-class humbug in every sense of the word. He is just good anywhere.

O, my heart! With the heart right, with the fountain clear, the stream will be clear. With a good tree the fruit will be good. And I declare to you to-night that the hardest work a man ever tried to do is to be a Christian without religion; to be a good man with a bad heart.

Why there are just scores sitting in front of me to-night that if it were literally true that we have wild beasts and serpents and other venomous things in bodily form in our hearts, as they are typically there, I would hate to be close round some of you, for fear I might get bit before I could get out of the way. O, God, give us clean hearts and clean hands.

And then I will say, to be practical all along the line, did you ever look at your tongue until you saw that? O, these tongues of ours! These tongues of ours! We Methodists pour the water on, and the Presbyterians sprinkle it on, and the Baptists put us clean under, but I do n't care whether you sprinkle, or pour, or immerse, the tongue comes out as dry as powder. Did you ever see a baptized tongue? Say, did you? Did you ever see a tongue that belonged to the Church? You will generally find the tongue among man's reserved rights. There come in some reservations, and always where there is a reservation the tongue is retained. The tongue! The tongue! The tongue! Pambus, one of the middle-age saints, went to his neighbor with a Bible in his hand and told him: "I want you to read me a verse of Scripture every day. I can 't read, and I want you to read to me." So the

neighbor opened the Bible and read these words:
"I will take heed to my ways that I sin not with
my tongue."

Pambus took the book out of his hand and walked
back home, and about a week after that the neighbor met him, and he said: "Pambus, I thought you
were to come back and let me read you a passage
of Scripture every day?" and Pambus said: "Do
you recollect that verse you read to me the other
day?" "No," said the neighbor. "Well," said
Pambus, "I will quote it: 'I will take heed to my
ways that I sin not with my tongue.' And," he
said, "I never intend to learn another passage of
Scripture until I learn to live that one." O that every
man, woman, and child in this house to-night would
go away from here determined to live that passage
of Scripture: "I said, I will take heed to my ways
that I sin not with my tongue. I will keep my
tongue from evil and my lips from speaking guile."
O me! Shakspeare told a great truth when he said:

> "Who steals my purse steals trash, ...
> But he that filches from me my good name
> Robs me of that which not enriches him,
> And makes me poor indeed."

These violators of character—I will venture the
assertion there are many, many, many here to-night—
if every word you said about people in this house
were posted up there in legible words, here to-night,
you would immediately leave this house and never
be seen in public again. "We ain't going anywhere where they put up every thing we say for
folks to look at." Now, I look at my tongue till I

see it. There is many a man that in other things may do well that at last will lie down in hell forever, and say: "I am conscious I am tongue-damned. I would have gone to heaven if I had n't had a tongue."

My tongue! And I say to you to-night the best thing we can do with our tongues is to speak well and to speak kindly of all men. I dare assert here in my place, when you take me from this sacred stand that I occupy, I defy you to put your finger on a word of mine against the character or reputation of any body. But I am not talking for myself up here. Understand that. Once in Jerusalem a great crowd—it was 1,800 years and more ago, as the legend goes, or the allegory—a great crowd was gathered in Jerusalem, and they were gathered around a dead dog, and they stood and looked, and one of them said: "That is the ugliest dog I ever saw." Another said: "O, he is not only the ugliest dog I ever saw, but I do n't believe his old hide is worth taking off of him." Another said, "Just look how crooked his legs are." And so they criticised the poor dog. And directly one spoke up and said, "Ain't those the prettiest pearly white teeth you ever looked at?" And they walked off and said: "That must have been Jesus of Nazareth that could have found something good to say about a dead dog." O, me! I like those people that always try to see something kind in people in their ways and walks of life.

And then, I ask you again, did you ever look at your feet until you saw them? There is a good

2

deal in that. "Thy word is a lamp unto my feet and a light unto my path." O, Lord God! I would follow in the footsteps of Him who led the way to heaven. There is no circumspect Christian who does not see to it that his feet are kept in the narrow way that leads from earth to heaven. A Methodist, a Baptist, a Presbyterian, a Catholic in a ball-room! Their feet, that they have pledged should follow in the footsteps of Christ, are there cutting the pigeon-wing to music! Now what do you think of that?

And I hear this expression: They say, "Well, our Church do n't object to it." Now, I would say a very strong thing here—and I hope you will take it in the very spirit in which I say it, for I never said a kinder thing or a harder thing than that— you never shall hear a truer thing. Whenever a Presbyterian, or a Methodist, or a Baptist, or a Christian, or a Congregationalist, or a Catholic says that their Church do n't object to dancing and theaters, and all such things as that, they could not tell a bigger lie if they would try in a hundred years! Thank God, there is not a Church named after Christ on earth that has not thundered out after these things with all the power they have got.

"Our Church do n't object." Well, now, the Episcopal Church being a Church in authority, how they did thunder against these worldly amusements? That little Church you belong to may not. That rotten little thing! I would not stay in it long enough to get my hat if it did n't.

I was sitting in a train some time ago, and the

train rolled up to the station, and just up on the platform, near by, were three ladies. One of the ladies said to the other: "Are you going to the ball to-night?" The other lady said "I ain't going." "But," she said, "I forgot; you are a Methodist, and you do n't go to such places. I would not be a Methodist. I want to enjoy myself." The other said, "Yes, I am a Methodist, and, thank God! I do n't want to go to such places." "O," said the other one, "I would not be a Methodist." And the train rolled off, and I felt like jumping on the top of that train myself and hollering, "Hurrah for Methodism!" And whenever she goes into copartnership with ball-rooms, and with all of the worldly amusements that embarrass the Christian and paralyze his power—whenever the Methodist Church goes into copartnership with these things I will sever my connection with her forever. And I love her and honor her to-day because she has stood like a bulwark against these things, and denounced them from first to last.

One of the honored preachers of this town, a man whose good opinion I value highly, one of the noblest, truest ministers of this town, said to me: "I declare to you, our Churches are little more than a graveyard. We have been killed and almost buried by this tide of worldliness that has swept over our homes year after year." And that is the truth. And I can read a ten-page letter that I got from a citizen to-day, and turn every face in this house as pale as death. That man wrote as if he knew what he was talking about. There is many a

mother at twelve o'clock at night, in this town, that
can sing with the blood trickling in her heart,

"O, where is my wandering boy to-night?
He was once as pure as the driven snow."

And O, why, why, why would I take this carcass, and that carcass, and the other carcass that are
so offensive? Why would I bring them out before
this congregation? Nothing would make me do it
but to get you to take those carcasses that are de-
spoiling the very odors of your city, and bury them
out of sight forever. That is it. You all have
spent two or three nights looking at me. God help
you to look at yourselves awhile. And you will
think I am a beauty before you get through. I look
at myself from head to foot—my hands, my heart,
my feet, my tongue. I look at my ways and walks
and character in this community. Did you ever look
at yourself as a member of the Church? Did you
ever wake up some morning and shut your eyes and
lie there and say, "Well, suppose every member of
the Church in town were just like me, what sort of a
Church would we have? Suppose every member
of the Church in town prayed as little as I pray,
what sort of a Church would we have? Suppose
every member of the Church in town paid as little
as I pay, how long before the whole thing would be
sold out by the sheriff?"

O, my brother! it is well enough now and then
for a fellow to get a square, honest look at himself.
What sort of a Methodist are you? There is a man
that has promised to renounce the world, the flesh
and the devil and the vain pomp and glory of the

world, and he has promised on oath, before God and man, not to follow or be led by them. What is your life? There is that Presbyterian, consecrated to God by the most solemn ceremony that heaven ever witnessed. Now, what is your character? There is the Episcopalian; with the imposing hands of the bishop laid upon his head, and with a ceremony as solemn as eternity, he was dedicated in the Church to God last night, and to-night he is in the biggest ball in town, dancing his way to hell.

And no longer than this very year, in one of the cities of the South, one gentleman told me this: Said he: "I saw the Episcopal bishop lay his hands on the heads of a class of twenty, one night, and the next night eighteen out of that twenty were at a magnificent ball." Now you say, "I would n't have done that; I would have waited a week." Well, if a fellow is going to do it at all, he had better get right at it. Do n't you think that 's so? How long ought a fellow to wait after he joins the Church before he goes to his devilment? Now that 's it.

I wish I could get all the Methodists and Baptists and Presbyterians in this city, and all other Churches, to live just as they promised to live. I wish I could get all the Episcopalians in town to be as good out of Lent as they are in Lent. That would be good would n't it? And I never could see why a fellow ought not to be as good one time as another. Did you? I never could. And I 'm going to be just as good the year round as any Episcopalian in this town is during Lent. I reckon they all hope to die in Lent. If a heap of them die out of Lent the

devil will get them, in my judgment. In a great
many places they dance Lent in and they dance it
out. Like the Irishman talking about holidays in
America—said he "Instead of hanging our heads
and sorrowing over the crucifixion of our Savior,
we Americans fire it in and fire it out."

Now, I do n't pick out any denominations and
say any thing about one denomination that I would
not say about another. There is no denomination-
alism in this. I have no purpose and no desire in
my heart to say one thing about one denomination
that I would not say against another. That is true.
I am just talking true things, and any night you
come here if you do n't like the way this is rattled
off you can rack out of here just the minute you
please. For I propose, God being my helper, to
speak the truth as I see it, and I do n't care what
men or devils or cities or earth or hell may say, I
am going to preach, while I do preach, what I believe to be the truth.

And I will tell you Christian people, if you
think the devil is going to surrender any ground in
this town until every inch is covered with blood
you do not know the devil as well as I do. I will
tell you that. I have been fighting his majesty
several years, and I declare to you that he is always
ready for a fight. He has possessed nearly two-
thirds of this city for nearly forty years, and if you
think he is going to make a voluntary surrender of
his territory you do not know him. He is going
to fight and fight, and every child he has got is
going to help him; you can put that down. And

I tell you there is another thing; there is a heap of members of the Church going to help him, too. They will that. Some places the devil goes to he never has any thing to do himself. He puts his hands in his pockets and goes round and gets members of the Church to run his devilment for him. They do his work cheaper for him than any other class. He does n't have to pay them, and they board themselves. In some towns the leading ball-room dude is a member of the Church—the fellow that gets them all up and runs the thing.

I look at myself as a member of the Church. O me, brother! when you see yourself as a member of the Church, as a professor of religion, it will do you good. I will ask you again, did you ever look at yourself as a father? O me! how close you get to a man's heart when you talk to him of his family. Brother and sister, did you ever have your innocent child sit on your lap, put its little arms round your neck and imprint the kiss of innocence on your cheek? Have you ever looked on your lovely children lying in their bed and said: "Of all children God ever gave, my children have the purest and best of fathers?" You can go home to-night and wake up your little Willie. Get him quite awake and ask him "Who is the best man in this city?" He will answer, "Why, you, papa." Ask him, "Whom would you rather be most like?" and he will reply, "Why, you, papa." Ask him who is the the best man in the world, and he will say, "Why, you, papa." He has got no sense. And that is why we curse, and damn, and ruin our

children. They can see no harm in us, and just as
we do they will follow and imitate us. A single
man may drink as a single man, he may swear as
a single man, he may lead a godless life as a single
man ; but as a married man you had better call a
halt, and ask where you are leading your children
to day by day. You may sit in the chairs of this
hall night after night; you may simply have your
curiosity excited; you may simply come here to
laugh, but when you gather your children in your
arms and see that your bad example is leading them
to death and hell there is no joke about that—no
laugh about that! God pity me and pity you in
our relations towards those that lean upon us; and
if there is any fact in my history I bless God for in
my heart to-night, it is the fact that not a sweet child
of mine ever looked in my face when I was not a
Christian, trying to serve God and set it a good example.

Did you ever look at yourself as a mother? Of
all beings that earth claims its blessings from, it
looks as though a mother ought to be the best.
Mother, what is your life before your children?
Consider yourself! Did you ever look at your children till you saw them? Wife, did you ever look
at your husband till you saw him? Husband, did
you ever look at your wife until you saw her? If
there is any body in the world I would have get to
heaven, it is my wife; and there is a husband who
never talked ten minutes to his wife on religion;
and there is a wife who never opened her mouth to
her husband about the way of life. O me! when

we think of a home that has been Christless, what a sad thing!

And then we ask you again, did you ever look at this city until you saw it? Did you ever take it by streets and blocks? Did you ever count the bar-rooms in this town? Did you ever count the beer-gardens in this town? Did you ever count the number of men that went in and out of the bar-rooms and beer gardens? I bring this question square before you. Did you ever count the number of soiled doves that curse this city and curse themselves? O my God, when we look at these pictures we have to shut our eyes and drop down upon our knees. We say, " God deliver us and God speed us." Did you ever count the billiard-tables in this town? Did you ever count the gambling hells in this town? No wonder this one writes and that one writes, " Jones, God bless you! turn loose your guns, and do your best to wake up the Christian people and show them how this town by streets and blocks is drifting to hell every day."

Now, I am going to stick to truth while I am here, and I say to every man and to every influence in this town unfriendly to Christ and unfriendly to the Bible to fight back. I do not look for any thing else. I want to say right now that I like to see things moving up, and if you can say any thing worse of me than I can of you, lamm in, and I will beat you to the tank in that line, may be. Pick every flaw you can in every sermon, and if I can not pick more flaws in your life than you do in my sermons, I will yield the feather to you. I say to

you now, we propose to get your eyes open so that
you can see yourselves. That is the first sight you
ought to look at. Then look at St. Paul. When
he went to the city of Athens, so wholly given to
idolatry, it stirred his heart within him. I have
heard Christian people say that they had no feeling,
no enthusiasm, no religious fervor, but never since
I joined Christ's Church have I been devoid of religious fervor and enthusiasm. The man who goes
about like a corpse, with no feeling, no enthusiasm,
that man is either dead to all intents and purposes,
or he has closed his eyes to what is going on about
him. When that great man visited the city of
Athens, so wholly given to idolatry, it stirred his
heart within him. And he went over to Mars'
Hill, pointed to the inscription, "to an unknown
God," and preached that grand sermon generated in
his soul as he walked through the streets of the city
and saw that it was wholly given to idolatry; and
I tell you to night, when we see ourselves and our
city and our surroundings as they are, there is hope
for us.

There is just one thing more I want you to do—
that is, to see the cross. It is the hope of the
world. It is the balm of Gilead. It has the power
to save. It is the redemption of the race. O, my
brother, that fourteen years ago and a few days I,
a poor, wretched, ruined, lost sinner, walked up to
see my father die. O, how I loved that father, and
how I broke his heart. I have wished a thousand
times that I had my father back just one hour that
I might lean my head on his bosom and hear him

speak the words of kindness and advice he has spoken to me in the past. As I stood by his dying couch he took my hand in his bony hand, and a heavenly smile rested on his face just before he passed out of this world. He did not die; he did not die. His faculties were as bright and his hope as buoyant in the very agonies of death as they ever had been. As I took his bony hand he said, "My poor, wayward, godless boy! You have almost broken my heart, and you have given me so much trouble! Won't you tell your dying father, now, that you will meet him in the good world?" I stood there for a moment convulsed from head to foot. I said, "Yes, father, I will meet you in the good world." I turned away from that dying couch, and every step I have made from that time to this has been toward the good world. And I mean, with the grace of God, to keep my promise. I left that bed a wretched sinner, and looked to God. I looked up there and

I saw one hanging on the tree
  In agonies of blood,
He fixed his languid eyes on me,
  As near his cross I stood.

Sure, never, to my latest breath
  Can I forget that look;
He seemed to charge me with his death,
  Though not a word he spoke.

A second look he gave, which said:
  "I freely all forgive,
My blood is shed to ransom thee,
  I die that you may live."

Blessed Christ, live forever to save dying men.

SAYINGS.

Paralyzing Sins.—You say, "Jones, why do n't
you preach against stealing, lying, and drunkenness?" It is because that ain't hurting the
Church. Nobody has any respect for you old red-
nosed devils in the Church. They do n't notice
you. They have got no respect for you. Nobody
has any respect for you if you are a liar. Nobody
bothers with you if you steal. Nobody cares any
thing about you. I will tell you it is n't lying, stealing
and drunkenness that is cursing the Church and
paralyzing her power and ruining the Church of
God. It is these worldly amusements that are
sweeping over our homes and Churches, and paralyzing us and making us to-day little better
than a grave-yard. That is it. I never saw a
spiritual man in my life that would stand up and
ask me, "Do you think there is any harm in the
dance?" Why do n't you ask me if I think there
is any harm in a prayer-meeting, or I think there is
any harm in family prayer? You know there is n't.
And when ever you hear a fellow asking if there is
any harm in a dance, you can reply: "You lying
old rascal, you know there is."

The "Thirty."—When I was in St. Joseph
preaching, there was a story in the morning papers
to the following effect: "Jones is not doing much
with the Thirty." The next morning I would see:
"The Thirty were pretty well represented at the
meeting." I said to my friends, "What does this

'thirty' business mean?" "O," they said, "there are in this city thirty millionaires—thirty men of the world, worth over a million." These things were against them. Some of those men I found to be true, noble, Christly, and generous, but those who were not we did not make much impression upon. One of the old millionaires who professed religion joined the Church. Afterward I said to him: "Well, my brother, you have disposed of your soul, you have given it to God, but you have a heap harder job left before you—what to do with your money. You had better begin to unload now. Shell out now, for if you are ever dammed it will be by your money. Mark what I tell you." If I had one-tenth of the money some members of the Church have in this town, and I did not do any better with it than they do, the devil would get me as certain as my name is Sam Jones. And if you have got as much sense as I have and you do n't get up from where you are, the devil will get you too; you can put that down.

SERMON II.

"Receive us: we have wronged no man, we have corrupted no man; we have defrauded no man."—2 COR. VII, 2.

ST. PAUL knocked at the inner door of the
Church of Corinth. He was met by that Church,
and he was asked: "Upon what ground do you demand so great a privilege?" And he replied, "On
the grounds, first, I have wronged no man with my
tongue. I have corrupted no man by my example.
I have defrauded no man in any business transaction." Jesus Christ watched the doors of his kingdom when he stood among men, with the most
uncompromising and most untiring scrutiny. And
when the young man approached Christ, and would
have entered the kingdom, and Jesus looked upon
him as he asked the question: "What must I do
that I can get into the kingdom?" Jesus looked
at him and said: "Keep the commandments." The
young man said, exultingly: "Why, Master, all
these have I kept from my youth up." And Jesus
looked him in the face, and said: "One thing thou
lackest yet," and the young man walked away. I
suppose his disciples, if they had been as worldly
as we are, would have said: "Master, that's a
magnificent young man. He's a very rich young
man. He stands well in the community, and if he
only lacks one thing let's take him in. He will

30

give tone to the Church, and he will pay largely. We have few members of that sort, and he's got money to pay our expenses. Why, Master, if he lacks but one thing let's take him in." "One thing thou lackest yet," said Christ, and the young man turned and went away, and that's the last he heard of him. The disciples caught at the same spirit and taught men this: that you must deny yourself and take up your cross and follow Christ. They taught us if any man love the world the love of God is not in him; if any man have not the Spirit of Christ he is none of his.

A large Church membership does not mean much here now. It does not mean much anywhere, under any circumstances, and I thank God that with the state of things I now find in existence everywhere it does n't amount to much with this world, to say the least of it. We ought to quit asking the question, "What Church do you belong to?" but we ought to ask, "How do you live now? How have you been doing? Do you pay your debts? Do you live right, and live good, and keep the commandments?" Brethren, an open profession, an outward profession, that is n't backed up by the possession of the principles of Christianity, is not worth the paper your name is enrolled on. I want to see the day in this country when Church membership means consecration, righteousness, and godliness.

I'm a natural, innate, constitutional inborn hater of shams and humbugs, and above all humbugs that ever cursed this world, the religious

humbug is the biggest. That's so. I will give
you a little illustration : At Harvard, I believe it
was, there was in the college an old professor, one
of those thick-glassed old fellows, near-sighted, who
was a wonderful bugologist. He knew bugology
better than he did manology, and he was acquainted
with all the bugs from Adam down, and he had all
kinds of them in frames hung up around his office.
In their mischief, and as a joke, the students got
the body of one bug, and took the legs of another
and the head of another and the wings of another,
and put them together just like as if nature had
formed it that way, and they all trooped down-
stairs together into the old professor's room, and one
of the boys says: " Professor, what kind of a bug
is this?" and the professor stood up and took the
card on which the bug was pinned, and he cast his
eyes on it, and after looking at it awhile he said:
"Gentlemen, this is a *hum*bug.'   Now you have my
idea of a humbug. It's a fellow that has a heart
that belongs to the Church, and a head that is run
by the world, and his hands by the devil, and he's
just nothing but a sort of a compound. God deliver
us from humbugs in the Church! Let's be only
one of a kind, and let that be a good Christian.
If I were asked now what is the trouble in Cincinnati—the greatest trouble—a trouble you can't
overcome as easily as other troubles—I believe I
would answer that the greatest trouble in Cincinnati
is, that you have too many Churches here.

I don't mean to say there are too many buildings or too many pastors. I would not tear down

a church in this city, nor hush the voice of a single preacher. I would not demolish a single Church organization in the town, but I'll tell you the trouble. I will take this Church here for an illustration. Your minister, you know, is the pastor of two Churches, and he has a hard time of it, too, I tell you, for one Church is about as much as any preacher can look after. The one Church you have has an enrolled list of members, but you have a Church on the inside of that, and whenever a man gets on the inside of the inside Church, then he can talk about the communion of saints and fellowship of the Spirit, and walk with God. A man who gets inside of the inside of a Church is safe for all time. But how many get in there? I reckon, if you would call a meeting of the truly spiritual members, you could hold it in some little side room. You wouldn't have to call it in this great room. It would be lost here. A double handful of your truly spiritual members would look lonely in here, and you would have to get them in the parlor. That's a bad state of things. How many men in this Church—and there is no better Church in the city—love God with all their hearts, and love their neighbors as themselves?

I am willing for any body to have more money than I have, and more land than I ever expect to have, and more stocks and bonds than I can ever get, but I ain't willing for any man that walks this earth to have more religion than I have. I can get as much as a soul full, and that's about as much as an angel can get. If I am a Christian, I will be a

Christian; if I am a Methodist, I'll be a Methodist;
if I'm a Presbyterian, I'll be a Presbyterian; and
if I'm a Baptist, I'm a-going to be one all over,
through and through; but I wouldn't be a little,
old, dried-up, knock-kneed, one-horse, shriveled
nothing anywhere. Haven't you ever felt some
time away down in your soul that you wanted to
get above every thing? Haven't you had a desire
to rise up above the sight of this kind of little fellows,
that you can put twenty of them in a sardine-box?
Haven't you ever had a glorious feeling in your
soul that made you feel for a minute as if you
wanted to be a whale? You have never known
much about religion if you never felt in your soul
as if you wanted to be somebody—something—so
big that you feel as if you could fly up, and up,
and up; then you can know something about what
religion is.

Religion's a grand thing. There is nothing on
earth like it, and nothing in heaven better than religion. A poor, tempest-tossed, tempest-driven soul,
thrown hither and thither in helpless wandering, tired,
restless, and hungry, finds a haven there. O! how
dark it was once for me; how hungry this poor soul
was once. How like the crest of a wave! I knew
no rest. But I found it in religion. Religion!
Religion! It's a great word. In its etymological
sense it means that there is something in this small
universe that can take up a poor, wandering, hungry,
restless soul, and tie it back to God. Religion
means to bring the soul back to its moorings.
That's it. I have often thought of the picture of

the Lake of Gennesaret, and, as I looked at the calm, placid little lake, surrounded on all sides by rugged, towering mountains, I have thought that the winds of the storm could never ruffle its bosom. But if there was any place on earth where the four winds of heaven more fiercely contested for supremacy, it was on this little lake of Gennesaret. Christ was once riding over this lake in a boat with his disciples, and the Savior was below in the cabin sleeping, when suddenly a fierce storm arose, and the little ship began to toss and pitch and rock fearfully, and the disciples, trembling with fear, ran and aroused him, and said: "Master, wake up, we are engulfed. We will be drowned." Christ opened his eyes and raised himself up, and wiping the spray from his forehead walked up to the prow of the little ship, and gathered the waves up to him on his lap, like a mother tending her child, and the seas subsided, and the winds blew no more. And the disciples said: "What manner of man is this, that the winds and waves obey him?" Blessed Christ, with my poor soul, tempest-tossed and driven, I'll crawl up under the cross, and he will pull my poor, tired soul up in his great loving arms, and sweet peace will enfold me, and I'll walk away singing:

"Now, not a wave of trouble rolls
Across my peaceful breast."

Brethren, there's something in religion that will make a man of us, there's something in religion for preachers and people. The more religion a preacher has, blessed be God, the better it is for him; and the more religion a merchant has, the better it is for him; and the more religion a farmer has, the better it is for him. Blessed be God, religion is not only the best thing in the universe, but it is free for all.

"Receive us." Why? "I have wronged no man with my tongue." A man's tongue has a great deal to do with his religion, or rather a man's religion has a great deal to do with his tongue. We've got sanctified people all over this country. They are sanctified in a thousand senses except the sense in which St. James talked about sanctification. Hear his description of a sanctified man. Listen! "Pure religion and undefiled before God and the Father is this: To visit the fatherless and widows in their affliction, and to keep himself unspotted from the world." A man who has learned to manage this term has it right. I believe in sanctification as strongly as justification; but, brethren, sanctification means a great deal more, perhaps, than you have conceived. A Christian preacher in Augusta went down to St. James Church one night to a holiness meeting, a sanctified meeting, where sanctified people met. Next day he met the pastor of St. James Church on the street, and said, "I learned last night, for the first time, the difference between justification and sanctification." "Well, how is that?" said the pastor. "Why, I found out last night that justification meant to satisfy God with man and man with God. That is justification; and sanctification means to satisfy a fellow with himself, and I thought to myself, there's something in that as sure as you live. Justification satisfies a man with God and

God with man, and sanctification satisfies a man with himself."

I have heard people talk as if they were well satisfied with themselves, but I never found many in their neighborhood who were well satisfied with them. Whenever a man gets more religion than he has sense, he's going to talk foolishness right straight. Do n't let any body come and say I'm only talking sanctification. I am not. Some of the best men on earth practice and live sanctification. But you are obliged to have something more. You must get something. Lord Jesus, Master, help men to see that religion does not consist in what I profess, but it consists in how I live. I have no objection to a man's professing sanctification. It's as much my privilege to confess sanctification as it is justification. I do n't quarrel with a man as long as he lives on a level with what he professes, but when he gets down below that, I'm going for him, sure.

The tongue, said St. James—I ran off at a tangent for a while—is full of deadly poison. Many a person in Cincinnati—if you will go to their homes, and sit by their side, and put your ear to their heart—you can hear their heart's blood drip, drip, drip, and you say, "what does that," and they'll tell you an unkind tongue stabbed it there. God pity a man that will take his tongue and stab a man's character with it. I'll tell you another thing. This tongue is not only capable of stabbing Christ, but the tongue is the cause of all the trouble in our midst. It's not what we do, but what we say, that kicks up the mischief all around—it's what we say. I have known men who would leave home in the morning and go down to their stores and be as polite to their women customers, and palaver to them as sweetly as you please; but when they go home at night they talk to their wives as if they were old bears. Did you ever know a case like that, my friend? No? Did n't you see one in the glass to-night when you brushed your hair before you came to meeting? Many a time a good pains-taking wife has carefully arranged every thing to make home pleasant, and bring smiles to her husband's face, but before he has been in the house five minutes he takes that tongue of his and stabs his wife to the heart, even before her kiss of welcome is dry on his lips, and she goes up-stairs and buries her face in her hands and sobs and cries as though her heart would break. God pity a woman that has an old bear for a husband! Many a time a poor man who has toiled all day with heart pressure upon him because of his kindness to her at home, goes home-ward and before he has been in the house five minutes the woman that should be all to him stabs him with her sharp tongue, and he says, in his grief, "I wish to God I were dead."

I think the finest tombstone I ever saw, and the prettiest epitaph I ever saw, was when I was visiting an old friend of mine. After dinner he took me into the garden, and in the most prominent place there was erected a beautiful tombstone of white marble, in memory of his wife, and on it I read her name and the date of her death, and her simple epitaph was this line: "She made home pleasant."

I remember the old Irishman who said: "I hope I'll never live to see my wife married again." Brethren, let us be kind to wife, for she has left her father and her home and her mother and given up all things for us, and she gives her life to us, and we ought to be kind to her. Never let a word slip from your tongue that will bring a drop of blood from her heart. We should be kind and loving to our children, too. I remember once, at a camp-meeting, two or three years ago, I was talking to two or three of the brothers after dinner, and to one of them a little girl, a rosy-cheeked and bright-eyed fairy, ran up and asked him some question, and he snapped out a word to her that almost made her faint, so frightened was she. I cried, "You brute, you!" Brethren, you can almost crucify one of your children with one stroke of your tongue. How cruel it is. I know how it is myself. Sometimes when I was busy at work my little boy would bother me and I would snap at him and drive him away, but I afterward hunted him up and begged his forgiveness. But some of you would sooner die than do that. Control your tongue and be kind to your children.

Think of the picture! I look upon that sweet child with his arms around my neck and he looks with beaming eyes of love in my face for the last time; and when his little arms are forever folded on his breast and he has gone from us, I never want to go in my parlor and look upon my child and say, "O, how his icy cold fingers point my memory to the past, and to my hard words and actions to that angelic child." God give us Christly teaching. Brethren, get your tongues under perfect subjugation. This is one ground on which you can enter the inner Church. Get your tongues straight.

But upon what other ground must I rely? "Because I have corrupted no man by my example." Brethren, what we need now is a few good examples. You go home, mother, and seat your little lovely daughter on your lap, and ask her, "Daughter, who is the best woman in the world?" and she will say, "Why, you, mamma." "Daughter, whom would you rather be like than any body else?" and the sweet little child will say, "You, mamma." Ask the child such questions as that and she will answer always, "You, mamma." Ah, sister, that child is mistaken; yet she is that way—there's no doubt about that. The saddest thing a father ever said to me in all of my experience was this. I was a pastor of a Church then, and I have been pastor for eight years, and know all about the relations of pastor and people. I tell you, brethren, you can't love your pastor too much, or pray for him too much—he needs your examples and prayers. This brother said to me, about four weeks after I had preached a sermon in his town: "I heard your sermon on 'Home Religion,' and it waked me up." He was a man of intelligence. I said, "What about it?" "I went home," said he, "and studied my children four weeks, in all of their varied characteristics, and all of the phases of their character and life, and I reached a verdict." "What was that?" said I. "Well, I found out that my children have n't got a single fault that I or their mother has n't got, or a single virtue that we have not got; a direct copy of my wife and myself our children are."

Our examples! A father said to me once, and he was a conscientious, good man, too: "A few days ago I was in a grocery store, where they sold provisions in the front part and kept beer and other liquors for sale in the back room. I was in there buying groceries, when a gentleman came in and said to me, 'Won't you have a glass of beer?' Without a thought, although I was never in the habit of it, I accepted. I walked back, and the beer was drawn, and as I put it to my lips my little boy pulled at my finger and said: 'Papa, what's that you 're drinking?' I stopped drinking, and told the little fellow it was beer. After a while the child again pulled my finger and asked me: 'Papa, what was that you were drinking just now?' And I told him again it was beer, lager beer; and so it was again as we were going up the street, my child pulled at my finger again and said: 'What did you say that was you were drinking, papa?' and as he asked that again, O God, my God, I would have given all the world to have been able to recall that act. I am afraid that one act will make a drunkard of my child."

Our examples! Brethren, hear me. I shall never do, or suffer myself to do, or suffer any one else to do, in my home, in the radius of my influence, any thing that would or could curse mine or

any body's child. You can have cards at your
house if you want to, but until this world burns
down, I never will, so help me God; they shall never
be brought in or remain in my house. Do you ask
me why? Nine-tenths of the gamblers of this city
were raised in Christian homes; they are the most
polite and refined gentlemen in town, and if cards
in any Christian home ever made a gambler out of
a Christian boy, then so long as life shall last, I
will never have cards in my house. If demijohns,
and glasses, and bottles ever damned a member of
the Church's son, then, so long as I have given my
home to God, demijohns, glasses, and bottles shall
have no place there. And I will tell you another
thing. Old Brother Demijohn and old Sister Demijohn, you are just raising up drunkards by the
hundreds, and I reckon if God Almighty lets your
sort of folks into heaven, the very angels would
halloo out, " Brother Demijohn and Sister Demijohn,
have you got in at last?" And some women have
reached the degraded stratum where they are nothing more or less than bar-keepers for their husbands — stirring their toddies and mixing their
drinks. Next to the biggest fool that God's eyes
ever looked upon is a woman who stirs toddies for
her husband; but the biggest fool God's eyes ever
beheld is a woman that will marry a man with
whisky on his breath.

I know what I am talking about. I believe if
I had had such a wife as some drinking men in
Cincinnati have to-day, I would now be in a drunk-
ard's grave and a drunkard's hell this moment; but,

thank God, my wife never would touch, taste, nor handle, nor suffer it in her house. I have had a woman come to me, who in her young married life had indulged her husband and seen that his wines and liquors were carefully prepared for him—I have had her come to me with haggard face, and cry out, "O Mr. Jones, in God's name, help me to save my husband from death and hell;" and she gave her husband the first years of her married life in the encouragement of drinking! An old woman in a county in Georgia—I was preaching prohibition down there, and I never felt more at home preaching Jesus Christ to sinners than I felt down there preaching prohibition—I know that it's unpopular in Cincinnati. I have been preaching prohibition experimentally, practically, collectively, and personally for about thirteen years, and it's never hurt me yet, but whisky liked to have knocked me in about thirteen months. In one county where I was talking prohibition this old snaggle-toothed, wrinkle-faced hag said of me, "I hope God will kill that man before election day for trying to rob people of their living." This old Mrs. So-and-so had buried three husbands in drunkards' graves. My Lord, what sort of an old hag was that?

I'll tell you another thing; I don't know how the preachers have been preaching to you—they are all better men than I am—but if the occupants of the two hundred pulpits in Cincinnati will stand up and talk for law and order, sobriety and righteousness will prevail in this city. God wake up the pulpits and help the brothers to talk about things that are damning this city! One preacher will talk about evangelical methods, and another preacher will split hairs a mile long on real and unreal regeneration. I never hear a man read this text— with all due respect to the preachers—" Except ye be born again ye can not enter into the kingdom of heaven"—I say I never hear that text read from the pulpit but I wish you to add: "If we confess our sins, God is faithful and just to forgive us our sins and to cleanse us from all unrighteousness." Jesus Christ knew how to preach, brethren, and Jesus Christ touched that subject to one man, an intelligent man who staggered back and asked, "Why, how can this thing be?" Hear me, brother. God's Gospel is to teach a man to quit his meanness. Come to God, and let the Lord explain his own works and let God do his own work. I heard of a grand preacher who had a grand revival; he preached day and night for three weeks on regeneration, and he never had a single convert; but brother, I believe the Gospel of Jesus Christ is adequate to reach every sinner in this city.

I am not going to run the grand old ship of Zion about ten miles from shore. I am going to bring her to the land. Ten million sinners might look at the old ship away off and say, "There she is, but I can't get to her, for if I tried to swim to her I would drown." Brother, brother! Let's run the old ship in until her keel strikes the shore. Tell the world: "All aboard! This grand old ship is going by!" You can't get the old ship of Zion too close to sinners.

"I have corrupted no man with my life; my example has been right;" that's it. "I have wronged no man; I have set no bad example." In addition to that Paul said, I have defrauded no man in a business transaction. O, for hands like these to work for God and for man!

Talk about Ingersoll, I never met an *intelligent* man yet that had been damned by Bob Ingersoll. The only difference between Bob Ingersoll and any other fellow running after him is this: Bob Ingersoll plays the fool for $1,500 a night, and this little fellow runs after him and plays the fool for nothing, and boards himself. And I tell you Bob Ingersoll is going to continue to play that kind of a fool as long as this country gives him $1,500 a night to insult God and ridicule his precious Word; and yet you go to hear him. If I had a dog to go and hear him I would kill him. He couldn't come to my house any more.

"I have defrauded no man in any business transaction." Brother, let us look into this and do what it says; do what you say you'll do and quit defrauding men. Brother, hear me; a man who has $50,000, $100,000 riding in a $1,200 carriage and living in a $25,000 house, driving down the streets meets a poor old widow from whom he has stolen. I tell you if there is any hell, it's for that kind of a man. There's no use talking. I'll tell you another thing. There are too many men in this country boarding with their wives: no doubt about that. Let me tell you another thing—when the fellow does a clean thing, God Almighty will stand by

him. He will give him three square meals every
day if he has to put the angels on one-third rations.
Let's do right and defraud no man, and we will
have righteousness, peace, and joy.

Well, I have talked considerably over an hour.
I did not intend to. But hear me, let's think about
these things. I tell you I never—I tell you I never
want to see a revival in this city, or anywhere else,
that isn't bottomed on bed rock. Let's go down
until you hear your boot-heels grating and grinding
against the Rock of Ages. None of your corn-stalk
revivals! We want the sort of revival that will
make men do the clean thing. If we can have that
sort of revival I want to see it—but not corn-stalk
revivals. Do you know what a corn-stalk revival
is? Well, if you were to pile up a lot of corn
stalks as high as this house, and burn them up,
there wouldn't be a hodful of ashes. We want a
revival of righteousness; we want a revival of
honesty; we want a revival of cleanness and purity,
of debt-paying, of prayer-meetings, of family prayer,
and of paying our brothers a little more salary.
That's the sort of revival we want. The Lord give
us this sort!

One more illustration in conclusion. Some
months ago a man was fearfully crippled in his
right leg by a railroad accident. It was fearfully
mangled and bruised. They wanted to amputate
the leg, but he said: "O I don't want to lose my
limb; preserve it if you can." They watched at
his side until at last the surgeon said: "My friend,
the crisis has come when we must amputate your

leg." He said: "Doctor, has it reached that point?" "Yes," said the surgeon. "Well," said he, submissively, "if there is no chance to save my leg, get your knife and go to work." When they got all ready and laid the patient on the table to commence the fearful operation, the surgeons desired to administer chloroform, but the mangled man said: "I do not want to take that; if I die I want to die in my full consciousness, but I want you to let me know by some sign when I begin to sink, so that I can breathe my spirit out in prayer." They told him that he could n't stand the operation without chloroform, but he said that he could. The doctor picked up the knife and said to the patient: "If you see me lay the knife down on the table you may know that you are sinking."

The doctor commenced the operation, and the man did not flinch. When he struck the arteries he laid his knife down to adjust them, and the young man took it for a sign that he was dying, and commenced praying. The surgeon picked up the knife and resumed his work. In a few minutes the operation was over, and he saw he was saved, and he turned to the surgeon and said: "Doctor, when you picked the knife up from the table and began your operation, it was the sweetest sensation I ever felt in my life." "What do you mean?" said the doctor. "I mean," said he, "that *those sensations meant life for me.*" Now, brother, when God Almighty throws down the pruning-knife it is a sign that you are sinking—the sword of the divine Spirit cutting through the tendrils of sin; but, thank

God, he has not laid down the sword. The sword of the Spirit means life. O brother, come to life in the presence of Jesus, and die in his love. God help us to take these things home with us!

------•------

SAYINGS.

INTER-COMMUNION.—We have taken down the fences now, we Christians, and for this occasion will have but one belief. The Baptist will take the Presbyterian by the arm and lead him over to the Baptist pond (for somehow or other the Baptists seem to have control of this pond), and on its banks they will feed upon Methodist grass, and there will be a great fattening. We have a combination of Methodist fire, Baptist water, and Presbyterian "hold on to what you've got," and we will have a glorious meeting. I feel it.

GIVE!—Once there was a large pond of clear water. Beside it ran a happy little streamlet. The pond said to its neighbor: "Why do you run so rapidly away? After a while the Summer's heat will come and you will need the water you now are wasting. Take example by me. I am saving all my forces, and when Summer comes I will have plenty." The streamlet did not reply, but continued on its way sparkling and bright, rippling over white pebbles, and its waters dancing in the sunlight. By and by the Summer came, with all its heat. The pond had carefully saved all its strength, not allowing a drop of water to escape. The rivulet had never changed its way, but had continued, making happy all that it had met on its winding course. The trees locked their green boughs overhead, and did not allow a sun ray to fall upon it. Birds built their nests and sang in these boughs, and bathed themselves in the pure water. Cattle drank of the living stream and delighted to stand upon the cool banks. But how was it with the pond? It was heated by the fierce rays of the sun. Its waters bred miasma and malaria. Even the frogs spurned it, and it became bereft of every sign of life. The cattle deserted it, and refused to drink of its waters. The little stream continued its journey, carrying its waters to the larger stream, to the rivers, and at last to the ocean, where God took it up in incense and kissed it and formed it into clouds. He harnessed the winds and hitched them to the clouds; and they journeyed inland until they came to this little happy streamlet, and then the cup was tipped, and as the streamlet got back its own again, a still small voice might have been heard, saying, "It is better to give than to receive."

5

Sermon III.

"Paul and Silvanus and Timotheus unto the Church of the Thessalonians which is in God the Father, and in the Lord Jesus Christ: Grace be unto you, and peace, from God our Father and the Lord Jesus Christ."—1 Thess. i, 1.

I READ for a Scripture lesson several verses in the first chapter of the First Epistle of Paul to the Thessalonians. I have read the epistles of St. Paul and St. John and St. Peter with some interest, and I trust with much profit; and after reading the epistles addressed to these Churches, I am ready to admit that, whatever men may say of the Church of the first century of the Christian era, all men must admit that the Church then had power with God and influence with men. And as I look out upon the Church of the nineteenth century, I find that in just so far as we have lost this similarity, and are unlike the Church of the first century, just that far have we lost power with God and influence over men. And I say again, just in proportion as we have maintained our similarity to the Church of the first century, have we power with God and influence with men. I believe this progressive age has improved every thing in the universe except religion, and men as they approach the religion of Jesus Christ, may well approach it cautiously, and light upon its truths like a honey-bee upon a flower, and extract the honey, but never deface its beauty or extract its fragrance. I believe in progressive

50

theology, but not in a progressive Christianity. Christianity impressed itself upon men eighteen hundred years ago as a soul-saving power, as a life-reforming power; and just in so far as it is a soul-saving and life-reforming power it still has God with it, and it still has power. Give me a progressive theology, but let me have religion in all Christian purity and power.

I sometimes think the Church to-day presents the picture of a little boy's copy-book at school. You see, he walks up to the teacher, who gives him a beautiful line as his copy. The little boy goes back to his seat, sits down and imitates the line of the copy set him by the teacher, then on the next line the little fellow will imitate his own writing, and down and down he gets worse and worse to the bottom of the page, and the last line the little fellow writes on the page is the worst line he writes. Now, Christ set the copy. The apostles imitated him. The next generation imitated the apostles, and so on down, until now the last page and line seem to be the most basely written of all. You say, is the world getting worse? Is man getting further from God? Are we losing the likeness of God altogether? No! There are more good men to-day upon earth than ever in its history, and there are more bad men to-day than ever in this world's history. If you think the devil is asleep, if you think bad agencies have retired, you have made a mistake.

Never in this world's history has the devil been so active, and his agencies more powerful than they are to-day, and this fact is a very potent factor in the world. God is depending on his Church to bring the world to him; the devil is depending on his crowd to bring the world to him. Just as God is powerless in this world without a faithful pulpit and a faithful Church, so the devil is powerless without his allies and his followers. Every good man in this country is an ally of God, and doing his best to save the world. Every bad man is an ally of the devil, and doing his best to damn the world. That is one reason why I want to find one city wholly the Lord's. I want to find one community where there is no servant of sin or of unrighteousness. I want to move my family into that community. I declare to you, as long as you have got one man in your community who is an enemy of God and the right, listen to what God says about him: "One sinner destroyeth much good." And if one will destroy much good, what will these ten thousand sinners all around here do? Brethren, if there was ever an age when we should look to primitive Christianity, and see what gave it such power with God, and such influence with men, it is to-day. If you think the soldier of the cross has nothing to do but just get up on dress parade once a week, or once a month, you do n't understand the situation; you do n't see it as it is seen by a great many of these old brethren. Well, when I was a boy they did n't have Sunday-schools, and they did n't have Church papers much. They did n't have Sunday-school literature, and they did n't have a great many things that I see now floating out be-

fore the public. Brother, when you were a boy infidel sheets were not circulated all over this country.
When you were a boy there was n't a bar-room for
every half-mile square of the American continent.
When you were a boy there was n't an infidel standing on the street corner in every town, talking and
showing his infidelity to every man. And now
that you know these things, do n't you want every
agency for good put around your home? For, I
tell you, your children, when you are dead and
gone, will be swept by this power into ruin and
desolation, unless like men you walk out to the
front and die in your tracks rather than let these
influences sweep over your home and your land.
That is what we want. I want you to let me talk
with you on this occasion for a few minutes about
the condition of things eighteen hundred years
ago, and what it is now; and we shall then learn
something from the lesson before us this afternoon.
There is a lesson here for every professing Christian man.

I am not here to parade the unfaithfulness of
the Church of God before the world; I just stop
long enough to say this: The meanest member of
the Church that ever lived in this community is
better than any of you men out of the Church; for
he tries to be good, but you have been mean ever
since you were born. I have no patience with you
trifling, cursing, drinking, godless men and women
out of the Church; and while I talk to the people
of God about their shortcomings, I want you to
understand, that you are meaner than a hundred of

them put together; so do n't you take special comfort to yourself now, while this is going on.

Now let us look at this subject as it presents
itself in the light of God's truth; and, brother, truth
is powerful for God and for you just in proportion
as you hear and obey the truth. Paul in the letter
before us, begins thus: "Paul and Silvanus and
Timotheus unto the Church of the Thessalonians,
which is in God the Father and in the Lord Jesus
Christ; grace be unto you and peace from God our
Father and the Lord Jesus Christ." Paul and
Silvanus and Timothy had preached the Gospel of
the Son of God at Thessalonica some months before
the date of this letter, and after leaving Thessalonica, or rather while they were there preaching
the Gospel, men heard the Gospel, believed the
Gospel, and obeyed the Gospel, and he organized
them into a Christian Church in this heathen city,
and then leaving on his missionary tour, after an
absence of some time—I know not definitely how
long—St. Paul addressed a letter to the Church at
Thessalonica in this language: "Paul and Silvanus
and Timotheus unto the Church of the Thessalonians, which is in God the Father and in the Lord
Jesus Christ." Now he here locates the Church of
God: "the Church of the Thessalonians, which is
in God the Father, and in the Lord Jesus Christ."

Now every truly Scriptural Church is located in
the heart of God, and God lives in the heart of
every Christian Church. The term, "in Christ
Jesus" and "having Christ Jesus in you," are in-
terchangeable. If any man be in Christ Jesus he

is a new creature; and if Christ be in you, he is formed in you the hope of glory. Brother, having Christ in you, and being yourself in Christ, mean pretty much the same thing.

Our Savior said to the race: "Behold, I stand at the door and knock; if any man hear my voice, and open the door, I will come in to him and will sup with him and he with me." And, O, what a privilege it is to open the door of my heart and let Christ in. What a privilege for him thus to be my guest in my own heart. I am ashamed of every thing I have to offer him. I am ashamed of the home I give him when he is my guest. Blessed privilege! Christ my guest! And then he says: "You shall sup with me now. I have been your guest in your heart; now you shall sit down; you shall be my guest, and you shall sup with me. I will be host, and you shall sit down at the table of my own heart and be fed with Heaven's bread and angels' food."

I am the guest of Christ, he is my host. Brother, you know what that means. I want to say at this point that you can run Confucianism without Confucius, and you can run Mormonism with Joseph Smith and Brigham Young in their graves, but you can't run Christianity without a personal, abiding, indwelling Christ. It is not a question of how you have been baptized, nor what Church you belong to, but the question of questions is, Is the Lord Jesus Christ embodied in your heart, and is he an ever-abiding guest? That is the question. The Lord Jesus Christ must abide in the hearts of men, so that we can say: "I am crucified with Christ, nevertheless I live; yet not I, but Christ liveth in me." And it is this ever present, abiding, loving, reigning Christ in the soul that gives us power with God and influence with men.

"But," says some one, "I have made profession of religion." Well, what if you have?" Have you got religion in your heart, and can you say, "The life that I now live I live by the faith of the Son of God, and the love of Him who gave himself for me?" "I die daily," said St. Paul. The first thing I do when I rise from my bed is to fall on my knees and die to this world, its pleasures, its profits, its friends, its emoluments, its losses; and I live to God, I live to righteousness, live to all that is good. That is it. The Church of God is implanted in the great heart of God, and God lives in the heart of the Church.

If I wanted to find God I would seek him in the hearts of good men and women. Whenever I am close to a good man I am close to God, for every good man is the home of God, and dwells in the heart of God himself. Well, now, the Church partakes of the nature of each individual member forming that Church. If a pastor has four hundred members in his Church, or if he has two hundred members, and fifty of them are good men and women, who love God and keep his commandments, and one hundred and fifty others are indifferent and careless and godless and Christless, then you see what sort of a Church he has. Three-fourths of it are astray from God and duty, and one-fourth pro-

claiming the love and teachings of Christ in their
character. You see what sort of a Church that
presents. Why, in the time of slavery, brothers,
if a man had two hundred slaves, and only fifty
of them were able to work, would n't he have had a
hard time making a living for his slaves? So with
two hundred members in a Church, and only fifty
of them active, that Church has got all it can do
to look after those one hundred and fifty invalids,
and has no time to go out and work and bring the
world to Christ. Do n't you see?

How many members attend the prayer-meetings
in this Church? How many do you have Wednesday nights? Do you say about twenty? Well, I
would sell out and quit, if that is the case. I'd
sell out on credit. I would no more put my wife
and children in such a Church as that—mark
what I say—I would n't suffer my children to be
raised in a Church of that sort. Now, you can run
that line if you want to, but mark what I say.
Every man in the Church who has religion goes to
prayer-meeting. You ask, How do I know? I
know because I have got religion, and it walks
about with me. You see I know what religion will
do for a fellow. I got it thirteen years ago. I was
right there when the thing happened, and I know
just exactly what it will do for a fellow. I have
tried it.

I will tell you another thing. Whenever you see
a Church and community run down that low religi-
ously, there are very few women in that community
that God can count on. I tell you when the devil

gets the help of a man's wife on his side, she has
very nearly gone nine-tenths of the road in the
direction of her husband's destruction. Sister, what
is the matter with your husband on Wednesday
night that you have n't got his arm to bring you
out to prayer-meeting? What is the matter? Is it
a fact that he has got no wife, and his wife has got
no husband? Is that the trouble? There are a
great many women in this world that I think, when
I look at their husbands, ought not to change their
names at all, but let their husbands go by their
name. They married such a little lump of nothing
that their husbands ought to go by their wives'
names, so that the people could ask of them, "What
was your name before you were married?" I think
that would go in first-rate. I reckon you will put
a little tin horse in his stocking for him every
Christmas, won't you, and buy him some candy.
Some of you look disgusted at this point. That is
the sort of look I once saw a woman wear when I
was doing my best to lift her poor drunken boy out
of debauchery. She was sitting back making noses
at me. Many a woman will stand right by and
hear her husband getting a going-over by some
friend. But the preacher, she thinks, must be very
careful what he says, or she will turn her nose up
at him. Yes, and the devil has got a mortgage
on that nose of yours, too. He is going to foreclose
some of these days, too. These are facts, and facts
are stubborn things, you know. You can not get
round a fact.

Suppose that with a Church of two hundred

members we have twenty that are full of faith in God and duty, and one hundred and eighty that stand out careless and indifferent—what can such a Church as that do? Only twenty of you able to fight, with one hundred and eighty hospital rats to look after! Do n't you see why we make no inroads on the world? Do n't you see why it is that you have n't had one hundred genuine conversions in the last ten years? Now you see the reason of things, and my plan is to take a common-sense view of the facts. I like to deal with facts. You can 't get round a fact. Theories you can brush out of the way, but when you come to a fact you can not dig under it, and you can 't jump over it; you have to meet it.

"The Church of the Thessalonians, which is in God the Father;" that means in every good word and work. That means in every thing that will help the world to be better and against every thing that makes the world worse. "Which is in God the Father, and in the Lord Jesus Christ." Then Paul goes on: "We give thanks to God always for you all, making mention of you in our prayers."

O, what a privilege it is for a preacher to pray for his congregation—his Church.

I never preach to a congregation for whom I have not prayed. I would be afraid to preach to a man for whom I had not prayed. I do thank God that always before I am called into the pulpit it is my privilege to go to God in prayer. There are a great many styles of preachers in this world, and a great many styles of preaching. I reckon every

man has his own style. If he copies after no one
else he is what we call an original character. God
never made two men alike. If he did, one of them
was of no account. You can put that down. A man
is potent just as he is himself. Now, the general
pulpit style of America is about like this: "Here
I am, Rev. Jeremiah Jones, D-o-c-t-o-r of D-i-
v-i-n-i-t-y, saved by the grace of God, with a message to deliver. If you repent, and believe what I
believe, you will be saved, and if you do n't you
will be damned, and I do n't care much if you are."
That is the style. That's the general style of the
American pulpit everywhere—except in this city,
of course. Brethren, I won't make any charges
against you. A great many preachers go into the
pulpit with a ramrod and a pump. They ram back
every thing that they think will hurt, and pump out
every thing that is pretty and nice—and the people
are just dusting to hell by the thousand. At every
conference you notice a delegation going up to the
bishops from the leading Churches. One delegation will go to the bishop and will say: "Bishop, we
want you to send us a preacher this year that is
popular with the young people." Another delegation will go in and say: "Bishop, please send us a
preacher that is popular with other denominations."
Another crowd will go in and say: "Bishop, please
send us a preacher that is popular with sinners."
And another crowd will go in and say: "Bishop,
please send us a preacher that is popular with every
body." But I tell you, I have never heard of a
delegation going up to conference and asking the

bishop: "Please, sir, send us a minister that is popular with God Almighty. We want a preacher that walks and talks with God." O, my, when you get this sort they will turn this country over; no doubt about that.

St. Paul prayed for the Church of the Thessalonians, and it is the duty of a preacher to pray for his congregation. I have no doubt some of these preachers here have been wrestling with God at midnight, on their knees, after all their members were asleep. O God, bless and save my people, these preachers have long been praying. Now what have you been doing? It takes just three things to make up a good sermon—thought, study, and prayer. You, men, associate that with every sermon you hear. Think you that I do n't have to study and pray over what I am saying? If I did n't you would n't want to hear it. You associate with sermons study, and thought, and prayer, do n't you? Now, some preachers say that they do n't have to study any. They say they open their mouths, and the Lord will fill them. Well, so he will fill them. Just as soon as you open it he will fill it with air. That is all that I know of that he will fill it with.

There is many an old air-gun shooting around over this country. Is n't that about all you can make out of that? These fellows do n't have to study.

We had one of them once in Georgia—I do n't know how many more we had. He said he did n't study; he just opened the Bible, and the first passage he struck was his text. He had Herod cutting off Abraham's head, and he had John the Baptist in the fiery furnace. They had him up before a conference, and the presiding elder said: "Brother, I understand you do n't study." The good brother responded that he did n't have to study; he just opened his mouth and the Lord filled it. "But," said the elder, "did n't you state awhile ago that Herod cut off Abraham's head?" "O yes, I said that." "Did n't you tell them that God put John the Baptist in the fiery furnace?" "O, yes, I said that, too." "Well," said the elder, "you can go on out. You can't get any new license from me. God does n't tell lies, and his Bible is true; and he did n't tell you any thing about Herod cutting off Abraham's head, or about John the Baptist being in the fiery furnace." So much for those who open their mouths for the Lord to fill them. Let me tell you, God never does any thing for a fellow that he can do for himself. God is n't going to run around posting lazy preachers that do n't study. He has got too much else to do. You associate with a sermon prayer, and thought, and study—and it just takes those three things to get ready to preach—and there is no preparation without them. You show me a preacher that does n't study, and I will show you an air-gun. Of course there are no air-guns here, but I am speaking of those in Georgia.

The next thing to an air-gun is an old powder-gun—one with nothing in it but powder. Nobody ever gets hurt with that. It is like a fellow shooting at birds without any shot. The birds enjoy it as much as he does; none of them get hurt. But

whenever a fellow puts in powder and shot, and puts
on a great cap from the ammunition of God, and
lays the barrel on the rail and takes careful aim,
and fires and hits—that's the time. After he hits
the fellow he can stop and apologize: "I did n't
mean to hit you there. I aimed here." But it's all
right. That is one of the preachers who aims where
he hits and hits where he aims. The greatest blessing any community ever had is a game preacher—
never afraid of the devil. And the greatest curse
is a time-serving preacher who is afraid of hurting somebody's feelings if he does his duty. Poor
little fellow! You should send him over some
molasses candy this evening and let him suck it.
Now, it takes two things to make a good sermon, and
that is a good preacher and a good hearer, and when
you get a good preacher and a good hearer together
then you are going to have a first-class sermon.
Well, if I must study, and read, and pray in order
to get ready to preach, what must you do to get
ready to hear? The Bible says a good deal about
that. It says: "Take heed how you hear." It
says: "Be not forgetful hearers, but doers of
the work." If you want to be blessed in your
deeds, get ready to hear. How will you get ready
to hear? By thought, and prayer, and study. Just
precisely as a man gets ready to preach, you ought
to get ready to hear.

Now, for instance, here is a woman. One fact in
her history is, that she is always made happy under preaching. One day a preacher went home
with her from Church, and says: "Sister, how is it

that you are always made happy under preaching, I do n't care who preaches, or what sort of a sermon it is?" "Well," said the woman, "you are the pastor, and you come round once a month and preach, and I spend thirty days in praying God to bless his word and make it effective in my soul ; and do you reckon that after thirty days of earnest prayer the Lord disappoints me? So it is a good sermon to me, I do n't care what it is to other people."

When you get ready to hear, you are going to be profited by the preacher. You can take the best seed in the world and scatter it out here, and you need n't expect to bring any crop ; but you plow the soil, and put in the seed, and till the ground, and har- row it, and in due time comes the harvest. So you can take the best seed from the granaries of heaven, and scatter it about on the ground of men's hearts, and you need not expect any return from it, but if you take the plowshare of faith and prepare the ground, and harrow it over with supplication, then the seed falls down into good ground and springs up and bears fruit; some fifty, some sixty, and some a hundred-fold, to the glory of God.

Brother, it is just as necessary that you prepare your heart to hear as it is to prepare your ground for the seed. This is the seed of the Gospel falling upon your heart, and if there is no preparation for the seed there will be no harvest. Get ready to hear. How many people have been on their knees wrestling with God, praying, " God bless this sermon to-day to my soul ; God prepare me to hear his word." How many of you have wrestled with

God that the power of heaven may rest on the word, and that you may be prepared to hear?

Prayer, that is what we want. Praying men and women, and the preachers that will wrestle with God and people that will wrestle with God. Now, we do n't want any special preachers. God can put up with any sort of preachers at a meeting if he can just have the power in his work—and you pray the power down from God. That is the way to get it. I can stand here and preach for a week and nothing will be accomplished unless you get the power of the Holy Ghost on the word.

And, brethren, what we need now is not a fresh preacher, but the Holy Ghost falling down on us, and we want to call him down, to pray him down, and we want a dozen or two hearts lifted up in prayer, so that before the first prayer gets up to God the answer will meet it half-way, and by the time the prayer gets to the ear of God the blessing is down here on the people. That is what we want. I think of a brother, one of the most wonderful workers for Christ, I ever knew. He was at Huntsville, Ala., and I wondered at the power of God that came down on the people. I knew several were praying. One night about 12 o'clock I was sleeping in the room with a young brother, who went there with me, and another gentleman, and they were disturbing me with their snoring, and I put up with it until after 12 o'clock, and I knew I ought to go to sleep, and I woke them up to help me move my bed into the parlor, as I wanted to lie in there. So they helped me into the parlor, with my bed, and

6

as we went into the parlor we walked right up on
our host—one of the best men under the skies—
praying after midnight on his knees, in his parlor;
wrestling with God. And my brother told me that
he walked out in the hall that same night at three
o'clock, and there was the brother still on his knees
and still wrestling with God for the power of the
Holy Ghost upon us. I told my brother, "Something has got to happen from this praying, when you
see God's people wrestling all night in prayer that
heaven's blessing may rest upon the people." Brethren, what we want here is men that are so busy
praying at 3 o'clock in the morning that they won't
have to preach at all. I want this settlement saved.
O, God, let down thy power.

Charles G. Finney, perhaps the most powerful
preacher that ever stood before an American audience, carried around with him an old brother, Nash.
The old brother seldom went to Church, but when
Brother Finney would start to preach, he would
fall on his knees in their room and begin to pray.
One night, Mr. Finney said, he began to preach,
when in a few moments the power of God came
down on all the congregation. He could almost
hear the audible steps of God coming in the aisles
of the church, and he said every sinner in the church
was converted to God, and every Christian made
happy. He never saw such power in his life. As
he walked out he said: "I know Brother Nash has
had a big time with the Lord to-night, I know he
has." He started to walk on to where he lived
with Brother Nash, and when he got there Brother

Nash was lying flat on his back on the floor. After
he got quiet Mr. Finney said: "I suppose you had
a great time with God. God has been upon us with
power." "Yes," said Brother Nash, "I was praying, and God came on me with such a baptism that
I prayed for the same thing on the Church, and he
stayed with me and went to the Church, and I stood
up and praised him, and sat down and praised him,
until I fell on the floor and shouted praise to God
for sending such power to rest upon the children
of men."

I tell you, my brethren and sisters here this
afternoon, if we can get men and women who will
pray God's power down on us, you will see things before another week that you never expected to see just
right here. Now, mark what I tell you. Lord God
Almighty, pour upon these people the spirit of
prayer, so that we carry it with us every moment.
Mr. Finney said: "I have never seen the power
of God rest upon a people until the spirit of prayer
has taken possession." Now, brother, let us leave
Sam Jones out of this meeting. This is God's
work. Let us give God the glory. He will glorify
no man on earth. As soon as you look up you will
see the power of God down upon you. Prayer,
prayer, that is what we want. Mr. Story, I believe it
was, illustrated this question. He said he was pastor
of a Church for eighteen years, and each successive
year God poured revival fire upon his people, and
hundreds and thousands of souls were turned to
good. "And," he said, "I frequently wondered why
it was that God blessed such an unfaithful pastor as

I am." He said: " At last I was standing by the bedside of one of my people, when perhaps he was dying, and he took my hand and said: ' Dr. Story, I am going to leave the world and go home to God. I want to thank you for much help you have been to me as my pastor. I have been poor and not able to do much for you, but I have done what I could, and for the eighteen years since you took charge of your Church, I have spent every Saturday night in prayer that God might pour his power upon you.' " Now, when you want power, you get on your knees; for I tell you the power of the pulpit is with the pew. I wish we had some good prayers here. I wish we had some women that walk and talk with God, and God would hear them as they cried Amen! Pray without ceasing—your work of faith and labor of love, and patience of hope.

Now, first, the Church was located in the heart of God; secondly, it was a prayerful Church; thirdly, it had works of faith, labors of love, and patience of hope. These are the three component elements of a Scriptural Church—works of faith, labors of love, patience of hope. What is a work of faith? It isn't a work of sight or knowledge. What is a work of sight? See that farmer plowing along between those rows of corn that wave on each side of him like a sea of green. Look at him as he plows between the rows. He can almost hear the joints of the corn cracking and popping under the pressure of its growth. As he plows he looks upon the corn. That is a work of sight. He can just see his crop coming on. What is work of knowledge? I heard two darkies coming along one day and one of them said: "I loves to work for So-and-so." The other says: "Why?" He answers: "Because I knows that just as soon as the work is done there is the money." That is a work of knowledge. What is a work of faith? I will tell you. Let me illustrate. Suppose you knew that old Colonel So-and-so was going to get religion to-morrow and join the Church. Suppose you knew that, what would you do? You would go and see him this evening and talk and pray with him. After it was over, would not you want to say, "I had a finger in that pie; I went and talked and prayed over him." Don't you know human nature so well? Well, what's a work of faith? It is go and see the old colonel this evening and pray that to-morrow he may be converted, and pray with him, because God says, "according to your faith so be it unto you." You well know what it is to pull on a cold collar. It takes a good tame horse to do it. You hitch him up of a cold, frosty morning, hitch him to a big load, and he sets to and pulls it off like a mule—that is what we call a work of faith. It is pulling on a cold collar. That kind of a horse you can hitch to a tree on a frosty morning and he will make a hundred set pulls at it—that is what we call a work of faith, pulling on a cold collar. I knew a fellow once who had a wagon load of wood to haul to camp and it was a cold morning. He hitched up his horses, but they would not pull a pound. He put a boy on each horse and then he ran them up and down, riding about two or three miles, and got them warmed up and then hitched them up and they pulled right off.

You notice how a preacher, Baptist or Methodist, in this country starts a meeting. The first thing you know he starts raking his members up and down the road for a week or ten days. He is getting the Church warmed up. They would not pull a hen off her roost till you got them warmed up. After you have warmed up a brother he will pray powerfully, but if you did n't he would n't pray one bit—running on feeling, you know. But he is a sight when you get him warmed up. Now, my doctrine is, I will serve God and do right, feeling, or no feeling. That is my doctrine. I never stop to ask how I feel. I just do what it is God wants done or what it is the Church wants me to do. A dog will run a rabbit when he feels like doing it, and when he does n't feel like it, he won't. If I were you, and all run to feeling, I would hunt rabbits. I reckon you would make a good rabbit dog. You ain't fit for much else. Now, a work of faith is to go right along and do what God and his Church wants you to do, and ask no questions; that is a work of faith. What is faith? St. James says: "If you will show me your faith without your works I will show you my faith by my works." I will show you what I believe by the way I do. And if you will find me a man that is busy for God, I will show you a man that has got works of faith and will do any thing whether he feels like it or not. A heap of people think if they do a thing when they do n't feel like it that they are hypocrites. Well, we will talk about that some other time.

Now, what is the difference between a work of faith and a labor of love? There is nothing in kind—it is a difference in degree. For instance, the first day I joined the Church I went home at night and my wife pulled the Bible down and said: "We will have family prayers." I took the Bible out of her hand and it almost shook me from head to foot, and my first impulse was to lay it back on the table. I read a chapter, however, and got down and prayed. The perspiration just poured off me. O, it was hard. It was a work of faith, but I just kept on praying, and prayed night and morning in my family until it has got to be the most delightful moments I spend at home—the time I spend in family prayer. Here's a man who the first week went to prayer-meeting. It was a work of faith, but he kept on going, till now he is impatient for the prayer-meeting to begin. He looks on Wednesday night as better than any other night in the week. Here's a weak faith. Get at it, whether you like it or not, and keep at it, and then it becomes a labor of love. An old brother gets up in meeting and says: "I feel it is my duty to pray in my family, and I feel it is my duty to pray in public, and I feel it is my duty to support the Gospel." You old hound, you, you didn't get half a mile on the way to glory, yet you are running on duty!

"I feel it is my duty to do so and so." Sing it out; you have heard such people, have n't you? I thank God this thing of religious duty is played out with me. I tell you what it is with me—it is a pleasure; it is a privilege. Why, brother, I use family prayer and public prayer, and read the Bible and visit the sick and give to the poor, just as a bird does its wings, to carry me where I am going to. Do n't you see I use these things as I use the passenger trains, to ride on to take me where I am going? What would you think of a man starting from home who would go trotting down the railroad on foot? You ask him why he does n't take the cars, and he say: "Well, I feel it my duty to go on foot." You know, when they first built engines they put only two wheels on them. They would run and make schedule time, but schedule time was only just three miles an hour, and it was all they could do to pull one car. After a while they put a jack under that engine and put eight more wheels under it, making ten in all, and that engine will cut along at the rate of fifty miles an hour, and will pull forty cars if you couple them on. That is the difference between the little two-wheeled fellow and one of the sort they run now. Brother, you have got your two-wheeled business out; you will make the schedule time of three miles an hour. Brother, there are lots of your little two-wheelers saying prayers and reading Bibles. I want the good Lord to get under some of you old brothers and put eight more wheels under you. I want you to have family prayer and visit the sick—and make public prayers—and do every Christian work, for that is what Christians do who have the wheels to roll on. The difference between a stationary engine and a locomotive is that the former stands still, while the latter has wheels, that is all. Now, brother, get up and let God put more wheels under you. That is what you want. You are making three miles an hour right along, but the devil can catch you whenever he wants to. It is no trouble for the devil to catch you, and keep up with you, or lie asleep an hour or two, and then catch up again, and give you a smiling and smashing up. Lord, give us wheels enough to keep out of the way of the devil. Just think of it. Three miles an hour, and on my journey home! "Angel band, come bear me home." Well, if you ever get there, angels will have to take you, for that thing you are on will never do it.

Now, listen, it is a labor of love to do any thing, and do it cheerfully. The Lord loves a cheerful servant; a cheerful servant loves the Lord. Any thing the Lord wants done, do it cheerfully, gladly, lovingly. Hear that. Give cheerfully, work cheerfully, labor cheerfully at any thing. Brother, I have been asked the question many a time, "How can you stand so much work?" I don't know but one reason for it, and that is, I have gone along cheerfully and gladly from the day I started until now, and I believe if I had gone along slowly and complainingly, I would have worked myself into the grave years ago. Brother, I believe cheerfulness is the journal that keeps down the heat. You need to get more oil, some of you, or you will burn up before you get to perdition. Cheerfulness! Do gladly what the Lord wants done. My hour is out. One or two words more and I will quit you at this hour. Paul says: "Remembering, without ceasing your work of faith, and labor of love and patience of hope, . . . For our Gospel came not unto you in word only, but also in power, and in the Holy Ghost, and in much assurance."

Now, brother, what we want at this meeting is a Gospel of power—mark the expression. How will you get it? You know when God wants to launch out his laws into force to do work for himself, he does n't count to see how many noses he has got. He goes by weight. He puts up scales and weighs us. Do you understand it? There is many a great two-hundred-pound professor around this country, and you put him on God's scale and he does n't weigh an ounce. He has a great, big, fat body; but if you could pull out his soul, and show it, you would say: "What is that starved, shriveled, shrunken thing you have got there? Why, it has n't had a square meal in ten years."

SERMON IV.

TRUST IN GOD, AND DO RIGHT.

"Trust in the Lord and do good; so shalt thou dwell in the land, and verily thou shalt be fed. Delight thyself also in the Lord, and he shall give thee the desires of thy heart. Commit thy way unto the Lord; trust also in him, and he shall bring it to pass."—PSA. XXXVII, 3-5.

THESE three verses which I have read cover about all the ground that you and I have ever been over or ever need go over until we have stepped inside the pearly gates. In each of them there is a precious promise, and in each one of these promises are conditions. I sometimes think we look too much to the promise, and too little at the conditions. I believe there is only one unconditional promise in the Book, as pertains to life and salvation, and that is the promise, you remember, God made to Adam when he was wretched and unable to comply with the conditions. God said to him in that lost and ruined estate: "The seed of the woman shall bruise the serpent's head." And this put Adam right where he could comply with the conditions, and since that all promises in the Book are conditional promises.

You might ask me: "What do you mean by conditions?" These railroads running by, yonder, haul passengers, for instance, on certain conditions. I know of but two—one is, get your ticket; the other is, get aboard. And just as soon as you com-

ply with these conditions, then all the speed in that
engine and all the comfort of that coach is yours
to your destination. And when a man complies
with the conditions of God's promises, then all the
power there is in God and all the comfort there is
in the Divine Spirit is his. And the world must
learn this fact. It is not so much a question of
who I am, but to what am I intrusted. There's a
good deal in that. I start to cross the Atlantic in
a paper box, and as soon as my box gets wet it
comes to pieces, and down it goes, and I go down
with it. If I start in one of those grand ocean
steamers, then all the strength in her hull, and all
the power in her boilers, and all the skill of her
officers is mine, and, thank God, I'll never go down
until she does. If I commit myself to the power
of the flesh, I am no stronger than the thing I commit myself to; but if I commit myself to God, I'll
never go down until God does, and he never goes
down. His course is upward all the way along.

These promises, as I said, are conditional promises, and we would be astonished to know how
many of these promises there are in the book.
Some man once compiled all the promises there are
in the book, and made a book of them, and it was
very large; and seeing the advertisement an old
Christian man wrote to the publishers for a copy of
"The Promises of God," but they answered him
that the edition was all sold, and the book was out
of print. He buried his face in his hands and cried,
"'The Promises of God' out of print! How sad;"
and he walked into his room and opened his Bible,

and the first page was covered with precious promises, and he said, "Thank God, this is not out of print." This book is full of them, and I sometimes think the reason we do n't realize more out of these promises is because we look too little to their conditions.

There is not a condition in life but what these promises go down to them and up to them and around them. There are thirty-two thousand precious promises in this book. There is a promise of the Father to us all. That 's the precious part of it, and one wonders that such a Father could be so good to such children as we are, and my present joy and my eternal hope are based on the fact that I can look up in his face, and say, " Father, my Lord and my God and Jesus." I feel that God is my Father, just as I feel that you are my brother. A man who realizes that God is his Father can realize in the deepest sense what it is to love his neighbor. There is a great deal in that too. We are not close enough together in this world. We are divided. I do n't mean by rivers—I do n't mean by geographical stretches, but I mean that we are divided in that every fellow has rigged him up a little concern of his own and gets himself off from every body else. There 's too much of that.

These promises are rich to us in proportion as we can realize that God is our Father, and that we are the children of God, and therefore brothers and sisters in Christ. I would scarcely consider my sister worthy of the name of " sister " unless she was better to me than to herself. I would n't own my brother if he did any thing that was too good for me. I would be ashamed of him, and I would despise myself if the best place in my heart and home did n't belong to my brothers and sisters. Good Lord, knock out this step-brother and step-sister business, and help us to be blood-kin to one another. That's what we want.

These promises come to us all alike, and they come to us as the children of a great Father, and they come to us in all conditions of life, and there is a promise for you and one for me;—a promise for me in the morning, at noon, and at night; a promise for me when I am living and a promise for me dying; a promise for me on earth and in heaven. There is not an inch of the way from the hour you gave yourself to God until the end, that you do not put your foot down on a precious promise that will rest your body, and on which you can pillow your head at night.

I appreciate the old woman that took the preacher home to dinner one day. She was preparing the dinner and the preacher picked up the Bible off the table, and was reading it at random, when he noticed the letters "T. P." marked often on the margin, and when she came in he said, "What does this 'T. P.' stand for that you have here?" She said, "Where do you see it, now?" He said, "Why, here, opposite this verse, 'Bread shall be given him.'" "Why," said she, "those letters 'T. P.,' written on the margin of my Bible there, stand for 'Tried and Proven;' I have tried them, and proven them to be true." And so, brethren, we should do likewise. We should have

our " T. P.'s " and be able to say, " I have tried the
promises of God, and proven them to be true."

These promises come to us in all their righteousness and fullness, but we had better stop and stand
a few minutes on their conditions. There is too
much of this harping on the Divine side in this
world. Every fellow thinks if the Lord would swap
sides with him he would run in first rate. We want
to do the running ourselves, and have God do
the repairing. We are all perfectly willing to do
God's part of the thing, but none is willing to do
his own part of the business. God will never get a
liking for you. That's your own job, and some of
you have got a mighty tough job. God will never
quit drinking whisky for you, and nothing in God's
world will keep a man sober who is pouring whisky
into his hide. Christ and whisky won't stay in the
same hide, at the same time.

I know when a man opens his mouth on the
ruinous effects of whisky he is dubbed a " political
preacher," a politician drumming for some party. I
do n't go much on party myself. That's so. I want
the political parties of this country to crawl up out of
the mud and wash themselves from head to foot and
put on clean clothes before I have any thing to do
with them. Instead of breaking down the political
fence and getting in on them, I do n't think I would
go in if they were to invite me in.

I was running on politics? Well, if there is one
class of people in this country I can not pray for
it's politicians. These politicians I can not pray
for. Some power whispers back when I try to,

"Do n't talk to me about them." Do you know a pious politician in America to-day? Do you? Rack me out one; I want to see him powerful bad. I've been hunting for one for years. I ain't on politics, but I wanted to say this much.

I've got the profoundest contempt for a man or woman that will drink wine, beer, or whisky. It's these things that are debauching humanity. And another thing I want to say. A good many of you are drinking beer or whisky or wine for your health. The devil is in it, and he does n't care whether you drink it for your health or not. He does n't care how or why you do it—all he wants is that you do it. If the Church of God in America would quit drinking whisky and vote on this infernal whisky question they could starve out half the lager-beer saloons in the country in six months, and vote the balance out of sight, for half of the saloons in Cincinnati are run by Church members—I do n't say Christians. God bless you, a Christian won't drink that stuff. I got religion thirteen years ago, and I know what a Christian can do.

There are a dozen preachers here who know more than I ever will. They're posted on a thousand things I never even heard of, but I'll say this much; there are two things I know well, one is what a fellow has to do to be religious, and the other is what he must refuse to do to be religious. I know these two things as well as any one, and that's about enough for this occasion.

Look at the conditions. "Commit your way to God and trust in him and do good, and you shall

dwell in the land, and verily you shall be fed."
There is a promise covering earth and time, and
the wants of the world; and I am glad to say to
you that there is not a physical want of my nature
but what this world stands with outstretched hands
to give it to me. I've heard of people starving to
death, but I never saw them. I never saw the
coffin of a man who had starved to death. I've no
patience with people who starve in this country—
not a particle.

If you want a sure successful life in this world
in every sense, the Bible says: "Trust in the Lord
and do good." How will I get every thing I want
for my physical man? "Trust in the Lord and do
good." Trust in God and do your duty—that's it
exactly. There's a heap of trust in this country.
There is the trust that makes men stand with hands
held out a-waiting for God to drop something in.
He will take every thing you give. That's one
kind of trust, and that's about nine-tenths of the
faith in this country—a catch-all-that-comes faith.
That's true. Always begging for something—Lord
bless you, if that's your faith. The country is just
a nation of beggars—that's the truth about it.
Yes, it is, too—religious tramps knocking at God's
door begging. I've a contempt for this sort of
thing—I have, too—always on the beg.

I've children, and when they hang around me
and beg for something, I don't give it to them; but
when I carry home presents and playthings for the
little ones, and get there at midnight, the first thing
that greets my ears when I awake in the morning is

not the little fellows in there begging for something, but they have got hold of what I have brought them, and have found it in the other room. And I hear one say: "I've dot the best plaything;" and another says, "Ain't this nice?" and "Ain't that a good papa to bring us all these nice things?" and as I lie there I think in my heart, I'm glad I brought these things. So God has been bringing us things, and all we want to hear is that he is around, and we are right after him begging for something, and never show gratitude for what we have received. Lord, have mercy on us. We don't deserve any more.

As I said, I don't go much on the divine side of the question; I look for the assurance that God is faithful to what he promises. There are lots of preachers who are everlastingly preaching on the God side of redemption, on the Divinity of Christ, and the authenticity of the Scriptures, and of the mysteries of redemption, and the incarnation. La me! the devil doesn't want any better joke on a preacher than to start him off on that line. If I ever see a fellow on the divine side of the Gospel, he puts me in mind of those disciples who had been fishing all night, and Christ walked up to them and said—I can imagine I see them all languid and depressed with their ill luck, and hungry—"Cast your net on the other side of the ship, over there." And they said: "Why, Master, we fished all night and got nothing." "Put your net on the other side of the ship;" and they did, and it broke with fishes.

There's many a preacher fishing on the wrong side of the ship—on the God side of the question. There's no fish over there. You ask one of them how many fish he has caught, and he will say: "Well, I haven't caught any, but I have had a lot of fine bites." Good Lord, help us to see that the fish are on the man side of the Gospel, and attend to our own business and let the Lord attend to his. That's determination. Let's stand on our side of the Gospel. Let us try to save souls. It's his business to create souls, and let him attend to his business. You are the fellows to bring them in, and Christ will attend to the rest and see that his blood cleanses us from all sin. If I want to dwell in the land and be fed of it, all I need do is to trust in God and do my duty. We have plenty of trust.

St. James gave us a clincher at this point when he said, "Show me your faith without your works, and I'll show you my faith by my works." That's the test of a man's faith. A man is judged by faith here, but by works hereafter. Every man must go before the judgment bar on the merits of his life. "Because I hungered and ye fed me, come in." That's it. Faith without works is dead! dead! dead! "Trust God, and do your duty."

Kind friends, a better race of people never walked the face of earth than those of Nashville. I love them for their prayers and sympathy. One day they tried to impress on me the fact that I ought to accept a home in their midst and accept kindnesses to me and my family. I said: "I don't need any house. I have a better house now than any of you.

I just live all around here, and when I get there
your wife gives me a better meal than she gives
you, and I get a better room than you do; and the
fact of the business is, I'm getting along better than
you all." Trust in God and do your duty, and
every thing in this country is wide open.

I'll tell you what's true. Since I gave my
heart to God I have had three square meals a day—
you can tell it by my looks—and plenty of good
clothes, and have any of you more than that? If
you have, what's done with it? Get it out here.
You won't have it long. While you do have it it's
a heap of trouble. I mixed with some of the old
rich fellows in one town, and I told 'em I wouldn't
swap places forty-eight hours with any of 'em.

I don't want to run a three or four-hundred-
thousand dollar concern for my board and lodging
and clothes. I've got too much sense for that.
John Jacob Astor was walking on Broadway one
day, and two fellows were walking behind him, and
one says: "Jim, would you attend to all old Astor's
business for your meals and clothes?" Jim said:
"No; I'm no fool." "Well," says the other,
"that's all old Astor gets." He owned twenty
thousand houses in New York, and he couldn't live
in more than one of them to save his life, and I
live in that many myself, and I get along as well as
he did. I'm not bothered with the thing. Money
is like walking-sticks; one will help you along, but
fifty on your back will break you down. Money is
like salt water; the more you get the more you want.
When you are full you want it worse than ever.

If a fellow has ten thousand dollars he wants twenty; if he has twenty he hankers for forty, and so on, and when he has a hundred thousand dollars he is a great, big, downright lump of selfishness from head to foot. If I were to follow the earth's plan—I have a wife and little children—I would go to work and buy two or three thousand bolts of linen, bleaching and domestic; buy five thousand cases of shoes, two or three thousand suits of clothes for my boys, and build a big warehouse and fill it with flour, and lard, and hams, and I am laid up then for hard times. I want to have plenty, you know. I would rather have my little home than have the job of keeping rats and thieves off the building, and I'll have an easier job. I can get to sleep when night comes. There's a heap in that. I met an old fellow in the city some time ago when the banks were shaky. He said: "I'm troubled; the money interests of this country are in an awful condition; and our banks have locked up what we have." I said: "Why, I did not know that." He said: "Why, the papers are full of it." "I never read any thing about banks," I answered; "I'm not interested in that part of the paper."

Brethren, I'll tell you one thing; you may let every bank in the country break, and they won't get me for a nickel—I have n't any thing to lose. I never want to be afraid some one would steal what I had before I wake in the morning. They would n't steal it if they knew I had n't more than I wanted. Trust God and do right, and you won't starve. When I joined the North Georgia Conference I was bankrupted—I've never got over it, in fact—but it did n't bother me.

I was put on a circuit that paid the preacher the year before $65. I had a wife and one child, a horse and $8—that was my assets. I took charge of the circuit, and the thought never struck me that I could not live. I was glad I had a place to work for Christ. I had to give my note for $120 to get a house—that was twice as much as the preacher got the year before. An old brother in the Church said to me: "You'll starve; you can not live on this circuit." I said, I'm going to stay here. Well, I did my best. I think I preached about five hundred times a year on circuits when I first started, and along about April of the first year my wife said to me: "Every thing is out, money and provisions and all."

Brethren, did you ever notice how every thing gives out at once, coffee, flour, and so on? I said, "Wife, it'll all come right. The Bible says so, and I'll starve to death if it is n't true. I have done my duty the best I could." It was not more than an hour after this that a neighboring brother drove up with a wagon load of stuff, and I had more in my house then than I ever had since. "Trust in God and do your duty." I said to my wife then, "We'll stay right here and not say a word, and if you and I and the child do starve we'll let 'em think we died of typhoid fever. Whenever you put your trust in God and do your duty you'll come out ahead every time." I'm sorry if any brother is uneasy about his salary. Do your duty. No work is hard if Christ is with us, and will bless us in our work.

I would n't give the spirit of the old negro woman down South for all of the alleged faith of some Christians. She was coming down the street with a big basket of clothes, singing happily as a lark, when a citizen said to her: "Good morning, aunty, you seem to be as happy as a lark this morning." "Well," said she, "I is, boss." "Have you any money laid up?" "No, boss, I has n't." "A home of your own?" "No, boss." "Well, how do you live?" "I washes for it," said she. "Suppose you get sick and could n't work, what would become of you?" Said the old black woman, cheerfully, "I neber s'poses any thing of de kind, boss. The Lord is my Shepherd, and I ain't going to want." I would n't give the spirit of that old woman for all the money in America, when it comes down to facts.

I have seen some members of the Church who said they were starving, and I thought it was a good thing. And I 've seen some preachers nearly starving, and I remember a minister who despised the way the people had of putting off punched nickels on him. He said it was scandalous. I said: "You need n't complain, you 've got the drop on them; you put off punched sermons on them." That 's about even.

"Trust in God and do your duty," that 's it; and I 've never yet known a faithful, sacred man to want, and that 's all we can have in this world — what we eat and wear. Said one of these rich fellows to me, "Jones, do you want us rich men to scatter our money all over town? What would be-

come of us?" I said you'll have it back in twelve
months. All you lose will be only one year's interest, that's all. They will have it again if it's
turned loose to-morrow. That's true.

Affinities sometimes determine some questions.
"Trust in the Lord and do good." Do your duty,
and this world has never witnessed the fact that
you should not be cared for in this life. I do n't
mean that a man should turn loose and do nothing
in the world but sing and pray. It is my religious
duty to work as well as pray. I never saw a real
lazy man in my life that I had any confidence in his
religion. A lazy preacher—of course you have n't
any in Ohio—is a man God will not have much to do
with. A fellow gets religion, he gets it in his blood
and muscle, all over, from head to foot, and it makes
an industrious man out of him. It'll make a
woman industrious. There are women in this world
who have n't struck a lick of work with their own
hands for years. They board and lie around and
about; all they do is shop, shop, shop. Hell is full
of such women as that! That sort can not go to
heaven.

I do n't care how much you work—it's Christian.
If you're worth a million dollars, what's that
compared to the wealth of the whole continent?
And yet you think you are some one if you own a
few nickels! They're the poorest thing a fellow
was ever loaded down with. You can scatter nickels
along the way ten feet apart, and you can tole a
man into hell with them. You know what sort of
animals you can tole. I'm not reflecting on any

one here, mind you. "I'm just insinuating a reference," as the old fellow said. "Get all I can— keep all I have," is the curse of the world and the Church. That's it.

Take the next promise: "He will give you the desires of your heart." That's a bigger promise than the other. Do you know how to get every thing you want? "Delight thyself in the Lord." There's too much moping and sad religion in this world. It's not religion—it's not Christianity. That's what I mean. Many a Christian is moping through this world with a long face, as if his father were dead, and left him out of his will, without a cent. If the Lord God, my Father, had done that I couldn't look worse than a great many of these Christian people. Some of us think it's a sin to laugh.

One good sister went away the other night and said: "I don't like so much levity." Poor soul, I hope you're much better by this time. If you take a tonic to-day you'll be still better to-morrow. "I don't like so much levity." Call this levity? Crack these jokes one at a time, and you'll find every one of 'em has the red-hot sting of a hornet tangled up in it, and you'll get stung. If you think it's levity it's because you have a levitous mind. There is no levity in this world; so it seems to a fellow who has dyspepsia, but not to a naturally healthy man. The only levitous thing about it is, I hold up the looking-glass, and you people laugh at your carcasses reflected there.

Religion never was intended to make our pleasures less, and in eternal loyalty to God I yield the palm to none, and no man shall unchristianize me because I do n't mope about like some of these fellows. If they want dignity wait until I die, and I 'll be as dignified as any of you. Just wait. What 's a preacher any more than a man? How can a religious man be any more sacred? Tell me that. I would n't do a thing at home that I would n't do at Church. Want to drag the Church down? No, I want to drag home up. Some people are solemn, serious, and very pious at Church, and they 'll come to Church pious and sleek and say, "I do n't like that merriment." You ought to have your neck broke.

The reason why the Church makes no progress in this world is because every fellow goes at it as if the Lord was working him to death and paying him nothing for it. That 's about it. If this sad, solemn, drooping, dignified piety is what makes your religion, I want it before I die, but I do n't want it until just about a minute before I die—I do n't want to be loaded with it while I live. If religion means I shall mope and cry and must not laugh, it would be too short to stretch myself on it, and too narrow to curl myself up in it. "Delight thyself in the Lord." Have you ever been to a prayer-meeting in this city, or a town prayer-meeting?

The preacher walks in solemnly and almost noiselessly, and the old brethren come in and scatter around the church as far apart as possible; one brother is called to sing and another to pray, and then after prayer they 'll go home sneakingly and call it "growing in grace." O Lord, what a lone-

some time they have had. The Lord does n't go
within a mile of 'em, and the devil gets in. I
would as soon pray to make a shade-tree out of my
walking-stick as try to grow in grace at a meeting
like that. It's a disgrace to us, and yet the old
corpse says: "I do n't like such merriment at
Church, and so much levity at Church. I wish
you would make us cry." I do n't believe there's
a bit of piety in crying. There's no meanness
in laughter. I tell you as long as the light of
my Father's face shines on me I am going to carry
a smile through the world. Whenever a man can't
laugh, he's in need of a liver medicine. There's
something wrong with him. Many a fellow in this
country has mistaken a disordered liver for religion—
a miserable old dose it is to carry. I do n't care
whether a man laughs or cries at Church. I want
to know whether he's a good husband or father
and a good neighbor.

I want a religion that will keep me straight,
and not one that keeps my mouth shut and makes
me look pious, and enables me to cover up my
meanness with my looks. The matter with the
Church is, it is hidebound. Some of you do n't
know what that expression means. It means that
your hide gets full and wants loosening up, and
you have got down in your coffin and you need a
thorough shaking up.

We have disgusted the world with our religion—
it's not attractive to the race, because our religion is
without joy, gladness, smiles, and songs. I want
every man to go with a quick step to prayer-meet-

ing, and for their first song let them break out on
"All hail the power of Jesus' name" with a rush,
and call on some brother to pray with a rush, and
let him drop on his knees and pray with a rush, and
let him stand up and sing with a rush, and talk with
a rush and go home with a rush.

"Commit yourself to God, and he will bring it
to pass." That's the biggest promise in the book.
How will you get all things? Commit yourself to
God. So it is with man. You go to a stable and
get a horse and buggy, and you can drive and
guide the horse as you please. He wants to go
everywhere, but will go anywhere he is guided.
Pull on his left rein, he goes left; pull on the right,
he goes to the right; say "whoa," he stops; knock
the lines on his back, and he goes forward. That's
the way with religion.

God has lines and guides you by them, but
sometimes you are balky and won't go, and he pulls
on the lines, and your mouth gets away up under
your ear, like the old mule that is balky and won't
go; and the mule will point his head in the wrong
direction, but the body goes the way the mule
goes. Stand here some night, and see that sister
headed for the theater on Wednesday night. God
wants her to go to prayer-meeting, and he will pull
on that line; and the devil wants her to go to the
theater, and he pulls on that line.

She's like a dog following two men on the
street—you can't tell to whom the dog belongs.
But you follow them out to the forks of the road
where the two men separate, and then you'll know

whom the dog belongs to. So, stand in this city on Wednesday night, at the forks of the road, with the prayer-meeting here and the theater there, and, as she comes along and reaches the forks, then you'll know whose servant she is. If you go to the theater Wednesday or any other night you are the devil's dog. The faith that believes every thing, and does nothing, is worth nothing to a man.

Do n't criticise me, but criticise yourself. You can pick a thousand flaws in my sermon, but look out for yourselves. You can't say any thing worse about me than I can about you. If there's any thing I despise it's a dull time. I like to see things move up. You can not harm me. Some men open their mouths to laugh, and you can drop a great big brickbat of truth right in. It's the biggest thing a man has—a laughing mouth. A man can be pious and laugh, but let him not laugh at the truth!

SAYINGS.

THERE is not an angel in heaven that is proof against bad company.

THE Bible was not given to teach me the way the heavens go, but to teach me the way to go to heaven.

A BIG nose is a sign of intellect; a big mouth, character; a big chin, courage; and big ears, generosity. Some of you pastors ought to get ear-fertilizers; for there are more little 'possum-eared Church members in this country than you can count.

Sermon V.

THE LOSS OF THE SOUL.

"For what shall it profit a man if he shall gain the whole world and lose his own soul? or what shall a man give in exchange for his soul?"—MARK VIII, 36, 37.

CHRIST JESUS, the author of this question, the author of this text, was a wonderful preacher. He was wonderful in that he was always practical. No man could leave an audience to whom Jesus had preached, and say: "Well, he discussed some theological dogma I was not interested in. He was arguing some ecclesiastical question that I felt no personal concern for." But Jesus had some things to say to every one. Why, when he preached he looked over at the farmers present, and said: "Listen, you farmers, you tillers of the soil. The kingdom of heaven is like unto a man going out to sow seed." He looked over at the fishermen present, and said: "Give me your attention. The kingdom of heaven is like a net let down into the water." When Jesus preached to the house-carpenters, he said: "Give me your ear. Take heed how you build." And when he preached to the housewives present, he said: "Hear; the kingdom of heaven is like unto three measures of meal in which you put the leaven, and when you go back you will find the whole lump leavened." When he preached to the merchants and business men present, he looked

94

them in the face and said: "You men who run on profit and loss, what shall it profit you, if you gain the whole world and lose your soul?"

This was a practical question eighteen hundred years ago; it is a very practical question now. This country is running on profit and loss. This is a nation of bargain-makers; a nation of traders. We commence trading in this country about the time we begin to talk. Little boys will swap knives; little girls will trade dolls. We begin to hunt up bargains as soon as we learn to walk. The merchants who draw the most customers are the merchants who put up "Big Bargains" in great letters over their store doors. Every one is hunting bargains.

This is a question, brethren, practical now—it reaches every body. Why? It is true. You can't get a Congressman to speak on any thing except the tariff; and that's the only difference now between the two great national parties—the tariff. And that question has got to be a sort of differentiated difference. Why, if a daughter is going to marry to-morrow, the would-be father-in-law does n't measure the to-be son-in-law's brain force, nor his nervous energies, but he measures his pocket-book and his capacity for making money. If you want to get a big collection now in the Churches out of the pockets of God's people, all you need to do is to convince them beyond reasonable doubt that God will give them two dollars for every one they put in the contribution box; if you do that, you'll get a whopping big collection on that occasion.

This is the question now of all questions—the question of profit and loss, and this question comes home to every conscience here to-night. You men who add up your debit and credit columns day after day, stop a moment and ask yourselves this question: "What shall it profit a man if he gain the whole world and lose his soul?" I believe it was Talmage who said once: "A man is very unwise to make an exchange like this—his soul for the world." He said there is n't a piece of property in the world, in an eternal sense, for which you can get a deed, or that you can get any insurance upon.

If I were a merchant in Cincinnati and had accumulated my fortune and decided "now I will buy me a beautiful farm and move out into the country, to recuperate and rest at my ease the balance of my life; I will find me just such a plantation as suits me—its mansions, its out-buildings, its bottom-lands, its table-lands, its woodlands, its brooks, its springs, its all; here is the place that suits me exactly;" but before a wise man will count down any money for it, he will go to the Books of Deeds and Mortgages and Liens to see if there is any thing against that property. No man will count his money down for a piece of property until he is certain he can get a clean title. Before you count down your money and make the trade and enter it in writing and take possession of this property, suppose you look around. You may take the property, and before you are in possession of it ten minutes old death may come along and say, "Off these premises," and off you go. How many men in this world have I seen just fixed

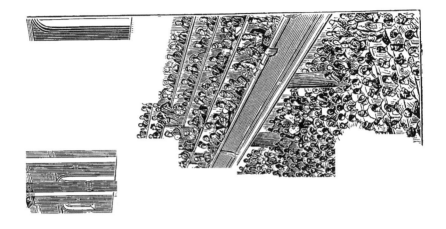

up for living well; their home just finished and furnished nicely and every thing arranged for comfort and long life and old age, and in just ten months after they have finished their place, black crape was hung on the front door knob and the hearse was brought up before their residence. How much of that thing have you seen, my brother?

In my own town I can remember almost a dozen places which men have arranged, and rearranged for comfort and ease, and just after every thing was well arranged, death came along, and there was a coffin in the house, with the shroud, and the weeping wife, and the crying children that came instead of peace and enjoyment. If I could build a palace and so arrange its doors and windows that death could not come in on me, I might make a trade like this; but death comes in here with fearful grief, and enters the palace and the hovel alike, and there is no power that can do away with it.

Suppose you had a piece of property and you wanted it insured, and you asked the insurance agent to come up and see and examine the premises. The insurance agent starts up with you, and when you get to the front gate you see flames bursting out of the basement or the cellar of that building. The insurance agent turns round to you and he says, "Good-bye, I can't insure that property, it is already on fire down in the basement." What about the insurance on this old world? Geologists tell us it is on fire away down in the basement, and Vesuvius and Ætna are but the chimneys to the conflagration below, and the molten lava flows year after year and never ends; God's word for it, this old world shall be burned up. Astronomers have swept their telescopes across the skies, and have told us that a dozen worlds have disappeared in the last few decades; they tell us, at first they look like other worlds, then they turn a deep blood-red, showing that they are on fire; and then they turn to an ashen color, showing that they have been burned to ashes; and then at last they disappear completely from all human eyes.

What, give my soul for a piece of property I can't get a title to; and if I could get a title to it, I can't get any insurance on it! Another thing: In our Southern city of Atlanta, on one of our prettiest streets, there is a very beautiful lot. Go there and ask the real-estate agent: "Why does n't some one build on this lot?" and he will tell you: "Sir, because every man that ever had any thing to do with that property has got into trouble about it. He buys a lawsuit." It is as true and as deep as nature, that every man that ever had any thing to do with this old world has got into trouble about it. The most miserable man in this city to-night, is the man that has got millions of dollars. I do n't know who he is, nor where he lives, and practically, by the grace of God, I never want to know who he is.

Some one said: "God showed what he thought of riches by the people he gave them to." I do n't know whether there is any thing in that or not. Many a man is wallowing in luxury and wealth in this world, many a man who has given himself up to money making and money accumulating, and enjoying himself—for what? I say: "You old fellow, you're a fattening hog that does n't know what he eats corn for." In trouble about it? I can say this much: Here's one man that was born poor, and raised poor, but I have held my own, and I have been at it so long I've become used to it, and it does n't hurt me a bit in the world—poverty does n't. That's the plain truth about it.

I 'll tell you another thing: One of our millionaires down in Georgia was a liberal man in the highest sense of that word, and when disaster brought him down to pennilessness and nothingness in finances, he said, " I went into my room and fell down on my knees and prayed, 'Lord God, explain to me why my money has all been swept away. I did my duty I thought; I have divided with the poor and given to the Church, and now it is all gone. Lord, Lord, explain it to me. I am in trouble about it.' I opened my Bible on my knees, and my eyes fell instantly on this passage, 'It is easier for a camel to go through the eye of a needle than for a rich man to enter into the kingdom of heaven.' When I read this I just clapped my hands and said gladly to God, 'I will have infinite life if I die a pauper.' "

You give a man much money these days and he gets very independent of God! That's true. I am surprised at a man getting so stuck up with a little money too. Here's a fellow worth one hundred thousand dollars; he thinks he's rich. Here's a man that's worth five hundred thousand dollars;

he thinks he's rich. Suppose you are worth five
millions, what's that compared to the city of Cincinnati? Suppose you own the whole city of Cincinnati, what's that compared to New York City?
Suppose you own both cities, what's that compared
to the whole United States of America? And suppose you own all America, what's that compared to
Europe, with all its wealth? And suppose you own
the whole world, and every bit of it is yours, you
could put two such worlds as this in your pocket,
and go up to the Dog Star and stay there all night,
even then you wouldn't have enough to pay your
lodging. What are you cutting up about? Putting on airs with a couple of thousand dollars. "What
shall it profit a man if he gain the whole world
and lose his own soul?"

Brethren, hear me! A man's wealth doesn't
consist in the abundance he possesses. I tell you,
the richest man in this city, in my opinion, is the
man who is contented with his lot. "Godliness
with contentment is great gain."

What does a man want with a pile of money
when he has to work the life out of him to make
it, and has to work twice harder to keep it after he
does make it? What does he want with it? It's
just like what you hear when an old millionaire
dies. You can hear one neighbor of his meet
another on the street and say: "Mr. So-and-so, the
millionaire, has just died, and left all his money,
by his will, to the bar-keepers of the town." "Why,
what do you mean?" says the fellow. "Well," says
the neighbor, "he didn't do it directly, but he did

it indirectly; he left it to the boys, and the bar-keepers will soon get it all."

Mark, fathers, who hear me to-night. Look to the interests of your soul and the interests of your children. Let me say this to you: "If I could provide a little competency for my wife, who has given me and my children all her life, I would n't leave a dollar in this world to any one of my children; if they're any good they won't need it, and if they ain't, leaving it to them will make them of no account." That's logic, brethren, as resistless as eternity. You can't dodge it. Many a fellow in this country says, "I ain't making this money for myself, I'm just laying it up for Sallie and the children." Yes, and you will give your life for money, and hoard it, and lay it up for Sallie and the children, but if you could see Sallie and the children six months after you are dead—Sallie with her new teeth and the boys with their fine turn-outs, you'd be surprised to see how well Sallie and the children get along without you. You would that.

I heard of one old man who gave his life for money, and spent his time getting money and pil-ing it up for his wife and children; and the preacher told me he was visiting at the house about six months after the old man died, and they put him in one of the garret-rooms. When he went in he saw a picture, with its face to the wall, standing over in the corner, and he went to it and turned it around, and saw it was the old man's picture. They put it away off there, and turned its face to the wall. That's a pretty bad state of things, is n't

it? And that old man had given his life, literally,
to money-getting. Let's see something bigger than
a dollar, and something better than stocks and
bonds. I will tell some of you here to-night, you
may be kneeling on your bonds, but I am kneeling
on the promises of God, and I'll be standing up
when you've been swept down forever.

Do n't any body say I'm talking against riches;
I ain't; I am glad we have rich men, but I despise
an old rich hog. I do. I am glad of every wealthy
man in this country. A great many think that
money is the root of all evil. That's a mistake.
The Book never said that. It says the love of it is
the root of all evil; and there are more poor men
going to hell for the love of money—on the principle that white sheep eat more than black sheep—
because there are more of 'em.

I've gone into cities and looked at the large
stores, gotten up, engineered, and run on the brain
of one man; and I've said, "I do n't begrudge that
man his money, for, I declare, a man that takes a
business like that on his mind has n't a minute in
the year to give to God." That's true! "They
that will be rich fall into divers temptations and
pierce themselves through with many sorrows. It
is easier for a camel to go through the eye of a
needle"—and that means the arch simply of the gate,
and the only way a camel can get through at all is
to unload his burden off his back.

One of the old millionaires down our way sent
for me once, and he said: "Mr. Jones, I want to
talk to you. I have given my heart to God and

my hand to the Church." I said: "Old brother, you have done all that, you have given your soul to God, but you will find it is a thousand times easier to manage your soul than all this money you have piled up here. You will break into hell about that sure. You'd better begin to stir your stumps and give some of that money away pretty soon, for you're right smart behind with God."

I am not talking against money. The best man this world ever saw was the richest man, and that man was Abraham. He could have left one of his servants more than Vanderbilt left all his children, and yet Abraham was one of the best saints this world ever saw. Thank God for every rich man who loves God and uses his money wisely. Don't say now I'm preaching against riches.

I'll tell you one thing: Riches you get wrongly will not only curse you, but it will curse your family after you are dead and gone. I was talking this evening about the ill-gotten gains of some man in Atlanta. A poor family was found by a reporter starving to death, and nearly frozen in the late cold spell, and when they came to find the cause, it was learned that they were making garments for a house in Atlanta that was paying them fifteen cents a dozen. That sort of money will turn into brimstone, and you will carry enough brimstone to hell with you to burn you forever, if that's the way you get your money. I will tell you another thing: Fifteen cents a dozen for making garments is the essence of communistic fire that will burn this country up some of these days.

"What shall it profit a man if he gain this whole world and lose his own soul?" A man ought never to buy or sell any thing without remembering that he has got a soul in his body to be saved or lost. What will it profit a man now if he gain the whole world? My brethren, we do not expect to get much of it; be as lucky as we may, we can not accumulate much. There is a certain class in this world I have a great contempt for. We have paupers down in our country, and we have what we call poor-houses, where we put our paupers, the old and decrepit and the helpless that have no home, nor board, nor friends, and we furnish a house and a home for that sort; but the finest specimen of a pauper that I ever saw was a young man twenty-five years old, who had no money and no religion, no stocks and bonds and no hope of heaven, no house nor horse, and no peace with God through Jesus Christ. There is the finest specimen of a pauper that this world ever saw. That tall fellow back there is serving the devil for nothing and boarding himself, or rather he is making his poor old mother board him. You are the meanest wretch this earth ever saw.

Men supported by their wives who sit at the needle sixteen hours every day to support a drunken husband, or a no-account son; that is serving the devil every minute for nothing, and making his poor, helpless wife or mother support him. O, how poor is a character like that. I think when a man gets to where he won't support himself, and his wife has to do it, it is time then for the decent

people of that community to tie a rock about his
neck and drop him gently in the river, and say
nothing about it; don't mention it. And, I venture the assertion, you have a thousand just such
cases in this city. I hate to see a man boarding
with his wife when his wife is rich; but, O my!
how I do hate it if he's boarding with his wife
when she is poor, and has to work for a living.

What will it profit a man if he gain the whole
world—if he gain all there is in it, and lose his
soul? O, how inexpressibly foolish it is in a man
to get none of the world and then die a pauper,
and be a pauper in hell for all eternity. I said
many a time, if there are any people in this world
that I do want to be religious, it is the poor white
folks and negroes. Many of them never have any
thing much in this world, and then they die and go to
hell, eternal paupers. It is the most awful thought
I can conceive of. Those old fellows who have
carriages and horses, and drink twelve-dollar cham-
pagne all their lives, they can afford to be damned,
if any body can; but those fellows who have never
had any thing here can not afford it.

The Lord save the poor people of this city, if
those who have plenty won't be saved! I am in
for the poor people of the city. God save them.
I hope they will come and fill every chair and pew
in this hall. I have known some preachers, and
all they wanted in the world was just to see one
old major or old colonel come in and take his seat,
and they would not look at any body else except the
old major or the old colonel and see whether they

were impressing him or not. Look here, you have found one preacher at least who do n't go much on these colonels and judges and majors. Who are they? The old red-nosed colonel and the old foul-mouthed major, I would n't wipe my feet on one at my front door. I have never seen one that was of much account after you got him. What do you want with him? His habits have been so bad, and his life has been so crooked, that when he joins the Church he has just to stand and fight the devil all the time, and if he stops only long enough to spit on his hands the devil has him all at once. Now, I am not after them. Let those other preachers, if they want to, run after the old colonel and the old major and the judge; but God give me the blood and muscle and the brain of this country to be relig-ious, and the blood and muscle and brain that have not been debauched in sin for forty years.

"What shall it profit a man if he gain this whole world and lose his own soul?" Now, breth-ren, when we consider this world, it is a glorious world. Thank God for such a world to live in for threescore years and ten. If I want water, three-fourths of the earth's surface is covered with water; if I want light, I have the meridian splendors of the sun by day, and at night he sprinkles the heaven like a swarm of golden bees; if I want flowers, well—

> "Full many a flower is born to blush unseen,
> And waste its fragrance on the desert air."

If I want books, the millions of shelves laden with precious works bid me come and read; if I want friends, there are fourteen hundred millions of beings around me, and God says take them every one for your friends; if I want bread, hundreds of millions of acres of the harvest field wave towards me and tell me, Here come and satisfy your hunger; if I want gold, the bowels of the earth are full of gold; if I want any thing that man could desire, and that sense could ask for, this world says, Here it is, come and take it. And I know that God has prepared a grand world for us hereafter, because he has made such a world for us to live down here in a few days.

But, brother, now you begin to talk about eternity, and this world is n't worth much. Here is a picture in London: A man—an eminent banker—was stricken with meningitis; he sent for the doctor; the doctor came and examined him, and said to him: "You have meningitis; three hours and you are gone." The banker turned his whitened face up into the face of the doctor, and said: "Have you spoken the truth?" "Yes, I have spoken the truth." "Well, doctor, if you will keep me alive until to-morrow morning I will give you a hundred thousand pounds." Half a million dollars! The doctor looked at him and said: "I have prescriptions to give and remedies to administer, but I have no time to sell. Time belongs to God." That shows you about what this world is worth when a man comes to die.

Look at Cornelius Vanderbilt. He had just said to William, "I leave you seventy-five millions," and to his other children and wife twenty-five millions. Here is a round one hundred millions. " I am the money king of America, and I give and bequeath this to my children." And then he turned over on his bed and looked on the face of his Christian wife and said, " Come, wife, now you can sing to me, ' Come, ye sinners, poor and needy, weak and wounded, sick and sore.' " The money king of America lay dying a pauper upon his bed. Call that success? God help me never to succeed that way.

If I have one thing to be grateful for it is this, for when my father bid me good-bye he simply said, " Son, son, make your father the promise that you will meet him in a better land; " and I shook his hand and told him good-bye; and my father did not leave a nickel in my hand. I believe if he had left me twenty thousand or fifty thousand dollars that I would have gone immediately and invested it in a through ticket for hell, and that I would be there this minute. Recollect, fathers, if your children are of any account they do n't need your money, and if they are of no account every dollar you give them will sink them down! down!! down!!!

Now a moment or two and I am done. We look at the other side of this question. I have nothing to say against this world. Be comfortable; have your good home if you can; have comfort all around you. God has put enough here for every one of us to have a good home and be comfortable. But, my good brother, always look for eternity. Get ready; prepare, prepare. I can not afford to give my soul to this world. No, sir; no, sir. My soul! my soul! Why, sir, hear me a moment on this, my soul. The time will come when my soul will take my body and lay it down just as a boy throws down his ball when he is tired playing with it.

The time will come when my soul will take my body and lay it aside, just as you have laid aside some old implement about your house or farm that you won't use any more. My soul! The time will come in the future when wife and children shall gather around my dying couch, and the doctors press their way into the circle, and my soul, just a moment will watch and wait, and then it will push the doctor back from my dying couch and overleap the circle of friends around my bed, and above stars and moon it goes, and overvaults the very throne of God.

My soul! My soul! Shall I give it in exchange for this world? No, sir; no, sir.

A father in one of the Southern cities said to me: "Two of my boys are dissipated, and, O, my money will ruin my boys, and I know it." Said I: "You say you've got money enough to ruin them both?" "Yes." "And you are certain it will ruin them?" Said he: "Yes." Said I, "I'll tell you how to dodge that thing." Said he: "How?" "Well," said I, "give me this afternoon $20,000 a-piece of those two boys' money for the orphan home out here, and you go home to-night and say to Tom and Henry, 'I have given Sam Jones $20,-000 of each of your money, and the very next time you get drunk I am going to give him $40,000 of

each of your money; and further, on your third
drunk, I will make him a deed for that orphans'
home for every dollar I have got.' And," said I,
" you will straighten them boys right out—you will
that." And before my money should damn my
children, I say to you to-night, I would give it all
to the orphan homes of the country. Well, as I
said, I told him what he should do with his money,
and, strange to say, he never gave me a cent. I
am afraid he will be in the pit before his boy is.

You can go down among the rich bottoms of
the Missouri and Mississippi Rivers and there you
find the most impure water; and you find the most
malarious atmosphere in the rich bottoms of the
Mississippi and Missouri Rivers. You can go up
among the old red hills of Georgia, and the clearest
sparkling water you ever saw gurgles up through
the old red clay, and the sweetest atmosphere blows
over the old red hills of Georgia. Among the rich
of this earth is the most corruption, and the most
wickedness, and the most guilt. Among the poor
of the earth you will find the sweetest virtues and
the noblest characters. Let us live among the poor.
Let us have a good atmosphere and good water.

And I will tell you, brother, that when a man
gets drunk on money he is gone. You preachers
are not candid with him. You do not tackle him
as you should. When an old fellow gets drunk
with whisky his friends go to him and say, " Look
here, old fellow, you are going to the devil. I wish
you would quit and keep straight." His wife pleads
with him. The minister pleads with him. Every

body pleads with him. But when a fellow gets drunk with money, bless you, his wife does not say any thing about it. She enjoys the "creetur" herself; she does not say, "Husband, you are going to perdition." The preacher does not tackle him; he is afraid to. There's many a man in this town drunk with money. Have you, brethren, been up to tell him "You are drunk with money, and the devil will get you?" You never tackle such men. You just say, "I want the favor of these old rich fellows, because I know if I bother them they will get mad with me and neutralize my action and neutralize my power, and I can not do any thing;" and you think "The best thing to do is to let the old fellow alone. I do n't want to antagonize him, but just make him pay his way along." O, sir, when a man gets drunk on money nobody bothers him then. He just goes on and on, and to perdition he goes forever.

"What shall it profit a man if he gain the whole world and lose his own soul?" We will make this discussion a little more practical and bring it down to where we have a practical interest in it in every sense. I want to say to you right now, I do not know what it is keeps you from being a Christian—you men sitting there. I can not tell what it is keeps you out of the Church and away from God, but I will say that whatever it is, whether it is a dance, or a dram, or licentiousness, I do not care what it is that keeps you away from Christ and out of the Church, you can put all those things together in one common pile and point to the pile and say: "That is the price I put on my immortality. That is the price I have sold it for."

That young man says: "I would join the Church, but I love to dance." That young lady says, "I would join the Church, but I love to dance." Well, young lady, go on. We will say that you go to 200 balls—that is a big allowance, is n't it?— and that you dance hundreds of sets. By and by you die without God and without hope, and down into the flames of despair you go forever; and as you walk the sulphurous streets of damnation you can tell them: "I am in hell forever, it is true, but I danced 400 times, I did." Now, won't that be a consolation?

That man out there says: "I want to join the Church, but preachers think a man ought not to take a dram and be a member of the Church." Supposing, brother, that you roll out forty barrels of the best Bourbon in the United States and drink it, every drop, and then die and go to perdition. You can tell them in hell: "I am in hell forever, it is true, but I drank forty barrels of the best Bourbon before I got here." That will be a consolation, won't it. That's remuneration, is n't it?

What do you want to dance for, young lady? Of what use is it to you? If I had to marry a dozen times—and I am like the Irishman who said he hoped he would not live long enough to see his wife married again—if I had to marry a dozen times, I would never go to a ball-room to get my wife. Do you hear that? I used to dance with the girls, but when I wanted to marry I did **not**

go to the ball-room to get my wife. Many a fellow
got a good one in the ball-room, and many a fellow
did n't. God gives a man a good wife and somebody else gives him a bad one. What good does
it do you to be able to dance? Take the best girl
in this town after her family is reduced to a fearful crisis by her father's business reverses. Now
they are poor and that girl must earn a living. I
will introduce her to a dozen of the leading citizens
of the town, and give her a worthy recommendation
in every respect. She is just what every body would
want as a music teacher, as a clerk, or in any other
capacity; but let me add as a postscript to the recommendation, "She is a first-class dancer," and that
will knock her out of every job she applies for in
this world. And so with every sin. And I declare to you to-night, that the thing that keeps us
away from God and out of the Church, that is the
price we put on our soul.

There is a man. He says: "I would be religious if it were not for so and so," and I never
think of this that I do not think of an incident in
which a husband sat by his wife at a revival meeting. When the penitents were asked to come to
the altar he was asked by his wife, "Come, won't
you give yourself to God?" He shook his head
and went home. That night she said to her husband, "I saw you were affected. I wish you had
given your heart to God." He said, "Wife, I can
not be a Christian in the business I am in." She
said: "I know that." He was a liquor dealer.
And she added: "Husband, I want you to give up

10

your business and give your heart to God." He said : " Wife, I can not afford it." " Well," she said, " how much do you clear every year on whisky ?" " Well," he said, " my net profits are about two thousand dollars a year." She asked : " Husband, how long do you reckon you will live to run that business ?" " Twenty years in the natural expectation of things." " How much is twice twenty thousand dollars ?" " Forty thousand dollars." " Forty thousand dollars ? Now, husband, if you could get forty thousand dollars in a lump, would you sell your soul to hell for that sum ?" He said : " No, wife ! no ! I 'll close out my business in the morning, and I will give my heart to God right now. I would not sell my soul for four thousand million dollars." O, that you all could see what keeps you out of the Church and from God. That is the price you have placed on your immortal soul.

Now, a word in conclusion. The soul—that is the other thing. There is the world and here is the soul. Now what ? My soul with its immortal interest ; my soul that shall live forever ; my soul that will shake off this body by and by, and lay it aside as a tired child does its toys ; my soul that shall throw this body down and fly away from it ; shall I give my immortal soul for this world ? No, sir, I can not do that. What then ? I will give my soul to Christ. He is worthy of it ; he died to save it.

Yonder is a parliament. Adam has just fallen and subjected the whole race to death, and now the reverberating thunders of God's wrath are heard

athwart the whole moral universe, and the announce-
ment is made in that parliament, "Adam—man has
fallen. The great federal head of the race has sinned
and fallen;" and a voice from the great I am
spoke out, "Who will take man's redemption on
his shoulders and bring him back to life?" I imagine the archangel standing up in that presence and
shaking his snowy wings, and saying: "This task
is too great for me." I imagine Gabriel might
stand up and say, "I shall blow the trumpet that
will wake the dead, but this task is too great for
me." But all at once there was One who stood up
in that presence and said: "I will take man's redemption on my shoulders." And the angels began
to wonder, and it has been the cause of increasing
wonder ever since that he should become the Redeemer; that he should become man that he might
redeem the race and be our Savior.

Brother, you read some years ago about a ship
in the Atlantic Ocean that sprung a leak away
down in the bottom of her hull. The announce-
ment that the ship has sprung a leak is made by
the captain, and the pumps are got to work; but
they will not pump out the water as fast as it
enters by the leak. The only hope for the safety
of the vessel is that some one will risk his life in
order to stop the leak. Volunteers were asked for,
and one man spoke up, "I will go down and stop
the leak." He went down and down—to the upper,
then the lower, and then the third deck, and then
he reached down into the water and worked there
repairing the leak until he became perfectly ex-

hausted. Then the pumps began to work, and by
and by the old ship grew lighter, and the captain said :
"The leak is stopped, but let us go down and see
about our friend." They went down to the third
deck and saw his body floating on the water. They
brought him up and embalmed his body, and when
land was reached they carried it ashore and buried
it. And the spot was marked by a tombstone on
which was the epitaph :

"THIS MAN GAVE HIS LIFE THAT ALL OF US MIGHT LIVE."

And the names of those he saved were all engraved
below. And they bless the memory of that man
and say : "If he had not died we should have been
lost."

And yonder is the old ship Humanity, and now
the waves of God's wrath and judgment begin to
pitch and toss her, and drive her on the rocks, and
she is about to go down forever, when the Son of
God sees her, and I see him come from the shining
shores of heaven as swift as the morning light, and
throw his arms around this old sinking ship. She
carries him under three days and nights, and
he brings her to the surface on the third morning ;
and then God grasps the stylus and signs the
Magna Charta of man's salvation, and then at the
blessed moment it is written : "Whosoever believeth
in the Son of God shall not perish, but have everlasting life." I will give my life to Christ ; he gave
his life for me, and he is worthy of it.

Down South, before the war we used to put a
slave on the block and sell him to the highest bid-
der. Sometimes he would run away, and we could

not get him on the block, but we would sell him on the run. "How much for him running away?" Well, brother, when God Almighty turned this world over to Jesus Christ, he turned it over on the run, running away from God, running away to hell and death, and the Lord Jesus Christ came as swift as the morning light, and overtook this old world in her wayward flight, threw his arms around her, and said: "Stop, stop, let us go back to God. Let us go back."

O Jesus Christ, help every man here to-say: "I will go back. I have strayed long enough. I will go back now." Will you, brother? God help every man to say: "This night I have taken my last step in the wrong direction, and have turned round." That is just what God wants sinners to do—to turn round—to turn round. Will you to-night say: "God being my helper, I will stop; I will turn my attention to heavenly things and eternal things; I will look after my soul, if I starve to death?" Will you do that?

Sermon VI.

Cornelius, a Devout Man.

There was a certain man in Cesarea, called Cornelius, a centurion of the band called the Italian band, a devout man, and one that feared God with all his house, which gave much alms to the people and prayed to God always.—Acts x, 1, 2.

THE first century of the Christian era produced some of the most remarkable characters of this world's history, and one of them was this heathen man, Cornelius. His character was remarkable in that it was symmetrical. It was well rounded. It presented a perfect whole. A perfectly educated will is one which says to the Divine Will, "Thou orderest, I will." "Thou commandest not, I will not." In other words, a perfectly educated will is a will in perfect harmony with the will of God. We Christian people have a great deal to say about crosses and sacrifices and losses. You know what a cross is? Now, I will tell you where the Christian finds his cross—when God's will is one way and his will another. Now, there 's your cross. But when you whip your will around into a parallel line with the will of God—now the cross is all gone—and you say: "The joy of my heart is to do the will of God." Delight yourselves in the will of the Lord and he will give you your desires, because your will is in perfect harmony with the will of God.

Character is but the soul, in all its phases, in

118

perfect harmony with the will of God.   Religion is loyalty to God.   Religion puts me in harmony with the will of God, so that whenever the chords of my heart are touched by the Divine fingers, there is music that would charm an angel's ear.   When I visit the sick I get the sweetest music of earth from my being, and every thing in me is set in perfect harmony with the will of God.   Character is the result of the harmony of forces.   There is a world of beauty in harmony.   I once sat in the parlor of a friend's house, and his oldest daughter sat at the piano running her fingers over the keys.   To the right of her stood her brother putting a banjo in perfect tune with the chords of the piano.   To the left was a sister with a guitar, and near by was another brother tuning a violin.   All these instruments were put in perfect harmony with the chords of the piano, and when all commenced to play together, there was music that would have charmed the heavenly hosts.   When a man is in harmony with every thing, if he is in harmony with God's will, he loves all that God loves, and hates all that God hates; and if he is not in harmony with God's will, he is out of harmony with all that God loves, and in harmony with all that God hates.   If you are in harmony with God's will, you will love every thing God loves, and hate every thing that God hates.   You love the right and hate the wrong, and you are godlike in character.

Cornelius's character, as I said a moment ago, was wonderful and striking in that it was symmetrical, and now, to-day, I propose to present this portrait of this heathen man to this congregation. It is the Scriptural portrait of this man, and when I look at it and then take my eyes away for a moment, I am ashamed of myself and of every man on the face of the earth. I am, for I tell you after the blessings of 1,900 years of Christ and all that accrues by reason of God's goodness to the race, as it marches on, this world does not present, in the noontide blaze of the nineteenth century privileges, such a character as this heathen man Cornelius. "Cornelius, a devout man,"—that is the first thing that God tells us about this man. He was a devout man. This term devout is a very significant one. It is a broad term. We have various adjectives and epithets by which we describe men. Sometimes we say he is a zealous man. Sometimes we say he is an earnest man. Sometimes we say he is an intellectual man. Sometimes we say he is a very humble man. Sometimes that he is very prayerful. Sometimes we say he is a very generous man, a forgiving man; but when inspiration tell us Cornelius was a devout man, it covers the whole ground in one word, and says that he was noble, and generous, and true, and all that makes the character of the Lord Jesus Christ lovely in the sight of man—a well rounded character. Cornelius was a devout man, or, in other words, a thoroughly religious man. I do n't care where he lives, whether in Europe, Asia, or Africa, such a man is worth his weight in gold in any community.

What a man does is the test of what a man is. I frequently ask, What is Mr. So-and-so worth? And some man with only the statistics of the tax-books before him, says he is worth three hundred thousand dollars. That is the only way you can tell what a man is worth—by going to the tax-books—and then, generally, you can multiply that by five before you reach it. I ask what another man is worth, and they go to the same source, and say he is worth ten thousand dollars. Here is one who, according to the tax-books, is worth ten thousand dollars, and another who is worth three hundred thousand dollars; but measured, according to God's rule, that man who is worth ten thousand dollars is worth a thousand times more to God and humanity than the other. After all, it is not how much a man is worth, but what sort of a fellow has got it. I have found that out. A man who is not religious in every thing is not religious in any thing, for religion is eternal, uncompromising loyalty to God and the right. A man who is religious at all, is religious everywhere and in every thing. That is it. That old adage—it has grown to be an adage—"religion is religion and business is business," enters practically into the life of the Church, and culminates in an expression like this: "I do n't believe in mixing politics and religion," and it is always uttered by the man who has no religion to mix with his politics. He who has no religion to mix with his politics is a demagogue and a trickster. I would not mix a drop of politics with my religion for all the world, but I want all the religion I have to go into my politics. It helps it.

Cornelius was a thoroughly religious man. There

11

was a moment in his past when the question was settled once and forever between his soul and its God. " By the grace of God I will be religious." Until a man reaches this final decision there is nothing in all the means of grace that can ever make him a religious man. My theology is summed up in three lines. God can not arbitrarily make a man good, nor can the devil arbitrarily make him bad. If you want to be good, God stands pledged to help you by all the means of his omnipotence. If you want to be bad the devil will help you. The last remark was unnecessary. There are so many living witnesses here to-day who will testify to the truth of it. The man who says: " I will be religious," wakes up heaven and hell with a single utterance, and God will roll an unfinished world aside to help such a man.

Now, brethren, I settled the question once, and forever. I will be religious. Then, I want to tell you, it is astonishing how the mountains will melt down, and the valleys will fill up, and how God himself will not only stand at the other end of the line, but will walk back down the line and tell me to take his arm, and walk and talk with me clear home to heaven—an earnest man, a man that means business. Well, now, suppose I decide: " I do n't know about this question. If I can be religious, and be something else, too, all right; but I do n't like this single-handed business." Well, now, I want to say this much. You have got to make a choice if you are ever religious.

My wife has given her life to me and to my

children, and I say here to-day, if I could leave my
precious wife above want I would do it, but I
would n't, as a matter of choice, leave a child of
mine a dollar in the world. You think I do n't
know what I am talking about now. If I were
going to hunt the worst thing that was ever per-
petrated, do you know I would n't go to hell, and
I would n't go to heaven to hunt it? I would just
came to this city and get one of your debauched,
drunken sons-in-law. My Lord! hell itself can't
beat that. Some of you know how it is, do n't you?
Is n't it awful? Your precious Mary married to a
brutal, drunken husband! And she lives consciously
every moment, embraced in the arms of a drunken
wretch, and every child that God gives her is half-
drunkard the day it is born. My God! can any
thing be worse than that? And God Almighty
says he has got something against your whole community when he lets the devil put that sort off on
you. Did you ever notice that? If a fellow is
worth about $200,000, it is astonishing how the
devil can run in drunken sons-in-law on him. You
had better look out, old fellow. That's the hand
of Heaven, and there's truth in what I am saying.
No, sir, if success means success in this world and
success is business, it may mean permanent, eternal
failure and bankruptcy, for I dare assert it is true
of many rich men that have sunk down to hell.
They could not go into joint copartnership in hell
to-day and buy with all their millions a drop of
water to cool their parched tongues. And you tell
me that is success! No, sir, give him success, but

I take religion, and then when the last hour shall come, if I die at the rich man's gate with the dogs for my doctors, to lick my sores, I will be lifted out of a pauper's body into Abraham's bosom to live forever and ever with God. Let me be a Christian, poor or rich, high or low. Let me be loyal to God, living right and doing right—"a devout man," a religious man. I like that sort of men. I like a man that is religious every time you meet him, and religious everywhere he goes, and religious in every thing he does.

I never had much confidence in a man that would do things when he goes to New York that he would n't do here at home. You have some of that sort here. A fellow that's sober as a judge at home, when he goes on a fishing tour can not get along without a keg of whisky; and he drinks it all the way along, and claims to be pious. And that is n't all. You not only take it along, and that's wrong in itself, but there are not half of you that take it who do not lie about it afterwards. That's one thing about sin. It not only makes a fool out of you, but makes a rascal out of you at every crack. That's as true as that the sun shines. I never have seen but one man in America that would stand up and say he drank whisky and never told his wife a lie about it. Have you got one here to-day? Is there a man here who drinks whisky who never told his wife a lie about it? If there is, stand up here, I want to see you. I expect some of you would have stood up but your wives are with you and you do n't want to be caught in a lie.

"A devout man." That means a religious man;
religious everywhere under all circumstances. That's
the sense of this text: "Cornelius, a devout man."
Thoroughly religious. When a pastor has that
class of members in his Church he can bank on them,
and everywhere. He knows just as well where to
go and what to ask for as he knows his name.
Good Lord, fill every Church in this city with
thoroughly religious people, and then we will take
this country for God. "Cornelius, a devout man."
Now listen: "And"—you notice that copulative
conjunction in there—"and feared God, with all
his house." Do you notice that when we talk about
people we never use the copulative conjunction?
We use the disjunctive "but." Did you ever notice
that? You ask about Brother A, and the answer is,
"Well, he's good, but he does n't pray in his
family." "Well," you say, "how about Brother
B?" "Well, he's a good man, a very good man,
but he seems to like his dram." You ask, "How
about Brother C?" "Well, he's a mighty nice,
good man, but he does n't pray in his family and
does n't always come to Church." Well, you ask
again about So-and-so, and you are told, "he's a
mighty good man, but he'll just knock you down
in a minute if you bother him."

When you have gone all round, whenever you
have asked about any body, they do n't talk more
than two minutes before they begin to use this con-
junctive. They say, "He's so and so, but he's
also so and so." You can take this disjunctive conjunction "but" and chip character all to pieces

with it in a minute. Now, God tells us Cornelius
was a devout man, and—do n't you see?—"and."
I like that "and." You can just take any fellow
in this town and say all about him. "He 's good
and kind." Then you commence to "but" him,
and the first thing you know you butt him off the
bridge, and that 's the last of him. Lord have
mercy upon us. Is the world a multitude of gossipers
and slanderers, or is it a fact that nobody can say three
good words about us without telling something
mean about us? Is that so? People say, " She 's
a pretty good woman, but if she gets mad with you
she will never make it up;" or, they say, "She 's
a right good neighbor, but she wants you to pay
back every thing you borrow;" or, "She 's a mighty
good wife, but I tell you if her husband does n't
do to suit her she will give him brimstone." I
mean those Georgia women, of course. That kind
of thing has never occurred here in this city. I
know you women just show in your faces that you
are like angels. You look as if all you needed was a
pair of wings, and you would go to glory without
any further ceremony.. It does tickle me just to
see you women put on an air of injured innocence.
"You know I 'm just as innocent as can be. I
never quarreled with my husband in my life, and
I never said a cross word to one of my children."
Sister, if you have n't done this, I will get you a
pair of wings before night and start you on to glory.

"A devout man, and one that feared God with all
his house." Now, listen. When Cornelius got religion, he got it all over; or, if you like the expression

better, it got him all over from head to foot. That is the first thing that happened to him, and he then feared God with all his house. Then the wife was religious and all the household were religious. And, I tell you the grandest sight angels ever look on in this world, is a father who takes the wife by the hand, and the wife leads the eldest child by the hand, and the eldest child the next, and so on, and to see that father and mother just leading their children right into the pearly gates for ever and ever—the whole family housed in heaven—that is a grand sight on earth and it is a grander sight in heaven.

But I tell you the saddest sight that God's eyes ever looked on—and he has seen the whole Mississippi Valley blighted with death and yellow fever; he has seen whole provinces of China starved to death; he has seen the flood of war covering almost half of the world—the saddest sights God's eyes ever looked on, is a father who takes the wife by the hand, and the wife who takes the eldest child by the hand, and both leading them to the brink of the river of death, until at last father, mother, and children all leap into the river that is lined from source to mouth with human wretches floating on to death and hell. There are hundreds of such families in this city going to hell—father, mother, and children, the whole group, hand in hand, and arm in arm. Is it yours? Is it yours? Is it yours, sir? If there is a deeper, darker place in perdition than all others, it seems to be for the husband and father, who willingly and deliberately turns his back on God, and grasping his family, leads them down to hell. And I want to tell you men in this town, if there is a man who has a good Christian wife, a praying, earnest Christian woman, and that mother is doing all she can to save her children, and the father is doing all he can to undo the mother's work and prayers; who, when his wife prays, sneers, and when the wife strives to lead the children to God strives to lead them away by his example; that if there is a more intolerable hell for any one, it is for that man who tries to undo the work of a Christian wife, and in spite of her prayers and tears, drags her children down to hell. And that's you, sir; and that's you, sir; and that's you, sir. O it were better for you that you never had been born, than to curse the life of a good wife, and damn the children of a good mother. If I have any thing special in reference to my wife and children to be grateful for, it is this: I have no living child that ever looked into my face when I was not a consecrated Christian man. God gave us one when I was wrecked and wayward and godless. That little child lived and looked in my face when I was godless and profane and wretched, and God took her to heaven; and I have often wished that Bickersteth had told the truth when he said—and if it be true it is the sweetest thing poet ever said—"A babe in heaven is a babe forever." And I have thought of that lovely one there, with my mind made up, I shall live a Christian as long as God gives me a child to look in my face, and when I get to heaven I will fall down and beg pardon of that sweet little angel that she ever saw me when I wasn't a Christian.

Now this riffraff, these low-down scoundrels round this town that have no wife or children, they may, in a sense, afford to swear, and drink, and sin; but when a father sins he sins with a vengeance, because every wicked act of his life is an impediment in the way of his children, that God himself must pull them over before they can ever get to God and glory.

"A devout man, and one that feared God with all his house." No, sir; if you ask me which I would rather see, all my family religious, or enjoy the inheritance of a Vanderbilt, I will say I had rather see one of my sweet children converted to God than to be presented with a hundred million dollars. The Atlanta *Constitution*, the other day, had a notice of a note to the editor of the Asheville (North Carolina) *Times*, in which a man wanted to get the address of Sam Jones, with an intimation that some man out there had died and left him a large legacy. Well, that item went the rounds and this person saw it and the people got excited about it, and came to me and asked if I had seen it. I told them, yes, I saw it; and they said, "Are you going to send on your papers and your proofs?" Said I, "No." "Why?" was asked. "Well, in the first place, I don't know but what it is some trap; and in the second place, I am getting along so well without a legacy that I think I will just keep on this way. I am doing swimmingly without one, and God only knows what would happen to me if I had one. So

I've gotten along first-rate, do n't you see?" Ninety-
nine, I had like to have said—and I think it is
true—ninety-nine cases in a hundred, where you
leave your children $20,000 apiece, without the
heritage of a good name or a Christian character to
go with it, you are leaving them enough to buy a
through ticket to hell; and they will invest in it,
and check their baggage through, and never stop
until into hell they go. That's the truth.

"Yes," you say, "Jones is preaching communism." I am not. I tell you to-day, there is n't a
man in this country that fights communism stronger
than I do. I have no sympathy with this low-
down rack of God's creation going round doing
nothing and wanting every thing that every body
else has; and I have no sympathy with the fellow
that has got a big pile of it and won't give any
away. That's the way I feel about it. I have
found out that money is like a walking-stick. One
will help you along if you are lame, but fifty loaded
on your back will break you down. That's so, and
the matter with some of you people is that you are
loaded down with money. Money is like guano;
if you put it on too thick it will burn up every
thing. And so money, if you load on too heavily,
will spoil a man. The richest man the world ever
saw was also one of the best. Abraham could have
bought out Vanderbilt and scarcely have missed
the money he checked out of the bank to pay for
Vanderbilt's estate, and yet he was one of the best
men on earth. It is not so much the money as the
sort of fellow that has it. That's it.

"Feared God with all his house." Now, brother, if there is a sight that charms my soul it is a family devoted to God—father, mother, and children, all in love and harmony with God. What a grand sight that is! I have been trying to finish a little cottage home at my house for several weeks, for my wife and children, and I told my wife the other day: "When the last nail is driven and the work is complete, we will get our friends together, and we will dedicate this house to God." Said I: "Wife, it will do our children good to know that they sleep in God's house; that they eat in God's house; and that every thing they do here is in God's house. Let us tell them: 'Children, your mother and father have given this house to God; we are God's children; we are your elder brothers and sisters. We are all children of God. Let us help each other to be good and to do right.' Then I said: "Wife, nobody will ever ask us to play cards here. They would no more play cards in this house than if it were a church. And nobody will ask us to let them dance balls here; nobody will want to dance in God's house. And nobody will ask us to give wine suppers here. This is God's house. Let us protect our home and protect our children by giving our house to God." She said: "It's a bargain." And so I have a house for my children that is God's house, in which to raise them, as if they were my little brothers and sisters and children of God.

Let me tell you, if every house in this city were dedicated to God this afternoon, at three o'clock, there would be some moving out, would n't there? My! my! Old Brother and Sister Euchre, old Brother and Sister Progressive Euchre would have to rack out, would n't they? And I reckon when you get backed up into heaven, for you never will get there unless God backs you there, as you are headed from it now—and God will have to turn you round or back you into glory, one or the other—I reckon if one of your sort were to get in there at last, to your astonishment, you would hear it said, "There come old Brother and Sister Euchre. Here they are!" And it would be the biggest wonder in heaven when the angels of God see old Brother and Sister Euchre dropping in. And then there's old Sister and Brother Demijohn, and old Brother Ballroom and Sister Ballroom. Whenever you dedicate your house to God the first thing you will have to do is to wash the devil's fleas off you. You can get the fleas of the flesh off with essence of peppermint, but it takes essence of damnation to do any thing with these moral fleas.

O for a house dedicated to God, a home dedicated to God, where the mother lives in the atmosphere of prayer, where the children are brought up under the most sacred influences that either heaven or earth know any thing of. I tell you, brethren, if there is a spot on earth of which it can be said truthfully, that angels encamp round about it, it must be the home that is devoutly consecrated to God, with a good father and good mother and all the children consecrated to God. Do n't you like that?

"Feared God, with all his house." Now, you see, Cornelius got religion himself, and the first thing you know it broke out all over his family; and now I tell you that there's a varioloid type of it that is n't catching. You know that, for there is n't one of your children that caught it, sister. The varioloid type—nobody knows you had it. They just put you in bed a day or two and you were out before any body found out you were sick. The varioloid type of piety has taken possession of this country, but it is n't catching. But you get one of the old-fashioned, confluent cases of small-pox, and every body will catch it that goes into the room. This varioloid type of religion that you see nowadays is n't catching, but you take an old-fashioned case, and when a man has got it, the first thing you know his wife will get it, and it will break out over the family, and the whole family will be consecrated to God.

You hear people say that minister's children are worse than any body else's children. I say that's a great big lie. There is n't a word of truth in it. I want to tell you what my observation teaches me, that the minister's children are better than any body else's children. I know men in Georgia to-day, raised by Methodist, Presbyterian, Baptist, and Christian ministers that any man in this city would be glad to call father. I do n't go much on the preacher who has n't got a religious family, though there are circumstances that we ought to weigh mighty closely. I am afraid he has n't got religion himself unless it has taken possession of his

household. I know one thing, one of the best
preachers in our State has the worst children, but
that is because the combined influences of city life
and the evils which are centered there have tempted
and carried off his boys. And I know another
thing; if I turn loose a godless child into this
world, when I come to die you can go to my tombstone and chip in large letters: "Here lies the
most arrant hypocrite this world ever saw." If you
have got religion right, the first thing you know
your whole crowd will get it. That is my doctrine.

"Feared God, with all his house." Brother, the
darkest, gloomiest spot on earth is the home where
there is no Christ and no piety and no prayer. A
prayerless house is the home of the devil, and his
children live there. Well, now, what else? First,
he got it himself; and, secondly, it took all over his
household, until wife and children and servants, all
were religious. Then what came? "He gave much
alms to the poor." See how the thing spreads—how
it grows out and develops, and takes hold of all the
land. I like a liberal fellow. I will tell you this:
What a man gives is a test of what a man is. You
take a man in the Church that is stingy; there isn't
a preacher in this crowd that has any hope at all for
him, or any patience with him. If I had charge of
some Churches in this world, filled up with low-
flung, stingy members, that were as stingy as some
of them are, I would have no faith at all that I
could accomplish any thing, and I would be afraid
the devil would get the last one of them, and I

would have to pray mightily to keep from being glad that he did. You know a man is in a pretty close place when he has to pray that way. Have you ever been that way, brother? If you have n't, then you do n't know some of the close places I have been in. I had one of that sort of members once send his wife for me when he was sick. He wanted to see me, as he was about to die. I went there, and he wanted me to pray for him. I said: "Pray for you?" "Yes," he said. I said, "What for?" He said he wished me to pray that he might get well again. Said I: "I can't do that, brother." He asked why. I told him: "I try to be honest when on my knees, and if I were to get on my knees and pray God to let you live, and he were to ask me what I wanted you to live for, I could n't tell to save my life. I do n't know what I want you to live for. You won't pray, and you won't do any thing else. What would I tell God I wanted you to live for?" I staid there a few minutes, and when I got up to leave he said: "Do you need any corn?" I told him I needed a load or so, or could use it, and said he: "I 'll send you a load down." And he did, and I do n't know whether any body else made any thing or not, but I got a big load of corn out of that man. Brethren, there 's many a man in this city that, if an honest preacher were to be asked to sit down and pray for God to let him live, the preacher could n't honestly do it. What do you want him to live for? He does no good in the Church; he won't pay, he won't pray, he won't do any thing.

The other day I picked up the Atlanta *Constitution,* and I saw an item concerning a Georgia man who was dangerously ill in New York. My heart leaped up as I saw it, and I said: "Lord God, do n't let —— die. We can't get along without him in Georgia. There is no good work going on that he is not up to his elbows in it. Lord, do n't let him die." The next telegram I read he was getting better, and he got well and is now back in Atlanta.

I would n't pray for that first fellow, I could n't; but just as soon as I saw that —— was ill I was praying for him. He is only twenty-eight or thirty years old, a merchant in Atlanta, a first-class fellow. There is but one trouble with him, and that is his stinginess. Why, sir, he is worth $20,000 and only gives $1,500 a year out of it for God and religion! I mean he is worth $20,000, and we can't get more than $1,500 a year out of him. One of your 'possum-eared fellows, is n't he? If I were to bring him up here and set him down beside you fellows he would scare you to death. Why, we were taking up a foreign missionary collection and this man stood up and said to the pastor: "I gave last year the best sister boy ever had to the foreign missionary field. This year I 'll give you $500 for foreign missions." O, my good Lord, give us some of that sort here. Give us one of that sort, to wake up the old fogies; just to show them what a fellow can be, you know.

Good Lord, help us to see that heaven is all around us here. I can stand right where I am and throw a rock into the middle of heaven. It is all about us. You say you will go to heaven when you die. Lord bless you, if you do n't get to heaven a few times before you die, you will never get there after you die. There are some preachers in this country who spend about one-third of their life on heavenly recognition—preaching heavenly recognition. Well, you will never catch me on that lay—heavenly recognition. I am like that old preacher in our State who said he did n't study about heavenly recognition. He said: "What I want is earthly recognition. Brothers, please recognize me down here; help me along down here. I am in a heap of trouble, and what I need is earthly recognition. When I get to heaven, and get a crown upon my head, and a harp in my hand, and sit down under the shade of the tree of life, I won't want recognition then, because I will be already elected for all time to come." I like that, and I like a generous man—a man that never has a dollar that is too good for God and the right. You have some generous people here. Thank God for every one you have got.

Sermon VII.

All Things Work Together for Good.

"And we know that all things work together for good to them that love God, to them who are the called according to his purpose.—Rom. viii, 28.

WE can say there is but one single exception in all the universe to the truth of this utterance, and God makes that exception all through his book. Every thing in this universe, except sin, works for the good of those that love God. There is nothing in sin, or of sin, or about sin, or around sin, or above it, or beneath it, or connected with it in any way, that can ever work for any body's good. What you have done that is wrong, what you ought to have done that you did not do, God can never make work for your good. If you have staid away from a prayer-meeting, God can never make that work for your good. If you have neglected your duty, God can never make that neglect work for your good. There is no provision of grace to make up for any body what he has lost from the neglect of duty.

Now recollect, if you are a Christian and love God, every thing you can not help, every thing you would have warded off if you could, every thing you would have conquered if you could, every thing in this life, except sin, works for good; and God himself can not make sin work for any body's good, be—

138

cause sin is the reversal, the throwing out of gear
the machinery of our nature. When we begin to
go wrong we reverse the machinery of our nature
and run it backwards. You can no more work for
God when you reverse the machinery of your nature
than you can make your sewing-machine sew when
you run it backwards. One is as impossible as the
other. All things work for good when you are running in harmony with God and in a line with God;
for, after all, religion is nothing more than harmony
with God. When you walk up to your piano, and
touch a key in that elegant instrument, and that key
is out of tune, and out of harmony, it is out of harmony, not only with the rest of the keys of the
piano, but it is out of harmony with every thing
in the universe that is in harmony. But when the
piano-tuner walks up to that piano and opens it,
and takes out his instruments and works away at
that particular string until he gets it in harmony,
then that key is in harmony with every thing in the
universe. And religion is getting in harmony with
God. Then every thing moves along harmoniously, adjusting and setting the Ten Commandments to music. Is it not so? When God bids
me do this or that he touches a chord in my nature in sympathy with his own divine heart, and
then we are in harmony with all. God wills and
wishes it, and he will make every thing in this
universe conduce to our present and eternal happiness.

"And we know that all things work together
for good to them that love God." There is the text.

There are three classes of people here this afternoon, and these three classes represent the whole world. The first class we mention are those that know they love God. Thank God, there are such persons on the face of the earth, persons who know they do love God. There is another class here, and those in that class do not love God; and about nine-tenths of us make up the third class, persons who do not know whether they love God or not. Sometimes they think they love him. Sometimes they think they do not. Nine-tenths of the world are made up of do n't-know-what-to-thinks. O, how numerous they are! But what is the use of going on in that way? If I were a ten-year-old boy and you asked me, "Do you love your mother?" I should reply: "Yes, sir, I do." "How do you know?" "Because when I do what mother says for me to do I feel good about it, and when I do something mother told me not to do, I feel bad about it." "Well, what other reason?" "I love her, and I love to hear her name reverently and kindly used." "Well, what other reason?" "It makes me feel bad for any one to speak unkindly and irreverently of my mother." Now you ask me, "Are you a Christian?" "Yes." "Do you love God?" "Yes." "How do you know you do?" "Because when I do what God tells me I feel good about it." "How else do you know it?" "Because when I do something he told me not to do, I feel as bad about it as I can." "How else do you know it?" "It does me good to hear people praise God and speak reverently of him, and it gives me a horror to hear any one blaspheme him." I have as many reasons why I love God as I had why I loved my mother.

The love of God is not necessarily an emotional feeling. I hear people talk a heap about feeling that they love God. I never stop to see whether I have feelings or not. I never inquire about that. Some people say they never want to do any thing unless they feel like it. I have seen preachers that are always gadding about, and are extremely anxious that all the members of their congregation shall be visited. Then there are preachers whose minds and hearts are in their Church, and they would rather be whipped than go and see any body. This brother deserves a thousand times more credit than Brother Gadabout. If pastoral visiting would have saved this town, it would have been saved long ago. God never said that people should be saved by pastoral visiting. He said that the Gospel is the power of God unto salvation. And I have a great deal more respect for the brother who would rather talk and preach the Gospel than go and see any body than I have for the brother who would rather be running around all the time. I tell you how I feel about it. I do not care whether a minister ever puts a foot in my house all the year round or not; but I will say one thing: When my wife and children visit my pastor I want him to preach enough solid truth to keep them going the whole week, instead of running and gadding about, and getting in my wife's way, and keeping things disarranged all the week while she is looking for the preacher.

I want my preacher to let my family visit him

at the house of God. I never saw people that
quarreled about the pastor not visiting them that
amounted to much, anyhow. If you treat a preacher
right, and give him a good, square meal every time
he calls, he hasn't any more sense than to come
back again. If a preacher doesn't come to see you
it is your fault. Isn't that so, brother? Christ
told his disciples when they went to a place, to go
to one house and put up there, and not to be running about all over creation. He knew what he
was talking about. But if I could not preach much
I would make it up in visiting. What I lost in
dancing I would make up in turning round. You
quit bothering your preacher about coming to see
you and help him in his work! If he has one
thousand members in his Church you make yourself useful and help him to look after the other nine
hundred and ninety-nine. I used to have some
members of my Church everlastingly at me to visit
them. One family bothered me more than any of
the others, and when I did make a call I made it
a jumping, bouncing class-meeting, and they never
bothered me any more. If some of you pastors
would do the same you would not be bothered as
much as you are.

Now I branched off from the subject I was discussing. I say whether we feel like it or not, let
us say: "I am going to do what I consider is right."
I am not inquiring this afternoon whether there is
an emotional feeling toward God in my heart.
What has Jesus Christ said? "Hereby ye know
that ye love me because ye feel that ye do so?"

No, he never said that; he said: "Hereby ye may know that ye love me because ye keep my commandments." God, love, and loyalty are synonymous in this sense. Loyalty to the right—absolute eschewing of the wrong—is proof to them that love God that they do love him.

Our text might read this way: "All things work together for good to them that keep the commandments of God." That is about the practical meaning of it. Well, now, if I am loyal to God straight out through and through, then the promise is: "All things shall work together for good." Well, I might stop here, but I wonder what that word "good" means. Suppose we give it this interpretation: "All things shall work together for the riches of God's people." Temporal riches— temporal prosperity? Why, if it had read that way there would not have been a word of truth in it, because, generally speaking, God's people are poor people.

Most people can not stand prosperity. Now, if you are going to be rich and religious both at the same time and place, all right, and if ever you get to heaven you will wear a bright crown there; no doubt about that. But I will say one thing to you, you had better look out along that line. Some folks think I have some spite against rich folks, like all poor white trash, but I have no spite against any body. If there is any body good to me it is the rich. If there is any body kind to me it is the rich. I think so much of the rich people of this country that I shall not let the devil get them if I

can help it, and I am going to talk to them when I
feel like it. How many genuinely Scriptural pious
rich women do you know in town? I do not
mean, how many belong to the Church? I know
the Church will get them in, and it's glad to get
them, religion or no religion. I ain't talking about
that. How many genuinely Scriptural, devoted,
pious rich women have you got in your city? How
many pure, noble, consecrated, self-sacrificing, pious
men who are millionaires have you got in your
city? Now, I never said there were not any. I
never said how many. I ask you, how many?

Prosperity! God never said: "All things
shall work together for the prosperity of God's
people." They could not stand it. Some folks
could not go to heaven out of a three-story house.
That's a fact. I do not say I am one of those who
could. I never tried it and never will, I reckon.
Prosperity—I do not want any thing to come between me and my loyalty to God. I like Agur's
prayer: "Give me neither poverty nor riches; feed
me with food convenient for me; lest I be full and
deny thee, and say, Who is the Lord? or lest I be
poor, and steal, and take the name of my God in
vain." The medium is best. Let me have "sufficient unto the day," with the blessed assurance that
I shall dwell in the land and shall be fed.

God never said: "All things shall work
together for the health of God's people." I
think some of the most afflicted people I ever
met in this life have been the best, and I think
sometimes most of us would get along better if we

were sick more. Take an ordinary Methodist, now a backslider, and strike him down with a six weeks' spell of typhoid fever, and you can do more to get him better spiritually than by preaching 500,000 sermons. Shake a sinner over a coffin and turn him loose, and he will hit the ground running every time. David said, "It was good for me that I was afflicted." It is a mighty hard matter to keep a big, fat, sleek Church member straight; but get him down for a day to where he is pretty near to death and eternity and it has a good effect. It is wholesome.

It is said of Jenny Lind that when Goldsmith first heard her sing, as he walked out of the opera house, somebody said, "Goldsmith, how did you like her singing?" He said, "Well, there was a harshness about her voice that needs toning down. If I could marry that woman, break her heart and crush her feelings, then she could sing." And it is said that afterwards when he did marry her and broke her heart and crushed her feelings, Jenny Lind sang with the sweetest voice ever listened to; so sweet that the angels of God would almost rush to the parapets of heaven to catch the strains. Sometimes violets send forth their sweetest odors when crushed beneath the foot. Some of the most religious people have been the most deeply afflicted; and if there is one prayer I have prayed from the depths of my heart it is, "Lord, if I am to save my soul at any cost; if I am to lie on a bed of pain for thirty years, if that is necessary, let me begin now, and suffer till I draw my last breath, rather than to be joyous and healthy in this life and then enter into the other world and into a life of interminable suffering. Lord, whatever is necessary to save my soul let it come on me. Save my soul, good Lord, at any cost to me." That is the way we ought to pray. I used to think when I first became religious that if I got sick or my wife got sick, "That's a sign God doesn't love me." But now I know that God loves me with all his great heart.

Then he did not say: "All things shall work together for the honor of God's people, for the popularity of God's people." I tell you, sometimes if you do your whole duty you will be very unpopular. Did you ever notice that if you want to be popular in society you must not be much of a Christian? You must, of course, belong to the Church, and you must agree with every body. Don't disagree with any thing. If you visit the house of a friend, and they have cards, don't say a word against them, but say: "Some people object to them, but I don't see any harm in them." O how much of that sort of nonsense there is in the Church! And if they have dancing, tell them, "Our preachers don't like it; but to save my soul I have never seen any harm in it." And if they want to go to the theater, tell them, "Yes, I was a young girl once myself, and I used to go to the theater." When the apostles preached the truth, it is said but one of them died a natural death. Those that loved to preach the truth languished to death in dungeons, or were burned at the stake, or stoned. It is not a very popular thing to be an earnest, zealous Christian. It is not. God never said: "All things are working together for the popularity of God's people."

You take a popular preacher, a preacher whom every body likes, whom the gamblers like, the liars like, the drunkards like, and there is something wrong. Whenever liars and gamblers and hypocrites and backslidden members like me, I'll tell the Lord: "I am wrong, I know I am. There is something wrong about this thing."

I have noticed another thing. You recollect the Pharisees and Sadducees had no use for one another. They hated each other, but when Christ came along they clubbed together and let in on him. Here is a backsliding Baptist sister, and there is a backsliding Methodist sister. They have no use for each other under ordinary circumstances, but when a preacher comes along and knocks the bark off of them they join against him, and it is astonishing how intimate they get. They meet at the theater or at the card table, and there are a great many points on which they agree, and when they meet they join in the fight against this one or that one.

Now I believe in voting. This country is running a good deal on voting, and so on, and I want every lady in this house that enjoys religion, and has cares at home, who goes to the theater, who shines at social parties and dances, just square dances—she has not cut the corners off the thing yet—I want every lady here that really enjoys religion, and goes to these places and plays cards and

dances, to stand up. I want to see you. Stand
up, every one of you! If I were one I would
stand up and be laughed at and say: "Here is
one." What! none? But I will tell you what
such persons will say now. They will say: "I
do n't enjoy religion. I will admit that. I have
got religion, but I do n't enjoy it." Now listen to
me: There is but one reason why you do n't enjoy religion, and that is because you have n't got
any to enjoy. It is the most enjoyable thing a
fellow ever struck, and the question would be with
me, How can I keep from enjoying it? Got religion, but do n't enjoy it!

God never said that "all things shall work together for the worldly honors of God's people."
He never said that. I am glad the Lord's people
do n't take many honors in this world the way it
goes now. I am glad they do n't take any good
Christian and run him for President the way they
run them now. I am glad of that. I tell you if
a man were all right and they were to run him for
President, would n't they smirch him? Take
Blaine and Cleveland. Ten years of close application of warm water and soft soap would not
wash off the smirching and vituperation that was
thrown on those two men in their last race. If
what was said against those two men were true,
they ought both to be in the chain gang. I am
glad the Lord's people do not have things in that
way. I do n't want to be President if they put
more mud on me before I get there than I can
wash off while I am there,

Worldly honors! They are not for God's people. What *does* this mean? "All things work for good." What is this "good?" It is n't health. It is n't happiness. It is n't prosperity. It is n't worldly honors. What is it the Lord means here? Now, let us come to the true text for a moment: "All things work together for the salvation of them that love God." Salvation is the greatest good this earth ever heard of or can experience. Now, I can see into the text, and see into a thousand things. "All things work together for the salvation," for the present, and eternal salvation of them that love God. A heap of strange things happen in this world, sister. You say; "Well, I can not see, to save my life, how the loss of my husband could work for my good. I can not see how the loss of my sweet child can work for my good. I can not see how the loss of every dollar of our property can work for my good." O how strange things have happened! Well, now, you see that clock on the mantel at home. You walk up and look at that clock. You take it down and look at the dial, and look at the works, which must be put together by a clockmaker. I took my clock to pieces once, and after I had put it together again I had sufficient wheels left to make another clock. I could not get it right. It had been made by a clockmaker, and only a clockmaker could put the wheels in their proper places again. When you look at the works of a clock you say: "Well, well, all those wheels can not be necessary. There is one big wheel turning slowly and another one fast. There is a great big one turning backward and a little one forward." You say a clock like that can not keep time. You put the dial back and the clock ticks on and strikes the hours, and you say: "It does keep time. I do not care how it looks." Now, God sets up in heaven the largest clock of all, and we can not see the machinery. Here is health and peace in your family. Well, that is a little wheel moving forward. The last dollar of your property is swept away. Well, that is a big wheel turning backward; but all things work for you, and work harmoniously in one direction for your present good and eternal salvation.

When I was at Columbus, Ga., I walked through an immense cotton factory. I was shown all the machinery, that which cut the hoops around the raw cotton, that which picked the cotton, and I followed one machine after another, from one floor to another. I watched some machinery carding cotton, others pulling it on to reels. At times I would say: "Look here, surely this is not the way to make cloth. If I did not want to make cloth, I would do just as you are doing." But when we got to the last machine, on the fourth floor, there was a pile of cotton cloth bundled up ready for the market. I looked down the line of machines and said, every machine in this factory works together for cloth; and, sister, by and by, when you step into the heavenly gates, you will look back and say: "Every thing in my life worked for good." O, how true these things are!

My father used to say: "My son, if you do that

I will correct you." When I got off by myself I said: "Papa is so cruel to me. Sometimes he whips me for doing some things, and if ever I get grown up I am going to ask papa what made him do that." But I was not eighteen when I found that my father had corrected me for things that would have ruined me if I had been left alone. When you get to heaven you will say: "God brought me to salvation the only way he could have brought me safely thus far."

"All things work together for good." A man once gave me this illustration of the text. He said he was sitting out under a tree in a garden eating a biscuit when he saw a little ant climbing upon the plank. He watched it, and said: "I reckon this little ant is in search of food." He had dropped a crumb, but the little ant was going in the opposite direction to it. He put his finger in the way of the ant to direct it to the crumb, and the little thing seemed to lose patience and want to quarrel with him, and it seemed to say: "Why do you stop me? I am hunting food for my young." The ant started off in another direction, and he dropped his finger again in front of the little ant, which seemed to be madder than before, and it seemed to say: "O, you great intelligent creature, why do you stop me? I am hunting food for my young." He dropped his finger in front of the ant again and again, and each time it seemed to say: "Why do you stop me? I am in earnest search of food for my young." He said he dropped his finger in front of the ant until he directed it to the crumb,

and when it picked the crumb up it seemed to say:
"I am so glad you put me in the way of finding this.
Here is more food than I could have found in a
month if you had left me alone." In this world
when we are moving in the wrong direction, down
comes the providential finger of God, and you say:
"I know I have the worst luck of any body."
And we stand and quarrel with God and ourselves.
We start out in another direction, and just about
the time we think we are about to succeed, down
comes God's providential finger, and we say: "Just
look at that!" In this way God drives us right to
the gate of heaven, and when we walk in there we
say: "Glory be to God. If we had been left alone
we would have gone to perdition, but he has driven
me right to the joys of everlasting life."

Providence means going before. I believe in
Providence as strongly as I believe in any thing.
Here is a wagon train moving westward. A horseman
lopes ahead, picks out the camping-place, buys the
provender for the stock, and arranges every thing.
That man was the providence of the wagon train.
Providence goes on ahead to arrange and plan
every thing. Now let us in God's providence from
this time say: "I will go along, and trust in God
that every thing will work together for good.
Though he fall he shall not be utterly cast down,
for the Lord upholdeth his hand."

I hold a baby's hand as it walks. Its foot
strikes something, and it falls with a force that
would crush its face. But I hold up the baby by
the hand, and I say, "Baby, I am so glad you had

my hand. If you had not held it you would have ruined your little face on the rocks. I have sometimes gone along and fallen, and I have thought I was gone forever, but the Lord had my hand and held me up, and I say, "Bless the Lord! If he had not held my hand I should have fallen down into eternal despair."

One day my two little boys ran ahead of me on the sidewalk. Directly I noticed they were back again holding by my fingers. Well, I thought, "What does this mean?" I loooked ahead and saw a few steps in advance a lot of cattle on the sidewalk. Just as they saw the cattle they ran back and got hold of my fingers and continued to laugh and play, as much as to say: "We were afraid when we saw those cattle alone, but now we would laugh and play if all the cattle in the world were here, for we are with father." Let me say to you, if you have got hold of God's hand, you are safe. When dangers and disappointments beset you, you laugh and rejoice. Lord, help and bless us, and save us.

SAYINGS.

WHAT WE WILL BE.—We had a talking meeting in Trinity Church, Atlanta, in which I took up the different parts of an engine as an illustration of the various machinery of the great engineering power of the Church. One fellow got up and said, "I would like to be the boiler of the engine where the power is generated." Another said, "I'd like to be the cow-catcher, to keep the way clear." Another

said, "I'd like to be the head-light, to light up the
track." Another said, "I'd rather be the whistle,
and sound the praises of God all over the country."
Another said, "I'd like to be the cab and protect
the engineer." And so they went on; until one got
up and said, "Brethren, I am perfectly willing to
be the old, black coal they pitch into the furnace
and burn up to generate the heat that moves the
train on to glory." Ah, that is it. If we had more
of the old, black coal sort, to pitch into the furnace,
we would carry this train to heaven. O God, if
necessary to the salvation of this city, let me be the
coal, and be consumed in drawing this people to God
and heaven.

BUT ONE QUESTION.—In the great work of
redemption, I have but one question to ask: "Lord,
what wilt thou have me to do?" I'll never stop
to ask God what he is going to do and how he is
going to do it and when he is going to do it; but
the question that engages my mind is, "Lord, what
wilt thou have me to do?" I never preach on the
divine side of the Gospel. The water is deep out
there, and little boats ought to stay near the shore.
I'd want to be a first-class swimmer if I should go
out in the depths of divine mysteries and inquire
of God what are the divine plans and the divine
modes and the divine "when" and the divine "how."
These are questions that never bother me at all. I
simply want to know what God wants me to do, and
if he'll tell me, I'll do that and trust him for the
rest.

Sermon VIII.

Eternal Punishment, or the Logic of Damnation.

"Because sentence against an evil work is not executed speedily, therefore the heart of the sons of men is fully set in them to do evil."—Eccles. viii, 11.

THIS is a wonderful old book we preachers take our texts from. In the book of Genesis we read of the creation of the world and the origin of man. God devotes one book to tell me of my origin, and the thousand chapters that follow tell me where I am going. We spend an hour here to-day on the pathway to the grave. This text belongs legitimately to the conclusion of the sermon, which is the answer to a question I want to ask you. I want first to ask the question, and I want us to spend twenty or thirty minutes trying to answer that question, and then we will let God answer this question; for we ought to be willing that God should answer all questions that pertain to life and salvation.

The question which I now propound plainly stated is this: "Why will you continue in sin?" Now, as simple as every word of that text is, may be we can spend a minute or two profitably in consideration of these words, "Why will you continue in sin?" I don't ask why you happen to be already a sinner. That involves three logical ques-

tions, which we have not the ability to discuss. I
do n't ask why you have come out to this service a
sinner. That will involve exculpatory statements
on your part, which I have not the time nor disposition to hear. But the question plainly stated is
not, "Should you remain in sin?" or, "How you
are a sinner?" but, "Why will you leave here an
impenitent sinner?" And we narrow the question
down a little, and we put it in this shape: "Why
will *you*?" I do n't mean the one behind you, nor
the one in front of you. I mean you. God bless
you! This is a very personal matter.

You can't get any body to die for you; you
can't get any body to stand in your stead at the day
of judgment and be damned for you. You stand in
your own shoes, as if you are the only individual
that ever violated a law of God. This is pre-
eminently a personal matter, and we do n't ask you
why the world continues in sin or why the members
of the Churches continue in sin, but we ask you,
"Why will you continue in sin another day, another hour, another week?"

We say first: Is it because you are ignorant as to
the nature of sin? Does any man in this congregation give me as his reason for living to-day in
sin and living on in sin, because he does n't know
what sin is? Is there a man here this evening that
does n't know it is wrong to drink, wrong to violate
the Sabbath, wrong to live in neglect of his Christian duty? Do you plead ignorance of the nature
of sin? The world stands convicted at this point.

You let a member of the Church do wrong, and

you are the first one to see it. You let my foot
slip, and you are the first man to see it and talk
about it; and your criticisms upon the life of the
Christian people are an everlasting demonstration
that you know what right is, and that you know
what wrong is. You know there is a vast difference between the way we look at men in Church
and out of Church. The world expects something
of a man in Church. I am glad it does. The world
does n't expect much of you, and if it did it would
be very much disappointed. Here is the difference
between a member of the Church and a man out of
Church. The member of the Church is a white piece
of canvas, and if any thing is sprinkled upon him
it makes a spot easy to discern. But that old sinner is a black, dingy piece of canvas, and you can
just take any thing and rub upon him, and it does n't
show at all. You let me go into a bar-room and
take a drink of whisky, and it is wired all over the
country, and read in every newspaper at the breakfast table to-morrow morning. You go in and take
a drink every morning and nobody notices you.
This is the difference between a gentleman and a
vagabond. You let me go out on the streets and profane the name of God, and it is flashed across the
world, "Jones is in the city, swearing." You can
swear every day. Nobody notices you. Nobody expects any better of you for it. That is the difference between a gentleman and a vagabond. I thank God, I
have lived to see the day in my State when nobody
will swear or drink whisky but vagabonds. You
do n't like that? Do you? I do n't blame you.

I would not either. Fifteen years ago I would have
felt very much insulted if I heard a preacher say
that. The truth is the same now that it was then,
but, O, what a different fellow I am now from what I
was then. Drinking is the habit of a vagabond,
and profanity is the habit of a vagabond; and if
you will be profane and swear you lack that much
of being a gentleman. No gentleman will profane
the name of God, and whatever else you lack, I am
sorry to say that many of you come that much short
of being a gentleman.

Ignorant of the nature of sin! Will you say
you do n't know your life is wrong? Every man
answers back, and says: "That is not my excuse.
I know what right is, and I know right is right.
I know what wrong is, and further than that, I
know wrong is wrong." Then we stop here and
ask you this question: Is there any man that says,
"The reason I live in sin is because I do n't know
what the consequences of a sinful life are?" I
know, forsooth, because this nineteenth century is
wicked; there is a hell. I heard a minister say
once, "That science is going to demonstrate that
there is no hell." Said I, "When that delegation
comes back I want to be on hand when they report." Science knows as little about hell, and what
is in hell, as science knows about the birthplace of
God. The biggest fool I know is that fool who
gets into the biggest, broadest way to hell, and stops
by the way and tries to persuade men there is no
hell. The biggest fool is the man who spends his
probationary existence in arguing that there is no

hell, and then lies down in hell forever, realizing that there is one. You poor dunce, what do you know of what is down there? Did you ever attend a Universalist meeting? I was at a Univerlist meeting one day, and that day all the red-nosed drunkards and gamblers and rascals of the town had the front seats and amen corners. All I want to know of a preacher is, who has got the amen corners?

God pity you living in sin. What is to become of you? Let this book speak out, and this is the only book that says any thing of the other side of the tomb. I will keep to this book until you find us something better, for this book says that "the wicked shall be turned into hell with all the nations that forget God." I believe in a bottomless hell, and I believe that the wicked shall be turned into hell. I do believe that the righteous have hope after death, and eternal life is the legitimate end of a good man. I mean to say that God will not punish a single person except he fly in the face of the required law laid down on every page of this book; except he lay his hand over every scar in his heart and says there is no scar there. I do believe if a man lives right he will get to heaven, and those who do wrong will go to hell.

Do you think there is fire there? I do n't know whether there will be any before you get there, unless you take something with you to burn you through all eternity. Every sinner carries his own brimstone with him. No sir, that man says he knows the legitimate end of a sinful life is hell;

and if you will tell me how long sin will last, I
will tell you how long hell will last. "It is not
because I am ignorant of the nature or consequences of sin that I continue in it," may be your reply
to my question. Then what is it? Are you indifferent to the results? O, how many men meet
truth without a tremor in their muscles. When a
man reaches this point, when you can't move him
with truth, he is immovable.

What stolid indifference we meet on all sides!
Men know their life is short, and that they may be
in their coffins before to-morrow evening's sun, yet
they are indifferent to their condition. "Indifferent?" You say, "I know what preachers think of
me, and neighbors think of me as indifferent, but
down in my heart I think and feel more than any
body has discovered. I have gone home from
Church with my Christian wife, her arm in mine,
and I have heard my soul beat with conviction, but
I would not have my wife hear it. Thank God,
wherever else I went, I was never indifferent to the
great truths of eternity. No, sir; it is not indifference. I look as if I were, but I am not."

Then, we ask, Is it recklessness? Is it because
you know the truth and will dare the truth? Is it
that? Recklessness is a poor thing in any world?
O, how reckless some men are. We see that Alpine
hunter as he walks on the narrow paths, with preci-
pices on both sides. He realizes his risk, yet he
walks on across the path, while the very dog that
walks behind him will wince and turn. I have
known men who seemed to be so reckless that they

were unwilling to live on to their three-score years
and ten, and lie down and die in the natural order of
things. I see them at twenty years of age begin to
drink, and they drink on until thirty years of age.
They know they are about gone. "One year more,
just twelve months, is all I can last," they say.
Yet the poor fellow goes on, and seems to be griev-
ing for damnation. And I see him walk out on
the street, all besotted with whisky, and pick a
quarrel with a friend, and that friend shoots him
down, and he leaps from the sidewalks of the city
into hell. God pity you! After all that has been
said and done you will go, within twelve months, to
a drunkard's grave! Forty years old, and before
you are forty-one you will fall into a drunkard's
grave! How is it?

Recklessness! You say, "I know wrong is
wrong, but I won't heed it. I curse publicly. I
drink openly. I sin with a high hand." God pity
you! If I were going to sin I would crawl off in
some dark corner and never let my example be
seen to lead on any others. How reckless poor
humanity is at times concerning the truth! It hurries
on to the edge of the precipice, and stands and
shudders but a moment, then makes a leap, from
which there is no recovering forever.

"No, sir, it is not recklessness!"

Then I stop and ask you this question: Is it
because you are satisfied in your present condition?
Thank God, no man was ever satisfied with himself
as a sinner. Twenty-five years of the gall of bitterness and the bonds of iniquity have persuaded me

14

that no man would ever be satisfied with himself as a sinner. Like the rough sea, you have no rest. You are devoid of peace within your breast. Thank God, he will not let a sinner lie down and sleep on his way to hell.

"No, sir, I am not satisfied with myself."

And when those innocent children throw their lovely arms around your neck and look up in your face, in all the innocence of their nature, you say, "Of all the women that God ever gave children to, I am least calculated to lead them to God and everlasting life."

"Satisfied with myself? No, sir. Nobody can say that away from God and on his way to perdition."

Then we will ask again, is it because of your inconsideration? I know sometimes a man will look at a thing and then look off. Do you know what bar-rooms are for, and billiard tables, and cards, and germans? They are tricks of the devil to keep your mind off of yourself. Sometimes men get conviction of the Divine Spirit, and they will go and dance it off; drink and swear and gamble it off. God pity a man who has convictions and will dance and curse them away; convictions that a lost spirit would give the world if he could have. If the devil can keep you busy all day in your store and make you dance yourself to sleep, he has got you pretty safe. There are members of the Church that rent houses for bar-rooms. You are a joint stock owner of that thing, and if you can tell me how a man of God can be a joint stockholder in a bar-room, then you have explained to me one of the profoundest mysteries of moral science. Every man belonging to a club is a joint owner of that bar-room. I have been expecting some of the high-bred gentlemen to come forward and defend the club. If I had such a nice thing I would just hire news-papers and defend it. And I will tell you that no bar-room, that no deck of cards, can be defended in heaven, on earth or in hell. You could not hire a decent idiot to sail into me on that question. I suppose some of you are mean enough to sail in, but you have got too much sense. I can associate with members of the Church, who belong to it, but when you set in to defend it, I would not wipe my feet on you. I am perfectly willing to give you all the time that I am not engaged in preaching.

"It is not because I am satisfied with my present condition. It is not because I won't think. I have thought, but doubts arise about these things."

Is it because you are leading a sort of compromise life? Do you say, I am going to be religious after a while. There is not a lost spirit in hell that has not said the same thing. You are going to be religious to-morrow. All that is within you, between you and eternal despair, is your heart that beats, and if that heart stops beating you are gone forever. "No," you say, "it is not because I am leading a compromise life."

Is it because a spiritual apathy has taken possession of you? O, how men sleep over their eternal interests! A man sleeping on the edge of a precipice, and he may go over forever! The wife of Mr. Rogers, of Marietta, Ga., was indisposed one morning. He sent a servant down street for quinine, and when he returned with it, his wife took the prescription, mixed it and swallowed it. She then went to the door and said, "Husband, that was not quinine I took just now." He ran hurriedly to the drug store. "What is that you sent my wife?" And the doctor answered, "I have sent enough morphine to your house to kill a dozen persons. I did it by mistake." He ran back and got another physician and they went to his house and commenced to administer emetics. A death-like stupor came over her, and she turned to her husband and said: "Please, sir, let me go to sleep." "O, no, if you go to sleep you will not awaken this side of eternity." They walked her up and down the floor, threw cold water on her face and continued to administer emetics. Again the death-like stupor seized her and she said: "Please, sir, let me go to sleep five minutes." "O, wife, if you sleep five minutes you will never waken up again." And they worked and wearied until four hours passed away, and then the doctor said, "Now we have saved her." I have seen thousands with that death-like stupor upon them, and they say, Just let me sleep these last precious verses through, and as the last note dies away they are asleep, and when they awake they will open their eyes in hell. God pity a man that will sleep his eternal interests away.

You say it is not ignorance as to the nature of sin; it is not the consequences of sin; it is not because you are leading a compromise life; nor because of inconsiderateness; nor because you are sleeping through your interests. Is it because you have a conquered peace that defies all the batteries of Heaven? Bishop Pierce was preaching at a camp-meeting in Georgia, and among those attending there was a man not a Christian. He was an old man, and sat out in the straw in front of the bishop. The bishop said, when he sat down, "Something said to me, 'You are preaching the last awakening sermon that man will ever hear,' and the good power came to me, and I turned it upon the head of that old sinner." He sat and turned and twisted in his chair, and bit his lips, and when the bishop quit preaching he got up, went to his cottage and barred the door, fastened the window, and prostrated himself on his face. By and by his wife came and knocked for admission, and the only answer she received was the groans of her husband. She looked through the cracks of the door and saw him prostrated on his face. She went back at 3 o'clock and he was in the same position. At sundown the battle was going on; at 12 o'clock that night the contest was still going on, waxing hotter and thicker, but grander in its results than the battles of Waterloo, or Gettysburg, or any battle that earth ever saw. At sunrise the next morning it continued, and at 9 o'clock it yet went on. At 1 o'clock the wife was standing opposite the cottage, and she saw the door fly open and she ran up to him. She could tell by the cold marble of his countenance that he had conquered. Yet it took him twenty-five hours to do it. That old man lived and died, but he did not have to fight any other battle.

You have got to surrender to God this evening. The hell-spirit is here, and you have got to expel this spirit out of your heart. It may not take you twenty-five hours; it may not take you twenty-five seconds to fight the last battle. How long will we go on in sin? How long will God forbear? Where does hope end, and where begin the confines of despair? Will you take the step this evening from which there is no recovery?

In Ecclesiastes, chapter eight, eleventh verse, is the logic of damnation. Because sentences are not speedily executed; because justice does not crush you down immediately, are you to go on to ruin? Because there are ten years between me and eternal punishment, shall I spend these ten years in sin? Because God is good, shall I keep on in wickedness?

If that drunken man knew that in his next drunken dream God would send him to hell; if that profane swearer knew that the next oath he swore God would send him immediately to hell, they would not drink or swear any more. Do n't think because the sentence is not speedily executed you can keep going speedily on. God help every one of us this evening! I recollect that day in my experience when I could look my precious wife in the face and say, "I have drank my last drop, wife." I recollect when I could look my friends in the face and say, "I have sworn my last oath."

Do n't put it off any longer, until you are gray-headed. Choose you this day whom you will serve. If I were a young man I would want to be religious. If I were an old man I would want to be religious. If the Spirit of God in Christ had always been cruel to me, I would serve him for what he was to my mother. O, how good he was to her. How he charmed her to his loving heart, and how sweetly she died! If Christ had always been cruel to me I would love him for what he was to my precious father. I would love him for what he is to my precious wife and children. I will love and praise him forever for what he has done for me and mine.

SAYINGS.

THE STORY OF ZACCHEUS.—Repentance! Repentance! I think I never, in my experience as a preacher, found a soul that was willing to give up sin, give up all sin, and stay at that point with the white flag run up, that God did not go to that soul. I recollect in my own experience, I thought I had cried a heap, and I thought I had mourned a heap, and I went along mourning and crying, and I gave up such sins as I thought I could get on best without, and when I quit crying and mourning and threw my sins down, I was at once conscious that God was my friend and that Christ was my Savior. How did they get religion when Christ was on earth? He saw Zaccheus up a sycamore tree. I don't know what he was doing there. But Christ saw him. Zaccheus was a rich fellow, and, I suppose, had pretty high notions, and Christ said to him, "Come down, Zaccheus, this day salvation has entered your house." And Zaccheus started down that tree, and got religion somewhere between the lowest limb and the ground. At any rate he had it before he hit the ground. He said: "What I have taken wrongfully from any man I restore it to him fourfold." He had a good case of religion in him when he hit the ground, there is no doubt of that.

ETERNAL LIFE.—Blessed be God, I believe in eternal life. I can not live with any other thought. Just thirty years ago I tiptoed into my father's parlor, one morning, and they said: "Be quiet, mamma's dead!" I was not old enough to understand it. I walked up to the casket and looked down upon my mother. She looked paler and sadder than I had ever seen her, and when they removed the lid father kissed her, and elder brother kissed her, and I kissed her, and I said: "Precious mamma's lips are so cold." She has been buried in the State of Alabama thirty years, and if I were to go down there to-morrow and dig the earth off of my mother's body and disinter her bones, I suppose I could gather them all up in my hands, and as I stand there looking at my mother's bones, I would say: "Great God, is this all that is left of my precious mother?" And as I stand looking at those bones my knees smite together, and I am in despair, and all at once a voice speaks audibly in my ear, and says: "This corruption shall put on incorruption. This mortality shall be swallowed up of immortality." And I look up, and say, "Thanks be unto God that giveth us the victory through our Lord Jesus Christ."

Sermon IX.

"For the grace of God that bringeth salvation hath appeared to all men, teaching us that denying ungodliness and worldly lusts, we should live soberly, righteously, and godly, in this present world."—Titus ii, 11, 12.

THE honor of Christ and the salvation of our own souls depend largely upon our holding proper views of the Scripture and practicing its precepts. Ignorance is a sort of heterogeneous compound that neither God nor man can do much with. The fact is, we must know something before we are capacitated to do something, and all intelligent action is based on intelligent thought; and there can be no intelligent thought unless we first know some things. The man who really knows one thing well is on the road to know a great many things, and the trouble, perhaps, with a large mass of humanity is, they have never known one thing well.

"For the grace of God that bringeth salvation hath appeared to all men, teaching us," instructing us, qualifying us. Teaching us what? "That denying ungodliness and worldly lusts we should live soberly, righteously, and godly in this present world." That is, in plain English, teaching us that we must cease to do evil, and learn to do well.

Conversion is a very common term in the Church and in the pulpit. Sometimes we use it in

a very vague sense. Conversion, Scripturally, means
simply two things: first, I have quit the wrong;
and second, I have taken hold of the right. No
man is Scripturally converted until he throws down
the wrong and walks off from the wrong and walks
up to the right and espouses the cause of the right.
Religion is a two-fold principle, or rather it is a
principle that enables man to discern the right and
to do the right, to discern the wrong and to make
him hate the wrong. There are two elements in
every pious life: 1. Negative goodness; 2. Positive
righteousness. Negative goodness is not religion.
If negative goodness were religion, then one of
these lamp-posts out here would be the best Christian in town; it never cursed, nor swore, nor drank
a drop since it was made; it never did any thing
wrong. If negative goodness were religion, then a
stock, or stone, or mountain, would be the best
specimen of Christian this world has. Negative
goodness is, perhaps, one of the halves of religion;
but genuine religion, Christly religion, means not
only that a man is negatively good, but that he is
positively righteous. There is no power in a negative position or in being negative. Christ Jesus
saw this, when he told his preachers to go forth
affirming and preaching the Gospel, not to go con-
futing the denials of infidelity. I never uttered a
sentence in my life to prove that the Bible is true.
I never spent five minutes in my life trying to
prove there is a hell. I never spent fifteen seconds
in the pulpit in my life trying to prove there is a
God. Nobody but a fool needs such argument. A

man told me once: "I don't believe there is a God. I don't believe I am any thing but mortal." Said I: "If I were you I would get me a little more hair and a tail and be a sure-enough dog—I believe I would."

There is, as I said, no power in a negative force, and none in a negative position of any sort. We are not sent forth to deny any thing that any body says, but we are sent forth to affirm something. An aggressive Christianity is always affirmative. I am sorry for the preacher that has backsliden far enough to try to prove in his sermon that there is a God. I am sorry for the preacher that has got so low down in his theology that he is trying to establish the fact that there is a hell. I know of men trying to establish the fact that there is no hell. A gentleman said to me the other day that the fact was nearly established. I said to him. "When did you start your exploring party down there, and when will they return to report?" He said he had n't started any body and he was n't looking for them to return. Said I, "How are you going to prove any thing about it then?" And I want to tell you this much: The assertions of the word of God on all these questions stand unshaken to-day, and a little colored child of three years old in this city knows just as much about hell as any living scientist. I suppose some of the dead ones know more about it. There's many a fellow that has written hell out of his theology here, but he won't be in hell fifteen seconds till he will jump and say, "My Lord! What a mistake I have made in my theology."

Bob Ingersoll was speaking on one occasion—I have a good deal of respect for Bob Ingersoll, a great deal more respect than I have for some members of the Church. When Bob says he does n't believe the Bible and does n't pay any attention to its precepts, they say they believe it, but do just as Bob does, you see. I can't stand that. And it is n't theoretical infidelity that is cursing this country; it is practical infidelity. Well, Ingersoll was lecturing—I believe it was in Milwaukee—and there were standing up in the corner of the platform where he was speaking three or four drunken men, talking in an undertone. That crowd felt they ought to take the amen corners on Bob; and all I want to know about any fellow is who takes the amen corners on him; and when you find Bob preaching you will find the amen corners filled with old red-nosed drunkards and other vagabonds of the town; they have rushed up and taken the amen corners. When Bob made the assertion, " There is no hell, and I can prove it to any reasonable man," he got the attention of that crowd, of course. They were interested at this point, and one of them straightened himself up, and staggered up to Bob and put his hand on his shoulder, and said, " Can you, Bob?" He said, " Yes, I can." " Well," said the fellow, " do it, Bob; and make it mighty strong, for I tell you that nine-tenths of us poor fellows in Milwaukee are depending on how you make that thing."

So we say we never need to try to prove any thing that the Bible asserts. We are to preach the word to the people and the Bible will take care of itself. The Bible was the guide of my mother. It was the stay of my father's life; it was a lamp unto his feet and a light unto his path, and he bequeathed it to me as his richest gift to his wayward boy. And I say to you to-night, take all other things from me and my home, but leave me my Bible.

> This precious book I'd rather own.
>   Than all the golden gems
> That e'er in monarchs' coffers shone,
>   Or on their diadems.
> And were the seas one chrysolite,
>   This earth a golden ball,
> And gems were all the stars of night,
>   This book were worth them all.
>
> Ah, no, the soul ne'er found relief
>   In glittering hoards of wealth;
> Gems dazzle not the eye of grief;
>   Gold can not purchase health.
> But here a blessed balm appears
>   For every human woe,
> And they that seek that book in tears,
>   Their tears shall cease to flow.

Bless God for the Bible, which is the guide of my life and the inspiration of my soul.

We said a moment ago that its positive and negative features—these two combined—give the Christian life force and power. There is no power in electricity until you bring the two forces, positive and negative, together. You see that negative electricity gathering about the trunk of this old oak tree? That tree has withstood a thousand storms, and now we see this negative electricity climbing up its body and settling in its foliage, and now the positive electricity passes over it in the cloud, and negative strikes positive, and the two forces come together in the top of this old oak tree, and it comes with a crash and splits that oak tree from its topmost twig to its lowest roots. There's power. There's omnipotence. And so in the life of every good man who is negatively good and positively righteous. Look at George Whitefield with his whole nature surcharged with negative goodness and his life full of positive righteousness. We see him going out to Moorfields near London at three and four o'clock in the morning; and with 10,000 lanterns blazing all around him, he preaches the Gospel. Before daylight and sun-up he has a thousand penitents and a thousand converts, and does more before breakfast than all the pulpits in London could do the year round. That looks like business.

Negative goodness! The Lord knows I have a contempt for the goody-goody members of the Church. Old Brother Goody-Goody and old Sister Goody-Goody are just goody-goody, and so good they are good for nothing! Have n't you seen 'em? I believe in doing good. I like goodness. I despise every wicked act that a man can do. But I tell you this, I have had members, as a pastor, who would work and do their level best, but every three or four months they would get drunk in spite of every thing I could do. When they were sober they went up to their eyes in religion and in work and in righteousness. I hate this thing you call drunkenness, and no man hates it more than I do; but I would rather have a member of the Church who gets drunk every three or four months, but works when he is sober, and does his level best, than one of these sober fellows that ain't of any account anyhow, and that might just as well be drunk or just as well be dead. God pity these lazy, shiftless fellows. All they want in God's world is somewhere to sit down and somewhere to spit. Spitting room is a big thing with lazy men.

Teaching us that we must quit the wrong; "that denying ungodliness and worldly lusts. we should live soberly, righteously, and godly in this present world." Teaching us this fact, and the first lesson Christ ever taught man here was this: "You are a sinner; you are a wrong doer; you ought to cease to do evil; you ought to forsake your sins." And I will say right at this point, I could never lay any claim to the salvation of Jesus Christ until I bound all my sins up in one common bundle and threw them all down, and walked over the river of resolution, and set fire to the bridge behind me, and stood and watched till the last expiring spark dropped into the water. Then I turned my back on sin and said, "I am in now for salvation or nothing;" and I hadn't got fifteen steps from the bank of that river till I was in the arms of God, a saved man. And I declare to you to-night, you men of the Church who say, "I can't live without sin," that no man ever found God, and no man was ever converted, until he quit his sins. That's all there is about it. When I stand up and preach against sin and sinners, the Church cries, like Macbeth in the tragedy, "'Lay on, Macduff.' Give it to him. He

ought to have it." But when I preach at the
Church and say, " You men who profess to be Christians, you are living in sin," they say, " O, he's one
of these sanctificationists, and he's putting on airs."
You want me to give it to these old sinners, but let
you alone.

Ah, me! brother! If God Almighty expects
these sinners to quit sin, what does he expect of
you who profess to love him, who profess to be
Christians? That's the way to talk it. Cease to
do evil and learn to do well. I want to say here
in my place to-night, that I profess to know a few
things along this line, and propose to say them to
that member of the Church that dances and attends
theaters and plays progressive euchre—and that's
the best named game I ever heard. Progressive
euchre! Progressive euchre!—double-quick to hell,
right along. And I say another thing. There is
no progressive euchre player in this house that
ought not to be indicted for violating the laws of
the State and be put in one of the jails of this
county. How do you like that? It is just gambling scientifically, magnificently, gloriously, socially,
and so forth. That's what it is. And I'll tell you,
in our State we can indict a man and put him in
the penitentiary for playing progressive euchre with
his neighbors any time, and I want to see the day
come when, if Christians haven't got faith enough
in the Lord Jesus Christ and their profession to
bind them to decency and right, the law will help
us to make our members decent. I do, I do, sure.

And the man who is running these things—I

tell you the truth, brethren—that man never was converted, that man never has repented, that man is still in the bonds of iniquity and the gall of bitterness. You ask me why? Well, I got religion fourteen years ago last August—I was right sure there—and it knocked that card-playing, theater-going system out of me right there! And I have never had a symptom of it since; and whenever the day comes in my religious experience that I want to play cards, and want to drink whisky, and want to attend theaters, I want to drop down on my knees and tell the Lord: "My religion is played out, sure. I never felt this symptom since I was converted, and now, Lord, as with most Methodists, my religion has left me. Give it back to me again." That's the way I talk; and all I can say of you Presbyterians and Christians and Baptists that are not on that line is, you never had any, because you can't lose yours, you know! When our members go to the devil, we say, "They have lost their religion," and when your members go to the devil, you say, "they never had any." Well, it doesn't make any difference which way it is, the devil has got them, sure.

"Teaching us that we must cease to do evil and learn to do well." This is the Christian truth that teaches me to deny ungodliness and worldly lust, and to live soberly as to myself, righteously toward my neighbor, godly toward Him unto whom I owe so much. Now, here are the three positive attitudes of the Christian: 1. He is a sober-minded man in his relations toward all the world around him. 2.

He is honest in his dealings with his fellow man,
and 3. He is godly in his conduct toward his Maker.

I like one of these sober-minded men that takes
a particular view of every thing and goes for the
long run all the time, and cares nothing for counting the present results, but is looking to the great
long run. He is the same every day, and the same
under all circumstances, and the same everywhere;
he is just as good in New York as he is in Cincinnati.

There is many a fellow that is a good Christian
in this city, but if he were to wear an indicator
when he went to New York, when he got back his
wife would quit him, in my candid judgment. I like
a religion that keeps me as good off of my knees as I
am on my knees; just as good on the outside as I
am on the inside; just as good in New York as I
am at home; just as good anywhere and everywhere
and forever, as my promises and my vows demand
I should be. I like that sort of Christianity—a
sober-minded sort, that regulates all my life. I like
that.

Sober-mindedness—that's the regulating force
of every good man's life; that makes him step along
in an even, smooth way toward the good world.
Some people think heaven is away off yonder, and
some think hell is away down yonder, but I want
to tell you that heaven is on a dead-level with every
good man's heart, and I want to tell you the way
to heaven is a dead-level. Christ dug down the
mountains and filled up the valleys, and the way to
heaven is a dead-level, and the way to hell is a
dead-level, and there is only one road in the moral

universe, and one end of that road is hell and the other end of the road is heaven, and it does n't matter so much who you are, as which way you are going. Do n't you see? Soberly, righteously, a sober-minded man.

You look at that stationary engine out yonder at the saw-mill. You see little governors playing around over the steam chest, and you see there that saw as it runs into that large log. That 62 inch circular saw runs right into the log, and the little governors let down, and additional steam is thrown against the piston head, and you see that saw wade right along through the log and run out at the other end, and the little governors lift up and let off the steam, and the saw runs at the same revolution to the minute, whether it is in or out.

There is the Christian man, like Job. O, my, he was a sober-minded man. In prosperity, and when adversity came, and the last dollar was swept away from him, Job run in and out of the log; and he was running the same revolutions to the minute when he ran into infirmity and disease and pain, and as he ran right through and came out, running the same revolution to the minute, he said: "Though he slay me, yet will I trust in him." And when they placed the charge against his character that he had sinned and done wrong, he went right along through that and came out on the other side, and the Lord God said to him, "Job, take my arm and walk with me, and I will make your latter days more prosperous than your former days."

I like a sober-minded man—a man who will do

the same thing all the time; not one of those men who will do something during the revival meeting, and who does n't recollect that he did any thing out of the revival, and one day he will shake your hands, and another day he will hardly know you when he meets you on the street. I do n't like one of this persimmon-headed sort of fellows; I want a fellow who knows you when he meets you, everywhere, and will do the same thing everywhere and under all circumstances. Sober-minded! A Christian man ought to be sober-minded, and rest on this one promised—" all things work together for good to them that love God "—sober-minded as to ourselves and righteous towards our neighbors.

I will tell you if there is any thing that religion demands of a man, it is that he be downright honest. Honesty! As somebody said: "An honest man is the noblest work of God,"· and that is the grandest utterance outside of the lids of the Bible. "An honest man is the noblest work of God!" And when I say an honest man,- I do n't mean a man simply that pays his debts—some of us ain't honest enough to do that. What this world needs right now is a larger course of downright honesty; that 's it. I will tell you, the Church of God will never take this world until we get honest. There are too many men in the Church boarding with their wives— agents for their wives. I want to die the day before my wife appoints me her agent. Do you hear that? What!—a man in the Church of God and a prominent character, and that man living in a $30,000 house, and riding around in a $1,200 turnout, while the poor widow woman whose money he has is walking these streets with scarcely bread to eat! If there is a hell at all that man will go there as certain as God is just.

Honesty! We want in this country men in the Church of God who will do what they say they will do. That's it. Why, sir, a man's Methodism isn't worth any thing to him in this country, and a man's Baptism or his Presbyterianism isn't worth any thing to him. You go down to a store to-morrow and want a thousand dollars worth of goods on credit, and the fellow says: "Can you give me any security?" "No; I am a Methodist." "O, Lord! You can't run that thing on me here." And let a Baptist go down there and say: "I'm a Baptist and I want credit." "Law, me! If you will come in here and let me show you how these Baptists have gouged me, you would not play yourself off as a Baptist." And so with every denomination. I tell you to-night, the Church will never do the work God wants her to do until she is honest— honest towards God and honest towards man. I want to see the day come when all the Churches in the world will have the character in commercial life that the old Hardshell Church has in Georgia. Down at Athens, in that State, an old Hardshell walked in one day to a store and said to the merchant: "I want a couple of hundred dollars' worth of goods this year on credit." The merchant looked at his old hat and jeans pants, and concluded that was not the sort of a man to trust, and told him he would not give him the goods. The fellow turned and walked out, and the merchant asked a clerk in the store : " Who is that man ?" " That's Mr. So-and-so; he belongs to the Hardshell Church up here." The merchant went out after him and said : " Friend, come back here. Are you a Hardshell?" He said, " Yes." " Well," said the merchant, " you can have all you want ; you can have all I have here in this store on credit for as long time as you need." And down in Georgia the Hardshells will turn a member out of Church for taking advantage of the homestead exemption act, or going into bankruptcy, just as quick as they would for stealing; they will that.

Honesty ! I like that. We have collection laws all over this country, and we have ruined our people; we have made our people dishonest by our laws—that is the truth about it. They are so constructed that a man can, by a mere technicality, wipe out all his debts, and compromise with his creditors.

Out in Waco, Texas, last year, there was a merchant thrown into bankruptcy, and he compromised his debts at a hundred cents on the dollar— just think of that—and paid it, every cent. He compromised his debts at a hundred cents on the dollar! He was a fool, wasn't he? He was a fool! They say in one heathen country they make every holiday a day for general handshaking among all enemies, and every fellow pays every dollar he owes in the world. That's a grand holiday, isn't it? They are heathens, though, ain't they? They must be heathens if they do that way. Make friends with all my enemies and pay every dollar I owe every holiday! Nobody but a heathen would do that, would he? Righteously do the right thing; do the right thing.

And I want to say that those bankruptcy and homestead laws have been the curse of this country in all ages of it. I want to see the day come—and I beg your pardon for the expression—I want to see the day come when you can sell a man's shirt off his back to pay his debts. I'd rather die than to be in debt, and have things that other people ought to have. That's the way I look at it.

You say, "Yes, you are talking mighty big." Yes, and I've talked little, too; I want you to understand that. The devil bankrupted me for both worlds, and when God converted my soul and I was called into the ministry, I was hundreds of dollars in debt, and I know how a man feels. I know how it cows a man, and I know how I have gone up with $2.50 at a time to pay a debt, while my wife had but one dress and I had one suit, and we were living at starvation rates, my wife doing her own ironing and her own nursing, and I splitting the wood and working and saving every nickel I could to pay my debts; and in spite of that I have heard of men saying: "If that fellow, Jones, would pay his debts I could have more confidence in him." I paid every cent, thank God! a hundred cents on the dollar, and I was just as good a man after I paid as I was before. And, thank God, that a poor man can be an honest man! Thank God, that is true.

I'll tell you the sort I find in my Bible. It is
related that Obadiah borrowed $500 from Ahab
and died before the money was due. After his
death Ahab sued the widow for the debt, and levied on her and her two children for the money.
They could levy on children in those days, and
they were to be sold in this case to pay the debt.
The mother was in distress, and she hunted up—I
had almost said a lawyer, but she never went within
a mile of one, God bless you. She hunted up
the best old prophet of God on the face of the earth.
She stated her case to him and said: "My husband
died owing this money and they have levied on my
two children to pay this debt. What must I do?"
The old prophet looked at her and said: "What
have you in your house?" The poor woman replied, trembling: "Nothing but a pot of oil, and
that is to embalm our bodies with." The prophet
never said a word about the homestead, but he said:
"You go and pour out that oil and sell it, and pay
that debt." She went home and borrowed vessels
and drew enough oil out of the pot to pay the old
debt, and she had more oil left afterwards than
when she commenced to draw it. That was God
Almighty standing by an honest woman, do n't you
see? I have seen it repeated again and again, and
I tell you that God Almighty will take care of honest men, if he has to put the angels on half rations
for twelve months.

I was once appointed to a certain work in a certain county on a Georgia circuit. The year before
the whole country was blighted with drouth. The

people had not made a bale of cotton to twenty acres, when they ought to have made a bale to every two acres.   Corn was not a paying crop, and merchants were pressing their claims.   I commenced preaching righteousness.   I said: "I know your soil has been parched by the drouth, I know your crops are failures, I know you are poor, but" I continued, "listen to me.   If the sheriff comes on you and takes your house and your stock, and your all, let him take them, and then walk out with your wife and children, bareheaded and barefooted, so that you can say, 'We are homeless and breadless, but my integrity is as unstained as the character of God.'"

O, for an unstained character!   That is what we want in this country.   O, for an honest man!   I tell you there are too many men in this country who have widows' and orphans' legacies in their pockets, and, I am sorry to say, too many of that sort have broken into the Churches of this country, and every dollar of that money that you keep in your pocket as a preacher, and in your treasury as a Church, the devil will make you pay back with compound interest.   He well knows that that is his money, and he does not loan his money without interest, and big interest at that.

"Teaching us that we should live righteously." Righteous men—I like righteous men.   James Thomson, the poet, was righteous in this sense. Lord Lyttleton says of him, that he wrote "no line which dying he could wish to blot."   You are a merchant.   Can you say on your dying pillow, "I

16

never performed a deed which I would now undo?
Samuel, the prophet, was a righteous man, and when
he walked out to his burial place, all Israel gathered
around him, and the clear voice of the old prophet
rang out as he asked these questions: "Whom have
I cheated?" "Whom have I defrauded?" "Of
whom have I received a bribe of money to blind
my eyes?" And all Israel answered back, "No
one." O, that was a grand victory.

But, brethren, the man who does not recognize
his obligations to God is but half a man at best.
I have my relations toward my family, and my relations toward my country, and my relations toward
my God. I will meet the demands of my children
and my home. I will meet the demands of my
country. I will meet the demands of the God that
made me and them. I am good for all worlds. A
godly man is one that does every thing with reference to the great eye of God that is looking down
upon him, a man that is godly in his life and character, and that does right toward the God that made
him. Where do we find examples of godly men?
St. Paul, the author of this text, was a godly man.
He lived for God, and counted all things as lost
that he might please God. In his dying moments
he sat in his dark dungeon and wrote in his last
letter to Timothy: "The time of my departure is at
hand."

O, what a thought! St. Paul meant to say to
him: "I shall have a cold supper to-night and a
cold breakfast in the morning; I shall sleep on a
hard bed to-night, but I shall take dinner in heaven

to-morrow with God and the angels." He talked about his departure as a school boy talks of leaving school for home, and when his head was severed from his body God stooped down, picked up that bloody head, and placed a crown of everlasting life upon it. He was a godly man, and God will take care of that sort of man, living or dying.

Just such a man as this died some months ago, and when his large family of Christian boys and girls stood around him, he struggled for breath in the last extremities of life. Just as his moments were drawing to a close he seemed restless and wanted to speak. His children's attention was attracted by his looks, and they said: "Father, is there any request you wish to make? If so, tell us what it is." He caught his breath and said, "Bring—" but, breaking down, he could not utter another word. His children gathered close around him and said, "Father, tell us what you want." Again he said, "Bring—" and could not utter another word. The children bent over him, and said, "Father, what do you want brought?" Presently his system relaxed in death, and with all his remaining energy his lips uttered the words:

> "Bring forth the royal diadem,
> And crown him Lord of all."

Then the soul swept out of his body and he never breathed another breath. God help us to live righteously, soberly, and godly in this world, and to look forward with blessed hope to the glorious appearing of the great God and our Savior, Jesus Christ.

At times within the past ten years I have thought of going back to the practice of law, and of accumulating a fortune that my family might be provided for, and of preaching the Gospel in after life; but with the blessed hope of God before me I have continued right on. My eyes are on something better, grander, and nobler. When kind friends in Nashville said: "Here is a ten-thousand-dollar home, and we will give thousands in bonds if you will make your home in our, midst," I replied: "No. In our own quiet little cottage my wife and children and myself love God and are striving to get to heaven. Excuse me. I love you just as much as if I accepted it." Then my wife said to me: "Husband, I am prouder of you for that than for any other act in your history."

And I want to say to this congregation that I am getting higher and higher. I sympathize a good deal with the eaglet caged up yonder. Now a kind friend, pitying its drooping condition, opens the cage door and lets it out. I see it leave its cage and turn its eye to the sun and to the mountain-tops. Its ruffled feathers begin to smooth down, and it raises its wings and shakes them for a moment. I see it fly up into the air and poise itself on its wings. It looks back toward the cage and utters a scream, as much as to say, "Farewell, cage; farewell, imprisonment and weary hours!" I see it fly higher and higher, until at last it steadies its wings just in sight, and I hear it scream again. It seem to say, "Farewell, earth and imprisonment and cage and dreary days." Higher and higher it ascends and sails aloft to light on the mountain top, free as air. Brethren, the soul of man, that has been ruffled by ten thousand cares, some of these days will look toward that blessed hope of God, plume its wings, and fly upward. And the higher we go earth shall hear our voices, growing the fainter, saying, "Farewell, cares, imprisonment, and earth!" Higher and higher we shall go, until at last we fly off in a bee-line for the other world. Brethren, let us get above worldly care and sin and temptation, and let us strike a bee-line for that home beyond, where sin and suffering are felt no more. May God bless you all, and may you ponder over these words in the spirit in which they have been uttered. If you do not like any thing that has been said, and if you come and apologize, I will forgive you, for I never bear malice to any body in this world.

SERMON X.

" And let us not be weary in well doing, for in due season
we shall reap if we faint not.—GAL. vi, 9.

BRETHREN, I want to preach from two sides of
this text to-night, one-half to you as Christians
and the other half to you *brethren*—I mean what I
say—who are not Christians. You are my brother,
but I shall preach the first few minutes from this
text to Christian people.

" And let us not be weary in well doing, for in
due season we shall reap, if we faint not." God
says if we do n't weary in well doing, we shall reap.
I trust that in thirty days from this good hour
every Christian here can write " T. P." opposite
this verse in the margin of his or her Bible —" tried
and proven " to be true. God says if we would
not grow weary in well doing we should reap—
reap a harvest of husbands and wives and sons and
daughters for garners in the sky. Now, brother,
this is a declaration with a promise attached—if
you won't grow weary in well-doing you shall reap
a harvest.

I wonder what that " well-doing " referred to
in this verse is? I will drop back a few verses
and find out. Brethren, first, well-doing in a
Christian life is this : " Brethren, if a man be overtaken in a fault, ye which are spiritual restore such
a one in the spirit of meekness ; considering thyself,

190

lest thou also be tempted." Thus I learn from the lesson before us that the first duty of every Christian man is to ignore himself, and crucify himself, and live only for the good of others. We never have much trouble after we have gotten rid of ourselves. My biggest job is managing myself, and I'd rather undertake to control and manage Cincinnati than to manage myself.

I can get the police to help me manage Cincinnati, if I can get *them* straight to start with. I can get the Law and Order League and the Committee of One Hundred, and get help from various other directions, to help me control this city. I'll tell you another thing: I hope when God blesses Cincinnati with another election—I refer not to any previous election, or to any man who ever held the office of mayor—but I trust that the next mayor you have will enforce the laws of the city if he has to die in the ditch in his endeavor to keep it straight. I'll tell you another thing: If I were a citizen of Cincinnati I would die by the Law and Order League. I would stand up with the citizens of the Committee of One Hundred until my feet flew from under me. I would go into every thing and stay with every thing that looked towards law and order. Understand that? It is your only safety as a city; it is the safety of the commonwealth of each State, and the safety of municipal corporations—the enforcement of law. Law is made not for good citizens, but for bad citizens, and there isn't a law on the statute books of Ohio that is odious to law-abiding people. What do you say to that? I am ready now and ready forever to die by the laws of my State, good or bad. I am branching off from my text, but what I have said is Gospel just as much as any thing I could say.

God bless you people of Cincinnati, and rally you round the code of your city, and the laws of your city, and help you to stand by them and to see them enforced, and if any fellow does n't like these laws let him emigrate—you have no use for him, nohow! This is a free country. If he does n't want to stay in a law-abiding city, why, let him emigrate, and if you all have n't money enough to buy him a ticket, if he will write me a letter I 'll furnish him a ticket, for the sake of the love I bear to you all. Law and order, righteousness, let it reign on earth, and let all good citizens stand by it. That's it! If I were mayor of this city next Sunday and Monday, there would be a thousand fellows in your lock-ups, and station-houses, and jails, on Monday night sure. Put that down!

Every man in this town that opened his bar-room on Sunday I would put in jail, if I had to call out the militia of the city to help put him there. Every bar-room door that is flung open in Cincinnati on Sunday is against the law, and in direct opposition to the law of your city and of your State; and, brethren, in the name of God, let 's enforce the law, or let 's call our Legislature home, and quit paying them to go up there to Columbus and enact a set of rules and laws that they do n't intend to carry out. Abolish the Legislature, burn the code, or make up your mind to stand up for law and order. God bless

the Law and Order League and the Committee of
One Hundred!

If there's a saloon-keeper in Cincinnati that
does n't like the way things are run, tell him to
emigrate, demijohn and all—you would n't miss
him! You can well spare twenty-nine hundred
saloon-keepers and beer-gardens, and then have one
hundred of them left, and the Lord knows that's
enough. A hundred saloons ought to do you, if
you ain't the greediest crowd I ever struck. If we
can't do any thing with law and order on these
saloons, let's starve them out. I understand that a
good many of them have got to that point now that
they can't settle their bills. They say they never
saw business so dull in their line in their life.
Thank God for dull business along on that line!

Brethren, stand by your Law and Order League,
by your Committee of One Hundred, and by your
mayor in the enforcement of the law, and not only
stand by your mayor, but tell him if he does n't pitch
in and enforce the law he can never be elected dog-
pelter in this town, much less mayor again. The
mayor is n't the boss of the town. He's the servant
of every body and any body, and, brethren, let's
make our servants do what we want them to do.
That's the way.

Law and order! Why, see what this little movement here has already done. You've shut up the
theaters here on Sunday, and I'll tell you, if you'll
push the battle on you will do like the citizens of
St. Joseph, Mo. When I went there, an honest
preacher, the pastor of a Church in that city, came

to me and said: " "Brother Jones, do n't open your mouth about the liquor traffic here or they 'll put dynamite under the house you sleep in and blow you up." "What?" said I. "They 'll kill you before twenty-four hours if you ever denounce the liquor traffic, and they 'll do it with dynamite," said the preacher, earnestly. " If they blow me up with dynamite," said I, "I 'll get a fine momentum, and I 'll keep on all the harder. The tendency of the flash of this thing is upward, and it 'll give a fellow a good start. I like that."

Well, out there in St. Joseph I turned my guns loose on that traffic, and in less than thirty days from the time I left there they had overhauled the 180 bar-keepers, found 180 true bills against them, indicted them, brought them up before the court, and they walked up to the judge and took solemn oath that they 'd never sell another drop of liquor on Sunday if the judge would only be light on them that time and let them off. They knew they were doing wrong, and they persisted in it until they were brought up sharply. Law and order has got to prevail in this city, and if it does, you 're going to see another state of things in Cincinnati. You good people are in the majority.

It is all a great big lie about the hoodlums running this town. I know some of the best citizens of this city are Germans, and I have received letters while I have been here from German citizens that have brought joy to my heart. Thank God for every German in this city that is for law and order! Thank God for every American here that is in favor of law and order! In this democratic country, I mean republican country, the majority rules. In a republican form of government the majority always rules, and the good citizens of this town are in that majority; and, now, let's come forward and dare to assert ourselves in favor of law and order and righteousness.

Well, I must come to my text. What I have been saying is good gospel, and it will do your children good after you are dead and gone if you will follow that kind of gospel; and the Lord knows I did n't come to this city to get up a shout-and-go-round corn-stalk meeting, where they all shout and afterward go on with their devilment, but I came here to get up a Ten-Commandments revival, a Sermon-on-the-Mount revival, and to preach righteousness among the people.

I will tell you another thing; the responsive hearts and the responsive presence of the people here in this hall to the Gospel as it has been preached have convinced me that Ohio and Cincinnati are overwhelmingly in favor of law and order, and may God bless you for showing it.

But, brethren, I must return to my text: "And let us not be weary in well-doing, for in due season we shall reap if we faint not." The first duty of every man is to ignore himself and his own purposes and desires and intentions, crucify himself and live only for the good of others. That's it. O, how I love to see a self-sacrificing man—a man that loves humanity better than he loves himself. I like that sort of a man. He is an honor to his race and a blessing to the world.

We have a man down our way in Georgia; he's a little Methodist preacher on a circuit now. Whenever I walk into the presence of that man I think he's the largest man I ever looked at, and he just expands in my presence when I look in his face, and I get whittled down until I feel I'm no bigger than a mole-hill beside a majestic mountain. Why does he look so large? Because, when I look into that face, I'm looking into the face of the most unselfish man I ever saw. He doesn't care one cent for himself. He doesn't live or do for himself, but every thought of his life, every act of his life is, "How can I help some one else?" He's the happiest man, and the most glorious being I ever looked at, and I trace it all to the one source, that he's so supremely unselfish. He just lives for other people. Brother, you'll never be worth any thing until you can get yourself down and get your foot squarely planted on yourself, and say, "Now, you lie there. If you get up I'll mash your mouth for you." When you do that you get in a position where you can help some one else. Blessed be God, I have got myself out of the way, and have nothing to look after now but other people. There's nothing in the way now, and, with my whole self in the background, I have nothing to do but to live and act for others all the day long.

This text says: "If a man be overtaken in a fault, ye which are spiritual restore such a one in the spirit of meekness, considering thyself, lest thou also be tempted." Your first duty is to live for

your brother. I 've often heard people say, " I have
no time to look after other people. I 'm doing first-
rate if I can get into heaven myself. I 'm in big
luck if I can get there myself without looking after
other people." Brother, you 've made a mistake
here as long as eternity. Listen to me, if I just.
wanted to make sure of damnation I would just
settle it, " I 'll never try to help any body else in
this country. I will spend all my days helping
myself." What is hell at last? It 's the very
quintessence of selfishness, and selfishness is hell,
and there is not an element in hell that does not
enter into selfishness; and the supremely selfish man
has already lighted the fires of hell in his soul that
shall burn forever and forever. A selfish man! Just
as I am unselfish I am lovable, and just as I am unselfish I am a blessing to the world. Just as I am
selfish I am unlovable and a curse to the world.

" Live for myself!" Why, what is it that makes
a man sell whisky? Selfishness! What is it that
makes a man gamble? Selfishness! What is it
that makes a man steal? Selfishness! Do you
catch the idea? In all the devilment that people
have ever done in this world there is a seed at the
bottom of the tap root of the whole thing, and that
seed is selfishness. All that is good on earth to-
day grows in this soil we call unselfishness. Divest
yourself, brother, of all selfishness, and strike out
to do good for the world.

I will tell you another thing. As Christian
people we ought to join hands here now as a great
army of Christians, and march to the front hand in

hand, heart to heart, faith to faith, love to love; march straight along as Baptists, Methodists, Presbyterians, Lutherans, and Christians of all denominations. We must join hands and march to the front, and let us say to this grand army, "We will hang together, and stick together, and fight together, and die together, and we will all go to heaven together, or we will all go to hell together. We will stick to one another world without end!"

There's many a preacher that has been unable to get up a successful meeting in his own Church, and if some other preacher gets up a big meeting in his Church, and four or five hundred souls are converted and brought to God, this poor preacher looks as if he'd been sick for six months; he just goes drooping about. I don't mean any Cincinnati preacher—I mean a Georgia preacher. I have seen them. They were so glad their brother preacher was having such a successful revival that it was like to have killed them, they just fell off pounds and pounds. I mean these Georgia preachers—I haven't any reference to any Cincinnati preachers. I have seen that the case with a preacher; he couldn't be happy over another preacher's revival to save his life.

It takes a good deal of religion for some pastors to stand by and see the pastor of another Church having such a big time with a revival. It takes more religion there than anywhere else in the world. It does that! I have been along there. I am a human being, and all of us preachers are human beings. Brethren, I want to see the day come when you will rejoice in every good act, for there never was a revival in this town that didn't help every Church in the town, if they put themselves in a right attitude towards it. Every revival in any Church in this city, no matter if not more than five hundred are out, will do good to every other Church, if they put themselves in a right attitude to the work of Christ.

If I never had saved a soul in the world, and the Lord allows me in heaven with the workers that did save the souls, I'd stand and shout hosannas over the work of the others. It takes a good deal of religion to do that. We want religion enough to stand by and enjoy another fellow's doing what we tried, but were unable to do ourselves. It takes one hundred and eighty pounds of grace to the square inch right there to let me crow over and enjoy another man doing a thing that I couldn't do myself.

I have known preachers—Georgia preachers, you know—to try for two or three years to get up a big revival in their Church, and they couldn't get up any, and then they lammed in and preached hard against revivals. They tried to have them themselves and couldn't, and then they just lammed in and preached as hard against them as they could. Lord, have mercy on selfish preachers! If God will take all the selfishness out of the hearts of all the preachers, myself as well as others, we will be in a position to lead the ranks of God into the belching mouths of the cannons of the devil and run him back into his citadel and bombard it until we run him out and capture this world for Christ.

There are preachers in this town that have n't
been in this hall at all; and mark what I tell you.
The preachers of this city that have stood aloof—I
want them to hear this, I hope it will do them
good—when they saw God was with it and saving
souls, and yet kept away, will have to make out
that a clear case of insanity was upon them during
these meetings or go to hell, in my candid judgment.   I do n't care, brother, if he is your pastor
and does rack around to see you every week, and
talk with you on religion.   I tell you when
God Almighty's cannon and musketry begin to
roar, every loyal citizen will rush to the front and
help fight the battles.   If your pastor, brother, has
been hanging back, you tell him he ought to go
before a jury and be tried for insanity, and carry a
good certificate with him to the judgment, for he 'll
need it.

Selfishness !   Good Lord take the selfishness out
of our preachers and out of our Churches, and then
we 'll win this world to Christ.   We 're not running this thing for ourselves, but running it for
Christ.   .

Now, suppose an insurance company had a hundred agencies and agents in this town and they
were to pull against one another, undercut one another, as the Churches pull against and undercut
one another.   Let a disaffected member get mad at
one Church here because the preacher raked him
about progressive euchre, and leave, another Church
will say, " Come, live with us."   All the same
Church, all agents for the same house and com-

promising and cutting rates! Why, there isn't an insurance company in America that wouldn't send their inspector of agencies out here and discharge every agent in the town if they ran on that schedule.

Selfishness is the curse of the world, and unselfishness is a blessing to the world. You have as unselfish preachers in this town as walk the face of the earth. You have the others too; I never call any names, but every fellow knows his number. If this cap fits any preacher in this house let him wear it. If it doesn't fit you throw it away and get a better one. People say I arrogate a great deal to myself. But I do not intend to take any thing to myself. I don't want any praise from any body. I don't care what you think of me so long as you think well of my Savior and do what he wants you to do. There are no selfish aims or ambitions to be gained in this fight, and God has blessed me in proportion as I have been unselfish. I don't want any praise; as I said before, I'd just as soon you'd throw mud on me as praise me. Brethren, with an unselfish spirit, let's join hands and march on to glory and to God with this city.

In St. Joseph, Mo., those brothers gathered and worked and worked for weeks together, and there they are to-day with more than a thousand souls that they reaped since the union revival closed. And now, brother, here is a harvest-field of one hundred and fifty thousand souls away from Christ; and I hope every pastor will call his Church together on Sunday at 11 o'clock, and give them the plan of the battle, and tell them what he expects

them to do. And brother and sister in Christ, if
you never did a faithful month's work for God in
your life, and you never intended to do one month's
work, you tell your pastor next Sunday morning at
11 o'clock: "Brother, put me down in the list of
the soldiers that will go in to conquer or to die."
And if you will do that, in less than six weeks
from to-day I will show you fifty thousand souls
converted to God and added to the Churches. The
doors are wide open. O, let us fight this old world
and get in the rear of this old world, and drive
them into the kingdom of God, and there is nothing else here to do. And brother, let us go with
unselfishness into this fight, and all meet and pray
together, and then they will scatter out to the different Churches in the city, and save this town
from death and hell.

I will tell you another thing. Every man of
righteousness ought to join in the battle. And you
that are not members of the Church, surrender your
heart to God to-night, and Sunday morning at 11
o'clock come in and join some Christian Church,
and be one of the most valiant soldiers of the Cross
for the next five or six weeks in bringing to Christ
those around you. If a man is trying to help others
to Christ, it is the best evidence that he has got it
himself. Go to work, and go to work for Christ
now. As a good man said, "I will pay the balance
in good works as long as I live. I am going to
devote my life to God and humanity."

I will tell you another thing. You can't be too
patient toward one another. These new converts

will need your care and mercy and good will and help every day—mark that. I want to say, I frequently hear this question: Do Jones's converts stick? Now, let me tell you, I never run any insurance on them at all; no guaranty. I do n't run any guaranty on my converts. They may, every one, be in the penitentiary before this time next year. But I will tell you one thing, every convert of these meetings will average up with the Churches they join. Do you hear that? Average up with the Churches they join. A woman said to me once, "Brother Jones, we had a revival here two years ago, and seventy-five joined our Church, and now where are they, those seventy-five?" She said, "I do n't believe in revivals." I said, "Sister, ain't those seventy-five here in town?" She said, "Yes, but I never see much of them. Why," she says, "some of those converts are getting drunk." Said I, "Ain't some of your old converts getting drunk." "Well, yes," said she; "but some of the new converts do n't come to meeting." "Do n't some of your old ones stay away, too?" said I. "Well, yes," said she; "and some of the new converts play cards." Said I, "Do n't some of the old ones play cards, too?" "Well, yes." Said I, "Sister, the new converts will live right up with the old ones; some of the new ones are getting drunk, so are some of the old ones; some of the new ones play cards, so do some of the old ones; some of the new ones are staying away from meeting, so are some of the old ones."

It is not so much the weight and bigness of the

infant as it is what sort of a mother has God given
it to take care of it! There is many a Church in
this country—O, what mothers, what mothers, what
mothers they are! Ah, me, there is that mother
with her sweet, beautiful babe yonder who cares
nothing for it! She keeps it in the nursery, and the
mother does n't see it once a week or once a month.
O, such a mother is n't worthy of a child! She
is n't worthy the name of mother. The Church in
this town is a mother to its converts, and there's
many a Church in this town that cares nothing for
its converts. They hire a preacher to look after the
Church, hire him by the month, and pay him by the
month to look after the babies, and I tell you there
is a sight of them to look after. I would rather
preach three hundred and sixty-five sermons every
year for one of your Churches, than to look after the
babies for one week. It's a solid fact. It is whine
and whine, and cry and cry; and soothing syrup
and soothing syrup. How many bottles do you
reckon have been used in this Church? I suppose
you can go into the closet and find hundreds of
empty bottles of soothing syrup. And before the
pastor can get one fellow quiet, another breaks out,
and it is running with the spoon and bottle all the
time.

Obliged to do it! It is n't right the way we do
with our preachers; it is not right before God. I told
them the other day up at Trinity, that in some of
these Churches the whole Church will be in the
wagon, every single member of the Church up in the
wagon, some laughing, some cursing, some drinking,

some playing cards, some shouting, but the whole lot up in the wagon, and the poor little old preacher out in the shafts trying to pull the whole thing along. There goes the poor fellow under this big load, just tired to death, and here some fellow wipes his mouth after taking a drink, and says, "Jab him up a bit." I say, get out of that wagon and catch hold and pull or push at once. O, brethren of the ministry, God bless you, hitch up that crowd to the wagon, and get up on the spring seat and drive a while!

It is a heap easier for you all to pull the preacher, than it is for the preacher to pull you. Let us swap about with him; let us all get out of the wagon a while. And about the only time you get out at all is when you go down a steep hill, and then you get out and push. The Lord have mercy on that sort of a man. Live for others, work for others. Your preacher needs unselfish members. God needs unselfish members. The world needs you every day. The poor, weak brethren in the Church need you every day.

Now this incident. I read it a few months ago. It was related by Bishop Marvin. He said that in one of his charges once, when he was a young pastor, he commenced a meeting on his circuit at a church, and he said at that church there were from two to three hundred members. He commenced preaching, but the Church did n't get aroused. And he said when he had preached about two weeks, seventy-five had professed conversion and joined the Church, but the Church never got waked up.

And before the first day of next January—this was in July—before the first day of January seventy-two of the seventy-five had gone back to the world, just as bad or worse than they were before. He said right over there on that same circuit there was another Church, the most faithful Church he ever saw, with two of the most faithful class-leaders he ever knew. He commenced his meetings there, and the Church was on fire with love to God and man. And that is pure unselfishness, love to God and love to man. And he said while preaching at that church one night, he noticed an old blacksmith, dingy, black, and dirty, come in and take a back seat; and after the service one of the class-leaders came up and said: "Brother Marvin, did you see that old dingy, dirty blacksmith take his seat?" "Yes," he said. "Well," said the class-leader, "he is the worst old drunkard this country possesses, and I was glad to see him here." The bishop said: "You ought to invite him back again." "Well, I tried, but he was gone before I could get to him." "Well," said Marvin, "you must go to see him."

Next morning, bright and early, the class-leader rode up to the blacksmith's house and said to him: "I am mighty glad I saw you at the church last night, and I want you to come again." Said he: "I love to hear that man preach; he caught hold of my heart; but," said he, "look at these ragged clothes and this debauched body; and my poor wife in rags, and my children in their desolation; we can't go to Church; got nothing to

wear." "Ah," said the class-leader, "I know that;
but I am going to bring you a suit a-piece for the
whole family, and come with my wagon and take
you to Church." He did. On that night the
blacksmith, his wife, and two oldest children were
there, and knelt at the altar. The next thing, the
blacksmith and his wife and two oldest children were
converted and joined the Church. And when the
blacksmith walked up and joined the Church, the
sinners out in the back of the house said: "The
first time that old blacksmith goes to town and
gets drunk they'll lose him."

The meeting closed. They got him to pray in
his family; they carried him work to his shop, and
got the neighbors to patronize him, and kept him
busy at his trade; and before two years he had
bought himself a nice cottage and paid for all his
tools, and was one of the respected men of the community. About six months after these two years
were over the Western fever broke out in the settlement. People all took a notion to go West, and
the blacksmith said he thought he would go. And
the class-leaders said: "Sir, we don't want you to
live out West; the company is too bad, and we
want you to stay here with us, with your family,
and go to heaven with us." He said: "I can do
better with my children out there." They couldn't
persuade him, and in a short time a small company
started out West with about forty wagons, and the
blacksmith and his family with them. They crossed
the Mississippi River, and one of the company wrote
back, and among other things said: "We gather at

the blacksmith's wagon, and he reads his Bible and
offers family prayer with all the company every
night and morning." And when they got the next
letter they had arrived at their place of destination,
and they were almost afraid to open it, but it said:
"The blacksmith has gone right into Church with all
his family and gone right to duty." Every letter
they got said, "He is faithful to God and duty."

About six months after he went out one of the
class-leaders one morning got a letter with a black
margin all around the envelope, and he opened it,
and it was from the wife, bathed in her tears, and
it read: "My husband died shouting happy last night,
and went home to heaven, and he told me to write
back to his faithful class-leaders and tell them another one is saved by grace and gone home to God."

O, for that spirit of religion in this country!
That is what we want. O, my brethren, let us
stand by one another; let us die by one another!
There is too much doubt and hesitancy on the mind
of the people. I recollect when Sam Small was
converted. O, how dissipated that man was! He
told you all himself. I do n't go behind his back;
I have said all before his face that I say here, and
I am no prouder of my precious child, or of my
wife, than I am of Sam Small. Thank God for the
grace that brought him to me. When Sam Small
was converted to God I heard him talk once, and
my wife and friends said, "Sam Small has got
religion, just as sure as Sam Jones has got it; he
has got it, certain." He has. He has got the
right aim.

The first thing I did, I threw my arms around him and said, "Brother, come and go to work with me in the cause of God." The wise brethren walked up and said, "Brother Sam, you had better be very particular; if his foot were to happen to slip it would be death on you, and you had better be mighty particular now." "If he falls down," said I, "he shall fall on me; I will hold him up, and stand by him until I die myself." And thank God Almighty, he never fell on me. I have never held up a pound for him, but I have got so now, thank God, I can lean on him, and he is helping to hold me up. Glory be to God for the spirit that will throw his arms around a poor fellow struggling, and help him on to God!

I never see a poor drunken man but I want to throw my arms around him and keep them there. I never see a poor, weak brother come up that I don't wish I had nothing else in the world to do but to keep him out of temptations and keep him straight until he gets firmly on his feet. They need your nursing; they need your help. But O, what is the use of bringing them in and nobody taking care of them? Take hold of souls and bring them through to God. You who are spiritual go and love him, stand by him, do your best for him.

I learned how to love a man once by a game of town ball. When I was a boy we used to play town ball. But I will tell you what, if I had a dog and he were to go out and look at a game of base ball an hour, and then come back in my yard,

I would go out and kill him, I would. None of your base ball in mine. There is not a more corrupting thing this side of hell than base ball. Now, put that down. They all thought I had forgotten that. I never have had any use for it. The idea of a great big young buck twenty-five years old running all over creation for a ball. If your mother wanted you to cut a stick of wood she couldn't get you to do it to save her life, but you dress up in a fool's garb and run after a ball, the hottest day, until your tongue lolls out, you fool you. That isn't all. It is one of the finest fields for gambling in America. And that is not all. I wouldn't wipe my feet on any crowd that would go out and play base ball on the Sabbath. Those are my sentiments. I couldn't put it in any more concise way than that. I don't know whether you agree with me or not; but you understand me, I reckon, don't you? I will let my boy play ball until he is ten years old, but after he is fifteen years old I believe I will wear him out with work if I catch him at such foolishness as that.

Men, stand by one another and help one another, and when one falls down let us catch him immediately and straighten him up, and then call to other brothers, and say, "One of you get under this arm and one under the other," and let him hobble on toward glory, and when he gets into heaven his crutches will be there too, blessed be God. It is about the only way you will ever get to heaven. It is to go there as a crutch under some poor fellow's arm, and the only way he will get there is for you to play the crutch for him. O, thank God, the crutches and the lame have to go in together, and they rejoice together in the name of the good work.

Stand by one another! Help one another! Do your duty toward one another! And when a poor fellow falls down do not look at him and say: "Just look at that brother now; he joined the Church during the revival, and now is drunk; look at him!" There is the poor, fallen brother in the ditch; he is drunk, beastly drunk; and here are two brethren standing off, looking at him and saying, one to the other, " I told our pastor not to take him into the Church." Do you want to know whom God thinks more of, that one lying there, or these two? That sot lying in the gutter is better than a hundred such in the sight of God. That poor, drunken fellow is better in the sight of God than these Pharisees that will see their brother sink and then say, " Just look at him." A brother would run to him and drag him out of the ditch and stand by him and say, " You have done wrong, so have I, and we will quit now and try to live right."

There is many a poor fellow who has gone to hell from this community that Christian people never made one effort to save from death and hell. They just go to the dogs all around us.

I have talked more than an hour, and now I am going to close with just these words. I never preached on the subject that I started out on in my life, and I have gone off in this direction, and I hope God will use it to your good.

Now a word or two to you men out of the

Church. Let me say this to you: There is a great responsibility on you. You have seen rich men in the community; you have seen a rich man and you have seen all the poor people turn away; and you hear the poor people talk and say: "That rich man does n't care any thing about us poor folks." The truth of the business is, these poor people imagine that that rich man does n't care any thing about them; and when they see him they treat him coolly, and he does the same, for the poor fellows do n't know what else to do. Now you have imagined many a time the Church did n't care any thing about you and that these people did n't want to have any thing to do with you, and you have turned away yourself. Turn to the Church and say, "Give me help and assistance," and they will take you by the hand and take you to glory and to God. When you do that once, men of the world, you will be on the right direction.

SAYINGS.

THE BEST PAY.—I received this in the contribution basket last night, and when this much comes to me it seems as if there can 't be any thing better than this to follow. This little note was in an envelope in the basket last night; and it seems as if this little scrap of paper pays me for every lick I have struck: "Brother Jones, I am in your debt, sir, as follows: For quitting and swearing off drinking, $100,000; for quitting and swearing off from swearing, $100,000; for quitting all my meanness, $1,000,000; for learning to love our dear Lord better than life, $3,000,000,000. Credit, $1. I hope to be able to pay the balance by doing good the rest of my days."

Brethren, here's really the pay in this service. Thank God for the privilege of doing good. That's one reason why I never asked you, brethren, for a cent of money, and I told you I did n't want a cent, for I knew God would pay me, and here's the pay. If this man feels that way, how do you reckon his precious wife and children feel about it? Glory to God for bringing heaven to one home in Cincinnati! Thank God for every home that has been blessed!

I thought once to-day I would have all the communications I got in the basket last night compiled into a little pamphlet, for it's rich reading. One dear woman writes: "I have n't a cent in the world to give, but I want to tell you that you have brought me to the dear Savior, and he is mine, and I am happy in his love." I tell you in heaven we will be paid, when money and dollars and cents have been long ago forgotten. Thank God for pay that I can cross the river with—I do n't mean the Ohio River, but the river of death to the city of God!

Sermon XI.

"According as his divine power hath given unto us all things that pertain unto life and godliness, through the knowledge of him that hath called us to glory and virtue. Whereby are given unto us exceeding great and precious promises; that by these ye might be partakers of the divine nature, having escaped the corruption that is in the world through lust. And besides this, giving all diligence, add to your faith virtue; and to virtue knowledge; and to knowledge, temperance; and to temperance, patience; and to patience, godliness; and to godliness, brotherly kindness; and to brotherly kindness, charity. For if these things be in you, and abound, they make you that ye shall neither be barren nor unfruitful in the knowledge of our Lord Jesus Christ. But he that lacketh these things is blind, and can not see afar off, and hath forgotten that he was purged from his old sins."—2 Peter, i, 3-9.

LET us notice two or three of these verses as we go along. "According as his divine power hath given unto us all things that pertain to life and godliness." Did you ever face this fact in your religious experience that there may be a thousand reasons why some men do not succeed at law; that there may be a thousand reasons why some men fail in merchandising; that there may be a thousand reasons why some men fail in agriculture; but do you ever meet this fact, that there is no reason in heaven or earth or hell why any man should fail to be an earnest, faithful Christian? There are reasons why men fail in every other profession and every other calling, but there are no reasons why any

214

man should fail in being a successful Christian. If
I am not a successful, happy, earnest Christian, it is
not the devil's fault; it is not the fault of the grace
of God; it is not the fault of this book; it is not
the fault of any thing without; but my trouble lies
deep within.

" All things that pertain to life and godliness."
Let us face this fact a moment. If I am a good
man, I am a good man on purpose. If I am not a
good man I am purposely not a good man. Nobody ever was religious by accident. The grace of
God never made any man religious. The Bible
never made any man religious. Preaching never
made any man religious. These are all grand in-
strumentalities in the hands of God, but no man
was, and no man ever will be, religious until he
settles it once uncompromisingly and forever: " I
will be religious, whether I am any thing else or
not. If I fail in every thing else, I will succeed in
this. If I do n't do any thing else, I will do this."
With the great one who succeeded in the highest
sense—St. Paul—he says, "This one thing I do."
Suppose I succeed. I am a success for all worlds.
Suppose I fail in this and succeed in every thing
else. I am but a beggar!

The next verse reads: " Whereby are given unto
us exceeding great and precious promises, that by
these ye might be made partakers of the divine nature, having escaped the corruption that is in the
world through lust." What does that mean—
" Being made partakers of the divine nature? " This
is, perhaps, one of the plainest, clearest statements

of the beginning of a Christian life. Here is a man who has been, perhaps, intemperate at times, worldly-minded, covetous, wicked, wayward, godless, and now comes a pivotal moment in his life. Perhaps it is the death of his precious wife; perhaps it is the burial of one of his sweet children; perhaps it was an earnest sermon; but some time something somewhere touched his heart and touched his conscience, and he says to himself: " I believe I 'll decide upon a better life. I ought to be good. I 'm sorry I 'm bad. I would give the rest of my days to nobler, better things." He eschews evil and learns to do good, and on and on he walks away from evil and walks into good, and may be six months later there is a happy, joyous, Christian experience brought about. When was that man made a partaker of the divine nature? It was in that moment away back yonder when he said: " I am wrong, I ought to get right;" that moment when he said: "I 'm bad; I 'm sorry I am. I have offended God and lived in sin. I would seek the favor of God and live in righteousness." It was away back there that that man was made partaker of the divine nature, and he yielded to and responded to and fostered and nursed that divine touch, until, by and by, the divine seed implanted in his nature, budded and blossomed into a glorious religious experience.

I used to think that if God could n't get all the heart he would n't take any. I made a mistake there. Brother, if you will surrender God an inch of space in your heart to-night, God will occupy that space, and God will do for a man and do in a man just in proportion as God can get hand-room and foot-room to work. And God will work that space so well and the results will be so glorious that if we will surrender every space and every place, God will go on with the conquest until he shall possess the whole. But if you draw the line any way and say to God, "Thus far thou shalt go and no farther," then God will surrender to you the space he already occupied, and the last state of that man shall be worse than the first.

"According as his divine power hath . . . made us partakers of the divine nature." Is there a man here to-night, twenty or thirty or forty years old, that down in his conscience is saying, "I am bad ; I am sorry for it. I ought to be good. I want to be good?" The good Spirit of all grace has touched that man's heart. And now, brother, you foster and cherish and nurse and perpetuate that desire in your soul until it shall spring up and develop into a burning, hungering and thirsting after righteousness. Don't despise the day of small things. A great many in the Church and a great many out of the Church are waiting for some wonderful transformation. They are waiting for some wonderful something to possess them. A great many of us are alike. We want such an experience as that of St. Paul, for instance. Well, St. Paul was a wonderful man. He was big game, and God used big ammunition and big guns on big game, understand that. Paul—it took the biggest cannon of heaven, loaded to its muzzle, to bring him down, and it brought him down to surrender. And there's many a little fellow in this country wanting God to shoot off that same gun at him. And if God did, it would n't leave a grease spot of you, you poor little fellow. God is too merciful to turn such guns loose on your sort. God never shoots cannon balls at snow-birds. Do n't forget that. Fancy a snow-bird perched on the twig of a persimmon bush and saying, "I'll never move until a cannon ball hits me"—and that will be his last move.

"According as his divine power hath given us all things that pertain to life and godliness, through the knowledge of him that hath called us to glory and virtue; whereby are given unto us exceeding great and precious promises." O brother! how divine the truth that God always promises to help a man to be good if he wants to be good! And my theology at last, brother, is in but two sentences. God can not arbitrarily make any man a good man. If he could, we would all be good, for he wills that we should all be moral. The devil can not arbitrarily make any man a bad man. If he could, we would all be bad. My theology is wrapped in these two declarations : If you want to be good, say so, and God will help you; if you want to be bad, say so, and the devil will help you. I need n't tell you that. You know that.

" Exceeding great and precious promises"—promises that come down to me, and reach out to me, and overshadow me, and that are like a great granite rock under my feet as I walk on the promises of God. There is no bankrupting the soul that carries in its consciousness the promises of God. Now, brother, let us take a sensible view of this. Let's you and I not wait for any thing, but let's you and I decide to-night. "Yes, I want to be good, and I decide to be good." And that isn't all. "I believe God will help me, and I'm going to start out on that line to-night." The greatest curse of men is, they are going to be good after a while. "I will be good next year," and so on. Well, if you and I are ever going to be good, it is time we begun. And if we are never going to be good, let's say so and settle it forever.

Now after a start like this, he says: "And besides this, giving all diligence, add to your faith virtue, and to virtue knowledge, and to knowledge temperance, and to temperance patience, and to patience godliness, and to godliness brotherly kindness, and to brotherly kindness charity. For, if these things be in you and abound, they make you that ye shall neither be barren nor unfruitful in the knowledge of our Lord Jesus Christ. But he that lacketh these things—" Listen! "He that lacketh these things is blind and can not see afar off."

You see the seeming contradictory senses in which these words are put, "Is blind and can not see afar off." He can see all around him. He can see stocks and bonds and money, and worldly goods and fruits. Ah me! He is what you might call a near-sighted Christian. He can see every thing about him; he can see the profits and losses of each day's business; he can see his mansion and see his town property and see his railroad interests, and so on, right about him, but he "is blind and can not see afar off." Ah me, brother! It is these long-sighted fellows that win. This one that looks ahead into eternity can say, "My treasure is laid up at the right hand of God, where neither moth nor rust doth corrupt and where thieves do not break through and steal."

You can tell a near-sighted man. Nothing out of the range of his sight excites him or moves him. That man standing by you there—you see a cyclone coming, but he stands there without a motion of his body. These men that can not see into eternity, and can not see beyond, are never excited. They call these other men "religious enthusiasts." And I declare to you, to-night, we have got a great many near-sighted Methodists and Baptists and Presbyterians and Episcopalians, and so forth, in this city. That father, there, can see his boy going in business, and can see him succeed in business; but how about his boy's soul and eternity? He can't see any thing there. That mother can see her daughter projected into society, and see her marry well, and see her move off to herself and start well in life; but how about her daughter's eternal's interests? She can't see any thing there. O, the near-sighted people of this world. They are "blind and can not see afar off."

And listen : " And have forgotten that they were purged from their old sins." There is not an old backslider in this town but what, when you see him down, will say, " I sort of doubt whether I ever was religious. I do n't think I ever was a Christian." Forgets, you see! There is not a miserable back-slidden person in this community to-night, but what, when you bring him square to the issue, will tell you, " Well, I thought I was converted then, and I thought I enjoyed religion, but I think now I was mistaken." " Think now I was mistaken !" Have n't you heard that all around? " I 'm afraid I was mistaken." Poor fellow! He has got into things that have so engrossed him, and so taken up his time, he has forgotten all about how good God was to him, and how God blessed him, and how he had lived for months, and may be years. " Blind and can not see afar off, and hath forgotten that he was purged from his old sins." I do n't know what you 'll do with all this sort un-less you turn them over to us Methodists.

I want to tell you of another thing right along at this point. There are ten, there are twenty warnings in the Word of God to Christian people, lest they fall, lest they go back—there are twenty warnings to Christian people to hold fast their pro-fession of faith, to where there is one call to the sinner to come to repentance. And now what do you say? It looks as if there is danger along that line. Now, " giving all diligence." O me! A religious life is a pious life, it is an earnest life, it is an energetic life, it is a life in which every man ought to lay aside every weakness and the sin that doth so easily beset him and run with patience the race set before him.

An energetic, an enthusiastic life! Ah me! It is a life like that of St. Paul. When once convinced, and when once he swore his allegiance to Christ, from that moment until he passed out of the world he was a grand rolling ball of fire all through his life and all through earth. O brother! "Giving all diligence!"

I can tell when a man is in earnest. If you let me watch the first three months of that young lawyer's life after he has just chosen the profession of law—if you let me watch the first three months of his life after he makes his profession, chooses his profession—I do n't need any tongue of the prophet to tell me whether he means business or not. I see that young fellow choosing the profession of law, and if, instead of poring over Blackstone and Greenleaf and all the law books, I see him now spending his evenings with the girls and loitering around the street, I do n't need any tongue of the prophet to say that fellow will never get but one case and the sheriff will get his client.

I see a young fellow starting out to be a doctor. Let me watch him three months. I see him loitering away his time and spending his evenings in parties, and paying no attention to physiology and anatomy and hygiene and so forth. I turn around and I can see what he will be. He will have but one patient, and the undertaker will get him next day, and that will wind up his practice.

I see a preacher starting out who proposes to be a preacher; he never looks in a book, never thinks, never studies; he is going to open his mouth and let the Lord fill it. Well, the Lord does fill a fellow's mouth as soon as he opens it, but he fills it with air. I have listened to some men preaching an hour, and they didn't say one thing in the hour, and I got perfectly interested seeing how the fellow could dodge every idea in the universe and talk an hour. I just watched him.

I see a farmer the first three months of the year who, instead of cleaning out his fence corners and repairing his fences and turning his land and being just as energetic and active in January as he is in May, is loitering around doing nothing. I don't need any tongue of the prophet to tell how he'll come out farming. I have seen him down South. I have watched him, and I have told him before he started in how he would come out, too. Said I: "I'll tell you what will happen to you. You'll buy your corn from the West; you put in forty acres to the old mule, and before the year is out the grass will have your cotton and the birds will have your wheat, and the buzzards will have your mule and the sheriff will have you, and that's about where you will wind up."

But, on the other hand, when I see a young lawyer poring over his books day after day and night after night, burning the midnight oil, and I see the blood fading from his cheek, and his eye growing brighter every day, I don't need the tongue of the prophet to tell me there will be one day a judge of the Supreme Court, that there will be one day one of the finest lawyers that America ever produced. And so on.

You let me watch a fellow the first three months after he joins the Church, I can tell you whether he means business or not. I see him begin to lay himself out of his prayer-meetings and begin to neglect his duty, and begin to think that he has got more religion than he wants, and he'll run the rule of subtraction or division through it instead of the rule of addition, and I know just about where he'll land. You are there now. When I see a man come into the Church of God Almighty and say: "I'm going to take every chance for the good world; I'm going to get all the good out of every thing that comes my way or comes within a mile of me or ten miles of me," and I see him do his best and at his place and drawing in from all sources in heaven and earth, and see him as he begins to move forward in his Church and to be one of the pillars in Church—I don't mean p-i-l-l-o-w-s; you've got a great many of that sort of pillars in your Churches in this town, good old cases for others to crawl in and lay their heads on and go to sleep; that sort of pillows, downy fellows!—I know he is "giving all diligence."

I will tell you what surprises me sometimes. See old Brother A. go down Monday morning to do his business, and he puts all his blood and energy and money and muscles and tact into his business from Monday morning until Saturday night, and all the energies of soul and body are bent on pushing his business forward, and he is taking every turn, and using every means to do this; and then he comes to his neglected Church on Sunday morning and - takes his seat and sits there as quiet as the dead, and when the service is over he goes around into the study and says to the preacher, "What in the world's the matter with the Church? I can't see to save my life. She's not moving any." If that old fellow runs his business three months as he does the Church the sheriff would wind him up and settle him in bankruptcy. Talk about a man running his business as we do our Churches in this country! Ah, me! There is not a man in this house that does not know his business will go into bankruptcy and ruin if he devotes no more time to it than we devote to the Church of God.

I'll tell you what I have got a contempt for in the highest sense—a fellow that is a first-class lawyer and a tenth-rate Methodist; he is the best lawyer in town, but the worst member of his Church. Now, sir, that sort of a fellow isn't worth killing in any country in heaven or earth. I'll tell you another fellow that I have got a contempt for. It is this fellow: he is the best merchant in this city and he is about a fifteenth-rate Baptist. There is another fellow—the best doctor in this city, and as a Presbyterian he is the deadest failure in the town. Now, if a fellow is of no account anywhere, the Lord can sort of put up with his being of no account in the Church; but if he is a first-class any thing out of the Church, God wants him to be a first-class every thing in the Church, don't you see?

Isn't it strange, brethren—now I don't single out any class in this world and say aught against them—but isn't it strange how few really pious law-

yers we have in this country? Is n't it strange? It
takes less earnest effort to be a first-class Christian
than it does to be a first-class lawyer, and I'd rather
be one first-class Christian than to be every first-
class lawyer in the universe.

You take the physicians of the community. One
of my old brethren, a physician once, belonged to
my Church, and I got after him about not coming
out, and he said that he tried his best to get there,
but he could not. "Well," said I, "I'll tell you,
old fellow, if heaven was a sickly country, I do n't
believe I'd want to go there." "Well," he said:
"why?" "Well, I am afraid there will be very
few doctors there." I do n't know what in the
world's the matter, but there are so few doctors
that are pious, but when you do find one that is
thoroughly pious he is one of the best men on the
face of the earth.

What's the matter with our professional men?
Have they grown too big to be religious? Have
they grown up to where the Bible is considered
their mother's and their little children's book?
What is the matter? O, sir, listen to me to-night.
The grandest lawyers this world ever produced
were the men who loved and lived by this blessed
book I am preaching from to-night. The best
physicians and the grandest in the science in which
they worked were men who read this book and
loved this book, and when they came to die they
said, "Wife, put the Bible under my head, and
let it be my blessed pillow upon which I shall
breathe my last."

I do n't want any better evidence of the upstart than a fellow that gets too big to like the Bible; and I declare to you that it has reached the point in this country now, if a fellow has much to say about the Bible and the faith of this book, they will ridicule him, they will say he is a fool that believes every thing—they will that. O, my brethren, when I see a Newton as he comes down from his observatory, just now numbering and counting the stars as he swept his telescope across the skies, I see him lay down his telescope and walk down into his closet, and kneel down and pray to God, and walk out and say to his wife, "Precious wife, I got closer to God on my knees in the closet than I was just now in my observatory, as I was counting and numbering the stars." The little fellow has too much sense to believe the Bible! A big head in a man is a heap worse than it is in a horse. A horse will die in about a week, but the poor fellow lives on in the way of all the country—one of these knowing fellows. The Lord likes one of these fellows who says, "I do n't know much;" a man who drops down on his knees every morning when he first wakes up and says, "Lord God, go with me this day. I am poor and weak and miserable and ignorant and blind. O, Lord! I would not risk myself out of this room and out of my yard to-day unless you go with me. Take my hand, precious Father, and lead me, because I know not the way." The Lord likes one of these men that feels in his heart, "I have n't got sense enough to go to my front gate

and back unless the God of heaven will go with
me." That is my sort.

"Besides this giving all diligence, add unto your
faith, virtue." I like this rule of addition. I like
it. I want more and more, and still there is more
to follow. I want to be larger to-day, and better
to-day, and grander to-day than yesterday. And
the biggest reason in the world why I'd rather live
ten years longer in this life than to die to-morrow—
the biggest reason after all—is the fact, that in the
next ten years, if God lets me live, I intend to
eliminate much that is evil about me, and I intend
to grow and develop into a grander Christian man
than I claim to be to-night. My highest wish for
a longer period of life is that before the day of
crystallization, God may eliminate from me all that
is evil, and develop me into all that is good.

"Add unto your faith, virtue; and to virtue,
knowledge; and to knowledge, temperance; and to
temperance, patience"—enough to keep a man pious.
You will find that evil here is broad and deep as you
look out. "Add unto your faith, virtue." You take
these seven graces before us to-night. Now, six
thousand years ago God said "Let there be light,
and there was light," but this world enjoyed its rays
for thousands of years before any philosopher an-
alyzed it and told us what pure, white light is.
After a while the philosopher stepped to the front
and he told us that pure, white, physical light is
the symmetrical blending of the seven primary colors
we find in the rainbow—red and blue and orange
and green, etc.; that the seven is pure white phys-

ical light. Jesus Christ said to his Church: "Ye are the light of the world." They did not understand him. But Peter studied the question and stepped forth as the great philosopher in spiritual things, and tells us that pure, white spiritual light is the symmetrical blending of the seven primary Christian graces—faith and courage and knowledge and temperance and patience and brotherly kindness and charity. The seven graces will shed forth a light that will, indeed, light the whole world.

Now, brother, let us change the figure a moment and look at it in this way: we are building for eternity. Every man ought to look well to the foundation. Jesus Christ is the great foundation upon which we rest all our hope and all our experience and all our patience for time and eternity. Christ is the great bed-rock, and faith in him as we build this spiritual temple, faith in Christ, is the first rock put down. And we build this temple without the sound of a hammer. We build this temple out of divine material and according to divine direction, and the first rock I put down—the bed-rock—is faith; for "without faith it is impossible to please God." "He that believeth shall be saved." I may say that my heart rests upon this old book; I may say that I believe this book; I may say that I inherited a faith from my father and mother in this blessed book; I may say that there is not a single utterance of God that I doubt in my heart to-night. Call me a dupe and call me a fool, but tell others, when you say I am a dupe and a fool, tell them I am a happy one.

Faith in my Bible? I believe this book; I believe this book, and this book has blessed thousands
of men before I was born, and the best men on
whom I lean every day, whisper back in my ear:
"That blessed book is a lamp to my feet and a light
unto my path." This blessed book, that never mis-
led a human step and never misdirected a human
life; this book, with its morals so pure and with its
Christ so ennobling and elevating to the race—I
believe, I believe!

I believe in God the **Father** Almighty, maker
of heaven and earth, and in Jesus Christ, his only
begotten son, our Lord; I believe in the Holy
Ghost; in the Church of God. I believe—I believe there is power in God and virtue in the blood
of Christ and truth in the Holy Ghost; and, brethren, if I didn't believe that book, and believe God
is its author, and God is with me, I'd close this
book and close my mouth and leave this town on
the first train that left for my home. I believe my
Bible; and when the Christian people of this town
believe this book, we are going to take this book
and conquer the whole city. I believe, I believe in
God, as he is the Father of all men, preserver of
all life, inspirer of all that is good.

I believe in God, and now to this faith in God
and faith in the right, what is the next rock we
lay down? See how this will fit: "Add unto
your faith, virtue"—*virtus*, courage. Now, don't
you see that if a man believes he is right the very
next thing he wants is a courage that dares to do
right and dares to be true. I want to say at this

point that I am not talking about physical courage. I am afraid that Christian people are sometimes physical cowards. I do not want a man to be a physical coward, but above all things deliver me from a moral coward. I want to tell you that I have searched this book from Genesis to Revelation, and I find that God never did choose a man to do a great work for him but that that man was game from head to foot. God despises a coward.

Moral courage! Physical courage is not much. Physical courage will march me right up into the blazing mouth of a cannon without shaking a muscle in my body, but that is not much. I have known generals and colonels and majors and captains and privates in this last war that never had a muscle quiver in front of a cannon. Yet these same men after coming home from the war would quake and wince and whine in the presence of public opinion. Afraid of that! Afraid of that! And I will tell you another thing for which a fellow needs courage. There are a great many things in this world that stand looking a fellow in the face and shake their fist at him, and if he hasn't got the grit he will run, no doubt about it. And I say to-night every man that walks out before this world and would make it purer and better, that man shall, like his Lord, have his Gethsemane, and his Pilate's bar, and his Judas Iscariot and his Simon Peter and his cross.

I tell you another thing. I would rather face every cannon in America to-night, as far as I am personally concerned, than face the opinion of the *élite* society of this city. What a hollow, miserable, heartless, godless old wretch that society is! Why, you can get on the street cars of this town, so I have been told, that are filled with theater-going, dancing, godless members of the Church, and Sam Jones is their text from the time you step on until you step off. Some say he is a brute. Some say he is as ignorant as a Southern plantation darky. Some say he is a vicious man. Some say one thing, and some another thing, and they shell the woods for a fellow. It is like the barking of a " fise " dog after a fast train—you can see the little fellow run, but you can not hear him bark.

Right is right, and stand to it; and when the last storm of passion has swept over, God is with you. That is more than can be against you, and that is all that you need. You attack 'the ball-rooms in this town, and every dancing, worldly member of the Church, and every sinner, too, turns his guns right loose upon you.

And I will tell you another thing. I want to say this to encourage you good Christian brethren that need just a little more backbone. When they tell you Jones is low-bred, do n't you believe them, for it is a lie! When they tell you that Jones is ignorant, you tell them that won't do; that Jones will go into a class with any of them to-morrow, and let a professor examine them on any subject. What do you say to that? And when they tell you that Jones came from bad stock, you tell them that a purer, nobler woman God never made than my mother, and that a better, purer man God never let live than my precious father. I am from as good a stock as God ever made.

I want to tell you right now that I never was in society. I reckon that one reason for this is that I have been poor all my life, and they would have objected to me on that account. They would never have let me in, anyhow. They would have known that I would tell on them, and they do n't want any tales told out of school; I have found that out. But I did not mean to say any thing about society now. We shall take that up later. We will shake it, till it is ready to be turned loose when we get through with it.

There are things in your city day after day and night after night that are enough to make a thousand mothers and fathers in this town call a halt, and say: "You had better stop right here. This thing has gone far enough." I tell you, mothers and fathers, if you will open your eyes and look around you a little you will call: "Halt! halt! halt! I will shoot you down if you take another step." And I know when a man begins to talk about these things I know how little Miss Finnicky and old Brother Finnicky and the whole devil's crowd will sit upon him. I have been around before.

Courage! courage! Jesus Christ, the great exemplar in Christianity, preached his own Gospel, and when he did, do you recollect that on one occasion a vast multitude turned their backs on him and walked off in disgust; and Jesus turned to his disciples and said: "Will ye also go away?" And Simon Peter said: "Lord, to whom shall we go?

20

For thou hast the words of eternal life." I do not believe I ever preached the Gospel as plainly as my Master preached it, for I have never had a congregation to "rush out" on me, and if ever I preach to a congregation and see the people jump up and run out of the house, I will jump up, too, and holler, "Glory to God! I am preaching like my Master now." But that would not be any joke on me. Everywhere I have ever worked, God bless you, they would say you people in the city were so mean you would not hear Sam Jones. They would brag on me and curse you. That is about the way the thing would go.

Courage that dares to be right and dares to be true! If a thing is wrong, fight it fight it! If it is right, stand up for it if every man on earth is against you. Stand and fight and fight and fight and fight, and though you go down and think you are alone, I tell you that when the din and smoke of the battle has blown away and you open your eyes, you will find God and the angels and good men standing around you.

Courage, brother! Now what does this mean? One time Peter's courage failed him, and of all the times in the world it was the time that Peter's courage ought to have held good. Yonder his Lord, defenseless and alone, given over to his enemies, stood before that cruel crowd, and they spat upon him and buffeted him and plaited a crown of thorns and pressed it on his temple until the blood ran down his cheeks. And Peter stood there looking at it, no doubt, until his very blood boiled.

And there was the Son of God and the Son of Man, without a friend in the world he came to redeem. There Peter stood out in the distance, and when the fatal moment came the people approached him and said: "You are one of his disciples;" and Peter answered: "No, I am not one of his disciples." And then again they approached him and said: "You are one of his disciples." He said: "No, I am not one of his disciples." And, again, a little girl approached him and said: "You are one of his disciples;" and Peter cursed and swore with an oath, and said: "I do not know him." Brother, I do not object to the way God's Word is written, but I have wished a thousand times that when my Master stood there, without a friend in the world, and they approached Peter, I have wished that Peter had rushed up by the Son of God and said: "I AM one of his disciples, and I will DIE by his side." If he had done that I believe that God would have rushed every angel in heaven down to Peter's side before he would have suffered a hair of his head to be touched. And we have forsaken our Master when he did not have a friend in the world.

Courage! Courage! I tell you, this sickly sentimentalism that we have that God's people are a peaceful, quiet, and get-out-the-devil's-way sort of people is a mistake. Down in my State I have been preaching prohibition, and in Georgia I have gone into those counties where prohibition was being fought the hardest, and said: "Brethren of the Church, take a stand and hold it. Do not let a barkeeper, that has not got more than three gallons of whisky, and that bought on credit, come out on the square on election day with an old, rusty pistol in his hand that has n't been loaded since the war, and curse two or three times, and talk loud and run every member of the Church out of town. God have mercy on you pusillanimous wretches," said I. " Hold your ground, and tell them that if they can die for their infernal traffic you can die for your precious children." And I said, " Go on, and God's approval will rest with you."

There was a day when one of God's armies was battling with the enemies of God. Joshua, the commander, was fighting with all the ransomed powers at his back, and the enemy was being beaten down in front of the ranks of God's hosts. But Joshua looked up, and saw that the sun was going down, and he looked up and said: "O God, if you will give me two or three hours more sunshine I 'll put this army to flight and will win a victory that shall make thine armies famous forever." And God turned and told the sun to go back on the dial, and " do n't you move an inch until Joshua routs this army root and branch and sweeps it almost from the face of the earth." And I tell you God will make the sun stand still in the heavens and the moon not move in the Valley of Ajalon, if God's people ever have the courage to stand up and dare to be right and dare to be true.

Sermon XII.

"The wages of sin is death, but the gift of God is eternal life, through Jesus Christ, our Lord."—Rom. vi, 23.

THERE are two questions which always come up legitimately and inevitably between employer and employe, between a hireling and his master. If you seek to employ a man for a day, or a week, or a month, or a year, the first question he inevitably puts to you is this: "What kind of work do you want me to do?" And when this question is satisfactorily answered there is another, inevitable and legitimate, and that is, "What will you pay me for it?" These two questions are the very basis of all contracts for labor. There can be no intelligent contract for labor to be rendered you without the settling of these two questions, What do you want me to do? and what will you pay me for it?

There may be a great many persons here to-night who boast of the fact that they were never in the employment of any body, or never sustained the relation of a servant or a hireling in their lives. There is a very important sense in which we are all doing service and in which we are serving a master, though you may boast of constitutional liberty, and that you live in the freest country in the world, whose constitution guarantees to every man his life and liberty and property; and yet there is a fearful sense in which all men are servants and all

237

men are at work for a master, and there is a very
important sense in which pay-day is coming.

Whose servant am I?   Our Savior taught us
no man could serve two masters; he would either
hold to the one and despise the other, or hate the
one and love the other.   He taught us again, To
whom you yield service obey him willingly.   A
great many people say, When you bring me into the
moral world I serve no master at all; and if this
world is cursed with any class it is the man who
says he is neither good nor bad! You ask him, "Are
you a good man?" and he will say, " No, sir;" and
if you ask him, "Are you a bad man," he will say,
"No, sir."   Neither good nor bad!   If there is a
being in the world I have a contempt for it is a
character of this sort.

There are a great many of that class in this
world too—a so-called class.   " I am neither good
nor bad."   I ain't good enough to go to heaven,
may be, but I ain't bad enough to go to hell—yes,
and I reckon you'll force a moral issue on this universe, and claim that God made a third world to
put you in when you die; neither good nor bad.
La, me; how many men in this world sustain that
relation toward the truth and the judgment of God.

Hear me on this question.   Our Savior said:
" He that is not with me is against me.   He that
gathereth not with me, scattereth abroad," and the
lines are so sharply and so clearly drawn, that no
man can stand squarely on a line between the good
and the evil, between the right and the wrong,
heaven's best interests and hell, with its demoraliz-

ing influence. I say every man of us is either on
the one side or the other side of this line, and any
man that is n't good enough to go to heaven is going
to hell. That 's all you can make out of it. Neither
good nor bad! There are two classes in all communities that puzzle the balance of humanity.
Here 's one man in the Church—we 'll say a clever,
moral, decent sort of a man; he belongs to the
Church, and he 'll pray when called upon, and he
seems to make a good steward, but he does n't pay
his debts, and does n't act right toward his neighbors. Here 's a man that does n't belong to the
Church—he will stand out there, and he pays all
his debts, and he 's liberal to the poor, but he does n't
belong to the Church. There stands the Church
member and here stands the other fellow—the Church
member won't pay his debts and won't do right by
his neighbor, but he seems to be trying to do his
duty towards God and not to man. The other is
doing his duty to his fellow-men, but he is n't acting right towards God.

There 's another fellow says: " I 'd a heap rather
be the man out of the Church that pays his debts
and acts right to his fellow-men than the one in the
Church that won't pay his debts and do right with
his neighbors, but acts square to God. I 'd a heap
rather be this one." Brother, why do you want to
be a fool by being either one of them? I do n't,
and I not only do n't want to be either one of them,
but I won't be either of them. I 'm going into the
kingdom of Christ, and intend to do my whole duty
to God and to my fellow-men; and now when you

see a man do this you see a whole man—not one of these little half-and-half fellows; one trying to do what the Lord tells him to do and being mean toward his neighbor, and the other doing right by his neighbor but being wrong with the Lord. I don't think there's much good about either, but I'd a heap sight rather be the fellow in the Church, for if I'm going to mistreat any body it isn't going to be God—he's the best friend I've got. Listen to me. My first duty is toward God, and I will do right towards him; and my next duty is to my fellow-men, and I will do right towards them; and then when I do this I'm made up for both worlds.

"He that is not with me is against me. He that gathereth not with me scattereth abroad." A man must take sides on the great moral issues of the world, and he must take sides with one or the other of the two great contending forces. A man must be with God or he is with the devil in all his walks and ways. I grant you, it looks sometimes as if a man is dividing up the thing. A man is trying to serve two masters. It reminds me of a Union man during the late war, and he had more loyalty than any body. He sent every boy he had to the war, but he was running a powder mill on the Confederate side, furnishing powder to the rebels. What do you think of such a man? He loves the Union well enough to give his boys to die for the Union, but he says: "If I can make a little money by furnishing powder to the rebels, all right."

Many a man in this country loves a dollar better than he does his children. Put that down. I'll

tell you another thing. Many a man says he loves
the Church, and he will put all his children into
the Church, and he's renting a bar-room to a fellow
who sells whisky and demoralizes the town—renting, perhaps, even worse places than that—a soldier
of Christ running a powder mill over the line and
furnishing ammunition to the devil. I can take a
handful of copper cents and tole a fellow like that
to hell and eternal fire by just dropping the cop-
pers along about every foot or two, right up to
the fires. I can that. Better the man that gets
down off the fence, and takes one side or the other.
I like that.

In our State, in the prohibition fight, we had
Prohibitionists that were Prohibitionists from the
crown of their hat to the toe of their boot, and we
had anti-Prohibitionists all over anti, but then we
had a great many people that said they were not
going to take any stock in it—going to vote one
way or the other. The old fools, they belonged
to the devil, from the tip of their head to the end
of the heels. "Is n't going to take any sides at
all!" and the fellow is the sneakingest hound dog
in creation. He is that. What is he good for?
I'll tell you what's the matter. He's afraid if he
makes a move one way or the other some fellow will
crack his head. That's what's the matter with
him, and the day of election he won't go down town
at all. His wife says to him: "Husband, why
do n't you get up and vote this awful stuff out of
the community?" And he says: "I ain't well;
I'm afraid if I go out I'll get in a fuss; I do n't

21

want to be mixed up with fusses." You old, little
pusillanimous coward, you—that's what you are.

Let's come out on one side or the other on all
moral questions. If I'm for a thing, I'm for it.
If I'm against a thing, I'm against it with all my
might, and you can't wake me up on any question
any minute in the day, and find me on both sides
of the fence, or a-straddle of the fence, for I love to
see a man a man all over, and a man of conviction.
I do that. If I'm on the right side, I'm there to
stay; and if I'm on the wrong side, I'll come over
as soon as you show me I'm wrong.

Brethren, we may settle this question here to-
night, in five minutes. "Whose side am I on?"
We must settle it. A tree is known by its fruit.
A salty fountain can't send forth pure water. Sam
Small never told a bigger truth than when he said
the other day, "If I wanted to raise a mob in this
town to do unrighteous things, to fight God and
truth and right, I'd beat the long roll in every
saloon in this town, and I'd muster in the fumes
of lager beer and whisky the worst element hell
itself could generate and get up." Isn't that so?
I used to think these whisky fellows were the cleverest fellows in the world, but when I was done with
them, and began to throw some shot in among
them, my, my, I threw some shot into the dirtiest,
stinkingest places man's eyes ever looked into.
You can always tell what a thing is when you begin to fire into it; you can see the fumes of it in
the atmosphere when you're firing.

A heap of the people in this town, that stand

back and won't take one side or the other, are
allied with the worst influence of earth. That's
so. I recollect when the proposition was made at a
temperance meeting once, and when the time came
for the signing of the pledge of total abstinence, a
good pastor of the city said: "I ain't ready to sign
the pledge. I'm a good temperance man, but I'm
not a teetotaler. I believe a little occasionally will
help me. I'm as much down on drunkenness as
any body, but I want it understood I believe in temperance, though not in prohibition." About that
time a fellow sitting away over in the corner staggered to his feet and said, with a drunken leer on
his face, and with fumes of whisky on his breath,
"Mr. Presiden', that preacher (hic) just 'spresses
(hic) my sen'ments 'xacly (hic)." The preacher
jumped up and said: "Well, if that's the kind of
fellows I've got to go with, you can put me down
on the side of teetotalism forever."

When you begin to dilly-dally and waver about
religion, let me tell you, brethren, the devil puts you
down soul and body on his side. That's a fact.
I've often thought of the story told of that poor
girl over yonder at the dance. During the dance
she dropped dead on the floor, and the story goes
on to say that the devil came immediately and carried off her soul, but in a few minutes St. Peter
came running up and said: "Where's the soul of
that girl gone?" and somebody said: "The devil
has just come and taken it off." St. Peter rushed
after the devil in double-quick time and overtook
him. He said: "Hold on, sir." "What's the

matter?" said the devil. " You 've got a member of
the Church's soul there, carrying it off. You have
no right to that, sir." " Well," said the devil,
" you can take it away if you want to, but she died
in my territory."

As men live, so they die, and if you can 't afford
to die on the devil's side, let me say to you you 'd
better not go over there at all. You 'd better not.
If non-members of the Church want to play cards and
dance and drink whisky, we have no right to enter
protest; but I'll tell you whenever I find members
of the Church, who have sworn allegiance to Christ
playing cards and drinking whisky and going to
theaters, I 'm going to look them in the face and
holler out, " Traitor !" " Traitor !" " Traitor !"
That 's what you are—a traitor. Brethren, that 's
pretty strong, but when you go home if you 'll pick
me out any thing stronger I'll use it also. I
have n't any compromise to make. Many a one in
this town is kicking hard right now, too. They say
" Why it 's outrageous the way that man goes on
talking about the Church. It's ridiculous, and it
ought n't to be permitted at all."

I tell you only a hit dog will run and howl
every crack. There 's no law against it. If they
ain 't hit, I want them to hush. I got some letters
to-day that made me feel sad in my soul. I 've a
good mind to pull some of them out and read them.
It 's enough to make an angel shudder, just to think
what members of the Church in this city are guilty
of day after day and year after year. It is that.

Let 's take sides, brethren. Let 's come over on

God's side all over and forever, or let's quit it altogether and go on the devil's side. In one of the
towns in Georgia a member of the Church—a
different Church from mine—said to me, " Jones, I
want to ask you a question. What harm is there in
card-playing?" " Do you play cards?" asked I.
" Yes," said he. " You 're a deacon in your Church?"
" Yes," said he; " and if you will convince me
there's any harm in this thing, I 'll quit it forever."
Said I, " You 're already convinced of one thing,
ain't you?" " Why, what's that?" said he. " That
you ain't worth the powder and lead to kill you
out of the Church?" " Yes, that's so," said the
fellow.

" Well, then," I said, " I have n't got any time to
fool away with such fellows as you. If you were
any good I 'd stand here an hour, but you've con-
fessed you ain't worth the powder and lead to kill
you, and I have n't any powder to waste on such as
you."

Is there a man here that prays every day and
goes to prayer-meeting regularly, and pays his
quarterage like a liberal man, and gives liberally to
foreign missions—is there one like that that goes to
the theater, and dances, and plays cards and drinks
whisky? If there is, stand up. If you are what
God says you ought to be, and still you do these
things, stand up, and I 'll apologize for what I said
against you. I never will apologize to any of the
uncircumcised Philistines—I never will. If you
live right and do your duty, and I wound your feelings, I 'll beg your pardon, but if you 're living the

life of a hypocrite in the Church, I will not apologize for preaching the truth to you.

One side or the other; for or against; serving God or serving the devil, one or the other—that's the text. Are you a servant of the devil? "To whom you yield yourself for service, obey his service." Listen. "Keep my Commandments." Do you do that? No? Well, then you are not a servant of the Lord. "Deny yourself; take up your cross and follow me." Do you do that? No? Then you are not a servant of the Lord. If a man isn't a servant of the Lord then he's a servant of the devil.

Let's drop back on the first proposition. Go to your master to-night, the devil; ask him what kind of work he wants you to do. He wants you to profane God's name, he wants you to belie the Sabbath, he wants you to debauch your soul with whisky, for it is said: "No drunkard shall enter the kingdom of heaven." Is that the sort of work he wants you to do? Yes, it is. Not only does he want you to do that sort of work, but there are a hundred of you here that can say: "That's the sort of work he sets out for me year after year. He wants me to do those things that will degrade me in my own eyes, in the eyes of God, in the eyes of men, in the eyes of my family. He wants me to do every thing that's disreputable and that will doom me forever in the future." Isn't that so? How many men here to-night can testify: "That's the truth in my case?"

If this is the sort of dirty, disreputable work the

devil wants you to do, you ask the question, "What does he pay for it? What are the wages?" You ask yourself this question, for may be pay-day will come on you before 12 o'clock to-night, when the laborer is worthy of his hire, and your wages will be counted to you to the last cent. Brethren, it is well enough to stop and ask yourself this question, for none of us know how close pay-day is at hand. Old fellow, you want to settle this question, "What are the wages for the life of servile bondage in the service of the devil?" I asked an old fellow this question one day, and happening to meet him the day after, he said: "If I had stood up and told those people what my wages have been for my service to the devil in the past sixty-five years, it would have frightened them. All I've got to show is the worst family in Georgia, and a knowledge of the fact that neither myself nor my family will be saved. That's all I can show for sixty-five years' service to the devil."

Brethren, stop here to-night and ask, What are my wages? The wages of sin is death, damnation and degradation. You ask, is that so? I can dig out of your cemeteries in Cincinnati, O how many, who are fit representatives of the eternal truth I am talking of right now. What are your wages? Pay-day is coming. Suppose, we will say, I am a servant of the Lord; suppose I serve him and make him the delight of my soul and my heart. I wonder what he wants me to do? He wants me to do those things that will make every body think more of me and make angels think more of me. He wants me to do those things that will elevate me in time and make me fit and meet for heaven hereafter. In this delightful service of the Lord you must keep the commandments, and when you can do that then you can say, "O Lord, I can enter such service as that for nothing." You won't want any wages for doing that. You will gladly go and serve him forever. What does he pay? Cash enough to live on every day; and when you get old and wrinkled and gray-headed, and can not work any longer, he stoops down and picks you up and gives you a house in heaven to live in with him and angels forever. If these things are true, brethren, can you tell me how it is that the devil has a servant in the world? I'll tell you how he got you, and how he is keeping you, and the Lord help you to-night to break these chains and walk forth a free man from this time on.

Brethren, let's take one side or the other of these questions. You can't be on the fence and be saved. You must come over to one side or the other.

I can never forget the hours in my life when I turned this world loose and had no God to take my hand. O brother, for nearly a week I was wading and wading through the deepest trials. I had turned loose all my sins, and I could not find the hand of God. I was reaching up, saying, "Father, take my hand! take my hand!" And on I went. I felt like the veriest orphan in all the universe of God, and miserably I pressed my way along, the most miserable man in the world. Thank God for those awful hours! They have been so awful to me that my footsteps shall never go back over that road. God, let me die before I shall ever cross that weary quagmire again in my human experience, poor and wretched and miserable! This was the first cup presented to my lips—the cup of repentance. I drank it down; and O, what anguish and misery of soul I felt. The next cup God presented was the cup of justification, and as I drank it I said, " Well, surely, God has kept the good wine until now." O, none out of God can know how glorious the sinner feels when he hears the voice of God saying: " Son, daughter, thy sins, which are many, are all forgiven! "

The first cup God presented to St. Paul, he was stricken down in the road and struck stone blind. For three days and nights he groped his way in darkness until he reached the house of Judas, and when Ananias laid his hands upon him and the scales fell from his eyes and joy came into his soul, I suppose St. Paul thought, " Well, God has kept the good wine until now." And a few months after that St. Paul was caught up into the third heaven and poised himself over the city of God, and looked down on the towering spires and jasper walls and pearly gates, and his ears were charmed with the songs of angels and the music of the redeemed. I suppose as he looked down on that city of God that he said: " Well, verily God has kept the good wine until now." But by and by in his lonely prison at Rome God presented another cup, and St. Paul took his pen again and wrote to Timothy: "The time of

my departure is at hand." He just took that great
clod of a word which we call " death " and threw it on
one side, and he said: " The time of my departure
is at hand. I have fought the good fight, I have
finished my course, I have kept the faith." If we
had St. Paul down here to-night to conclude this
service, and he would just tell us what good things
God has in store for us, we would all leave here
shouting the praises of God for the glorious hope of
an immortal life beyond the skies.

I have thought of many things in reference to
eternity. I have thought this way: I have lain down
and dreamed of heaven, and I have stood up and
thought of heaven, and I have sat down and read
of heaven, and then I have sung of heaven, and on
I go; but, brethren, all the money I have got in
the universe is in this bank, and if it does n't break
I am a millionaire. I have felt it many a time.
All my calculations and all my interest is in that
direction, and if at the final day God should say to
me: " Depart, ye cursed, into everlasting flames," I
will turn my back and walk away from the gates
of heaven the worst disappointed man that God
ever drove away from his presence. No, sir. My
calculations are all that way. And then after awhile,
if I do succeed and step inside of the pearly gates and
turn around and see God and angels, and precious
mother and father and loved ones, brethren, I will
just bury my face in my hands and say, " Sure enough,
beyond all doubt or cavil, I am here, I am here."
And blessed be God, I just as fully expect to realize
that I am in heaven as I realize to-night I am here,

in fact more so. I may be mistaken about being in this city, it may be somewhere else; but when I get to heaven, there is no place in the world like heaven, and I will know I am there, sure enough.

Well, now I know what a servant of God will do for other folks, and we are all alike. I have been watching some things mighty close during the last few years. I was pastor of a Church, and in that Church there was one of the most faithful godly women I ever saw in my life. Her husband was wealthy and she gave with a princely hand to the poor and to every good cause, and it was joy to her heart to do for the Master. And finally her time came to pass out of this world. I visited her in her last illness. She was dying of consumption, and had spent several Winters in Florida. When I would go into her room and talk to her she would frequently say, "I dread to die; not the result of death," she said, "but the agonies of death." And I talked to her and encouraged her all I could. She said, "I am so frail, I am so weak I can scarcely lift my hands, and, O! how can I grapple with physical death?" The last time I visited her before she died she motioned to the company present to leave the room—I suppose she did, for they all got up and walked out at once and left me alone with her. Then she said: "My pastor, I have some things of importance to say to you that I never want you to mention while I live, for the world makes light of such things, and what I say to you is as sacred to me as my own soul." She said, "You know I told you when you were here last that I was afraid of the agonies of death; not of what is beyond." "Yes, ma'am," I replied. "Well," she says, "I am not now." "Why," said I, "what brought about the change?"_ She said, "Yesterday I was lying in my room here and I put my handkerchief over my face and I was thinking of heaven, and, all at once a scene just as natural as life presented itself. It seemed that I stood upon the moss-covered banks of a beautiful river and the noiseless water was rolling gently by. All at once a little boat ran its prow out right at my feet, and the oarsman invited me into the boat. I stepped into the little boat and it moved off so noiselessly, and we disembarked on the other bank amid the shouts of the angels and the songs of the redeemed, and they carried me up a beautiful avenue to a palace, and we walked up to the door of the palace and the door stood ajar. They carried me into the palace, and I felt like a stranger in a strange place. They carried me up to the King and introduced me to him, and as soon as my eyes fell upon him I saw and recognized immediately that it was the world's Redeemer, my precious Savior, and I was at home from that time on. Now," she said, "I am not afraid to die."

Just a few days afterwards, as her husband sat with her, she called him in a whisper. He went to her. She said: "Husband, I feel so delightfully strange; what do you think is the matter with me?" He felt her hand and felt her arm to her body, and it was cold. "O, precious wife," he said, "you are dying." She raised her arms and clasped them round his neck, and said: "O, husband, if this is death, what a glorious thing it is to die." And she fell back upon her pillow and never breathed again.

Just eleven days after that I was walking along by the hotel, and the husband of this good woman said: "Mr. Jones, my little Annie is very sick. I wish you would come and see her." She was the only child of that man and the good sister that had died. As I walked into the room, there was little Annie, little ten-year-old Annie, sick with diphtheria. I walked in and took her hand and said: "Sweet darling, are you suffering much?" She said in a whisper: "Yes, sir; a good deal." I said: "Darling, do you want me to talk to you?" And she said: "Yes, sir; if you please." "What about?" I asked. She said: "I want you to talk to me about heaven." I said: "Well, darling, it is a great country, a glorious place, where little girls never suffer, and mamma is never sick, and where all is life and health and peace." And her little eyes fairly shone like diamonds in her head while I talked. And directly the doctors walked in and her father said: "Annie, darling, the doctors want to cauterize, to burn your throat again." She looked up so pleadingly and said: "Papa, please sir, don't let them burn my throat any more. Mamma has been calling me all the morning, and I want to go." "Why," he said, "sweet darling, if you go papa won't have any little girl. Won't you stay with papa?" "Well," she said, "they may burn my throat, but it won't do any good. I am going

to mamma." They burned her throat, and she lay
perfectly quiet a minute or two. Then she was visited by some Sunday-school children, and she
turned and said: "Won't you sing "Shall We
Gather at the River?" And she said: "I have
heard them singing it over there, and mamma is
joining in." The little children began to sing, and
just as they commenced the chorus, the sweet spirit
of little Annie left the body with a placid, heavenly
smile on its face, and went home to live with her
mamma forever. No wonder the old prophet said:
"Let me die the death of the righteous, and let my
last end be like his." "Mark the perfect man
and behold the upright, for the end of that man is
peace."

Peace! Peace! Now another incident and then
I will quit, just to show you the difference; a
simple contrast. I want you to see it. During the
last cruel war—and how cruel it was—a minister
in our State was summoned to Virginia by a telegram, which read: "Your brother is mortally
wounded. Hurry to the front." This minister
hurried to the front as fast as the trains could carry
him to the battlefields of Virginia. When he
reached Virginia he found his brother was wounded
sure enough fatally. He was in a country home,
and he made haste to the place, and when he walked
into the room where his suffering brother was lying
he went up to the bed and took his hand. He saw
immediately that death was doing its work, and he
said: "Brother, I am so glad to get here before
you die. Brother, I am so anxious about your soul.

You have been a wicked man all your life; I have prayed for you, and talked with you many a time. Now, brother, brother, will you right here surrender your heart to God?" "O," said the wounded man, "do not talk to me about my soul. I have thrown away all my health and vigorous days and despised God and religion, and now I can do nothing with every fiber of my body burning and aching. O, brother, I can not talk with you now about religion." The next day the brother tried his best to approach him again, but the wounded brother waved him off, and said: "Brother, I am tortured to death with physical pain. Please, do not trouble me now. I am unprepared and shall die unprepared, but do not torture me more than I am being tortured." He could not approach him.

It was the sixth night this preacher brother had sat by his brother's bedside. Loss of sleep and exhaustion and anxiety had reduced him so much and worried him so, that, as the wounded brother was lying quietly that night about twelve o'clock, he said to himself, "I will lie down on the cot and rest for a few moments. I won't go to sleep. I see brother is very low." And he said, "I lay down on the cot and, in a moment almost, was sound asleep." And while asleep he dreamed that his brother died with his mouth wide open, and just as soon as the soul left the body he saw the devil come in in bodily form and approach the bed, and walk up to his dead brother, and look down into his brother's mouth, and he saw that the soul was gone. And he said: "I thought that when the soul of my brother left his body it hid among the piles of wood I had piled up by the fire to keep the fire going, and the devil scented the soul, and started around to my brother's hidden soul, and as the devil approached that hiding place the soul flew out of the room, crying 'Lost! Lost! Lost! Forever lost!' And," said he, "in the distance I heard the wail of my brother's soul as it hurried out of the reach of the devil, and in the distance I could hear the shrieks and screams of my brother's soul as the devil fastened his talons in it forever and ever. And when I awoke up, agitated and frightened, the light had gone out. And," said he, " I jumped up and lit the lamp. I walked up to the bed. There was my poor brother, lying with his mouth wide open and dead. And I believe God shut my eyes in sleep to show me the scene that presented itself in that room."

SAYINGS.

FAITH is the principle on which Omnipotence slumbers.

GOD loves righteousness and hates sin. The devil loves sin and hates righteousness. That is the difference.

SERMON XIII.

ST. PAUL'S LAST WORDS.

"But watch thou in all things, endure afflictions, do the work of an evangelist, make full proof of thy ministry."—
2 TIM. IV, 5.

THAT is what St. Paul said to Timothy, and then he added: "For I am now ready to be offered and the time of my departure is at hand. I have fought a good fight, I have finished my course, I have kept the faith. Henceforth there is laid up for me a crown of righteousness, which the Lord, the righteous Judge, shall give me at that day, and not to me only, but unto all them also that love his appearing." Now, in the verse which we read as a text, St. Paul said four things to Timothy; and these words we might denominate his dying words— the last words of one of the greatest men God ever made. I have been frequently touched by reading the words of St. Paul to Timothy. I have seen the fatherly interest and the tender, watchful care that St. Paul bestowed upon Timothy, his own son in the Gospel; and now that they have had their last conversation, as they have preached and labored and eaten and walked and talked together for the last time; and as all earthly association and communication is cut off forever, and St. Paul is about to pass to his reward, he has something to say to Timothy.

How the last words of a dying neighbor impress us, and how the last words of a good father fasten themselves upon us! How the last words of a good mother are cherished by us! We can forget a thousand things father said while he lived, but we can never forget the last words of a good father. We forget a thousand things that mother said in life and health, but the last words of a precious mother linger with us like the memory of a pleasant dream. The last words of Paul to Timothy, and through Timothy to us! And O, how much St. Paul compassed in these three lines.

The first thing he said to Timothy was this: "Watch thou in all things." If there ever was a day in the world's history when the people of God ought to be vigilant and watchful, it is now. This watchful spirit is the sentinel of the soul—the sentinel on the outpost. I am commanded to be vigilant, to be watchful, because my adversary, the devil, is going about like a roaring lion seeking whom he may devour. I am commanded to be vigilant and to be watchful because I wrestle not against flesh and blood, but against powers and principalities and spiritual wickedness in high places. General Washington said whenever danger was imminent and the enemy was near by: "Put no one but Americans on the outposts to-night." And now while enemies surround us on all sides and press upon us in every direction, is it not best that we put none but the most vigilant souls upon the watch-tower, and that we put the sentinels that belong to our own souls on the outposts, the most faithful. It was death for a sentinel to sleep at his post. Do you wonder why they were so severe on poor fellows for going to sleep out on post? I'll tell you why. The safety, the peace, the lives of 60,000 men are in the hands of that sentinel out there on the outpost, and for him to go to sleep on post means to have the enemy charge upon a camp of sleeping soldiers and butcher them in their bunks. No wonder the general says to his sentinel on the post: "It is death to go to sleep on the outpost there." And I tell you another thing: The way God talks to us, it is mighty near death to you and me if we ever forget to obey the text, and fail to be watchful.

Another Scriptural term for this same expression or thought is this:

"Walk circumspectly."

Now, that word "circumspectly" is a Latin derived word, a compound word. It means "looking around you." The Indian walking in the primal forests of this country, inhabited by all kinds of wild beasts and reptiles, walked with perfect safety, because he walked circumspectly. The Indian bade his squaw and his children good-by in the morning and went into the wild forests, inhabited by wild beasts and reptiles, and they did not think of his safety. They knew that if the enemy approached him from the right, he saw him. If the enemy came from the front he saw him. To the left he saw him. If he approached from the rear, his keen sense of hearing and seeing detected it. If it was a wild beast crouched on a limb above his pathway, he saw him. If it was a hissing serpent underneath

on his pathway, he saw him. And the Indian
walked in perfect safety, because he walked circumspectly. Circumspectly! A man walks along and
looking ahead of him is not walking circumspectly.
A man who just looks to the right and looks ahead
is not walking circumspectly. If a man looks on
both sides and to the front he is not walking circumspectly. If a man looks to the rear and in
front and on both sides he is not walking circumspectly. If a man looks above him and in front
and on both sides and to the rear, he is not walking
circumspectly. But if he look above and beneath
and in front and to the right and to the left and in
the rear, and in walking looks around both ways and
all ways, then he is walking circumspectly, looking
in every direction.

I know not from what direction the enemy may
attack. I know not whether it shall be from the
left or from the right, from the front or from the
rear. I know not what sort of enemy it may be,
and I know not the direction he may come upon
me, and so I shall obey the Scripture and walk circumspectly, looking around both ways. Both ways!
Walking circumspectly! Well, I must not only
walk looking all around me both ways and looking
outward, but I must look within. Look at myself.
Spurgeon said all our enemies are comprehended
under three heads: The world, the flesh and the
devil. He said: "The devil is a cunning old
enemy. O, how cunning he is! but by the
grace of God I can conquer the devil. This old
world," he adds, "is a multitudinous affair with

ten thousand things to attract and seduce me, but by the grace of God I can conquer the world. But," he said, "Good Lord, deliver me from myself."

Nine-tenths of your trouble and my trouble is not on the outside at all. It is inside. There's where the trouble is. As I heard a brother say to-day: "You can go out in the world as much as you please, but you had better mind how you get the world into you." Sometimes we mislocate things, like the good old brother that called on Bishop Wightman. Down in Mobile, Alabama, the bishop had been holding conference, and a good old brother came up to him in his room one day and said to the bishop: "I haven't been to my Church in two years. I haven't been out at all in that time." "Well," said the bishop, "why is that, brother." "Why," said he, "they have got the devil right behind the pulpit." "What?" he says, "got the devil right behind the pulpit?" "Yes," he says, "they have. Just as soon as I walk into the church the first thing I see is the devil right behind the pulpit." "Why, brother," said the bishop, "what in the world do you mean?" "Why," he says, "it's the organ they've got in there." "Well," said Bishop Wightman, in his polite way, "I guess when you go into the church the devil is in there sure enough, but you do n't locate him right. He's not in there right behind the pulpit, but he's in you. He's in you. You've mislocated things. There's the trouble."

I heard a good old brother say once that when

a man got mad with him, he always spoke kind
words and said kind things. "Why," said he,
"when a man wants to raise a difficulty with me
and talk bad things to me, if I get mad, the devil
will come out of that fellow into me, and he'll
divide devils with me. He's got enough for both."
And the trouble with humanity is that they don't
locate things right. And without locating your
enemy, you can never fight him successfully. That's
the truth. The wisest general in this whole war
was the general, not that knew so much how his
troops were arranged, but who disposed his troops
by the arrangement of his enemy's troops, so that
his strongest point was just opposite the strongest
point of his enemy. And the Christian man, who
is best equipped to fight the devil, is the Christian
man who not only knows the strength of the devil,
but knows exactly where he is located and all
about him.

Watch! Your trouble, if rightly located, is
within and not without you. I would rather fight
a thousand enemies outside of the fort than to fight
one enemy inside of the fort. There are more dangers on the inside. And now let us see what we
have inside to betray us.

Well, let's see! Is there any body here troubled
with a spirit of neglect? That is a fearful enemy
on the inside—the spirit of neglect. I don't care
what else you have or don't have—if you have got
that you are betrayed. As I have said before,
you may take the best man in this city, he may be
every thing you want him to be, but you just let

him neglect to pay his debts and there is n't any body in this town will have any respect for him. Is n't that true? And we must reach the point where we see that the strength of the Christian is in the earnest, persistent discharge of every duty that God enjoins upon us.

Neglect! Neglect to pray; neglect to read the Bible; neglect to walk uprightly before God; neglect any Christian duty—the man who does it, does it at the cost of his soul. The spirit of neglect! Now if you take a man who has prayed night and morning in his family, just get him to leave it off at night, say for instance, or leave it off in the morning, for instance; and just let him to neglect it a time or two, and you know that the next thing that will happen is that he will quit it altogether. Just let a fellow neglect his prayer-meeting two or three times, and he gets so he won't want to go at all. Just let a man neglect to read his Bible for a few days, and he 'll get so he won't want to look at his Bible at all. O, the spirit of neglect! It has cost millions of souls!

Neglect! And every time Christ prefigured judgment, the fellow that was condemned was condemned for neglect—every one of them—and in no instance was one condemned for what he had done, but condemned for what he had not done.

Neglect! You let a man begin to neglect his business—it goes right down. Let a man begin to neglect his religion—it goes right down. Let the member of a Church begin to neglect prayer-meeting, he goes right down to zero. Let the member of the Church begin to neglect to pay the preacher, and the first thing you know he's a pauper. Do n't you see how the thing goes? And I tell you all, in every part and department of religious life, aggressiveness and fidelity is found in the fact that we do not leave any gaps down, but put them all up.

Neglect! Well, then, I will watch not only the spirit of neglect that might take possession of me, but I will watch my tongue. O, me! these tongues of ours give us more trouble than any thing and every thing else in the world! It is n't what we do, but it's what we say that keeps us in trouble every time. It's what we say. I will watch my tongue. I declare sometimes I almost wish I had n't any tongue. O, me! if we just had some way of regulating every word we utter, as a President can recall some minister or some consul that he had sent off somewhere—O, what a grand thing that would be! Brethren, I'd spend the next ten years in recalling—I think I would—I'd be busy at it, I'd be busy; and the only way I can do now is to watch my tongue. And I declare to you, if a man opens his door his dog runs out in the street before he knows it. It is astonishing how many things will come up, and come when he least expects it, upon his tongue.

I will watch my tongue. I will watch my temper. The noun "temper," is not in the Bible at all. The verb "to temper," is in the Bible. Do you know where we get that idea of the word "temper?" We get it from the blacksmith's shop, where the blacksmith, for instance, is shaping an ax and upsetting the blade of it; he heats the blade again and pushes it down into the water, and, taking it out, he watches it take its color, and again he pushes it into the water and takes it out and watches it takes it color, and then directly he passes it to the hand of the farmer and says: "I think that is tempered, but I do n't know. If you will grind it and take it out to that knotty pine log and throw it in a time or two I will be able to tell you whether it is tempered or not." And the farmer takes up the ax, and goes out to the knotty pine log and strikes it a time or two, and it is full of notches, and the edge all turned and gone. He takes it back to the blacksmith and says: "You missed it this time; look here, it is notched all over with gaps." And the blacksmith takes it and puts it in the fire again and tests it, and when the owner takes it out to the log, its edge is all right and he says: "This edge is perfect." That is where we get our idea of temper.

Many a time we have had our dispositions in the shop, and we have upset them and we have tempered them, and now we say, " Well, now, I never will get that way any more; I have got the edge all right this time; I got it tempered up in every respect," and the first old knotty log we get to, away it goes and the notches are all broke out and the edge is turned off, and we say, "La, me, it 's of no use for me to try at all; I did worse this time than I ever did before." Have n't you ever felt that? O, this temper of ours! A good temper will stand any thing without the breaking out of a gap or the turning of the edge.

There is a great difference between good nature and good temper. I have heard people say, "O, that person has less temper than any body I ever saw." Well, he is of less account than any body you ever saw, if you mean by that he is simply good-natured. I tell you it takes a man with immense temper, and when that temper is of the right sort, then it is you've got the finest character this world ever saw. I heard a lady say about a cook once, "That is the best-natured, kindest, cleverest, best girl in this world, and the only thing I have against her is, she is of no account in the world, that you ever saw." That's the only thing she has against her, "She is no account in the world, that you ever saw."

I like temper, but I want it to be on the edge right, and I want to be sure that that temper is managed right, and we can only have good tempers with vigilant, watchful care over them. The best way I ever managed my temper was to clinch my teeth together and not let my tongue run a bit. Your tongue is a sort of a revolving fan to the fire, and the first time you let your tongue go, you are gone. Did you ever try to clinch your teeth this way together and try to keep a padlock on your tongue when you felt as if you were going to get mad? Did you ever try to sit down on your tongue once? If you'll do it, you'll be astonished.

I will watch my temper, I will watch my tongue, I will watch my disposition, I will watch within, I will watch without, I will be vigilant, I won't be surprised by any thing. I am going to see my enemy approach, I am going to watch him as he comes, and I am going to meet him as he comes.

I thought after I was converted and went to preaching, that it was a man's duty to defend himself, and a man has to get mad always to do that; and I recollect a time or two when I got what I thought to be an insult, and there was a personal fracas. Well, the last one I had I got into the fuss all over, and it seemed as if the Lord had about turned me loose for good, and I just said: "Good Lord, if you take me back I tell you what I'll do; I will never get mad with any man on the face of the earth until he treats me worse than I have treated you." Well, sir, I have been now at it eleven years since I had the difficulty, and I never found a man yet that treated me worse than I treated the Lord, and until I do I am going to stay in a good humor with humanity. That is my doctrine. So I often think of the incident where Talmage went to the father of a boy and said: "My brother, your son "—a little boy about ten years old—"wants to join my Church. What do you say?" "O, no," said the father, "he does n't want it; he is too young; he does n't know what he is doing." After a while he consented, and Talmage told him that he had joined the Church. About three months after that the father met Talmage, and he said: "There, Dr. Talmage, I told you that my little boy ought not to have joined the Church." "Why?" said Dr. Talmage. "Why," he said, "no later than yesterday I caught him in a point-blank lie." "You did?" "Yes." "How old were you when you joined the Church?" He said: "I didn't join the Church until I was a grown man." "Well," he asked, "how many lies have you told since you joined the Church?" "Well," he said, "that's a gray horse of another color. I never thought about that. That makes quite a difference, doesn't it."

I will watch and watch in all directions, and see to it every day of my life that I watch the approaches of every enemy, and I'll fight them as they come.

Well, when St. Paul tells me to manifest always and possess always this watchful, vigilant spirit, then he says, "Endure afflictions." It is one thing to do the will of God and it is quite another thing to suffer the will of God. Almost any body is willing to be a hammer and strike for God, but very few people are willing to be an anvil and be struck for God. And there is quite a difference between the two. Almost any body is willing to go out and knock any body else down for God, but are you willing to be knocked down for God? That is the question.

I think one of the most impressive things I ever heard was of a young man belonging to the Young Men's Christian Association who was standing out on the sidewalk in a city, handing dodgers to folks out in the street, and pointing up to the room where they were going to hold the service. A gentleman who walked along with the crowd saw this young man hand a dodger to a fellow, and the man peeled away with his fist and had like to have knocked him down on the sidewalk, but the young

man regained his foothold and was ready with a
dodger as another came along. Directly another one
slapped him in the face as he gave him a dodger,
and the gentleman became interested in watching
how he took it; and he said he staid there, and, in a
few minutes, he put a dodger into a man's hand, and
the man caught him and mashed him right down on
the ground, and tore one of his coat-sleeves off, and
bruised him up generally. But he got up and had
another dodger ready for the next man that came
along. And the stranger went up in the room and
heard a young man talk, and he said, "Gentlemen,
I never heard a sermon in my life yet that impressed me, but I stood out here before your door
and saw how the roughs mistreated that young man
over there, and I saw the spirit in which he accepted it, and I walked in here to your meeting, and I want the very same spirit that made that
boy take all that in the spirit which he did."

Ah, brethren, "Endure affliction." It is the
hardest thing in the world to do so. Humanity
wants to fight back and kick back and talk back.
I have felt that a thousand times, and I never
fought back or kicked back or talked back in my
life that I was not sorry that I did it. The best
thing is to stand and hold out and let your enemy
kick himself to death, and he will soon do that
if you will hold right still. A soldier in the last
war said: "One of the hardest things I had to do
was to lie still under fire." And this affliction here
is nothing but the bearing and pressure and weight
of the "tribulum." That tribulum we get from the

old threshing-floor where the wheat was spread out
in the straw on the floor, and where a man got a
big long hickory pole and shaved it down thin in
the middle so it would have a spring to it, and he
came down on the wheat and beat away there by
the hour; and that was the "tribulum" coming
down on the wheat. Do you know what he was
up to? He was getting the wheat separated from
the straw and chaff. The tribulum is the weight,
you see, and when God comes down hard with the
tribulum he is just beating the wheat out of the
straw and chaff, and the great astonishment to me
is that the Lord will beat away so hard and so long
to get as little wheat as there is in us. And God
is obliged to be patient and, with tender mercy,
to beat sixty years on some of us and never get
more than half a peck of wheat after sixty years.

"Endure affliction." That is it. Bear whatever is sent upon you; and I will tell you there is
nothing like affliction. Many a time a man has
grown careless and godless and worldly in the
Church, and the Lord has tried every fair means to
touch him and move him. And there is a man now.
The doctor says: "I am sure it is typhoid fever,"
and on the fifteenth day he says to his wife: "His
case is getting a little doubtful." On the twentieth
day the doctor says: "You may prepare for the
worst." He hears the whispering—he is lying there
on his bed, and the old clock ticking so loud there
on the mantel—he hears the doctor talking to his
wife just outside of the room door, and he can see
his wife's lip quiver and see her wipe the tear from

her eye, and he heard the doctor say: "You can prepare for the worst." The twenty-first morning the doctor says, "He is a shade better, the crisis is come, he is turning, there is a chance for him."

The thirty-fifth day he is sitting up in a big old arm-rocker, with his dressing coat on, and his wife gone out of the room, and the children gone out of the room, and he says: "Well, thank God, I am up one more time in this world;" and he gets up and walks to the door by the help of the chair that he drags along with him; he turns the key and locks it, and he walks back and he kneels down between the arms of that old chair and he says: "Thank God; I am well one more time, getting well. He has spared my life, and now, God, on my knees I promise you, I am going to make a better member of the Church and a better father and a better husband than I have ever made." And he gets up off his knees and God blesses him, and he claps his hands and says: "Glory to God! He is so good to me." God had to take that fellow and put him on a forty days' case of typhoid fever to get him where he could bless him. Don't you see?

O, how much goodness in the Lord! He won't let us be lost until he has done his very best on us. I tell you, take almost any fellow and take him over a coffin a time or two and turn him loose and he will hit the ground running every time. He will do better.

"Endure affliction." Sometimes it doesn't last very long. I recollect a case down in my town where I was pastor. I worked on a fellow all during the meeting, couldn't do any thing with him, but he was taken down with bilious fever and he got to death's door. They thought he was gone. And, O, what promises he made that he would do better if he got well. And two or three weeks after he got better I said: "Brother B——, how are you getting along?" He said: "I am getting better all the time." "Well," I said, "how about your soul?" "Well," he says, "I'm afraid that isn't doing much better." "Didn't you promise the Lord that you would do better if you got well?" "Yes," he said, "Mr. Jones, I did, but I tell you a fellow is going to promise 'most any thing when he gets down as far as I did." "Endure affliction." Whatever is sent upon you bear without a word, for I declare to you there is nothing like patience under affliction. When the Lord's providence touches us, let us not fight, but lean up against God's arms, and perhaps he will lay the rod down and won't strike a lick. The best way to fight God is to run up to God. I found out when I was twelve years old that when my father wanted to lick me, the closer I got to him the better. I found that out.

St. Paul next says, "Do the work of an evangelist." Now you say, "That just had reference to Timothy; that does not have a reference to us at all." Do you know that God intends in the salvation of every soul that you should be propagandists yourselves? Did you ever think of that? The trouble is, you have turned the world over to us preachers, and you have turned it over to a sorry set, and we are not half running it, God knows. But I reckon we do the best we can with the material on hand. There is some hickory the Lord himself could not make an ax-handle out of unless he makes the hickory over again.

We preachers have had charge of the Churches and the salvation of this world now, in a sense, for eighteen hundred years, and we have just gotten one man in every twenty-eight to profess to be a Christian, and only about one in those twenty-eight is one when you weigh him up right. We are making big headway, ain't we? We preachers are good clever men and do the best we can, but God never intended that the world should be handed over to us. He intends that every converted man shall be a preacher in a sense, going out and doing work as an evangelist. Suppose that every member of the Church should this January say: "God helping me, I will win one soul during this year for Christ." Then the membership next January will be double if that promise is observed. And if the promise were renewed then, on the succeeding January the membership will be four times as many. And on and on and on and in this way, before your heads grow gray all over this Church could turn this whole city to Christ. That is geometrical progression, and God is going to convert this world just that way. Listen! When one-half of the world is converted to God and that half says: "One soul apiece to-morrow for Christ," and all go out and bring one soul to Christ, then every body is converted and a nation is born to God in a day! You see how it works?

One soul a year! It does look as if every Christian ought to win one soul a year, or go out of the business. If I could not do that I would just quit in utter despair, I would. And I want to say to you all to-night just this: Just a few years ago, down in Georgia, God stooped down and touched my poor, ruined, wilted, blasted soul and called it back to life. I started out the weakest, frailest thing, and I declare that when I went to Atlanta to join the conference I had no idea they would take me. I could not see how they would take such a fellow as I was and put him to work; and when they put me on a circuit I was the happiest man you ever saw; and when I got nearly home—I had not thought about what the thing would pay—a man stepped up and said: " Jones, that circuit they have sent you on never paid but $65 a year to its preacher." I listened, but that statement did not bother me a bit. I was happy that I had a place to go to work in. I commenced preaching six or seven or eight times a week, preaching and meeting in private houses, schools and Churches, working as hard as I could and working right on. I started out to do my duty toward God and man, and the three years I spent in that work were the happiest three years, it seems now, of all my life. And God saw to it that we had three square meals a day and respectable clothes, and that is as much as you have. Do you have any more? If you do, where do you put it? Some of you put it in the bank; some in railroad stock. Yes!

I do not reckon there has been a mind in this

century that has been under higher pressure than
William H. Vanderbilt. There were many things
about that man I honor—many things about his life
I would have the business men of this world emu-
late. I will say this much about him: the last evening, when he dropped out of his chair and fell to
the floor, when the railroad president was talking to
him—when he sat in that chair he was the richest
man in America; when he fell on that floor he was
as poor as I am. When I leave this world I want
my friends to say, " I am glad there is a good man
gone to heaven." When Vanderbilt died every
body wanted to know, " How will it affect the Stock
Exchange?" That seemed to be the only question
in New York City, " How will it affect the Stock
Exchange?" They did not seem to care much
about the man. They did not seem to have much
to say about his funeral. The whole thing rested
as on a pivot on that one question: " How will his
death affect the stock market?"

Now, sir, as God is my judge, all along through
my religious life, the one burning desire of my soul
has been to see others brought to Christ. I have
worked on and on and on, and I tell you, the happiest
moments of my life have been the moments when I
have seen men's souls given to Christ. The one
earnest prayer of my life has been, " God help me
to help souls to Christ." Brothers, how do you
feel about that? I may gather together a fortune,
but it may curse my children; but if I gather souls
to Christ, how grand that is.

This recalls the dream of a young lady—I

do not go much on dreams, but there was something impressive about this one. A young lady dreamed that she died and went to heaven. As she stood around the great white throne she saw that every one there had on a beautiful crown, and that beautiful stars decked each crown. She approached a sister spirit and said, "What do these stars represent in these crowns?" The sister spirit replied, "These stars represent the souls we have been instrumental in saving," and she said, "I thought I reached up and pulled off my crown and it was blank, and I began to be miserable in heaven. And all at once I awoke and praised God that I was still out of heaven, and I said, 'I will spend the rest of my days in winning stars for my crown of rejoicing in the sweet by and by.'"

How many of us here to-night if we should die now and go to heaven would wear a starless crown forever? May God help me as I journey through life to gather souls to God, that they may be stars — not in my crown, but, blessed be God, I would put them all in my Master's crown, and say to him: "You are worthy of them. You shed your blood and died that they might be redeemed."

Lastly St. Paul said: "Make full proof of thy ministry." I do love to see a soul go and work in earnest for Christ and work on until the work is completed, and then shout over the results. That is just what this means. I will illustrate this. I can get through quicker in that way. I had once in my charge, when I was a pastor, a precious good wife and mother. Fourteen years before that she married a young man, sober and industrious; but after their marriage he commenced associating with drinking men. He soon began to drink himself, and he led a very dissipated life for several years, and finally he was taken home with delirium tremens. One morning two doctors came and examined him, and they called his wife aside and said: "Madam, your husband will die to-day." She looked at the doctor and said, "No, he won't die to-day." "Well," they said, "madam, these symptoms that are on him never fail. He will die." "No," she said, "doctor, he won't die." "How do you know?" they asked. She said, "I have been praying for fourteen years to God to convert that man and save him before he dies. And," she said, "I have prayed earnestly and with faith, and I know he is not going to die. I do not care a cent about your symptoms." That evening the doctors came back and examined her husband, and said he was better. She said, "I have not been uneasy about him. I knew God had not converted him, and I knew God would not let him die until he was converted. If he were to die in the condition he is in, I would be an infidel. I could never have believed that God hears and answers prayer. I have been praying for his conversion for fourteen years, and I knew God would not let him die before he was converted."

. The man got better and he was converted, and he led a pure, good life for two years, and then, under some fearful temptation, he fell and began drinking again. She went back to God and prayed:

"Good Lord, save my poor husband at any cost. I will work my hands off to support my seven children. My God, save my poor husband. I do not care what becomes of us."

Two or three months afterward her husband was taken with articular rheumatism, the most fearful kind of rheumatism that ever afflicted humanity. There he suffered day after day, and he turned his heart again to God. He was the most meek and patient sufferer you ever saw, just trusting in God every moment. One morning when his wife was standing by he said: "Good-bye, precious wife. The moments are coming when I shall leave you, and when I shall leave you—and I owe it all to you and Christ—I shall go to heaven and pass into the joys of the blessed."

She stood over him until his last breath had gone, and his face was placid and calm in death. As soon as she saw sure enough that he had gone into eternity, she clasped her hands and cried: "Glory to God, he is saved! Now I will work my hands off to support my children." And that woman to-day is a precious Christian mother of seven children, and she is training them for a better life.

Mothers and sisters, when you get in earnest you will see this world with all its glitter and fearful influences. Now let us say: "I am going to pray for some persons and will never stop until they are converted." Will you do that and interest yourselves in souls around us? O, that every one in this meeting would save a soul for Christ!

Sermon XIV.

"And it came to pass when they had brought them forth abroad, that he said, Escape for thy life; look not behind thee, neither stay thou in all the plain; escape to the mountain lest thou be consumed."—GEN. XIX, 17.

I HAVE but three questions that I would propound to any man as he stands up preaching righteousness to me. The first question I would ask any minister of the Gospel is this: " Are you posted upon the subject which you are discussing? Do you know what you are talking about?" And when this question is satisfactorily answered, I will put a second one to him: " Do you mean kindly toward me?" And then I have but one more to ask, and that is: " Do you live what you preach?" With these three questions answered in the affirmative, I throw open the doors of my heart and conscience to any man who will so answer them.

We have selected as the text for this evening the four words of the seventeenth verse of the nineteenth chapter of the Book of Genesis: " Escape for thy life."

There is implanted in the bosom of every man an instinctive love of life; and also implanted by the hand of God in this same bosom, the fear of death. We all love life; we all fear death. There's only one thing in the universe that's stronger than my love of life and my dread of death,

279

and that's despair, and suicide is the last retreat for despair. I needn't stop here to argue the proposition that men love life and dread death. The thousands and the millions of dollars that are spent yearly for physicians, and remedies and patent medicines and mineral springs, and the sanitary features of your cities and your towns, is practical proof that I assert the truth.

I might stop here long enough to say that there are certain physical substances that we know perpetuate life; and that there are certain physical substances which produce death. There is such a thing as wholesome food for the physical man, and there is such a thing as poison—one perpetuates life, physical life, and the other produces death. These are plain propositions we all understand.

Man in his very nature is a trinity in unity; he has a physical being, an intellectual being, and an immortal or spiritual being. Just as it is true, therefore, that certain physical substances, wholesome in their nature, tend to perpetuate life, and certain poisons will produce physical death, just so certain is it, also, that there are certain lines of moral conduct that tend to perpetuate moral life, and certain lines of immoral conduct that produce moral death. If one is true the other's true. Cincinnati, with all her boasted financial standing, with all her intelligence, and with all her art, presents the picture every day to your eyes that sin is debauching and dooming and damning your people. I have but to walk out on your streets with my eyes open, and with my ears open, and I can see that thousands of people are lost, whether there's any death or hell, or not. They are lost to all that is good, and all that is pure, and all that is noble, and all that is true.

Brother, when a man is lost to the true and the beautiful and the good, what deeper, darker hell would you have than that? The exhortation of this text is, "Escape for thy life." The signification that is put on this text is that we should look at the power behind an exhortation like this. All that is beautiful and glorious in heaven on the one side, and all that is unutterable on earth and inexpressible in hell is just behind this exhortation, "Escape for thy life."

Sin is the one thing in this universe that can permanently damage a man, and eternally damn him. Disappointment may worry him, and grief may sadden him, and adversity may bring hardship and hunger to his life, but, blessed be God, sin is the only thing in the universe that can leave its permanent mark on character, a mark which shall last forever.

We shall take the moral law, and we shall take the Ten Commandments as the basis, largely, in this discussion. I am ready to say here this evening that I believe God wrote the Ten Commandments on the tablets of stone, though the infidel may say that Moses wrote them, or that Hume, the historian, wrote them; but I care not who wrote them; the citizen in this State that does not live on a level with the Ten Commandments deserves to be in the penitentiary.

"The transgression of the law!" There can be
no good citizenship where the Ten Commandments
are infracted. There can be no such thing as safe
political movement or social reform unless it is bottomed on the Ten Commandments. I stand on
these Ten Commandments, brethren, and when this
world burns to ashes I shall have a foundation as
enduring as the God that made me.

I will, however, discuss this in a practical way,
and stand squarely on the Bible principle and on
the God side of the questions. If you see this
matter differently from what I do, it will be because
you occupy a different standpoint. If you come up
where I stand you will see it as I do. If I go
down where you are I will see it as you see it, but
I'm afraid to go down there any more. I'm afraid
I might die there, and be lost forever.

I. We will take up first the sin most commonly
practiced among men, and that is *the sin of profanity.*
O, what a fearful sin, in all its aggravated guilt and
its general use in this land, is this sin of profanity.
Old men swear, and young men swear, and women
swear and children swear, and we're almost a nation
of swearers to-day as we walk up and down the
land. I want to show you what a profane swearer
is. I want to locate him; I want to tree him this
evening, and twist him out of his hole and let you
see him as God and his angels see him.

The sin of profanity! I read in these Ten
Commandments this: "Thou shalt not take the
name of the Lord thy God in vain, for the Lord
will not hold him guiltless that taketh his name in

vain." "Let your communication be Yea, yea, Nay, nay; for whatsoever is more than these cometh of evil." I will read you another of the commandments, "Thou shalt not steal." Here are two commandments, "Thou shalt not take the name of the Lord thy God in vain," and "Thou shalt not steal." You will break this first commandment, but you won't break this second one. You'll swear, but you won't steal. Why? Suppose I say that a man who will steal will lie and get drunk and curse. Well, you say, "That's a fact." Let us comment on this thing: A man who will swear will lie and get drunk and steal. "But," you say, "you mustn't go back that way. You may come this way as much as you please, but if you go back that way you'll get a fuss on your hands." Well, brethren, I've often heard it said: "It's a poor rule that won't work both ways." Let's run that down a little further.

There's a man sitting out there that will lie, but he won't steal. He will blaspheme the name of God and smut his lips with other utterances, and stilt himself upon his "honor," and yet that same fellow would curse the virtue of the purest girl in this city to-night if he thought he could do it without being overtaken in his guilt. There's many a man in this country stilting himself upon his honor. There are two commandments he will break, and one he won't break over. I have logic, I have human life squarely on my side when I say that when a man that has a condition of the heart and life that will let him persistently break one commandment, all you 've got to do is to turn him loose and he 'll break them all.

"Thou shalt not swear and steal." God said both with all the power of his nature. That man says: "I swear, but I won't steal." Why? "I can swear all around." Thou shalt not swear. "That 's nothing in my way." Thou shalt not steal. A fellow does n't go around that much before he strikes the sheriff and the judge and the jail. Do n't you see? Is it because you are afraid that the sheriff and the judge and the jail are round there? I want you to see this—that 's all! I assert it, with all the sincerity of my nature, that a man who will break one commandment habitually and persistently, if you 'll make every thing else even, he 'll break them all. He does n't care about God.

I made this proposition one day: "I want every fellow who went into the rebel army cursing, and did n't steal any thing, to stand up." Directly a fellow stood up over in the corner, and I said: "They must have kept things out of your reach, old fellow." That old fellow told a lie, or they kept things mighty close—one thing or the other. You take one of these swearing men at home and put him in the army and he will go out and steal a bee-gum and then he 'll steal a sheep and stay with a lewd woman all night and disgrace himself before God and men and angels. I tell you, brother, that sin in its fearful influence permeates our system, and when the cancer breaks out on your tongue it is in your blood from head to foot. If you stop cursing and put a salve on your tongue it will break out on your hand, and you'll steal something. It's in you, and you've got to get it out.

Profanity! How much there is of it in this land! A mother sends her little boy down street to get a spool of thread, and the little fellow walks three blocks, and O! he can't get back to his innocent mother until some wretch has sowed his little heart full of the seed of profanity!

O! how much profanity curses this State and this country! I often think of the grandmother of little Willie, who was on the train which stopped for a few minutes for some cause, and the two gentlemen who were carrying on their conversation, swore and swore awfully, and the grandmother jabbed the ends of her fingers into the ears of little Willie and compressed them tight, so that Willie would not hear their awful profanity. Willie sat still for a little while and then he shook his head and moved about, and he was so restless he would not let his grandmother hold her fingers in his ears; so she rushed up the aisle and said to the two swearers: "Gentlemen, my little Willie won't let me hold my thumbs in his ears, and I wouldn't have him hear this awful talk for the world; it's the height of impudence, and shows how you were raised, by sitting among strangers and pouring out your profanity in the ears of people." I could travel in perfect peace but for this one thing! These railroads have got up their sleeping-cars and their mail and baggage and express-cars, and they just lack one more car. I want them to put on a cursing-car for black-mouthed travelers.

Profanity! Profanity! I recollect on the streets
of my own town, when I was a boy, we were all
standing on the corner, and the minister passed by
just as I swore. He laid his hand on my shoulder
and said: "Young man, don't curse that man. It
is just like holding a coal of fire in your hand and
squeezing your fingers on it and saying 'Coal of
fire, burn some one else.'" I always thought of
that afterwards, that it was "Coal of fire, burn some
one else." That fearful, excuseless sin—profanity!
When the devil wants to catch a good man he baits
his hook and covers it up, and then they don't bite,
but when he wants to catch a profane swearer, he
throws in the naked hook, and says, "Fool, gobble
it down," and the fool gobbles it down.

Profanity! What does it pay you? Nobody
thinks any more of you because you swear. It
doesn't help you in business. It doesn't make
any body think any more of you; it doesn't make
your wife think any more of you. If you are a
professed swearer and user of profanity, you just
lack that much of being a gentleman, I don't care
what else you may be.

This excuseless and useless profanity! Boys,
let's assert our manhood, and our sense of justice
and the good that's in us, and let's say this afternoon, "I have sworn my last oath. Whatever else
I may be doomed for, I won't curse my way to
hell." Boys, let's quit this profanity. There's no
manhood in it. There's no beauty in it. There's
no business in it.

I heard a drummer say once that he went out

on the road with another drummer, who had different samples and was in a different line of business. Said he: "At every town I sold goods this man did n't sell any. At last, after he had failed to make a trade at a store I went to, when he walked out the proprietor said, 'Who is that man?' I told him. 'Well,' said he, 'you can just tell every drummer on the road that none of these cursing, blackguard fellows need come about my store to sell goods; I'll quit the business before I buy any goods from one of them.' The other drummer asked me, 'What's the matter?' Said I, 'It's not your firm, or your samples, but it's you. That man told me he would n't buy from a profane drummer.' The drummer said to this, 'If that's so, I'll quit now.' And he went on his way and sold afterwards as many goods as any other drummer on the road."

Escape profanity. It will degrade you here, and damn you hereafter. Escape profanity. Men, let's say to-day, from the depths of our heart, "I'll never swear again. Whatever else I may be guilty of I'm done with profanity forever."

II. How much *Sabbath-breaking* is done in this country! I want to locate you all for yourselves. I'll give you the worst Sabbath-breaking places in the country, one by one: San Francisco, first; New Orleans, Cincinnati, Chicago, St. Louis. That's their order. Bad order, too. San Francisco, first; New Orleans—the very cess-pool of hell itself, second; Cincinnati, third. I'll tell you another thing. With your theaters turned loose, with your bar-rooms turned loose, and your places of amusement turned loose on the Sabbath, and your base ball on the Sabbath, let me tell you, you're putting the red flag on the track. You put a red flag down on the track of that Cincinnati Southern Railroad, and when the engineer comes thundering around the curve and sees the flag two hundred yards in front of him, he reverses his engine, shuts the throttle dead tight, claps the air brakes on every wheel, and he'll burst that boiler into ten thousand pieces before he'd run up to within less than one hundred yards of that red flag. That flag means death and destruction to him and to all the passengers on the train behind him. I tell you when you people come sweeping around the curve of Sabbath-breaking and desecration, and instead of your city officers upholding the law they were appointed to uphold, they are defying the law; you may see the red flag down the track, and you'll have to reverse engine and down brakes or you're lost.

I'll tell you when the crackling flames and the dense smoke of your burning court-house lit up the sky on that terrible night of the riot, God ran up the red flag and said, "Call a halt." You'll never have law and order and safety and good government in this city until the strong arm of the law is upheld, and every violator of the law shall suffer the penalty, be he a millionaire or be he the poorest foreigner in the city. You can see it in the air. We're nearing a reform. The theater men say, "We're done Sabbath breaking." Brethren, hear me on this: The fact that these men have desecrated God's day, and have kept it up as long as it would pay, and until the Law and Order League brought them to taw—the transgressions connected with their past doings blot out all the glory that they would have if they should be decent in the future.

I tell you all, in God's name, this afternoon, forget not the commandment " Remember the Sabbath day to keep it holy." May the Lord redeem this city from Sabbath-breaking. As an American I thank God for every foreigner that comes to this country, who is a law-abiding citizen. I thank God for every single foreigner in America that is a representative of law and order and righteousness; but I deplore the fact that any country or government is emptying upon us men who desecrate the law of God and the law of man, and bring anarchy into our midst.

Let me tell you: If all the sins and iniquity committed in Cincinnati on Sabbath were reproduced in Atlanta the next Sabbath the whole concern would sleep in jail that night. In Georgia we have a God and a Sabbath, and they're as sacred to us as our wives and our children. Men break the Sabbath in groups and sections, and they all join in trying to wipe it off the face of the earth. If you'll find me a man that keeps the Sabbath holy, I will show you a man who will keep every other day in the week holy. Show me a man who will desecrate the Sabbath, and I'll show you a man who'll desecrate every other day in the week. This is as true as that I'm talking to you this evening.

25

May the Lord multiply the number of Sunday-keepers, and give us no other sort in this city.

III. *Gambling!* O, how much gambling there is in this country! From the Louisiana State Lottery up, I commence at the bottom, they are gambling! gambling! Let me tell you gamblers: The young man that wins at Louisiana State Lottery $10,000, has lost his soul, and lost his character ninety-nine times out of a hundred. If I ever have a boy that's fool enough to buck against the Louisiana Lottery, I want him to lose every dollar that he puts in. It will be better for him in the long run.

The truth of the business is that a good, honest plowboy, who plows furrows in the field for $1 a week, is better than one of these fast young men in this city that gets his money questionably, to say the least! When the plowboy gets his dollar at the end of his week's work he goes home at night and to his room, and when he slips off his pants he puts them under his pillow, and the eagle on that dollar sings like a nightingale, and lulls him to sleep. I like an honest dollar. They're the only dollars in this universe that will do a man and his family any good.

Louisiana State Lottery, gambling at cards and speculating in "futures!" I tell you these men who are called dealers in "futures" call it that to keep themselves from being regular blacklegs. I like the old greasy-deck plan the best. It is the more honest, for there you put up money on one side and then on the other, and things are in sight there with a vengeance! No "bull" and "bear" business about that. These little Church fairs with their little gambling schemes will never reform this country, and many of these things have set an example that has studded this country with gambling schemes and other dishonest transactions. Let's wash our hands and be honest if we starve to death! Let's earn our bread by the sweat of our brow!

IV. The *club-house* in this city is the place where you train many a fellow for the black-leg stable. Club-houses! I pushed it on to these club fellows in St. Louis, and they got after me and said, "Jones, you'll have to let up on this business." I said, "Come down to-night; I'm going to let down on you fellows with a vengeance!" There isn't a social club in this city but what has every thing in it that a good man will eat, and every thing in it that a bad man will drink. They have bar-rooms and card-rooms and billiard rooms, and there is nothing in God's universe that ever damned as many people as these three things. There's no logic in heaven or hell or on earth that a man can defend a club with! I feel sorry for a man when he joins a club. I do that! If you do make an impression on one of these club fellows, they ridicule him at the club, and they ridicule him out of it. You may call me narrow-minded and bigoted on these things, brethren, but the day will come when you will stand up like a man and say: "Jones, you're right on that!"

The difference between the club bar-rooms and the other bar-rooms is that the latter are for the

vagabondish drinkers. The club bar-rooms are behind the scenes a little, but they'll soon make vagabonds out of their customers. They teach a fellow
to drink and gamble, and then when he's learned
these things too well they kick him out. The
meanest thing in the world is first to damn and
ruin a fellow and then kick him out. You've done
that too. There are many of our Christian homes
in this city that are but gambling-houses, where
the children are trained to play cards. God pity
the man that can't run his house without a pack of
cards!

V. *Licentiousness!* This is a world of licentiousness all around us. A man in a certain town
said to me, "Jones, there isn't a pure boy living in
our city." I said, I'm sorry. If one-half of our
society is corrupt, O, then, when will the tidal wave
of licentiousness begin to sweep over the other half
of society? If our boys are all impure, when will
this wild beast crush our daughters' virtue, and our
mothers be no longer pure? God let my sweet
children with their precious mother sleep in their
graves before such a day ever comes to the United
States of America.

Licentiousness! As I look at this flood tide of
uncleanliness sweeping over our country, O, what a
harvest awaits us in the future! Look at our
asylums, our hospitals! They're full of the fruits
of licentiousness; and hear me, young man, that
unholy alliance you have formed, the fruits of that
alliance may be an innocent child born to you in
licentiousness, and recollect, as the basest woman in

Cincinnati bears that innocent child in her arms, that it's your mother's grandchild and your sister's niece.

Licentiousness! Young man, hear me on this point. I want you to determine to say: "Whatever we are, God help us to be pure. I will take no liberties with any woman that God lets me lay my eyes upon any more than I would not have another man take with my wife, my mother, or my sister."

The doctors of this country have said to many a young man: "You can't be virtuous and be healthy." Is there a doctor here that ever said that to a young man? If there is I want to look him in the face and tell him "You are a liar of the deepest dye." My daughter, your daughter, has the same nature and the same constitution as your boy, and I dare you by all the power in the Bible to walk up to my daughter and tell her she can not be virtuous and be healthy!

Boys, let's be clean. Let's shun this licentious river that is sweeping so many to death and degradation and hell!

VI. *Intemperance.* I am expected to take sides everywhere on this moral question, and he who would confine the matter of whisky to politics is a fool or a rascal. It is not a political question any more than "Thou shalt not steal" is a political question. It is a question of morals and belongs to the Ten Commandments. In Georgia you slip up to the ear of the great God and ask him which side he is on, and then put me down on the side with

God. When you have asked him, then slip up to the side of the suffering Nazarene that gave his blood and all for the amelioration of the race and for the salvation of men, and say, "Which side are you on?" and you need n't come back to me and ask me what side I am on, but just put me down on his side.

Go to the grave of the best wife, the cruelty of whose drunken husband broke her heart, and ask that wife, "Which side are you on?" and then put me by the side of that precious wife. Then dig open that little grave, three feet long, by the mother's side, and ask the little angel, "What side are you on?" and then put me on the side of the child. If I am with God and the angels, and good women and children, blessed be God, then I am on the right side.

Blessed be God for the privilege of taking sides on moral questions! I ain't a politician, and you could n't run after me fast enough to give me the presidency of the United States. I ask no higher honor than to preach righteousness and truth to the children of men.

Let's us quit drinking, boys! A dram cup in my hand broke my father's heart! Quit drinking, boys! It'll drive the unhealthy roses from your cheeks, and they'll never come back again! Quit drinking, boys!

SERMON XV.

"WHAT I HAVE WRITTEN, I HAVE WRITTEN."

"What I have written, I have written."—JOHN XIX, 22.

NOW, brethren, let us all be prayerful. Let every man that believes God hears and answers prayer, lift his heart continually in prayer to God while I try to preach in the name of my Master. I want to read to you three or four verses in different parts of this book—the Bible. Let us give especial attention to them, because they have much to do with the discussion that follows: "Rejoice, O, young man, in thy youth; let thy heart cheer thee in the days of thy youth, and walk in the ways of thine heart and in the sight of thine eyes; but know thou that for all these things God will bring thee unto judgment." (Ecclesiastes xi, 9.) "Let us hear the conclusion of the whole matter: Fear God and keep his commandments, for this is the whole duty of man." (Ecclesiastes xii, 13.) And then we read: "So then every one of us shall give account of himself to God." (Rom. xiv, 12.) And again we read: "And the books were opened, and another book was opened." (Rev. xx, 12.) And now we come to the text: "What I have written, I have written." (John xix, 22.

There are two "somethings" and one "some

one" that I had to do with yesterday. I have to do with them to-day. I shall have to do with them forever. "Conscience" and "record" are the two somethings and God is the some one. Conscience—Record—God. Conscience and record are like two index fingers pointing right up into the face of God, and God is the great index finger pointing to the final judgment. Conscience is that something running through my life approving the right, disapproving the wrong. Conscience when outraged is that something that will not let me sleep, no matter how soft my pillow. Conscience—that something that will not let me eat, no matter how richly laden the table. Conscience—that something in me that makes me drop my head in guilt and shame before the world. Conscience—where is the man in this audience who never felt the pangs and pains of an outraged conscience? The poet was right when he said:

> "What conscience dictates to be done,
>   Or warns me not to do,
> This teach me more than hell to shun,
>   That more than heaven pursue."

And I am right in saying upon this occasion that the most fearful sin a man ever committed in this life, is to sin directly and to sin persistently against his own conscience. Do you do that thing which conscience says thou oughtest not to do? Do you not do that thing which conscience says thou oughtest to do? Do you persist in the evil when conscience cries: "Stop! hold! murder! murder! don't do it?" Conscience—ah, me, brother! some one has said that an outraged conscience is the worm that shall never die, and the fire that shall never be quenched.

Where is the man that never outraged his conscience; that never did violence to his conscience? I have more admiration for that poor heathen woman who, in answer to the dictates of conscience, drowns her babe in the Ganges as it flows at her feet, than I have for any woman in this building who stabs her conscience. I pray you listen! Heaven is the home of conscience. You have felt its pangs, you felt them yesterday, you feel them to-day, and you may feel them forever.

Record: A man has a record just as a man has a conscience. My record is as much a part of me as my conscience or hand is; my record is as much a part of my immortal being as my hand or arm of my physical being; my record is as inseparable from that body as this arm is inseparable from my physical body. Your record is just as much a part of you as your hand is. You can not separate them. Do what you will, you can not remove them. I was sitting, some years ago, by the side of a soldier that had lost his arm up to the elbow, in the war. As I sat by his side he pulled up his empty sleeve and turned and said, "My, but those fingers burn and itch!" I says, "What fingers?" "Those fingers on my right hand." I said, "You have no right hand." He said, "That is true, but that whole hand and arm is as much on me in feeling, although buried on a battle-field in Virginia, to-day, as it was before I went to battle."

So your record can not be separated from you.

Every man's record is made up to this hour. Now, with the conscience outraged as many are in this house, with a record that condemns me, at every point in life; with the great God and the judgment seat before which I shall appear to give an account of my deeds, whether good or bad, is enough to bring men to their feet and make them see this in the light of eternity. You men who don't believe in hell fire—you men who don't believe in eternal punishment, if you can tell me how long a man's conscience can live and act, how long the record of guilt can live, I will tell you how long hell will endure.

I tell you, my friends, if there is not to be a final judgment when man shall be brought to a final bar to give an account of all the deeds done in the body, if there is to be no judgment hereafter, there are incidents and feelings and aspirations and fears and dreads about my being that can not be explained in time or eternity. Every bad deed of my life, every wayward act of my life, every wicked word of my life, have been so many fingers pointing me ever and anon to the great day in which I shall give an account to God, for the way I have lived, for what I have done, and for what I have said.

If you can tell me how long a lie will live, I will tell you how long eternal punishment for telling a lie will live. If you will tell me how long it takes time and eternity to gather back into nothing the guilt of butchering your neighbor and bring him back to life, I will tell you how long your conscience will be guilty for taking the life blood of your neighbor. I am not troubled about how long conscience may last, but I am troubled how long conscience may lash, for conscience and record go before the great white throne.

An old sheriff down in Georgia, named Zackey, was approached by his pastor one day, who said to him, "Come out and give your heart to God, and prepare for death; you are getting old." Mr. Zackey said, "I am not afraid to die." And he told him the truth. God never made a braver man in this world. There was no danger on earth he would not face in duty. He would walk up to the mouth of a thousand cannon. He never knew what the tremor of physical fear was. He looked up into his pastor's face and said, "I am not afraid to die." "That is true. God never made a braver man than you, but how about the judgment bar of God?" And the old man's lips trembled.

The Judgment, the Judgment. My God, I am afraid of the judgment seat of Christ; may I not be afraid to die! Some people say that the hour of death is the honest hour. That is a mistake. Many a poor fellow has passed out of this world with a smile on his face and gone into eternity to be damned forever. I never ask how a man dies; I care nothing about how he dies; you need not ask how I died, but keep the record of my life, and then if I live right you may know it. If you live right! I do n't want any evidence; I only want his conscience and record right. You men who have rejected ten thousand opportunities, look at your record to-night, take a survey of the field and the conscience in your bosom, looking up to God, and bring yourself so close to the throne that it may do you good.

If this Book teaches any thing, it teaches the final judgment; if you tell me there is no judgment, I declare to you in the life of sin I never look to my sins that all of them do not point their bony fingers toward a final judgment day—a day when each man shall give a final account. If I am to be responsible to any body on a judgment, then there must be a trial—for judgment implies a trial, a trial necessitates a time and place for hearing, and when I speak of judgment I am not talking to you of brimstone, but ten thousand things worse—the idea of being banished from God is a thousand times worse than hell itself, and a record that makes me droop my head for rocks and mountains to hide me from the face of God and the Lamb forever.

Judgment is a forensic term, and means simply the equitable adjustment of an issue, but in an ecclesiastical sense it means the final adjudication in heaven's chancery, when God shall summon men and angels alike around his great white throne and there sift the issue between himself and all created intelligences; and when God once says to you, "Ye cursed," there never shall be an after jurisdiction. The record of my guilt, as the glory of my commendation, will blaze forever in full view of my eyes as my vindication in heaven or my condemnation in hell.

Judgment! Let us strip this subject of all its

mystery. When a man has violated the laws of
this State there are but three ways by which he
can hope to escape. One is by force of law, another
by force of testimony, another by pardon, where the
governor extends his clemency and pardons the
criminal. Now I grant you that justice may be
defeated in many ways. A criminal may violate
the law of the State and fly from justice, and keep
out of the way of sheriffs and officers. He may
bribe the grand jury so that they will not find a
true bill against him. He may bribe the jury or
the judge that tries him, but when a man is once
arraigned before the criminal courts of this country
there are but three ways by which he can hope to
escape justice.

One way is by force of law. When a criminal
is brought into the court-house, and one witness
after another is introduced, and they prove his guilt
beyond reasonable doubt, and when the judge picks
up the Code of the State and says: "This man is
guilty, but the law of the State does not make the
offense a crime," the man is acquitted by force of
law. There is no law that says his conduct is
criminal, therefore he is acquitted.

I might stop here and run off at a tangent, and
say some things that would burn like fire. I understand that the jurors of the courts of Cincinnati
will take a solemn oath on the Bible to render a
verdict according to the law, and go into the jury-
room and perjure themselves, and walk out and say
they don't believe in the law. If you are one of
those men, you are a perjurer—a moral leper—you

swear to execute the laws of the State of Ohio, and try a case under that law, and walk out of your jury-room and say, "We don't believe in the law!" You ought to be in the penitentiary yourself, sir. And if I was the judge on the bench, I would order your arrest, and I would cause the last one of them to be prosecuted for perjury and put in the penitentiary, even the justices as well as the jurors. That is the truth about it.

But if the thing charged in the indictment is a crime, then he may be acquitted by force of testimony. When the jury, after hearing the evidence, say: "There is not sufficient evidence to convict, and we find the prisoner not guilty," then the prisoner is acquitted by force of testimony. But if he is condemned by law, and condemned by testimony, then there is but one hope, and that is the pardon of the governor.

Now, up yonder, before that tribunal, there can be but three ways by which men can hope to escape. You can not dodge God's ministerial officers and keep out of their way. You will come to the judgment! to the judgment! to the judgment! When we leave this room some will go this way, some that way, but every road you take converges right towards the judgment-seat of Christ, and if we never see each other's faces again, we shall meet at the throne of God at last. I can not dodge God's ministerial officers. "Whither shall I go from thy spirit? or whither shall I flee from thy presence? If I ascend up into heaven, thou art there; if I make my bed in hell, behold, thou art there. If I take the wings of the morning, and dwell in the uttermost parts of the sea; even there shall thy hand lead me, and thy right hand shall hold me."

No, sir! God Almighty will burn this world up and bring us to the judgment-seat of Christ. You can not dodge the ministerial officers already on your track. One of God's sheriffs put his hand on your head one day, and since that it has begun to frost. God's sheriff touched your eye one day, and you have been wearing spectacles ever since. God's sheriff touched your leg, and you are now walking with a cane along the streets. Wherever you meet men the touch of God's sheriff is upon them, and that means simply:

I have claimed you for my own!
I will take you by and by.

And then, again, you can not bribe God's grand jury. They have already sat upon your case, and the verdict reads: "The soul that sinneth it shall die, and he that believeth not shall be condemned." I know in this country that a criminal sometimes rushes up and defies the court and its authorities, but can you defy the court of God that sits upon the throne? Shall I rush up in the presence of the great God, who in the beginning held a great flaming mass on the anvil of eternal purpose, and pounded it with his own powerful arm, and when every spark that flew from it made a world—shall I rush up into the presence of such a God as that and defy him? No, sir! Shall I bribe the Judge of all the earth? No, sir! But when I shall be individualized at that final moment, and shall walk out into the presence of that great God, I have but three ways in which I can hope to escape.

One is by force of law. Now, hear me! I shake that little bundle of paper (the Bible) in your face, and if that little bundle of paper is true, it outweighs all this universe. If this book is true, I have in my hand a bundle of paper that does not weigh ten ounces, and yet it outweighs all the stars of the universe. If this little book is true—and we have to die whether it is true or not—you and I must meet God, and give an account of what we have done in the body.

The law of God. I want to say at this point that God will spring no new law upon you up yonder. Men say: "I do not like to read that Bible, it condemns me." If this law condemns you down here to-day, it will condemn you up yonder at the judgment to-morrow. You will be the same man. This will be the same book.

"But," says that man, "I have never violated many laws in that book." Well, listen: "For whosoever shall keep the whole law, and yet offend in one point, he is guilty of all."

How do you understand that? Yonder is a boat chained to a wharf on your levee. That chain has 100 links, but if I want to cut that boat loose, how many links must I cut? Fifty of the biggest links? Ten of the middle-sized ones? No. I need only cut the smallest link, and that boat is as effectually loosened as if I had cut them all. And he that breaks the least is as guilty as if he had broken them all. Suppose I want to go to Kansas

City. There is one right road to that place, and 1,000 leading in other directions. When I take one of the wrong roads I am as effectually out of the way as if I had taken every wrong road in the universe. And, brother, hear me: God looks not upon sin with the least allowance, and can any man stand up before the final bar and say: "I have never violated a precept of that book." Until you can do that, you can never hope to escape by the force of law.

The law condemns. The apostle tells us that " by the deeds of the law there shall no flesh be justified in his sight." The law is but a rule of action that prescribes what is right, and prohibits what is wrong. And, brother, hear me! If, in your past life you have ever violated a precept in this book, you can not hope to escape up yonder by force of law on the final judgment day. You are compelled to acknowledge: "I am guilty before God. I have violated precept after precept. I have not only done it repeatedly, but I have done it knowingly and willfully. I can not hope to be acquitted by force of law."

Then I say to you, how about the force of testimony? Now we have come directly to the text: "What I have written I have written." I just quoted before that: "So, then, every one of us shall give an account of himself to God." Know thou that for all these things you shall be brought unto judgment, whether these things be good or bad. Now we stand there before his final throne. "What I have written I have written."

26

I declare to you this evening that it is my belief and it is founded on Scripture, that every man and every boy of us is now writing testimony by which we shall stand or fall on the last judgment day. Greenleaf on Evidence tells us that the best evidence a case is susceptible of shall be produced. He tells us again that written testimony is better than oral testimony. He tells us again that the evidence produced must correspond with the allegation, and be confined to the point at issue. Now, brother, here is the best testimony (the Bible), and every word of it in God's own handwriting. Written testimony is better than oral testimony. Lumpkin, one of the grandest jurists that ever sat upon the Supreme bench of Georgia, said: "I would rather trust the smallest slip of paper than the best memory man was ever gifted with." Here is written testimony: Start an engine from New York to San Francisco, and there is attached to its side a little piece of mechanism which indicates the number of miles it has traveled, the stoppages it has made, and how long it stopped at each station, and if you want to know the record of the journey you need not ask the engineer a word. The little piece of mechanism on the side of the engine tells you its record. You go to the city of New York, and you see the Fifth Avenue Hotel with its 700 rooms. You see that it is lighted up day after day and night after night, some rooms burning 100 jets, some ten, some one. You step to the proprietor and say, "How can you keep an account of this gas? How do you know how much you burn?" and he says, "Come with me." You walk with him down underneath a double stairway. He strikes a match and lights a candle and holds it to the dial plate of the gas-meter. He says, "You see that finger trembling on the face of the dial? That indicates to the one-hundreth part of an inch how much gas has passed through this meter during the past three months. There is a record for you." And every man and every boy this evening can stand up and face this fact. "What I have written I have written."

Ah, me! the record of some men, the record of some boys who hear my voice this moment! If your wife could read your record just as you have written it down, she would spurn you from her presence and drive you ever from her home. There are boys listening to my voice whose mothers would drive them from their presence if they could read the last night's record of those boys. O, the record! Boys, every oath, every wicked deed, every midnight carousal, every debauched act of your life, is written in legible indelible letters, and shall sparkle forever on the tablets of your hearts.

O, me! Men sometimes say it makes no difference. Brother, it makes no difference whether you approached this hall in this or that spirit, but it makes an eternal difference whether you did right or wrong on your way here.

Record! Record! We sometimes say "as true as the Bible," but every record, every line on the tablet of your heart is just as true as the Bible is true. It is a secret record. God would not suffer an angel of heaven to touch that record. God

would not suffer the worst enemy in the world to
touch that record of yours.   God would not suffer
your precious mother to put her finger on that
record.   It is a secret record of the soul by which
it shall stand or fall at the judgment-seat of Christ.
True! true! Holy Spirit, shine on our record this
evening!   Let us read it now in thirty seconds—a
record of accumulated guilt that will drive us to
some power to save, some power to relieve.

Record! Record! Record! What is your record
as a Presbyterian?   On one side of your record I
see recorded vows of eternal constancy to God.   On
that page I see " I swear eternal allegiance to God
and the right."   Brother, what is your record from
that day to this?   Brother Methodists, with vows
upon you that would almost crush an angel, how
have you lived since you knowingly and intention-
ally made these vows to God?   Ministers of the
Gospel of Jesus Christ, what is your record since
the day God called you into his work, and you
promised to be faithful to God and to man?   O
Holy Spirit, shine on these records here this evening.   Let us see what we must meet at the final
bar of God.   I want to say to you that I would
frequently preach very differently but for record-
making.   I want to say to this vast assemblage of
fathers, husbands, and sons here this evening, that
while I preach the Gospel to others, I never forget
for a moment that I have a soul in my own body
that will be saved or lost.   God pity us here this
evening, and turn our eyes inward, to see these
records as God would have us see them.

What is your record, husband? What is your record, father? What is your record, son? There are hundreds of men here this evening, and the only reason you can hold up your heads, the only reason you can move among your fellows, is the consciousness that nobody on earth can read your record. It is hidden out of the sight of man. There are men listening to me now, who, if I could tear a page of the record from their heart and stick it there on that wall in legible letters, would shrink from this congregation, rush out of this hall and out of this town and never be seen within its radius again. O, brother, it is hidden now, but God's Word for it, every wicked act, every secret sin, shall be proclaimed from the house tops. Oh, fearful thought! Record! It was this that made the poet say:

"It is not all of life to live,
Nor all of death to die."

I know that you may drown out this record in a night's spree, but it comes back with all its power to condemn in the morning. I know that in the giddy round of pleasure you may drown its voice for the hour, but ever and anon it shakes, it shakes its horny hand in your face, and says: "Look! Read the record of yesterday, of last week, of last year."

"What I have written I have written." What have you written upon the record of your life? What upon yours? And upon yours? I stand here to condemn no man. I ask you, my brother, in all love and kindness, what is the record you have made to this hour? Some months ago a lady slipped a pedometer into her husband's pocket as he went out in the evening. He was a business man in the city, but every night as he left the supper table he said: "I have to go down to the store." On one occasion she put one of these indicators in his pocket, and when he came back she took it out and consulted it. The faithful little dial told her that her husband had walked seventeen miles that night. And she said to him: "Husband, where have you been to-night?" He replied: "I have been posting my books." She said: "Husband, that won't do. Do you post your books as you walk?" "No," he said, "I post my books sitting at my desk." She pulled the little indicator out and put it in his face and said, "There is the record of your work! Seventeen miles to-night. It is half a mile to the store, and half a mile back. Explain yourself." She made him explain, and it turned out that he had walked sixteen miles round a billiard table playing pool. And I tell you, my congregation, that within your bosom there is a faithful record being kept every day, and when at last God shall say, "Who art thou and what hast thou done?" the record has passed into the recording angel's hands, and he shall read line after line and page after page of guilt that is enough to damn the universe.

Record! record! Every oath has been recorded. Every wicked act has been recorded. Every unfaithful act has been recorded up yonder! O, my brother, how about your record? And I have found out another thing: Men talk one way with their tongue and write another way upon the record of their heart. A man stands up there and says: "I do not believe in God." Then he writes down upon the tablet of his heart: "I have just told a lie. I do. I do." A man out there says: "I do not see any use in revivals. I am as good as any body in the Church." Then he takes up his pen and writes within: "I have told one of the biggest lies I ever told. There is a big use in revivals. The world is going to destruction, and I am the meanest man in town." He writes one way and talks another. Brethren, I will know you by and by just as you are.

Record! record! There are men who hear my voice to-day who, if their record were to close with this hour, have sinned enough to damn the universe, and I beg you never to add another line to that accumulating record of guilt, which is enough to make the devil, when he looks at it, hide his black face under his wings! God pity us! May the pen drop from our palsied hands! May we never indite another line that may condemn us here or at the judgment bar of God.

"What I have written I have written." And I want to tell you that when once you put it down, it is down forever. The autobiographies we write on paper can be altered and underlined, but the autobiography you have written on the tablet of your heart can never be altered or erased. It goes down as it is. It abides with you for ever.

Record! record! record! At the age of 24 I was

brought face to face with the fact that I had a record sufficient to damn the universe. Brother, let me turn to Spencer; let me read him through and through, and having done so, I say to Mr. Spencer: "I have been charmed with your theory, but how about my conscience, my record, my God?" Mr. Spencer says: "I do not treat on those subjects." I say: "Of all subjects, I am the most in need of these." Then I turn to Brother Darwin, and after reading his evolution theories, I say: "But how about my conscience, my record, my God?" He says: "I do not treat on those subjects." I go to Mr. Tyndall and all earthly philosophers and scientists just at the time I need help and enlightenment, but they turn their backs on me and walk off. Now, with record enough to damn the universe, I stand with no philosopher to help me, and no scientist that can reach me. Brother, hear me! All the tears of my precious mother could never have erased one single line of this record. All the prayers of my father would have been wasted on this record. All the prayers of the Church would avail nothing. All the combined chemicals of earth could not have erased one single word of it. O, what shall I do?

And now, brother, I will tell you why I hang my highest hope of salvation on this blessed Gospel. When every other source had failed me, I took this book in my hands, and I sought the cross of Jesus Christ, and there, a poor, guilty, wicked wretch, I fell down under the cross. And the precious Saviour picked me up and pardoned all my sins. He blotted out this record of mine, and he took my arms and put them around the neck of God. And I love this religion and this Bible, because it proposes to do with conscience and with record and with God. And there is no other system in the moral universe that proposes to lead a poor man in these dreadful extremities. Aye, with record enough to condemn all men, I went to the cross. And now I understand that blessed old hymn:

> "There is a fountain filled with blood,
> Drawn from Immanuel's veins."

Bless God for that precious blood that saves a poor, lost, ruined sinner! I want to say to you to-day that my hope of heaven rests on this point. Fourteen years ago a poor, wrecked, ruined sinner, his blood washed away my guilt, and now my record has been washed out in the precious blood of the Son of God. Now take heed to the judgment. Charge me with Sabbath-breaking, charge me with infidelity, charge me with every thing, but there is the record, and the precious blood has washed out every page and every line, and I stand acquitted on the final judgment day by the force of testimony and the prerogative of pardon. Blessed be God! Acquitted on the final judgment day! Brother, brother, the hope of the world is the cross of the Son of God. Let us rush up under that cross, the lost, the wicked, and the wayward. Fourteen years ago I was the worst of the worst, and sometimes I think that God suffered me, in spite of my mother's prayers and my father's example, to go down to the gates of hell, that I might be sent back again to bring back the men closest to the gates of hell. God help you all! I care not who you are, he will not only pardon your sins, but he will separate them as far as the east is from the west. He says: "I will blot them out of the book of my remembrance."

O, brethren, let us turn our eyes to the hope of the world. This evening let us, on God's own terms of capitulation, run the white flag out of the citadel of our hearts, and God will tell the angels to get their wings and fly down to earth and convey peace and hope to every rebellious heart.

SAYINGS.

HOW TO KILL LOVING PARENTS.—There is a way to kill a mother without any weapon. The father of a lot of drunken sons said to me: "Jones, my boys are killing their mother, my precious wife. What can I do? What would you do? It does n't look as if their mother will live twelve months longer." "Well," said I, "I do n't know, brother, I declare! You puzzle me with that question, but I 'll say this much: If I ever raise boys at my house that are drunken debauchees, and they turn out to be drunken vagabonds, and just crush their mother's heart, some morning after they wake up sober, I 'm going to call them into their room and say: 'Boys, you are killing your precious mother by the inch. She is dying a hundred deaths! Boys, listen at me: Go up in your room and get the old, breech-loading shotgun, and put forty buckshot into each barrel, and walk down to the breakfast-table this morning, and put it to your mother's head and fire both barrels off. You shan't kill my precious wife by inches. You may bring your shotgun and shoot her down, but you shan't kill her by inches that way, boys.'" O, me! There's many a precious woman in this town that's dying by the inch, and you can run home to-night and put your ear to your wife's heart, and hear the blood drip! drip! drip! May God have mercy upon us.

THE HARDEST THING.—The hardest thing a poor fellow ever tried to do in this world is to give himself to God just as he is. He wants to fix up and brush up and arrange the matter. O how we do hate to turn just such a case over to God! We would like to make him about half-way what we want him to be before we turn him over. It is the hardest job a man ever undertook to turn himself over to God just as he is.

Sermon XVI.

The Prodigal's Return.

A Sermon to Men.

"I will arise and go to my father."—Luke xv, 18.

AS a congregation of fathers, husbands, and sons we will be together no more this side of the great day when we shall all stand before the great throne, and give an account each for himself. Brethren, give us your prayers and your attention, and I trust this service may bring a tide of love that shall sweep you all over the perilous bar into the great Kingdom of God. We shall read this afternoon, and make a running comment on, the Parable of the Prodigal Son: "And he said, A certain man had two sons; and the younger of them said to his father, Father, give me the portion of goods that falleth to me. And he divided unto them his living. And not many days after the younger son gathered all together and took his journey into a far country, and there wasted his substance with riotous living. And when he had spent all there arose a mighty famine in that land, and he began to be in want. And he went and joined himself to a citizen of that country, and he sent him into his fields to feed swine. And he would fain have filled his belly with the husks that the swine did eat; and no man gave unto him. And when he came to himself he said: How many

316

hired servants of my father's have bread enough and to spare, and I perish with hunger! I will arise and go to my father, and will say unto him: Father, I have sinned against heaven and before thee; and am no more worthy to be called thy son; make me as one of thy hired servants. And he arose and came to his father. But when he was yet a great way off his father saw him, and had compassion, and ran and fell on his neck, and kissed him. And the son said unto him: Father, I have sinned against heaven and in thy sight, and am no more worthy to be called thy son. But the father said to his servants: Bring forth the best robe and put it on him, and put a ring on his hand and shoes on his feet. And bring hither the fatted calf, and kill it, and let us eat and be merry. For this, my son, was dead, and is alive again; he was lost, and is found. And they began to be merry. Now, his elder son was in the field, and as he came and drew nigh to the house he heard music and dancing. And he called one of the servants, and asked what these things meant. And he said unto him: Thy brother is come, and thy father hath killed the fatted calf, because he hath received him safe and sound. And he was angry, and would not go in; therefore came his father out and entreated him. And he, answering, said to his father: Lo, these many years do I serve thee, neither transgressed I at any time thy commandment; and yet thou never gavest me a kid that I might make merry with my friends; but as soon as this, thy son, was come, which hath devoured thy living with harlots, thou

hast killed for him the fatted calf. And he said
unto him: Son, thou art ever with me, and all
that I have is thine. It was meet that we should
make merry, and be glad; for this, thy brother, was
dead, and is alive again; and was lost, and is
found."—Luke xv, 11-32.

I never feel I am any kin to this older brother.
Really, I don't know who he is. I don't know
what place God intends he shall fill in the vast
moral universe. This much I know: we live in a
fallen world. There are unfallen worlds. I reckon
the inhabitants of these worlds ought to have kept
their first estate, and they would not have had to
cry out when God threw his arms around a wandering, wayward man that has spent his all with
harlots. I suppose the unfallen world looks on
with astonishment and wonder, and they wonder
why it is God should be so good to this fallen world
when they never transgressed. Brethren, there is a
moral universe all around us. This young man, the
older of the two, occupies some place in that moral
universe. I hope, I trust, I believe, that there is
such a thing as mercy to cover his case. We will
leave him in the hands of God while we discuss the
other brother this evening—the one that is kin to
us; the one we have known all our life. If this
prodigal boy were not my brother I should never
think I am a man myself.

Let us take the parable just as it presents itself
to us, and we will modernize it so that we can get
hold of it and see it plainly; for this is one of the
most perfect pictures of human nature the world

ever looked upon. This parabolic illustration of a thing is but the photograph, the portrait of it; and here is one of the finest portraits of humanity that inspiration ever drew, for it is so lifelike—so like me, so like you, and so like every man of us. O, what a picture of human nature!

If Christ had never said another word but this I would have always looked upon the author of this parable as divine, for it stamps him as a divine person. "A certain man," he said, " had two sons, and the younger of them said to his father, ' Father, give me the portion of goods that falleth to me.' And he divided unto them his living." I have heard preachers say some mighty hard things about this boy; they said he was wicked, dissipated, and wild and profligate at home; that he was the worry of his father's heart, and gave his mother so much trouble. I don't know where they got that idea of this prodigal boy; they didn't get it out of the Bible, sure. Look here now: if that young fellow was prodigal and wild, and dissipated and wasteful, and his father divided with him his living, his father was a fool to start with. We will put it in that shape. This younger brother (according to the laws in those days, the older brother inherited the estate, and the younger brother had no legal claim on his father), this younger brother comes to his father and says: " Father, give me the portion of goods that falleth to me," and he immediately divided his living. Without a word of remonstrance or hesitancy or advice he turns over to this young fellow this great amount of property. The

face of the parable shows that, up to that hour, the
young man was praiseworthy, upright, industrious,
and worthy of the confidence of his father, so far as
all outward manifestations of his conduct were concerned.

I repeat it: A man that has sense enough to
accumulate a fortune, or sense enough to take care
of an inherited fortune, is too wise to turn over a
vast amount of property, without a word of remonstrance or advice, to a wayward, dissipated, profligate boy. He wouldn't do that—no father would—
and the very face of the parable shows that this
boy, so far as his father knew, was trustworthy. I
have always felt sorry for this boy when I saw the
preachers jump on him, and stamp on him, and beat
and kick him. I have! I feel sorry for many a
poor sinner, too. I wouldn't touch a hair of your
head, brother, if I could get the meanness out of
you without doing it; and every stamp and kick
and jerk I make at you is to jerk and stamp and
kick the meanness out of you.

If I could go through this country with Mrs.
Winslow's Soothing Syrup and get more souls to
Christ by having the sinners each take a teaspoon-
ful, I would invest every nickel I have in that
syrup. I would that! I am for the efficient thing,
for that which will make you cease to do evil and
learn to do right. That's all I have against you.
I haven't any thing else against you, for I love you
all as if you were my own brothers; but, O, how it
makes me feel bad and sad to see the way you do!
It hurts me on your account, and on your wife's

account, and on your children's account, and on account of humanity. I am your brother, and when you suffer I suffer; when you rejoice I rejoice. I am happy at every happy man I meet; I am sad at every dejected, sorrowful, sinful character I meet. I weep with those who weep, and I rejoice with those who rejoice. O Lord, lift us up here in Cincinnati, to where we can rejoice with those that rejoice and where there will be none to weep with and mourn with, and none to feel sad over!

Let's catch up the thought of this parable, and find our way back to God. "A certain man had two sons. And the younger of them said to his father, Father, give me the portion of goods that falleth to me. And he divided unto them his living. And not many days after the younger son gathered all together and took his journey into a far country." We may imagine this father divided his portion to the younger son, and the young man then spent a whole week in getting every thing in order for the journey.

We may say that his property consisted of camels, and sheep, and horses, and servants; and now he has spent the week in gathering all together; and we will say when Saturday night comes all the plans have been made, all arrangements have been perfected, and on Monday morning, bright and early, this grand pageant, this vast caravan, drives out in front of the old homestead, and the young man calls a halt to all movement, and stops, and hushes every thing into silence; and he walks back up through the front gate, and up the avenue on to the porch of the old homestead, and he takes his father's hands, and says: "Good-bye, father!" and we can see that father look upon him with eyes of love and mercy, and say: "Good-bye, boy!" and the tears course down his cheek; and then the boy turns to his mother to bid her good-bye, and the mother instinctively throws her arms about her boy, and says: "Good-bye, son!" and then she imprints a thousand kisses on his face, and she says to him: "Son, remember the instructions of your youth." The young fellow then deliberately turns his back on father and mother and home, and walks out of the front gate and bids the caravan move off, and they move off in grand style. It is a wonderful pageant, and mother and father linger on the front veranda and watch the procession as it passes out of sight and gradually winds its way over the brow of the hill and disappears from view. The father turns around and utters an earnest prayer, "God, look after my boy;" and the mother, with the tears running down her cheeks, says, "O, shall I ever see my boy again!"

On the boy moves with his caravan, and I imagine about sundown he drives out on a beautiful camping ground, pitches his tents, and arranges every thing for the coming of the night; and now I can see every thing in order, and every thing has been cared for, and now I see the young man as he unfolds his coat, spreads it out and lays himself down for the night's rest, and turns his eye to the heavens above him, and he begins to think, "This is the first night I have ever spent from my home.

This the first night I have ever slept from beneath the roof of the old homestead. This is the first night I have been where I could not hear mother's voice, and could not hear father's advice."

I have wished many a time that that boy, before he went to sleep that first night, had settled it in his mind, "This is my first night from home, and by the gracé of God it shall be my last, for to-morrow morning, when I arise I shall turn this caravan around, and will drive back to the old homestead." O, if he had settled that, how many hours of heart-ache, and anguish, and desolation and misery that boy would have avoided? O, poor, miserable, wandering boy, I've thought a thousand times of you, and wished you had turned around and gone back.

We see him next morning with renewed vigor rising early, and after a simple breakfast drives on and on, and the next evening the same scene is re-enacted. He goes to bed, and I think, "Well, young fellow, you see now this is your second night out. You're on your journey, two days away from home;" and I wish that night the boy had settled it in his mind, "This is my second night from home, and by the grace of God to-morrow night shall be my last. I will turn my face on my journey and will go back, and in two days I'll reach the old homestead." That boy would have been away from home only four days if he had done that. But on and on and on he drives, each night repeating the same scene; and at the end of the sixth day, Saturday night, he picks him out a pleasant camping-ground on which to remain over Sunday.

A boy never gets his own consent to break the Sabbath the first week he is away from home. The boy says, " I 'll tie up here, and rest. It is father's Sabbath and mother's Sabbath, and I will reverence this day." The boy was only a week from home then, you see, and he could n't afford to break the Sabbath. He winds up his first week on Saturday night, and he goes to bed, and as he lies there looking up at the bright, cold stars in the heavens he says, " I am six days' journey from home." The next morning is the Sabbath, and the sun rises gloriously and bathes the scene in a sea of light, and as he looks around on that beautiful Sabbath day he has the consciousness, " This is the first Sabbath I ever spent from home ; this is the first Sabbath sun that ever rose on me when away from my father's house."

I wish he had settled it that morning, and said, " By the grace of God as this is my first Sunday from home, it shall be my last Sunday from home." I 've wished a thousand times this wayward boy had turned his train around the next morning, and driven back to the old homestead. If he had, he would have been out just one Sabbath from home, and the next Sunday would have found him sitting by his mother's side, listening to her sweet voice, and by his father's side, listening to his words of counsel. O, if he had settled the thing that way, how many weeks of hardship he would have shunned, and how many hours and days of misery he would have avoided!

Monday morning finds him driving on and on, and I imagine that at the end of his second week's journey he drove into a magnificent, fertile country, and as he looked at the beautiful land and surveyed the situation, he said: "I believe this would be a good place to settle. I believe I will buy in this locality and settle down;" but something suggested to him the thought: "Well, if you buy here and settle down, you won't get more than settled before the old lady 'll come down here on a visit with the old man, and they 'll want to break in on your arrangements and advise you how to run things, and they 'll meddle with your affairs; and if you 're going to make out for yourself and create a name for yourself and build you up a fortune, the best thing for you to do is to pick up and get to where they won't visit you."

The fact is, the purpose of the boy's mind was this: he had been watching his father, and saw his old fogy notions and way of doing things, and he thought many a time, "If the old man would turn this thing over to me, I 'd manage the thing better than he does." Yes, and some of you fathers who turned things over to your boys—where are you now? If you don 't mind your boys, some of you, they 'll ruin you! You can 't afford to turn over to your son his part of the estate, and you must n't let your boys bankrupt your wife, their mother, and his sisters. Well, the boy watched the old man until he thought the old man was stupid, and he thought his old fogy notions would n't do, and his idea was, "If father will turn his estate over to me, I will be able to double, and triple, and quadruple it in value in less than ten years. My idea is to buy a magnificent plantation, stock it well with fine stock, build me a palatial residence, and arrange every thing in first-class order, and when I get to counting the money, then I won't mind a visit from the old folks. But I'll want to have matters all arranged before they begin to meddle and interfere."

Well, the prodigal boy drives on and on, and at the end of the third week he drives into another beautiful locality, and I imagine he says, "This suits me. This is magnificent ground here. I like this soil and climate. I like this altitude. I'll buy here." Then he begins to think, "Why there's a post-office in the settlement over yonder, and I won't be here three weeks before I'll get a long letter from father full of advice, and I'll get a long sentimental letter from mother, and they'll be doing nothing but advising and suggesting. The fact of the business is, if I'd wanted their advice I'd have stayed at home. I don't want to be meddled with and interfered with. I'm a whale, and if there's any thing bigger than that, I'm that!" Boys, haven't you often felt that way? Haven't you felt it crawling up your sleeve and running all over you, and you thought you were bigger than your father?

"Into a far-off country," and on he drove. I want to say another thing here. The boy's moving off in style; he's got plenty of money; he's no poor man; he's able to pay his way. I imagine him moving on with his great train of servants and

stock, until at last he pulls up before a beautiful
country place, and he says, " I guess I 'll sleep in a
mansion to-night. I 'll tie up at this good man's
house on the wayside here." Next morning, when
the time comes for him to depart, he turns to the
good man, and says, " What 's your bill, old fellow ? "
The old man says, " Why, it 's nothing. I 'm glad
to have had you stay with me. I won't charge you
a cent." The young fellow swells up, and he says,
" You can 't insult me, old man. I 've got plenty
of money. I 'm no pauper in this country. I do n't
want to be insulted by having any man treat me
like a pauper. Name your amount." That 's the
way! You 've been there, have n't you, boys?

I 'll tell you another thing ; whenever you strike
one of these I 'm-no-pauper fellows, if you 'll put
your dogs on his track they 'll tree him at a hog-
pen! There 's many a boy in this hall this evening that 's headed for the hog-pen ; and you 'll never
turn until you get there either, and some of you
never! "Able to pay my way !" I imagine when
his money did get scarce he sold some of his stock
and still had plenty of money.

On and on the prodigal boy drove, and when he
had reached a far-off country—then what? He
bought him a hundred thousand acres of the most
fertile land in the settlement ; he built him a palatial residence and stocked his farm, and he was a
prince in the land! I 've seen many a boy that
thought he was a prince. But when he reached
that far-off country, what did he do? He spent
all—not part of it—in riotous living! Listen,

again. When he had spent all there arose a mighty
famine in the land. Did you ever notice, brother,
when you 're out of money it seems as if every body
else is out too? Did n't you notice when you did n't
have a thing in the world you could n't get a man
to be your friend? Did you ever notice when
a man had spent his all there was a famine to him,
no matter what there was to other people? Ever
think of that, boys? O, how true that is! There
is a family down town here; they have n't a dollar
in the world, and there's a famine right here in
Cincinnati for them. Every grocery in town is
loaded down with flour, and meat, and all kind of
eatables, but there's a famine in their home. And
it was when they had spent all that there arose a
mighty famine in this land.

Now, brother, when you get to this point where
you see the famine, where you see how this young
man ended, we'll leave the young man there, and
let's you and I go back and come down round this
line! Brother, here's human nature; let's see
what there is in this for us. Let's see what's in
this life-like picture. When you were ten—and
you were twelve—and you were fourteen—and you
yonder sixteen, you were spotless boys, as pure as
snow. You looked up to your father's God, and
said, "Give me the spiritual portion that falleth to
me," and God turned over to you your mother's
prayers and your father's advice and Gospel influences, and the precious Bible given you by
your mother, and all good influences God turned
over to you, and then you started into a far-off

country. Do you know that a man can live in the same house with his mother, and sleep in the next room to his mother, and yet be in a far-off country from his mother! Do you know that? Do you know that a man may be in the world with God and yet be away from God? Do you know that? O, young man, I'm so glad that the purity of your mother and the sanctity of your home make you a great distance from it. I am so glad there's a place of purity for poor disconsolate ones on earth to resort to occasionally.

Young man, listen! You started out with your spiritual heritage; you went on spending your substance; you threw away your father's advice, your mother's prayers. O, mother's prayers, how much they are worth! You threw away the Gospel influences of your younger days. You threw away all that was good. You have been scattering, scattering! scattering it along the way, and there you sit to-day, and you haven't a vestige of your spiritual heritage left you. All gone! All gone!

"And when he had spent all, there arose a mighty famine in that land." O, boy, with the world full of Bibles, you haven't one! With other mothers praying, your mother has gone from you forever! With other fathers advising their children, your father has ceased to speak, and his lips are closed and cold in death! O, how desolate is he who has spent his all in riotous living!

I was preaching once, and, after preaching, I said, " If there is a man in this house that feels in his heart ' I haven't a thing left, I haven't a friend

left in the world,' come up and give me your hand,"
and immediately one poor disconsolate fellow arose
and walked up the aisle and took me by the hand,
and with a face that spoke more than words could,
he said: "Mr. Jones, I have n't a friend in the
world. I have n't any thing left on earth. It is
all gone, all gone." O, brethren, there was a mighty
famine in that man's land. O, what a thought! O,
what a thought! He had wasted all! Boys, where
is the Bible mother gave you? Where's the sweet
lullaby of your cradle? Fathers, where are the sermons that touched your hearts in your younger days?
Men of the world, where are the good influences
that should have made you happy Christians? All
gone! All wasted in riotous living!

"And when he had spent all there arose a mighty
famine in that land." My presiding elder told me
this incident once: "In my district, some time ago,
I was driving along the road, and I reached a country cross-roads grocery, and, as I drove along in
front, a poor, desolate, trembling man walked out
of the grocery and accosted me, and said: 'You
do n't recognize me, but I know you. We were
college mates, and graduated in the same college
class, twenty years ago. We joined Church at the
same time, but when I came out of college I got
into bad company, and I have been going from bad
to worse ever since. I've been on a spree, drinking
hard, and just now, when I went in that grocery,
desolate and moneyless, the barkeeper said he would
give me a drink for nothing, and I took hold of the
bottle, but my nerves were so unsteady I could n't

pour the whisky out, and the grocery keeper poured it out for me, and as I took the glass and raised it to my lips I felt my old mother's hand come down on my head, and she said :

> " ' Now I lay me down to sleep,
> I pray the Lord my soul to keep ;
> If I should die before I awake,
> I pray the Lord my soul to take.'

" ' My precious old mother had been in heaven twenty years, but I felt her hand just as I did in days gone by, and as she spoke to me I dropped the glass, and I walked out and met you.' " The presiding elder said that, when he passed on (so he was told afterwards), that fellow walked back into the store and drank the stuff, and he was carried out a corpse. That poor mother followed her boy to the very gates of hell, and had her hand on his head as he foundered on the rocks of hell and sank forever.

O, my, how a man can squander all and spend all in riotous living! "And when he had spent all," the parable says, "there arose a mighty famine in that land." And the next thing he did he joined himself to a citizen of that country; and when he joined himself to a citizen of that country that citizen put him into the field to feed swine. Recollect, this is a Jew; this young man was a Jew. What more disreputable work could a Jew be put at than feeding hogs? He put him into the field to feed swine.

Look here, brother, when a man disposes of all; when mother's prayers, father's advice, the Bible,

all good influences are disposed of, the next thing a
man is going to do after he has disposed of all is to
join himself to a citizen of this country, the devil,
and the devil puts him to work—puts him to blas-
pheming the God of his mother, violating the
Sabbath of his mother; puts him to drenching his
body with liquid fluid, which is but the essence of
damnation. Now, here I have said before that God
wants humanity to help him bring the world to
Christ; the devil wants humanity to help him damn
the race; and whenever a man joins himself to the
devil, the devil puts him at the work of damning
humanity; and every wholesale liquor house, and
every brewery, and every saloon, and every still-
house in Ohio is an agent of the devil, doing his
work.

"And he joined himself to a citizen of that country," and the devil put him to stilling whisky, and
the devil put him to running a brewery, and the
devil put him to opening a saloon, and the devil
put him to the work of damning humanity, and
that is the only work of every servant of the devil,
damning humanity.

I go to the Legislature of Ohio. I say, "Gentlemen of the Legislature, I want you to make the
sale of liquor in the State of Ohio free, and with
the freedom to sell it I demand the privilege
of debauching the children of your wives, and
cursing your homes." And I will tell you another thing: The Legislature of Ohio, if they
were asked by the bar-keepers of Cincinnati the
privilege of damning their own children, and break-

ing the hearts of the wives of the members of that Legislature—what do you think the legislators would say to that? I tell you it has reached the point in this country where the legislature of many States— and if this does n't fit Ohio they need not wear it; and if it does, I beg them to throw it away and get them a better cap—it has come to a point in many States of the Union where, instead of the legislature controlling the liquor interest, it is the liquor interest that is controlling the legislature. An old swill-tub in the House of Representatives making laws for decent people!

From a governor down to a dog-pelter, I would not vote for a man that touches, tastes, or handles whisky to save my life; and you can never redeem America with a legislature whose breath is tainted with whisky. You never can do it! God save the legislatures from the fearful curse of being controlled by the liquor element in this country! But "money makes the filly go;" you have heard that. Money makes the filly go. And I will tell you another thing: money makes the filly's son go, too. The earth swallow me up before I would lend myself to any influence and join any citizen of this country and help him to debauch and damn my race! I would die by the inch; I would walk up on a burning fire and be burnt to ashes before I would lend myself to an infernal alliance like that.

In Georgia (and I know it is true of other States), we have had men in the Legislature that just staggered around town drunk, on both sides of the streets, and they staggered into the legislative halls drunk.

They were not fit to be in the penitentiary, much less the legislature. God give us sober men—sober men to rule us and to make our laws! God save our codes and our statute books from the danger that liquor will do them all over this country!

"And he joined himself to a citizen of that country." Whenever a legislator joins himself to a citizen of that country he is going to do some bad work. Whenever a governor, a Supreme Court judge, whenever any influential man joins himself to the devil, he can play havoc among the rest of men. Now, listen again: "And he fain would have filled himself with the husks that the swine did eat." Now, you notice he went at the most disreputable job in the world, and when he went to feed the hogs he would eat the husks, and he fed the hogs on husks, and ate husks himself; ate the same thing he fed the hogs with. "He fain would have filled himself with the husks the hogs did eat."

Did you ever notice the fact that just what the devil makes you feed other folks he makes you eat yourself? Did you ever notice that nine out of ten of these beer-drinking fellows are puffed up with beer, so that if you would stick something in them it would run out by the gallon? Did you ever notice that nine barkeepers out of every ten die drunk themselves? Did you ever notice that? If you feed other people on liquor, the devil will make you drink it. If you pour beer down other people, the devil will make you gulp it down, and away you go. God pity a man that just sits and feeds out damnation to others, and then sits and enjoys it himself.

Ah, me, what an awful thought. Just what you feed other folks on you will feed yourself with. You are a gambler, and you win other folks' money, and the devil makes you sit right down to the table, and you lose it again. Did you ever notice that? That's just as certain as we are in this house this afternoon.

"And he fain would have filled himself with the husks that the swine did eat." O how low down we get, how low down we get. I took a bar-keeper into the church once, and he said: "Jones, I never sold liquor but nine months, and I stayed drunk those entire nine months. I could n't sell it without staying drunk; my conscience would not let me." I like that; that's a sign a fellow has got some conscience. It is a sign his conscience is not dead. But there are men in this town that sell whisky all the year round, cool, sober men. You who do this have no conscience; your conscience is dead; dead and buried forever, and God pity you.

"And he joined himself to a citizen of that country." Some of us have joined ourselves to a citizen of that country, and O, how fearful our lives are. What disreputable lives we lead every day. O, young man, you never could hold up your head again in the presence of your poor mother if you could get your conscience aroused once more. O, think what awful lives we have led, and then think how pure and good our lives might have been.

"And he joined himself to a citizen of that

country, and he sent him into the field to feed the swine;" and after this famine had pressed him sore, and he began to be in want, what then? "And when he came to himself"—O, brother, here is a point; let us look a minute. "And when he came to himself." What is the matter with humanity? What is the matter with you? What was the matter with me? I look back fifteen years ago. What was I doing? Wringing the blood out of my father's heart; making my precious wife cry her eyes out, and my little innocent ones threatened with no home, and with orphanage, and with want. What was the matter with me? Do you mean to tell me if I had been myself I would have done that way? No, sir.

I will tell you another thing: If you can get your eyes wide open this afternoon you will be turned around, a sensible man, and won't do as you are doing. A man of good, sound sense, to say nothing about religion, won't treat his wife as you treat her and love her as you love her. A man of good, hard sense won't treat his children as you treat your children, and at the same time love his children as you love your children. I tell you there is something wrong with humanity.

And that boy bid his father good-bye and started away, and spent weeks on the road, and spent months in feeding swine, and filling himself with the husks that the swine did eat, and all at once his eyes got opened and he came to himself. Look here, I can't help believing that there was a strange infatuation had hold of him. I don't know how you feel about it, but when I look back I say, "I

was n't myself, and there is no use talking about it."
And every son in this country that is running in his
mad career, he is mad with his wickedness, his intellect is beclouded, he does n't see himself, and he
does n't see the truth as it is. Now when that boy
came to himself he said, "Why, sir, who am I?
What am I? Where am I? What am I doing
here?" Look here, it will do you some good if you
will ask those questions this afternoon; "Who am
I? Where am I? What am I doing here?" O,
brother, you are away from where you took your
mother's hand the last time, you are away from
where your father's advice would have led you.
Where are you? Joined to a citizen of that country
feeding swine, damning humanity.

"And when he came to himself." Just here let
me say this much. I had gone along, and occasionally I had realized that I was n't living right;
I saw that my wife was fading away in grief;
I saw that my father was dying by the inch. At
last I looked around me and came to myself, thank
God, and I glorify his name forever for that day
in my history when I got my eyes wide open and
saw the deeds of my life, and saw how wicked I was.

O, brother, I thank God for getting my eyes
opened that day; and since then I have been singing, "Happy day, happy day, when Jesus washed
my sins away." I was a new man, a saved man,
and I went right about and left off my wickedness
from that day to this.

And when he came to himself what did he do?
He said, "In my father's house even the servants

have bread enough and to spare, and I perish with hunger. Here I am starving to death, with the best father and the best home a boy ever had." And when he got his eyes open what did he say? "I will arise and go to my father." I will arise. Look here, that boy got the whole secret of the matter in that one expression—I will, I will, I *will* arise and go to my father. When he said that, the miles between him and his father's house melted away; there was nothing between him and his father. "I will arise and go to my father."

I suppose the devil said to him, "Well, you are in a pretty fix now to go to your father." And did you ever notice this is just what the devil will do to you; he will take you by the heels and drag you through the mud holes of sin, and then make you get up and look at yourself and tell you that you ain't fit to go anywhere. Did you ever notice that? O, what a mean old devil he is! He said to this boy: "Just look at yourself now; you ain't fit to go home; you have no clothes and you are a thousand miles from home; you have no shoes, how can you walk? You haven't got a dollar to pay your way; you have no hat to cover your head. Ain't you a pretty one talking about going home?" But when that boy jumped up in his manhood and in his resolution, and said, "I will arise and go to my father," why, sir, there was God Almighty's excursion train run right up to the side of him, and it came to a dead halt, and God told him to get aboard, and that He would see him the balance of the way. If you will say that this afternoon and

mean it, God will do the rest. "I will arise and go
to my father; I am going, money or no money,
shoes or no shoes, hat or no hat, miles or no miles,
I am going."

And now we see him start back—no shoes, no
hat, no money, and a long way to go. Off he
starts and on he goes. And I imagine I see
him when on the way he comes across the mansion where he had stopped some time ago, and
where he had been insulted when the man did not
want to charge him any thing. I imagine he
looks at that place, and says, "I believe I will not
go in the front door, but I will get through the
fence and go around behind the orchard; I do n't
want to see those folks." And he climbs the fence
and takes the back way around the orchard until
he passes the house, and comes to a poor negro
cabin, and he says, "Auntie, I wish you would
give me some bread. I have n't got any money—
have n't got a cent to pay you, but I have got the
best father a boy ever had; and if you ever see my
mother and can hear her thank you once for any
favor shown her boy, you will be paid for it.
Please, auntie, just give me a little bread." That
colored woman gives him a pone of bread, and he
turns around and goes to the roadside and lies on
a pile of leaves and goes to bed. He learned that
from the hogs. He is going to bed, now; piles up
in those leaves, and sleeps all night.

The next day he passes on down the way; and
I imagine, as he went down the road, two neighbors were talking together, and one said: "Do you

remember that grand pageant going down this road some time ago, and the princely young fellow in his phaeton? It was the talk of the neighborhood for a whole month." And the other one spoke up, and said: "Yes, he stopped at my house, and I insulted him the next morning, because I did not charge him any thing." And then the first fellow said: "Did you see that dirty, vagabondish tramp go down the road this morning?" "Yes," says the other. "Well," says the first, "there was something about his face that reminded me of that princely boy that came down the road a few years ago. I don't know what made me, but I thought of that princely boy as this pauper and beggar." "O, no," says the other, "that can't be that princely boy." "But I believe it was the very same fellow."

Look here, citizens of Cincinnati. Here is a man who has been out West twenty years, and he comes back to Cincinnati, and a poor, bloated, besotted, drunken wretch staggers along the walk; and that gentleman who has been living in the West twenty years says: "Who was that staggering along there?" "That's Bill So-and-so, son of Colonel So-and-so." "That can't be he; Bill was one of the nicest young men in the city." "I tell you that is Bill So-and-so; he has been a vagabond for ten years." "Well, well, I never saw such a change in a fellow in my life." You just let the devil get hold of some of them and keep them awhile, and their own folks won't know them. That's what's the matter. I will have nothing to

do with a man that will despoil my countenance
and ruin my health so that my own precious
mother can't recognize me.

There is a grocery-keeper, an ex-barkeeper and
gambler in this town. I saw him two weeks ago.
He came to me and talked with me about religion,
and he came forward here and gave himself to God,
and I met that same fellow in the streets a day or two
ago and I did n't know him. His skin was clear,
and he looked well; and it is astonishing how the
Lord God can take one of these poor vagabonds and
make a new man out of him right away. And it is astonishing how the devil will treat you the other way.

And on and on he travels. He is going back
now, and I tell you there is no distance, no hard-
ships, no any thing to a fellow that is on his way
back. And look at him now; he is just as humble
as a dog; you can just say any thing to him now;
you can't hurt his feelings. Why, he is perfectly
willing to be kicked about by any body. He feels
that he has deserved it, and that's the difference
between going away and coming back.

O, my congregation, this afternoon, in all love
and kindness, do you see yourselves in this picture
as wandering off from God? And how many have resolved: "I will go back; I will go back." And
this poor boy suffered in sin, until at last he says:
"I will arise and go to my father, and will say
unto him, Father, I have sinned against heaven and
before thee, and am no more worthy to be called
thy son; make me as one of thy hired servants.
And he arose and came to his father. And when he

was yet a great way off his father saw him and had compassion, and ran and fell on his neck and kissed him. And the son said: Father, I have sinned against heaven and in thy sight, and am no more worthy to be called thy son."

I have thought about him many a time. I imagine he came up the road near the old homestead. And I have seen that prodigal approach and look down toward the old homestead; and there was home, and peace, and plenty; and there was the picture just as he had carried it from his youthful days—home, and peace, and plenty. And then he looked at the home, and then he looked at himself, and he says: "Just look at me; I am not fit to go any further at all; O, my, I believe I am willing to lie down and die; a place in the old cemetery will do me." And he sits down and says: "I can go no further; I won't go any further." And while he sat there his father saw him a great way off, the Bible says. His father saw him, and they were eyes of mercy that looked out that way; and his father ran to him, and those were legs of mercy that carried that father; and his father ran up to him and kissed him, and those were kisses of mercy that be imprinted on that poor boy's face; and his father spoke to him, and those were words of mercy; and the poor prodigal lifted up his face and said: "Father, I am no more worthy to be called thy son." And the father just clapped his hand over his mouth, and would'nt let him say another word; and he said to the servants: "Bring forth the best robe and put it on him; and put a ring on his hand and shoes on his feet; and bring hither the fatted calf and kill it, and let us eat and be merry, for this my son was dead, and he is alive again; he was lost, and he is found."

O, precious Father in heaven, I can recall the day when I was a poor, wretched, ruined man, despairing, dissipated, godless, wicked, and when I had sought thee and prayed to thee, and thou didst not bless me, I broke down and said: " I give it up; I am not worthy to go to my Father at all." And just when I broke down and said: " I give it up; there is no hope for me, in sight of the old homestead," my Father in heaven saw me, and his eyes were eyes of mercy; and he ran to me, and his feet were feet of mercy; and he flung his arms around me, and his arms were arms of mercy; and he spoke to me, and his words were words of mercy. And I said: " O, Lord, nothing but sin have I to give." And God whispered back to me: " And nothing but love shall you receive."

Blessed be God for the prodigal's return and welcome. Ring the bells of heaven, there is joy to-day. O, brother, every man in this house, every boy in this house, who wants to live and die under the roof of the old homestead in our Father's house, I want every one of you to stand up. Those who will say conscientiously: " I want to go back, and I want to live and die under the old roof and homestead in my Father's house," stand up. Blessed be God. O, angels, come and carry the news back that these prodigals are coming home.

SAYINGS.

UNTIL twenty-five years of age I was the big-gest fool you ever looked at, only when you look in the mirror yourself.

SALVATION in its highest sense is to love every thing God loves and hate every thing God hates. What I love and what I hate determines who I am.

I RATHER like the expression of that good old woman who cried out: " O, Lord, if you will only save me in this world, you shall never hear the last of it in the next."

THE JUDGMENT DAY.—Without such a day as this in the great future before us we might meet parties in heaven that would astonish us. We have known many a knotty, gnarly, hard-to-be-under-stood Christian in this world, and we have thought: " Well, if this man gets to heaven I would be sur-prised," and without such a day as that, if we should meet such a man in heaven we would won-der through all eternity " how could this man have got there;" but with a day like that before us, when God shall bring this brother before the great white throne, and shall strip him of all his idiosyn-crasies and shall show you all the pure gold of his character, and shall say to him : " Come, ye blessed," a universe will stand around and say " Amen" to this brother's commendation.

SERMON XVII.

A Sermon to Wives.

"But the fruit of the Spirit is love, joy, peace, long-suffering, gentleness, goodness, faith, meekness, temperance. Against such there is no law."—GAL. V, 22.

THE question before us this morning is "wives"— wives in all the tender relations toward those whom they love. For this cause a woman will leave father, mother, and home for her husband, and these twain shall be one. There is no more sacred relation than this. There is no relation in life that has so much joy and so much self-sacrifice as this holy relation, ordained of God. This man, this woman, mutually agree to take each other as husband and wife, and live together after God's holy ordinance in the sacred relation of marriage, and they further sacredly promise to agree to love, treasure, and keep each other in sickness and in health as long as they both shall live, and, forsaking all others, they cleave unto each other.

How solemn the rite of matrimony! How solemn the vows on that occasion, and your happiness and the happiness of your husband depend largely upon his unflinching and your unswerving loyalty to your vows. All trouble and all heartaches in this relation have been brought about by a want of fidelity to the vows made to each other

345

in the presence of God. " Whom God hath joined together let no man put asunder." There is no spot on earth that you enter more sacredly, and yet some enter more ruthlessly, than that belonging to husband and wife, and interference there may cost two persons their souls. It may cost you your life. There is no relation in life in which we need more patience and more forbearance and more of the forgiving spirit. There is no relation in life that you and I, as third parties, have less business to be interested in. " Busy-bodies" suggesting, planning, advising, have broken up the peace of many a home in this country. A mother-in-law, a father-in-law, a cousin, an aunt, a nephew, O if you could remember that God said it!—" Whom God hath joined together let no man put asunder." I believe I will let any body in the world talk to me about any thing and every thing except about what my wife is doing. If she has any faults I do n't want to know it. If she has done any thing wrong I would rather die than know any thing that would be unpleasant for me to know. I despise tattlers and gossip-mongers. You 've heard of 'em have n't you? I tell you, in this sacred relation about the best thing that you can do for those that have any trouble, is to get down on your knees and ask God to bless that woman and help her to understand her husband, and to bless that husband and help him understand his wife.

Nine-tenths of the difficulties of wives and husbands occur from the fact that they misunderstand each other, and the woman that will believe no ill of her husband and the husband that believes no ill thing of his wife, are the happy people in this life; and the reason the wife believes no ill is because she knows her husband is true to her, true to God, and true in all the relations of life; and the reason the husband believes no ill of the wife is because he knows her to be faithful to him, to her God, and pure and good in all the relations of life. I do n't think we ever made a greater mistake than to attempt to deceive each other. I would rather see my wife buried than catch her in a downright falsehood.

How can a woman ever respect a man that has told her one downright falsehood? Truthfulness, patience, a desire to understand the whole question— perhaps all these things are at the bottom of home felicity and home happiness. Now, in order that I may do as I should do, it is all important that I should be what I ought to be.

Now, we are not going to talk so much on what we ought to do as we are going to talk on doing. I must be something in order to do something. That old song that I was talking about the other day,

"O, to be nothing, nothing!"

we have sung and cried over until it has turned out to be nearly true; but I do n't want to be nothing. I am willing to be nothing until the Lord gets hold of me and makes me something, and then I want to be something all the rest of my life.

This morning we have an interesting subject. I

may be able to see many things more interesting, but I can discuss no question more profitable than this—the fruit of the Spirit. If there is a good woman, if there is but one true, good woman in the universe, I want that woman for my wife. If there is but one true woman and one noble woman and one pure woman, I want that woman for the mother of my children; and that is the sentiment of every man who lives on earth. Whatever all others may be, God give me a pure wife and good mother for those around my hearthstone that call her mother. We will flee away this morning into a higher and better experience and spirit. The fact of the business is, we have groped around in these old pastures of society and city life, and we have lived so long on these old pastures until the grass is mighty short, and you have to bite well down to the ground to get any grass at all.

The Lord help us up into the green pastures and beside the still waters, where we can feast and fatten on the grass of righteousness. Ain't you getting tired of the old pasture? Won't you be led out into the greener ones, and enjoy God in the best and highest sense? Then listen to this discussion. The fruit—the fruit! "The fruit of the Spirit." The tendency and end of all vegetation around us is to mature fruit. I look now at that grand old oak tree with its bare branches, and in a few more weeks, in the Spring, it will begin to bud and blossom and leaf out, and then I notice that it is gathering from all the stores in the atmosphere, and drinking in all the moisture at its roots, and by and by I see that tree pouring its vital fluid into the little acorn, and I see the acorn week after week growing, and developing, and expanding, and the old tree is bending all its forces and gathering from all resources and pouring its vital fluids into the little acorn, and still the acorn grows, until by and by I see the yellow, rounded, beautiful, matured acorn lying on the ground beneath, and then I see the grand old tree shed its leaves in the Fall, and see its forces going back to Winter quarters. That old tree, from the first bud on its branch until it shed its leaves, used all its efforts to produce ripe acorns.

Go into the garden in the Spring, and see that apple tree bud and leaf out and blossom, and the little apple appears, and then I see the tree bending all its energies and gathering from all sources, and pouring out into the little apple all its vital fluid, and I see the little apple growing, developing, and expanding, and by and by there's a ripe, juicy, red, luscious apple, and then I see the tree cease its efforts, shed its leaves, and go back into Winter quarters. The tree started out to mature ripe apples, and as soon as matured, it ceased. It has reached its ultimatum when it bore matured fruit. I grant you there are a good many intervening difficulties between the blossom and the ripe fruit; there are the cold frosts of April and the wintry winds of March and the worms that gnaw at the core of the fruit, but the tree answers the end for which it was created just in proportion as it overcomes all these obstacles, and matures the fruit for your garnering.

"The fruit of the Spirit!" In the vegetable

world around us, just as the end of the oak and apple tree is to mature fruit, so the purpose of every Christian life is to produce and mature Christian fruit. The fruit of the Spirit is love. This is the fruit that blossoms highest up the tree; this is the fruit that Christ raised upon the spiritual tree, which shed its blossoms on all below. "The fruit of the Spirit is love." Every Christian woman and every Christian man in this world, in the hour of their conversion, bud and blossom into this Christian fruitage of love. If there's any thing that's Christianity in the concrete, it is love. If there is any that is contrary to Christianity, it is ill-will, hatred. I do n't know how you feel, but I can tell you this much: The hour I was converted to God, I blossomed into this Christian fruitage of love. I recollect down in my town there was a fellow I had an uncompromising dislike and contempt for. I actually hated the man, and yet I did n't know the reason for it. Have n't you seen people you did n't like, and almost hated them whether you wanted to or not? The Lord loves every body. I know he does, but I thought many a time there were people the Lord did n't admire, to say the least of it; and I did n't admire this fellow from our town—I disliked him. When I was seeking religion I never thought of this, but after my conversion I met this man on the street, and I saw I loved him just as much as any body else, and I have never had any thing against him from that day to this. If religion does any thing for me, it makes me have love for every body that God loves, and that means every body.

Love! Fourteen years ago I budded and blossomed into a Christian life and love. There are a great many intervening difficulties between the blossom and the ripe fruit; I can tell you that. There are the cold winds of neglect, and there are the blighting frosts of temptations, and the worms of depravity that gnaw at the heart of the spiritual tree, but I answer the end for which I was created in Christ just in proportion as I overcome all difficulties, and by the grace of God mature my fruit; for this is a world of fruitage, a world in which I grow and develop and mature fruit, and after a while God will gather my fruit in heaven, and I shall have fruit and bread forever, and he or she who fails to mature Christian fruitage in this life, will have no fruitage to eat and rejoice over in the world without end.

There are a great many intervening difficulties between the blossom and the ripe fruit. Many a woman, when she tastes of the pardoning power, says she will love every body. Love is the sublimest passion that ever moved the heart of God. Love is the power of Christ—a power known unto men.

Mother, your control over your children is owing to your love for them. Your supreme command over your husband is largely owing to the fact that your love conquered and your love controlled him. Love will go a long way in this world. What you can't do by love you need not try to accomplish any other way. Love will argue, love will contend, and love will pledge itself, but above all things love can cry. That's a great thing. I have had my wife argue and contend with me over points, but I could always beat her at an argument or in a war of words, but I never had her yet to cry but what I surrendered right there and then. "Just quit crying, and I'll do any thing you say."

Sister, you have made a mistake if you use any weapon except love to fight with. Love! Now, at this point I must grow and develop the fruitage. Whatever there is to make you mad or angry, or resentful, or make you bear malice in your heart, here come in the worms of depravity, the biting frosts, the chilling winds, and it is my business to see to it I overcome all these difficulties, and mature Christian fruit. It is a sad sight to see a wife or mother who blossomed into this fruitage, and just about the time the little fruit made its appearance she let some one walk up under her spiritual fruit tree and flail the last particle of the little amateur fruit off her spiritual tree. Sister, you have had that done many a time. The saddest sight in the neighborhood is to see a spiritual tree standing stripped of its fruit, and the little amateur fruit lying all over the ground under the tree. Did you ever see anything of that sort?

Fruitage! I tell you, too, if they treat you as they did me you'd have no fruit at all. I must tell you how other folks do about maturing fruit. Down in Georgia, in the peach orchards, after the trees have blossomed, the farmer sees there's going to be a cold north wind and a clear sky, and he knows he's going to have a frost, and they roll logs and make big heaps of brush, and burn them all night, and let the heat and smoke blow over the orchard, and keep away the frost of the night. O, how essential it is to keep the warm fires of the Holy Ghost burning all around us to keep the deadly frost away. It is all essential for me that I pray to develop my fruit. Look at your apple tree in the garden. You see it in full bloom—and God never made a prettier bouquet than an apple tree in full bloom—you keep and preserve it just in proportion to the apples it bears.

"Three different years," saith the Lord, "have I sought fruit and found no blossoms. Cut it down. Why cumbereth it the ground?" The ax is laid at the root of many a good tree in this town. God has planted and dug and fertilized many trees in this town, until it seems his patience has almost given out. If we ever bud and blossom let us pray God to let us live long enough to mature ripe fruit. Love! Blessed Christ, thou art the one we would follow! Look how gloriously he matured his fruit. Of those who surrounded his cross in his last moments he said: "Father, forgive them; they know not what they do." Through all the cruelty and neglect and ingratitude manifested towards him Jesus bore a spirit of love and good will toward mankind.

Now, where there's love there's no enmity or malice or ill-will. A woman whose heart is full of love is happy; but a woman that runs love out of her heart is a miserable woman. You've been mad a whole day. Wasn't that a great day for you? I have known women who pouted all day. I can

30

stand a quarreling woman, but these pouters get away with me. They pout at the table, and they pout in the parlor, and they pout on the street. Now, my little Bob used to pout, but he got behind a door or under a bed to do his pouting. I liked that. If I were going to pout I would get under a bed and have my meals sent to me. Sister, when your heart is full of love your face will be full of sunshine, and you'll make home a happy place. Let me say this to you: Many a woman is always quarreling with her husband about staying home at night, and when he does stay home she's everlastingly after him, and God will have to reverse the universe before you can make that home lovable.

You quarrel with your husband to stay home, and when he does stay home you quarrel with him. "I've got the contrariest husband in the world. I can't keep him home a minute," says many a woman. You make home the happiest place in the world, and you can't drive him away. There are exceptions to the rule, of course; but, if home is the happiest place in the world, I'm going to show you that human nature will go where it can enjoy the most pleasant place on the earth. You can do any thing with your husband with this spirit of love. I have known mothers to manifest ill-will and spite toward their children. I'll tell you another thing: When a wife gets mad with her husband she can say the worst things in the world; but, when a woman gets mad with her children, she can be the hardest upon them. I have been in different cities and towns, and have seen some mothers' conduct toward their children—their married children. I know one mother who had her notions and mind fixed that her daughter should marry a wealthy young man; but the daughter did n't love him. And I tell you another thing: whenever a woman marries for money she is making herself a hard bed to lie in. I tell you, every woman ought to marry on the same principle my wife did. I neither had money, nor was I very pretty; it was a case of pure love. Well, as I was going to say, that mother had picked out some rich young man for her daughter to marry; but the daughter could not think that way and love that way, and she married another young man, and they did well in life and prospered; and God was good to them, and they had every thing to make life comfortable; but that mother, as unrelenting as death, never forgave that daughter. O, what a thought! Is there a mother in this town that do n't speak to her daughter and love her with all the tenderness of her nature?

O, mothers, will not the lower animals be a lesson to you in your conduct toward your children, and teach you to love them? What is it that could make me dislike my children? What could rob any child of mine of the love of my heart? Whatever our children do, let's win them by love, and keep their confidence, and train them for a better life. A mother that won't speak to her children! I do n't believe there's an old cat in town that would n't speak to one of its kittens; I do n't believe there's a lioness in the Zoo that would n't speak to its young! O, mother, shall you be more degraded than the lion or the cat or the mouse? If you will come to understand that, whenever pride takes the place that love ought to occupy, you are going to do a heap of mighty foolish and mean things. Whenever pride takes the place that love ought to occupy, how cruel pride is, and how selfish pride is, and how stubborn pride is. When you get that compound into a thing it is mighty bad—cruelty, stubbornness, willfulness, pride!

Sister, just open your eyes to the genial rays of the Sun of righteousness, and let love spring up in your heart and live therein, and live everywhere, and live under all circumstances, and say: "O God, if you will let me bud and blossom into this fruitage, I will gather from every source, from all points, from the heaven above and the earth beneath me, from all communion with God, from visiting the sick and giving to the poor, and from all good words and works will I gather and pour into this Christian fruitage of love!"

"The fruit of the Spirit is love." I am a Christian just as I love, and I am not a Christian just as I hate; and with love reigning in your heart and shining out on all, you are like your God, for God is love, and he that loveth is begotten of God.

I had two brethren in my Church once who fell out and quarreled, and they seemed like to have fought; and I tried my best to get them to settle up, but they wouldn't do it; and then I tried my best to get them to fight it out, but they wouldn't fight; but about six months after that, at a revival service, I looked over, and there I saw these two brothers hugging one another in the church. They made up all their difficulties, and O, how happy they were. I took one of them aside after service, and I said: "Brother, answer me an honest question. You have been mad six months. God says, when thou bringest a gift to the altar, and there rememberest if thy brother has ought against thee; first be reconciled to thy brother, and then offer thy gift. You prayed while you were mad many a time, didn't you?" Said he: "Mr. Jones, if I have acted the rascal I haven't acted the fool. I haven't been on my knees since I got mad." I like that! Some people will get on their knees to pray while they are mad with somebody. I found out that if I did the joke was all on me then. Whenever I get mad the joke is all on me then. I am hurting none but myself.

Let love through all your actions run and all your words be mild. I remember once, myself, a minister about forty years old met me with other brethren, and we commenced talking, and after awhile the preacher lost his patience and got mad, and said, O so many hard things to me; and I sat and enjoyed the whole thing, and started off and walked down street; and after I got down a piece, I heard some one calling after me, and looking across the street I saw it was the preacher, and he ran across the street with the perspiration pouring off his face.

Said he: "You're an awful hard man to catch. I've tried to find you so bad, to beg your pardon

for what I said. Do forgive me, and I'll never do
it again." Said I: "I've nothing to forgive."
Whenever you stay in good humor and they get
mad you may be sure they'll come back to you.
Do n't say any thing to them, and they 'll be racking over to straighten it out. Keep your temper
and love every body; and the Lord says: "When
a man's ways please the Lord, he maketh even his
enemies to be at peace with him."

The fruit of the Spirit is love, joy, and I believe
a joyless religion is a Christless religion, and every
religious life buds and blossoms into the fruitage of
joy. I like that old song,

> "Religion never was designed
> To make our pleasures less."

If any body ought to be joyous and happy it is
a Christian person. Christian wives, joy will keep
you in perfect peace if you make your home attractive to husband. Wear a smile always. You see some
wives and they are always moping, and she looks
as if her Father in heaven had just died and had n't
left her a cent in the world, and she 's so disconsolate!

If you would make home wear one big smile
always what a grand thing it would be. I love to
see every thing smiling. I love any thing that will
bring a smile. As I said the other day, let 's quit
singing, "The Sweet By and By," and sing the
sweet now and now. In joy make home pleasant.
Make home pleasant! A thing of joy is a thing of
beauty forever, as well as a thing of beauty is a
thing of joy forever. Try to be joyous and pleasant
for a whole week. Keep your faces straight, and

if they get out of shape let it be with a great, big smile as broad as the double doors on your parlor. I like a smile a mile long sometimes. Some of you can't keep your faces straight a week. If you will go home and be right joyous, and look happy for a week, your husband will say, "Well, if Sam Jones hasn't done any thing else in this town, he has changed my wife. I have a pleasant home." Many a poor fellow wants to see a brighter face on his wife, and sometimes we do so wretchedly we can't smile. The children see it all—the children hear it all. Many a woman whipped Billy, and Johnny, and Mary, and Julia, about fussing with one another, and the truth of the business is they had learned to fuss from their father and mother.

I do n't mean to say you women fuss with your husbands or husbands fuss with you, but I know a woman in Georgia that fusses with her husband, and I know you would n't have a fuss if you could see her. I asked a man once, "How often have you and your wife quarreled?" "We do n't quarrel," said he. "Do you mean to say you never said an unkind word to your wife?" "That's so," he replied. I turned to his wife and asked, "Do n't your husband ever speak unkindly to you?" "No, sir; never," she said. I looked at him again and asked, "Has n't your wife never given you one cross, crabbed word?" "No, sir; she never did," he said. I said, "I would like to get your pictures to take home with me—man and wife that never said an unkind thing to one another in their life!" Why not have it always joy and peace and pleasure and enjoyment? O, these little riffles—these little troubles?

We must gather from all sources and mature this fruitage. And then He said: "The fruit of the Spirit is love, joy, peace." It is grand to love and glorious to have joy, but how sublime to have peace growing and developing in the heart. I heard of a man who was put away up in a corner room of a hotel, and every morning he opened his eyes the first thing that greeted his ears was the tramp of men, and the jar of the horses' feet, and the roar of the street cars, and the confusion of the wagons. One morning he woke up and every thing was quiet. He did n't know what was the matter. "Have I left the city? No! Have I changed rooms? No; this is the same room! Is it Sunday? No! Then, what's the matter?" He got up and looked out, and there were the street cars and horses and men and wagons going and coming just as usual, but there was no noise. He looked again, and saw that the snow had fallen some ten inches deep, and all was going on as usual, but there was no noise—the snow deadened the sound!

Sister, let's stay under the snow clouds of peace, and let them fall down upon us, and you and we will have peace and quiet—peace at home, peace abroad. I like very much the old woman in Stewart County, Georgia, when my father was refugeeing South. Father was going along one day and drove up and asked: "Mother, is your husband in?" "No, sir." "I want to get some corn, if you please, for my stock," said my father.

"I think my husband has corn to sell, but he isn't at home," the old woman said. "When will he be home?" "Not before to-morrow." "I would like very much for you to let me have some corn," my father again said. "I can't do it; I don't know whether he has corn or not," the old woman said. "It's very necessary I get some," said my father. "But, mister," the old woman said, "I don't know whether husband would like it or not, and I would rather have peace at home than abroad," said the old woman finally. Sisters, think of that sometimes when your neighbors make suggestions to you about entertaining and one thing or another. You know how that thing works. Whatever pleases your husband, do that to please him. "I would a heap rather have peace at home than abroad. I don't live with you. I live with my husband, and would rather have peace at home than abroad"—that's what you should say.

"Peace, love, joy, *long suffering*"—do you know what that means? That's one of the greatest fruits. Long suffering means, I will bear it always. How many women sin and say: "I have borne that old thing as long as I am going to, and if she does it again I'll give her a piece of my mind." A piece of your mind? How big a piece would you give her? You ought to take that back and say: "I'll give her a piece of my tongue"—you can spare that! Long suffering!

The fruit of the Spirit is love, joy, peace, long suffering, *gentleness*. I love a gentle horse. A gentle horse has scarcely any value at all. I remember old John. He was a grand old horse. The children would go to the stable and climb up his legs, like trees, and they could drive him any way. If John were to run away a few times, he would n't have any value at all. A gentle horse—wonder if it 's the same as a gentle Methodist or a gentle Baptist? That sister yonder can get up in style for some entertainment, but when it comes to getting up clothing for the orphans, how she is n't there! She never was one of those Church members who could do any thing. I often think of the fellow who went to Dr. King, and said his wife and daughter wanted to join Church, and said he was ready to pay for his pew. If the devil lived in Cincinnati he would run you out of church—he 's always at meeting, and would naturally want a comfortable seat. " I 'll rent my pew, but if you want me or my wife or daughter to do any thing, we can 't do it. I 'll pay the pew rent, however." Dr. King said: " My friend, the Church of the Heavenly Rest is right around the corner."

Many a woman in this town thinks she belongs to the Church of Heavenly Rest. Nothing to do— husband pays pew rent, and does mighty little at that. A woman over yonder says : " That 's mighty little," but I have got to get down to many little things to strike you. " Mighty little! I think she has little to do." That 's so! I saw a great big fine horse once, a magnificently developed animal, but he would n't work to a thing but a little red-striped buggy ; but hitch him to that, and he would go a-clipping. He was a great horse in a little red-striped buggy, but he would n't pull a wagon or a carriage, or anything else! Sister, have you ever seen one of these striped-buggy Methodists racking out Sunday morning at 11 o'clock? You can hitch them up to any little entertainment, and they'll drive grandly, but you could n't hitch one of them to a prayer-meeting to save your life. He won't work anywhere but Sunday morning at 11 o'clock at dress parade!

Many a woman in this house this morning has n't been to Church any morning but Sunday morning for years. Those old hills are depopulated every Sunday morning at 11 o'clock, and when I speak of the hills, do n't think I mean aught against those good people. Some of the best people God ever blessed this earth with live on those grand hills around this town. By up-on-the-hill folks, I mean those folks who are up so high on the hill of pride they can't come down on the earth where Christ would meet them and bless them and save them. When I refer to up-on-the-hill folks, I mean folks that won't work to any thing under Heaven but a Sunday morning 11 o'clock buggy. Suppose you had a horse that would n't work to any thing but a striped buggy, and then would n't work to that even—what would you do with him? Suppose you could n't sell him, that being a swindle? Why, take him out and kill him; I would n't sell such a horse as that to any body. Taking this city, if you picked out your Sunday morning 11 o'clock crowd, what would you ask for them? If you would do like many stores, to sell dead stock, you'd have to start a five-cent counter, or you'd have to put 'em in bunches and sell 'em five cents a bunch, and then you'd have to beg a fellow's pardon for cheating him. The more of them you have, the poorer you are. Sunday-morning-11-o'clock _Christians ain't worth the powder and lead it would take to kill 'em!

Gentleness! I'll tell you another thing, sister—your husband is one of that sort, and it's your fault, too! When you were first married your husband wanted to go to meeting with you, but you wouldn't get up, and now he does not want to go, and the devil will get you both as certain as we are here to-day if you don't improve. Many a woman in this country has gone into partnership with the devil to damn her husband. In a Church down our way, at Eaton, Brother Dodge was pastor, and he told me he married a Christian girl to a young man who didn't belong to the Church, and in less than six months that Christian girl had her husband hard on the road to the devil.

It would be impossible for me to be a good man without a good woman to help me. Your husband will never be any better than you are. A woman must never follow her husband, but must take his arm and walk by his side! I don't believe in seeing a husband first and a wife next—husband and wife must be side by side! I don't believe a man has any more sense than a woman! I've seen many a woman who ought to have swapped places with her husband, to say the least of it. What does a great big first-class sensible woman want, toddling about in this world with a little old sawed-off, one-

horse man that is n't worth a cent? I would go to
the legislature and have my name changed, and
make him take my name! How would it sound to
hear one man ask another, "What was your name
before you were married?"

Here is another woman. Her husband comes
home and says, "Wife, let's go to prayer-meeting." "No," she says, "I've been thinking about
you; you look so care-worn and tired, I do n't
think it's best for you to go out at night. I am
going to rub your head." She's gone into partnership with the devil to damn that fellow. Sister,
you do your duty, or move your boarding-house.

Love supreme! Gentleness! Gentleness! A
woman can win with gentleness when every thing
else fails. I recollect a fellow who was gambling one
night, and when 1 o'clock came he jumped up from
the table and said: "Boys, I'm going home. I've
one of the best wives in the world waiting for me.
Why, she's so kind and gentle, if you all were to
come up home with me now, and I were to ask her
to get you all supper, she would do it." One of the
old gamblers laughed and said: "I've been hearing
of that sort all my life, but I never saw one."
Well, they all went up to see, and they rang the
door bell, and then he introduced her to his gambling friends, and said: "Wife, we're all hungry and
want supper." She invited them with smiles into
the parlor and said she would get supper as quick
as she could, and when it was ready they all sat
down and were waited on like princes, and when
the meal was over one old gambler turned to her

and said: "Your husband told us, but we would n't believe you were such a good woman. Tell me, how can you be such a wife to such a husband?" Her lips trembled, and the tears ran down her cheek, as she said: "My husband is a poor gambler, and I have prayed for twenty years that God would save him, but God does not answer my prayer, and the poor fellow will soon be dead; but I will make this life as pleasant as possible to him." The old gambler turned to the husband and said: "How can you be such a husband to such a wife?" And he jumped up and said: "Gentlemen, I am going to surrender to my wife to-night. I give myself to God and wife for a better life from this hour." And it is said afterward that man preached the sermon that won all these other gamblers to Christ. If your husband will not be good, and will go to hell, make it as pleasant in this world as you can.

"Gentleness, goodness, temperance." I 'll stop here a moment and say something about temperance, as I have n't said any thing about it since I have been here. If your husband wants to drink, tell him he can 't make a bar-room of your home. If he wants you to stir toddies for him, you must say: "Husband, go down town and let those fearful wretches that are damning people stir your toddies in the bar-room. I can 't do it." The biggest fool, sister—and I say fool as the Bible uses it—in Cincinnati, is the woman who will stir toddies for her husband and make them sweet and nice! Gone into partnership with the devil to damn her husband and make him die a drunkard!

Look here! whatever sin may be brought against my wife in my drinking days, the angels will clear her of that, for she never suffered a drop of the infernal stuff to be brought to her home! If my wife had sweetened my toddies for me as you do for your husbands—some of you—I would have been in a drunkard's grave before this. If there's any thing in the world a woman ought to hate it's whisky. Temperance! Go home this morning and gather up those demijohns and bottles, and take them into the back yard and knock them to pieces.

Some of you say, "I'll want some for my next entertainment." Yes, the devil will entertain you for a while, and that will be the end of you! Look here, wife, my Bible teaches: "Touch not, taste not, handle not the unclean thing." The best thing to do is to throw out every thing in the house that ever poisoned a soul or drove a man to degradation and death. One woman said the other day: "It's ridiculous the way Mr. Jones talks about cards. How can I entertain my husband without playing cards?" Have you an idiot for a husband? In the asylum the superintendent recommends cards, and if you go there you can see the poor insane persons playing cards!

Sister, send your husband to the asylum, and have him entertained there! What do you say? "Can't entertain your husband without cards!" Poor old soul! She must have been like the woman who was entertaining her husband at table, and they had a little spat, and she fired something at his head, but missed it and hit the motto up over the door, "God bless our home." The little boy said: "You missed pap's head, ma, but didn't you give the motto hail Columbia!"

Stop that progressive euchre business! Quit it. It's gambling as certain as God reigns in heaven! Whenever at a game of cards you put a party on this side and a party on the other, and put up a prize for the winner, that's just as much gambling as if the prize were a thousand dollar bill. That's playing a game of chance for a thing that's put up, and progressive euchre is gambling, as certain as death, and nobody but gamblers play it. Sister, I would hate to sink down to hell with the stigma on me that I lived and died a gambler. It is bad enough for men to gamble, but when women begin to gamble it's a disgrace to God's creation! Stop it! Stop it!

"Goodness, temperance, *faith*." I sometimes dwell on these things too long. Let's live right, and let them adorn our every-day life, and then, some of these days, we are going to have a glorious recognition up yonder!

Sermon XVIII.

MOTHER—HOME—HEAVEN.

A Sermon to Mothers.*

The Lord is my shepherd.—PSALM XXIII, 1.

I HOPE this sermon will be profitable to all of us. This is one of a series of services for women only, and is held with a special reference to mothers. There are three words that are very closely associated with each other in our minds, and perhaps mean more to us than almost any other three words. These words form the subject of this service: "Mother, Home, Heaven."

---

* Music Hall presented an unusual scene yesterday morning—a scene the like of which has not been witnessed since the hall was erected. Every seat in the auditorium and in the balcony and on the stage was occupied by a woman. There were old women bent with the age of years, their silvery hairs and halting step testifying that something unusual it was that brought them forth on such a damp, muddy, disagreeable morning; young women in their teens, and middle-aged women, maids and wives, society women and toilers in the house and workshop; women in silks and women in calico—women, in fact, of all kinds and of all nationalities. It was an audience seldom gathered together—an audience that only the eloquence and earnestness of Sam Jones could bring together, and it was well repaid for all the discomforts of the horrible weather that has been hanging in murky clouds over our heads for a week. Rev. Mr Jones is in his element when he has such an audience as this, and tears and sobs were many as he uttered some of his wondrous truths, and drew in vivid colors, and with an imagery rare, such pathetic pictures and graphic descriptions as would melt the heart of the hardest woman on earth His sermon was a powerful one, and many a mother present yesterday morning said "Amen" as he told of the fearful sins and shams of society in the world around The sermon was intensely interesting, and the report will be found well worth the reading by many women, and men, too, who were detained from yesterday's service.—*Cincinnati Commercial Gazette, January* 29, 1886.

Mother! What is home without a mother? How may I ever find my eternal home without a mother's prayers to inspire me and a mother's hand to guide me? History teaches us some valuable lessons on all its pages concerning this thought. Do you know that Nero's mother was a murderess? She gave to this world the most cruel man in the history of humanity. Lord Byron's mother was a proud, intellectual woman, worldly-minded in all her ways, and she gave to this world one of the most profligate, dissipated, intellectual autocrats (Lord Byron) the world ever saw. John Wesley's mother was a praying, painstaking, sensible, pious woman, and she gave to the world one of the richest and grandest characters; and to-day John Wesley's mother is the grandmother of one of the greatest religious denominations in this nineteenth century of ours. George Washington's mother was a good, plain, sensible woman, and she gave to the world, to America, a man that won the title, "The Father of His Country."

Some one said once: "If I could mother this world I could save this world;" and another said, "The hand that rocks the cradle rules the world." In a woman's meeting, some months ago (and I assert there is no more important meeting ever called together than a meeting of mothers), the question was sprung, "How old ought children to be before we begin to train them for God? to nurture them in the admonition of the Lord?" And one good mother said: "I think we ought to begin at six years of age with our children." A second said: "Why put off so long? Why not begin at the age of five?" And a third said: "I began with mine at four." Another good old mother said: "We must begin to train them in the paths of righteousness from the day we begin to train them to walk." At last a good old mother in Israel arose and said: "I'll tell you when to start: begin twenty years before the birth of the child with its mother?" O, sisters, if you will give a child a good mother she will see to the training of that child, and she will begin at the right age.

The mother! I want to say here, this morning, that, in reading the history of King Josiah, in the Bible, in a period of corruption and wicked influences, with nothing to bring him to a pure and holy life, I've often wondered at his being such a good man in the midst of such wickedness and corruption; and I can trace Josiah's goodness to no other source than to the fact that he had a good mother; and I say to you all, this morning, if you will take the Bible, and the preacher, and the Church, and all means of grace, and put them all on this side of me, and put my good mother on this other side, and ask me: "Which will you take, and endeavor to make your way to God the most successfully?" I believe I'd say, "Take the preachers, and the Bibles, and all other means of grace away from me, but leave me my good mother, for I believe she will succeed in carrying me to heaven." ·

A good mother is the greatest blessing ever bestowed on a family of children; and a godless, wicked, worldly mother is the greatest curse that ever blighted a home! I can understand how men can be wicked. I can, in a measure, understand how it is men can forsake God and live a worldly life; but the most terrible moral anomaly and monstrosity in the universe to-day is a godless, Christless mother, with innocent children playing around her home. O, mothers, of all beings in the world, God demands of you that you be the purest and the best! I have said this much as preliminary to what I shall read, discuss, and comment upon this morning—the Twenty-third Psalm:

"The Lord is my shepherd; I shall not want. He maketh me to lie down in green pastures; he leadeth me beside the still waters. He restoreth my soul; he leadeth me in the paths of righteousness for his name's sake. Yea, though I walk through the valley of the shadow of death, I will fear no evil; for thou art with me; thy rod and thy staff they comfort me. Thou preparest a table before me in the presence of mine enemies; thou anointest my head with oil; my cup runneth over. Surely, goodness and mercy shall follow me all the days of my life; and I will dwell in the house of the Lord forever."

I am glad, my sisters, that all commentators are agreed that David is the author of this Twenty-third Psalm. It makes little difference to me just now who is the author of the Nineteenth, or the Fiftieth, or the Seventy-third Psalm; but I am especially glad to believe that David is the author of the Twenty-third Psalm. You know that David was the shepherd boy who cared for the flocks of his father, and when he penned this psalm no doubt his mind ran back over his youthful days when it was his duty to care for his father's sheep. David remembered how, in the morning, he led the flock forth to the pasture, and how, in the afternoon, late, he brought them back to the fold. David remembered that it was his special care to see that all the sheep were provided for. When the little young lambs, by want of strength, could not walk to the pasture, he took them in his arms and carried them to pasture. And David remembered how, when the old and decrepit sheep were left in the fold, and could n't go to the pasture, after he reached the pastures in the morning, as the grass with dew was wet, and tender and sweet, he pulled up great armfuls of the tender grass, and in the evening carried it back to the fold for those old and decrepit sheep.

If I am young and without strength my Shepherd will carry me to the green pastures. If I am old and decrepit, and can not get to the green pastures, my Shepherd will bring the sweetest grass to the fold for me.

> "Even down to old age all My children shall prove
> My sovereign, eternal, omnipotent love;
> And when hoary hairs shall their temples adorn,
> Like lambs they shall still in my bosom be borne."

Blessed be God! Christianity, with its every truth among men, is the only institution that proposes to look after the gray hairs of the world! Mothers and fathers in gray hairs, defenseless and

friendless, when your children forsake you God
will take you up.

"The Lord is my shepherd." David remembered the day when the wild beasts came down
upon his sheep and carried off one of his lambs;
how he followed the beast and overtook and slew
it, and brought the lamb back to the fold. He remembered how water, and food, and shelter, and
every necessary comfort, were provided for his
sheep; and now looking over the picture of his
youthful days as a shepherd boy, he lifted his face
to God and said: "O God, as I am greater than a
sheep, and as thou art infinitely more great than I
am, so much more art thou my shepherd, and I shall
not want."

"I shall not want." There is a place in God,
mother, that you ought to seek—where no vacuum
left by the loss of any thing leaves a wound in your
soul. The time comes to us in our peace with God
where we can give up all, and yet praise God for
his love, and when it seems we have more left than
when God began to take from us. There is that
scattereth abroad and yet increase. I shall thank
God as he takes my children, for I shall want them
more in heaven than on earth. Did you ever read
that precious book, "Stepping Heavenward?"
Every mother should read that book. As you turn
its pages you will involuntarily write on the margin, "That's me; that's me." O, what a book of
light!

I recollect an incident of a father and mother.
The father was a physician, and their little Willie

was ill, and growing worse for several days, until at last his condition was critical. About midnight one night the mother came down and walked into the sick-room, where her husband sat by little Willie's bed-side, and as she entered she threw her eyes upon the pale, hard-breathing little invalid, and as she looked at him she threw herself on her husband's breast, and cried out in an agony of fear: " O, husband, God is going to take our little Willie away!" and she sobbed and cried aloud. Directly the husband looked up and said: " O, wife, do n't say God is going to take our child from us, but if little Willie is not better by daylight, we will give him to God." O, precious mother, that can see her child transplanted from the thorns and brambles of life to the roses of the paradise of God, and say: " I have given God a child!" Thrice happy that mother who has a child in heaven! That mother who has a sweet one in heaven is a better mother to those she has left than she ever would have been if God had not given her a child in heaven! O, how those little waxen, ice-cold fingers bind our memories back to many a hasty word and act scattered along our backward track, and, O,

> " How those waxen hands remind us,
> As in snowy cerements they lie,
> Not to scatter thorns, but roses,
> For our meeting by and by."

" The Lord is my Shepherd, I shall not want." I shall not want! I shall not only have protection, but if the enemy approacheth God will throttle that enemy. If I want food God will bring it me, and whatever my needs are, my sweet faith takes in all the providential beneficence of God, and I shall never lack for any thing. You will be happy the day you settle the question and say: I'd rather be the least of them and in rags than wear a royal diadem and sit upon a throne.

There are women in this city that the society of this town bow and scrape to in their presence, and they imagine themselves queenly beings, but the woman that bows in loving faith before God is the honored one among good women. Society! society! A leech of the heart, and when society shall fix itself upon your life-blood, it will draw the last drop of blood out of your heart, and you'll be a bloodless, heartless woman, and that's the worst thing God's eyes ever looked upon—a woman without a heart! You know what society does for a woman. A woman that enters society and goes the giddy rounds forgets her children, and God, and every thing, and she comes in contact with the most heartless creatures God ever saw, and by and by she is transformed into a heartless wretch like those around her.

I never went into society myself—they wouldn't let me in—may be because I was too poor, or else I would tell on 'em. I only know of it as society women who've been reformed have told me, and to tell the truth, I never did see many reformed society women. They're as scarce as hen's teeth, as the old saying is. God pity a woman that has forgotten God, and all she thinks about is: "How will I shine?" and "What spot must I rub next

to make it shine?" and "What will I wear next?"
or "I've been eclipsed at Mrs. So-and-so's house,
and here's another about to eclipse me;" or, "If
they jump up and crack their heels together three
times, I must jump up and crack mine four
times. I must try to beat this mean old thing."
Didn't you ever try to beat a neighbor on fine
houses and entertainments?

The Lord pity a woman that will sacrifice every
thing the Lord holds dear for the sake of trying to
outshine some one else! Good women try to shine
within themselves! Fool women try to outshine
others!! Draw your own conclusion, sister, as to
which class you belong to! The minute you begin
to talk about society there's a whole lot of poor,
ignorant, innocent women say: "I never heard of
that; no such thing as society." Yes, and you look
as if all you needed were a pair of little golden
wings, and you'd be off to glory!! Sister, you
know what I'm talking about! Let's turn loose
all things that interfere with heart, and sympathy,
and godliness, and let's bid them an eternal farewell!! A mother—a heartless mother—who in her
love for show, and love for criticism on that line,
and for the purpose of being spoken of in the
circles of society, will set wine, and beer, and
brandy on her entertainment table, will sacrifice the
sobriety of her husband and children, and doom
both to hell forever to have a little finer cham-
pagne, and have her society friends smack their
lips over it and say: "That's the best in town!"

I'll tell you another thing. You'll never reform

32

Cincinnati, or New York, or any place else from intemperance, and degradation, and death, until you reform the respectable people of this country! You can put that down. As long as mothers run bar-rooms at their homes, you can't blame men for running bar-rooms on the street corners of the town; and mothers who train their children at home to drink, can't blame the children for going to bar-rooms and getting it whenever they want it. I have known mothers to set out brandy and wine at their home, and in the gay flirtations of life the loved ones began to dissipate and drink; and I've had that mother come to me afterward wringing her hands, and with a look of infinite despair on her face, say: "Help me, for God's sake, to save my husband and children, for they seem already to be beyond the reach of the arm of God!" How many mothers in this house to-day whose heart is bleeding, drop by drop and hour after hour, because of their children's sins, and yet they have been contributing to the transgressions of their sons and husbands.

"Mother" ought to be the synonym of all that's pure, and holy, and good, but instead of that, it has reached a point in this country where mother means simply an idle name, and her interest and care for the souls of loved ones is no more than if they hadn't any souls to be interested in great questions at all!

There's a mother out there that has spent more time in preparing her daughter for the ball-room than she ever spent on her knees praying God to

save her daughter from hell! What do you expect
from the children of such mothers as that? She
will have the finest dressmaker in the town two
weeks on a dress for her daughter, and when that
dress gets home that mother will spend more time
altering that dress than she ever spent on her
knees in her life praying to save her daughter from
hell. What can you expect from women like that?
I've said many a time if I had to marry a thousand
times—and I'm like the Irishman who said, "I
hope I'll never live to see my wife married again"—
the further I could get away from the giddy pleasures and sinful amusements of life, to get me a
good wife just that much further would I go. I
would never go to a ball-room to get a first-class
wife. You can get wives in ball-rooms, but I
never said what sort. God gives a man a
good wife, and you know who gives him a
bad one.

Mothers, there are thousands of influences around
us to-day that speak out in unmistakable language,
"Call a halt." Let us turn our faces toward God
this morning and say: "The Lord is my Shepherd,"
and the Shepherd of my children, and we shall not
want for purity, or for honor, or for pleasures, or
for sustenance, or for any thing that is best for us
in life and in eternity. The way to keep yourself
from want is to keep somebody else from wanting.
The best way to get God's help is to pitch in and
help some one else, and God will help those that
try to help others; and if every mother in town
would do her best to try and reform her own home

and the homes of others, O, what a glorious country we would have.

One great curse of this century is idle mothers and idle daughters. There are women in this country who board around continually. They never turn their hands to any thing useful in the universe. They never stitch, they never hem a handkerchief, never darn a pair of socks for their husbands, and they never do any thing. All they do is to manage to get down to the breakfast table every morning before the dining-room is closed, and then they say sometimes: "It seems to me they could be a little more accommodating round here, and run the thing a little later than they do." They manage to get down to dinner or supper, and that's about all; and if they ever get out it is to go to some entertainment, or theater, or to some millinery shop, or to some first-class dry goods house. What's such an anomaly as that worth? Nothing in the universe. Nobody in this world can be any account and do nothing. Nothing! Why, if some of you women of that sort were to die to-morrow, and they were to keep it out of the newspapers, nobody would know you are dead unless it be those who miss you at the theaters, and the milliner would n't see you. I do n't know even whether your husband would miss you. I reckon, though, he'd miss you about the time the monthly bills usually come in. I reckon he'd miss you then!

Sister, no matter how much your husband is worth, if you are not necessitated to work for yourself, go out and work for others. I declare to you to-day, if I had the means and opportunities that some women in this house right now have, I'd visit homes, and make calls on the poor, and do every thing that would be of benefit to mankind. You see some women who say, "I haven't any use for this poor white trash," and nine out of ten of these very same came from that sort of stock. A generation or two back you'll find that some poor financier, or poor white folks, pitched in and made a whole lot of money, and you're their daughter or their grand-daughter, with an immense fortune to start with; and perhaps your husband came from the same sort of stock; you unite your fortunes, and you think you are princely people. A magnificent family—whose father may be was a rag-dealer. If there's any class of people in this world I've a contempt for it's these kind of people that say, "I haven't any use for this poor white trash," and you don't have to take the back track more than a mile on this sort of people before you find out who their grandfathers were and what they did.

"The Lord is my Shepherd, I shall not want." I'll say to you this morning that if you have confidence in God you'll never want for any thing. "He maketh me to lie down in green pastures." Sister, be conscious that God is your father and do your duty, and you will lie down in green pastures. That's a position of ease. "Lie down in green pastures"—not on the rocks or in the wilderness where the wolves prowl about, but "in the green pastures." I have nothing now, but when I get hungry I can get right up and go to eating all around me " in green pastures." " He leadeth me beside the still waters." O, what a gracious picture. I have seen this picture on the walls of a parlor. The young sheep at the edge of the pool with the old sheep in the water; the little lambs playing on the banks, and it reflected their antics and gambols; and as I looked, I seemed to hear the old sheep say: " We have had enough for this time, and enough for to-morrow, and enough for evermore;" and such a picture of contentment I seldom ever looked at before.

" The Lord is my Shepherd, I shall not want. He maketh me to lie down in green pastures; he leadeth me beside the still waters." David naturally jumped from the idea of the sheep to the idea of human beings, you see. Did you ever stop to think how close we were all to sheep anyhow? They say, " Two heads are better than one, even if one is a sheep's head," but sometimes you strike a fellow with both, and that's bad. We're a kind of sheep any way. It's natural for sheep to wander off and get lost, and when a sheep does get lost, it's the most defenseless thing in the world, and when you call it to come to you so you can shelter it, it just ups and runs away. You are that way, too. It's the most natural thing in the world for you to wander off from God, and when you do wander away, how defenseless you are, and while God has been calling you back all these years, you've been running the other way. O, how much we are like sheep! There are no real sheep here this morning, and therefore I am not afraid of offending them. Sheep! David gets away from the idea of the sheep, and he says, "He restoreth my soul." We 're getting to a point now, sisters. I want to impress on your mind, "He restoreth my soul."

When I was a pastor in the South I heard of the sickness of one of the members of my Church. I was called there, and drove out of town about five miles. When I got out of my buggy I walked up the avenue to a beautiful country residence and rang the door-bell. Some one admitted me, and I walked in. The husband met me soon, and I saw such a sad and dejected look on his face. He asked me into the parlor, and when I went in I saw that every thing there was covered with dust and all disarranged. Directly he returned, and asked me to walk into his wife's room. I walked in and up to the bed-side, and there on the bed was the pale, sick wife; her hand was hot with fever, and a hectic flush covered her face. As I looked into her burning eyes and into her sunken cheeks, she said: "O, how much I'm suffering?" A suffering wife—a suffering mother. I do n't believe there 's one man in a thousand that 's capable of sympathizing with a suffering wife, with a suffering mother. Sister, sometimes suffering is the fire that purifies the gold.

A suffering wife! Well, as I was about to say, I staid at this house of my member, and was invited to dinner. As I entered the dining-room I noticed every thing was dirty and disarranged. When we left the room the children burst in, and the mother said, pettishly: "Nurse, take these children away; they almost break my head with their noise. Keep them out, nurse." Well, dinner was announced, and, as I said, every thing looked as if it was pitched on the table—no knife at my plate, no spoons on the table. After eating in some way and getting through, I came into the sick-room again, and had prayer and read the Bible. When I left the house I looked back and said: "O, there's the saddest home I ever saw." Just three months after that, after preaching one day at a country church, a red, rosy, bright-faced woman ran up to me and said: "Mr. Jones, do come to dinner with us to-day." "I do n't know you," I said. "Well," said she, "you must go any way." "All right," said I, "if I must I guess I'll have to go."

So I got into my buggy and drove down the road after them, and they stopped in front of a beautiful country residence, and as we all walked up the steps three or four children rushed out on the porch and met the mother, and she took them all in her arms, and she hugged the little fellows, and romped and played with them like mad. We walked into the parlor, and I noticed how nice every thing was kept, and how regular it looked. Then we walked into the family-room, and every thing there was as clean as a pin and elegantly arranged, and we then went out to dinner. The dinner was fit for a prince, and she presided so elegantly, and the husband looked so happy, and the children looked so gleeful. When I got in my

COTTAGE HOME OF REV. SAM P. JONES,

buggy, after it was all over, and drove down the avenue, I looked back over my shoulder, and I said: "That's the happiest house I ever saw." And, sisters, that was the very same house I was at before. So changed I did n't recognize it. One time mother was sick; next time she was restored.

Sister, there's as much difference in your home with your poor soul drooping and perishing, and your soul feasting upon God, and growing in grace and righteousness. Just as much difference in your soul as there was in that home I described—in a physical sense. In a thousand homes I've known I've seen such a marked difference. If you will get your soul toward light, and get full of love to God and man, and go home to-day and live there two weeks that way, your husband will have to call in a neighbor to identify you. He'll say: "This looks like the same woman, but she does n't talk or act like it. I never saw such a change in a woman in my life."

I'd as soon expect the world to come to an end right now as to expect some of you to get full of religion, because you're so full of other things you can't throw them out! How do you expect God to live in your home with you? You've a card-room in your house, but is there a grace-room in your house? Did you ever build a prayer-room in your house for family devotion, and say: "O, Christ, be thou an eternal guest in my house, and live here and abide with me for ever?" Folks that have cards, and wine, and worldliness, and balls, never have any room in their house for Christ! Never!

We will never have redemption in this country until we get mothers restored to love and harmony with God. Never, never! Here are Mary and Annie. Mary is eight and Annie is six years old. Husband comes home to dinner, and wife says: "Husband, do you care if next Wednesday night I give a little party to the children?" " A little party?" asks the husband. " Yes," says wife, " a little party." " Why, wife, the children are too young to be talking about parties." " O, yes," says wife, " every body has parties for the children. It's just a little, little, little party, that's all." " Why, wife, I tell you our children are too young to be thinking of parties." " Well," says wife, " that has always been your way. The Lord knows I sometimes wish we didn't have any children; they're in jail all the time, and can't see any pleasure at all; and the fact of the business is, I believe you're going to ruin the children by the iron rod you're holding over them."

That's the devil's way. The devil came near getting old Job from bottom to top, when he got Job's wife against him and got her for him. You see, when the devil gets a woman, he has a power. Well, the husband talks against it until he sees he's got to let up or have a row. You know what that means, don't you, sister? He knows he's got to say " Yes," or you'll pout about the house a whole week. I mean the women that ain't here— we never pout. This thing has to be carried out. Well, the children have a " little party." What is a little party? Nothing but a big party with short clothes on. That's all it is! And what is a big party? It's nothing but the ante-room to the ball-room. What's a ball-room? It's nothing but the ante-room to the "german." What's the "german?" It's nothing but the ante-room to infinite and eternal disgrace and damnation!

Mothers train their children for the devil and hell, and by the time they're fifteen I'd as soon preach to a goat as to one of 'em! How many children have you seen in any of these meetings? It's gray hairs and grown-up people here. Our children, some of them, are trained by the circles they reside in to resist the word of God, and they're as impervious to the truth as if they were seventy-five years old in sin. My experience among men is, I take in ten adults to one child. What's the matter? Mother, when it's too late, too late, you're going to call a halt. Mark what I tell you. There are incidents and scenes occurring in every city in America to-day that make the mother faint and swoon, and drop down and say, "Almighty God, am I to blame for this?" Read the daily papers! There's been things in the papers since I've been here that ought to have made every mother walk into the family room and say, "Husband, children, we will call a halt!"

You say, some of you, "Why, Mr. Jones, if we do what you say, our children can't amuse themselves or have any pleasure." I'll say this much: If my children can't enjoy themselves without parties and dances, and cards, and all that sort of things, then they can move out. They'll have to find another boarding-house. They can't eat **my** bread and run on that line! No, sir! I say, "You can rack out of here whenever this home doesn't suit you." My Julia Baxter is only eight months old; and there are not five children in all Georgia that has more fun than mine do, and I won't let my children mix with these things! No, sir! The Lord pity our race that has degraded and groveled so low that it must go into all sorts of excesses to have pleasure.

Let me drop back a minute on two girls, **one** from this house and another from another house. You'll know them as soon as I show them. Well, here are pictures of two homes:

The first picture: Little Annie walks in. Annie is six years old, and says, "Mamma, please ma'am, give me some thread for my needle," and mamma looks at her and says, "Yes, there you are again, you little vixen. You've wasted more thread than you're worth to-day, and you're always troubling me. Get on your bonnet and get out of the way and go and play." Annie drops her head and walks off. Next day Annie comes in and says, "Mamma,"—mamma is busy at the machine,—"Mamma, give me some scraps for my doll dress." Mamma says, "I won't. You've wasted more scraps than you and the doll are worth. Don't bother me. Go away, and go over to Mrs. Brown's, and see if you can't devil her awhile." Little Annie drops her head and walks out of the door, and when she gets in the yard the tears come to her eyes and she sobs, "I wish I was dead—that's all I wish. Lord

knows, mamma never has a kind word for me."
The next day after, Annie comes in again and says:
"Please, mamma, loan me your thimble." And
mamma says: "Why, you little brat, you had that
thimble yesterday and lost it, and it took me an
hour to find it. I'll cut the blood out of you if I
see you with that thimble any more." Annie goes
out again crying, but this time she says: "I wish
mamma was dead now—that's all I wish." Next
day Annie comes in and says: "Mamma, may I
have the loan of your scissors?" Mamma snaps
out: "No, you can't. Do you want to stick your
eyes out, and be blind on my hands?" Annie went
on this way, day after day and year after year, and
by and by she grew to be eighteen years old. I
went to see her mother after she grew up, and
mother draws down a corner of her mouth way
below her chin and says to me: "I don't know
what's the matter with my Annie. She's the worst
girl in all this settlement, and Lord knows I've
done my best for her."

I'll tell you another thing: If I were a wid-
ower and Annie's mother were a widow, I don't
know which I'd take—the old woman or the
daughter. I believe I'd take the old woman—
she'd be dead and buried quicker. I have heard
fellows say, when they married a lady, the father-
in-law and all packed up traps and moved in on
him. I don't know but what it's right after all.
You ought to court the whole family and find them
out. It is a question whether a man can get a first-
class wife out of a third-rate family. Some of you

mothers are raising wives for men that will be ter.
rors. Mark what I tell you. I'm like the Irish.
man who said: "If I die there'll be one mon who
will regret my death." "Why, who is that?" said
a fellow. "It's the fellow that gets my wife," re.
plied the Irishman. This is an important question.
As you train and raise your children up so they
will do. What was the matter with little Annie?
The trouble was she was just like her mother.

Here is another picture: Little Mary walks up
to her mother who is sitting there quietly, and says:
"Mamma, please give me some thread." "Yes,
my darling, I will get it in a moment—I was just
thinking about you; I want you to be a good girl;
that is the one great desire of my heart." And she
gives Mary the thread. Next day she comes in
again. "Mamma, please give me some scraps for
my doll dress." "Yes, dear. I was just reading
a passage from the Scripture—'Remember thy
Creator in the days of thy youth.' Daughter, do
you know what that means?" "No, ma'am." "It
means you must commence now and be good." She
gives the child the scraps. Little Mary walks out
and says: "I just know I've got the best mamma
that any little girl ever had." Next day she came
in again. "Mamma, please let me have your
thimble." "Mamma is using it now, but I will
let you have it after awhile. But do you recollect
that verse I read to you yesterday?" "No, ma'am;
but I recollect what it was you said—I must commence to be good now; and after I went out, I
went into my room and kneeled down and prayed,

'God, help me to be like mamma.'" "Well, my darling, mamma has not said prayers yet this morning. Will you come into the closet with me?" And they went together and shut the closet, and about that time a thousand delighted angels rushed in. They wanted to get in and see what God was going to do for mother and Mary. And when the two came out little Mary still had hold of mamma's finger. A tear that would not stain an angel's cheek trickled down her cheek. An angel crystallized it in his hand and flew immediately back to heaven among the other angels and said: "Here is a crystallized tear of a sweet little girl that mother is training for everlasting joy and bliss and heaven." And so the home training goes on, and by and by there is a little eighteen-year-old girl, the pride of her mother's heart, a blessing to the poor, to the community, and to the Church; a blessing to all around her. And the community says: "Look what a sweet, pure girl Mary is!" Do you want to know how it comes? Mary is just like that sweet mother of hers. O, mother, you impress your character day by day upon your children.

SAYINGS.

TURNING ABOUT.—Rev. George Smith was preaching a learned discourse on the distinction between evangelical and legal repentance. He made the welkin ring, and many of his congregation had fallen asleep, when Uncle John Knight got up in his rear pew and said: "Please let me show what repentance is." "Certainly, Uncle John Knight," said Mr. Smith. Uncle John started right up the aisle—he was lame from rheumatism and stamped this way as he marched up the aisle slowly—repeating the words, "I am going to hell! I am going to hell! Now, George, listen," said he; "I will turn," and he wheeled right around. "I will show you what repentance is," and as he stamped along in the opposite direction, he repeated: "I am going to heaven! I am going to heaven! That is what repentance is."

MANY an old sinner who wants to go to heaven does like the man who wanted to go to Cincinnati so bad and yet got aboard a train going straight from Cincinnati to Chattanooga.

HELL and heaven have parallel tracks. Trains on the one go hellward; on the other, heavenward.

A LOCOMOTIVE engine on the track is the grandest thing you ever saw, but off the track it is a helpless lump of iron. So humanity is of no use on the highways of worldliness. "I am the way," says the Lord. Let us start out on the dirt road of dishonesty, and we will soon get our souls mired down in the dirt. I wish men could see that the soul has no more business off the way of Christ than an engine off on a dirt road.

SERMON XIX.

WATCH THOU IN ALL THINGS.

A Sermon to Daughters.

"But watch thou in all things, endure afflictions, do the work of an evangelist, make full proof of thy ministry."— 2 TIM. IV, 5.

WHAT this discussion has to do with the young ladies of Cincinnati, we may find out further along. These are the last words of St. Paul, that grand old man of God, to Timothy, and through Timothy to us, the sons and daughters of the race. He said four things to Timothy in this one verse, and these four things cover life in all its aspects and all its multiplied phases, and you may get something from each of those four things, and from all of them, that will make you in time honored by society and in eternity safe in heaven.

The first thing Paul said has special reference to myself, and was this: "Watch thou in all things." He believed we ought to be good, if we wanted to make those around us good. My first business is to look after myself, to see that I am straight myself, and then I am in a sort of attitude to straighten out others. First cast the beam out of your own eye, and then you can see how to cast the mote out of your brother's eye. Sometimes we are paying more attention to the mote in some one else's eye than we are to the beam in our own eye.

It is a hard matter for a giddy, gay, godless mother to have sweet-spirited Christian daughters, and it is very hard for a good and pious mother to stay very pious and have a set of giddy, godless daughters around her. "Evil communications corrupt good manners." A good mother may be wrongly influenced by her children, and I know an idle mother has a permanently bad effect on her children.

The first thing said here is, "Watch thou in all things." We have the same idea, though perhaps it is a little plainer, where we read, "See then that ye walk circumspectly, not as fools, but as wise." Many a trap, device, influence, and power in this world that have demoralized souls and ruined men and women, ruined them because they did not walk circumspectly. Circumspection is the sentinel of the soul, put outside to watch the approaches of the enemy. In military tactics you read that sentinels are posted on the outer edge to watch the enemy, and if you will read the manual you will see it is death to a sentinel to fall asleep on post. The safety of those hundreds of thousands of men here in the army is in the hands of the men on post out there. If you go to sleep and are surprised and disarmed by the enemy, it is death to you.

I tell you it is spiritual and eternal death to the soul for the sentinel of the soul to go to sleep. Nine-tenths of our trouble is that we have gone to sleep and our enemies have surprised, approached and overcome us because we were not on the watch. You must have a vigilant, watchful soul looking in every direction. Our Savior looked at this world just as it presented itself to him, and he said, "Awake, thou that sleepest, and arise from the dead, and I will give thee life."

Slumbering world, wake up. Rub your eyes, look around and see your enemies as they approach on every side. The enemies of mankind may be summed up in three words—the world, the flesh and the devil. I saw this illustrated once where a man said he had married three times (I do n't like that to start with) and the first time he married he married for riches, the second time for beauty, and the third time for intelligence. He said that in these three wives he got the world, the flesh, and the devil. If he gets to heaven he will have gone up through much tribulation.

"Watch thyself." My enemies are most of them within. I may have an enemy out yonder who wishes me harm and who will slander me, and who might shoot at me on the street, but that fellow can't do me any harm. People that talk about us never harm us. When you hear one man talking about another you can know that man is trying to drag him down to a level with himself—a level lower than the one he is on, and he wants to pull him down with him. Whenever you talk about any body you are trying to pull him down on a level with yourself. Let him stay up. You'll have more room if you let him stay up—you have more room down below where you are.

I like that old blacksmith who, in his shop one day, was told there was a man up the road who was slandering him and saying the worst things in the world about him, and trying to ruin his character, and he was advised to go up the road and whip him. Said the blacksmith: " I can take this sledge and hammer out more good character in three weeks than that man can ruin in ten years. I will stick to my work, let him do his worst."

No man can harm me from the outside—the trouble is always on the inside. I'd rather fight ten thousand on the outside than one on the inside. Our worst enemies are on the inside.

First I will watch my temper. If I were preaching to a congregation of men I would dwell at length on temper, for men are the beings who have so much temper. Of course the women have very little. Temper, temper, temper. The most lovely girl in Cincinnati to-day is the girl who has her temper under the best control. Find me a person without any temper and I'll show you a person there's very little in. I want a world of temper, but under first-class control. Temper to a woman and to a man is what steam is to an engine— it carries them along. If an engine can't work her steam out through the cylinder escapes but blows all the steam through her whistles, it's a nuisance to every body in the community; and the woman who lets her surplus temper fly out through her mouth is a nuisance to all creation.

Sister, a question of temper. Have n't you many a time straightened out your temper, and fixed it up nice and said, " I'll never get mad any more; I disgrace myself every day, but I've got this thing all right now, there 'll be no more trouble about me, you 'll never hear from me again? Pardon me this time. I pledge you I 'll never do that way again ; " and you get it all fixed up nice, and it is n't an hour before something comes in front of your temper, and it goes all to pieces, and just look at that. I wish I had that high-tempered woman here to-day. She is not here, but you may just tell her what I said.

Temper! temper! Temper under control. Whenever you feel like saying an unkind thing, say a kind thing, though you die. Whenever you feel unkindly toward a person, do him a kind thing; if you feel like acting unkindly, or have acted unkindly, go straight to him and do the kindest thing you ever did in your life. One way to overcome evil is with good, not evil. If any one speaks unkindly of you, speak a good word of him. If any one does evil to you, you do good in return. Return good for evil.

My temper is controlled largely by what I think and what I do, and if I think kindly and talk kindly about a person, I find my temper will be submissive; but whenever I attempt to say an unkind thing or do an unkind thing, my temper gets out of fix. That's the way with it. The most lovable sight in the world is four sisters, and each one is just as kind as can be to the others, and they never speak an unkind word the year around. The most lovable sight in this world, I say, is loving, sweet-spirited sisters, as kind to each other as they can be, and in all their conduct they show they appreciate one another. One says, "Sister, I'd

rather you would have this than have it myself.
Sister, you wear my hat, or my sealskin cloak, or
wear any thing I have that you want." The milk
of human kindness is always manifested where the
temper is under good control and in complete sub-
jection to the spirit and law of Christ. Be kind
toward one another, and you'll find a kind temper
is a blessing to all and a blessing to every one.

Then I'll not only watch my temper, but I'll
watch my tongue. O, these tongues of ours. How
much harm, sisters, we can do in one little visit
with these tongues of ours. The tongue! The tongue!

Reading Æsop's Fables, I find where the author
of the fables was told by his master one day:
"Æsop, I am going to have some elegant friends to
dinner to-morrow, and I want you to serve the best
food you can get as a dinner for them." Next day
the guests all came and were shown into the dining-
room by the host, and there was n't a thing on the
table but tongue. The master became angry and
said: "Here, Æsop, I told you to get up the very
best dinner you could, and here's nothing but
tongue." "O," said Æsop, "Master, tongues are
the best things in the world. It is with the tongue
we speak words of love and words of pleasure;
and it is with the tongue we say kind things and
scatter words of kindness. Tongue, master, is the
best thing in the world." Said his master, "Æsop,
my company is greatly disappointed. Suppose you
bring on the worst dinner you can to-morrow."
And the next day when the company entered, not
a thing was on the table but tongue. "Æsop,"

said the master, " yesterday you said the best thing in the world was tongue, and now you 've got tongue as the worst thing." " Well, master," said Æsop, " tongues are the worst things. We ruin men's character with the tongue. It cuts with more fearful effect than a sharp-edged sword. We spoil reputations and assail whole communities with tongues." I will watch my tongue.

I will be on the watch for another thing. "Watch thou in all things." I will watch my company. I will watch the sort of company I keep. There is n't a man or boy or girl in this country that is proof against bad company. There was a young lady that said to her father: " Do you care if I go to the ball this evening, father?" And the father replied : " Yes, daughter, I 'd rather that you would not go." " Why ?" asked the daughter. " Daughter, I do n't like the company you 'll be in." " I know, papa, all of them are not nice, but there will be some nice people there, and I am not afraid of the bad ones hurting me." About that time there fell a dead coal on the grate fender, and the father pointed to it and said, " Daughter, what 's that ?" The daughter said, " It 's a burnt out coal, father." " Pick it up—does it burn you?" " No, father." " Well, throw it down. Now what 's that on the ends of your fingers, daughter ?" " Why it 's smut, father." " When you go into bad company, if they do n't burn you, they 'll smut you every time."

Give me your attention just here on this idea. I do not see why it is young ladies take so much

stock in the dancing and frivolous young men of
this country. You can bring a solid, sensible,
thorough-going young man up, and stand right by
his side a full-fledged dude, and tell nine girls out
of ten, " Girls, take your choice," and they 'll take
the dude every one ! I 've seen a dude start down
the road with a hundred girls after him full tilt,
trying to catch him, and you never in all your life
saw such a scramble as there was there.

Here 's a young man ; he 's a flirter ; he gets $40
per month ; he 's a spider-legged, jockey-club sort
of a fellow ; you can see him and you can often
smell him, too. I know him better by smell than
sight. He 's a clerk in a town store at $40 a month,
and he dresses like a prince ; his opera bill is $25 a
month, cigarette bill $20, his livery bill $40 more,
and his board bill is about $40, and I can count
out $200 a month that it takes to run that boy, and
for the life of me he only gets $40 a month. One
of that kind down South was having a big time
with the girls, and the proprietor of the store he
worked in found out what he was doing, and one
day he caught him by the lapel of his coat, and
said : " Look here, young fellow, where do you get
all this money to foot these bills ?" " My step-
mother is sending it to me," whimpered the dude.

Who ever heard of a step-mother sending a boy
money ? I had the best step-mother this world ever
saw, and she never sent me a cent in her life. Many
a fellow in this country who says his step-mother is
sending him the money, is doing some downright
stealing, I tell you. If a fellow like that were to

come to my house and fall in love with a daughter of mine, and she with him, and she would some day ask me if she could marry him, I would inquire: "Do you love that boy? Are you going to marry him?" and if her reply were "Yes, sir," I should say: "Well, you had better hurry the thing up, for that young man is going to break into jail before he does into my family, and I do n't want you to be disgraced before marriage."

Some of these young fellows are having a big time, and some of you girls say: "O, my, is n't he perfectly irresistible? He's just exquisite!" I reckon you have reference to his perfume. That sort of a fellow is king of kings and lord always in some communities. Many a girl that marries a fellow like that does so at her own risk. I know one that married a fellow like that, and at the end of a year he had to leave town for something or other—they never knew what—and the poor girl looked sad and dejected for a long time afterwards. Girls, you take a terrible risk when you marry a fellow like this.

Well, I'll draw the reverse picture: Here's a little fellow 17 years old; he's got on a wool cap and jeans clothes, but he's a pious boy and goes to Sunday-school and Wednesday night prayer-meetings. He clerks on at that store, until by and by he's put into some sort of a responsible position; he belongs to the Church, is honest, and attends meetings regularly. One day I heard two girls talking as he passed, and one says: "Just look at that old thing now; is n't he a sight? He's the

worst thing I ever saw; he belongs to the Church—
he does, too; he's the strangest boy I ever saw;
look at that old hat he's got; why I would n't give
a flip of my finger for a fellow of that sort."

That fellow works on steadily, and he is pro-
moted to book-keeper, and the next thing we hear
of him he goes up into the country and marries
Mary Smith, one of the plainest, most sensible girls
in the whole settlement. They move into a little
cottage; the firm grows, and about ten years afterwards I see that young fellow's name at the head of
the firm, and he's one of the strongest and best
business men in the city, and he has built him a
nice residence over here, and his wife is one of the
best and purest women in the Church, and she's a
blessing to society; and there they are, going on in
grandeur and Christian beauty. You do n't have
to ask that Mary Smith where her husband is. He
was n't one of those spider-legged dudes that ran
away and left his wife.

Girls, watch your associations. Watch in all
things that pertain to righteousness, and make it
the rule of your life to love God and live in harmony with God and truth. Watch the company
you keep, the associations you make, the kind of
books you read. I will tell you books are your
company. I hate to see a girl who reads nothing
but dime novels. Some of these ten-cent-novel
girls will read Dickens and cry as if their heart
would break over Little Nell, but when they look
out of the window and see a poor barefooted little
girl with her feet nearly frozen in the cruel snow,

they won't shed a tear; but they will cry like forty over Dickens's Little Nell, and not over that starving little child out there. The Lord have mercy on these people that can cry over ten-cent novels and not be moved by the terrible suffering about them.

Balls! I'll see your parents later on the subject of ball-rooms. I want to tell them something that will reform them or make them mad—one or the other. Put that down. I am not here to arraign you ladies about playing cards. J. G. Holland said a big thing when he said "Cards is a game of starvelings, mentally and spiritually." That's a great big truth. God pity a home where more cards are played than any thing else. I wish you could have heard Mason Long or Steve Holcomb, the two reformed gamblers, talk awhile. I declare to you it would make you go home and throw every card in the house into the fire, and be done with them forever.

When I was preaching at Chattanooga, one afternoon, on the subject of cards, a mother and daughter who were there went home and resolved to play cards no more, and they burnt up all the cards in the house. That evening, when the boy came home, he said: "Mother, let's have a game." "No, son," said she; "I have played my last game." Said the boy: "Sister, won't you play with me?" "No," said sister; "I will never play with you again, and God forgive me for ever having played with you." The boy went to meeting, and was converted, and when he went home he said: "Mother, I'm glad you burnt the cards. I will never play again."

And the mother cried out: "Thank God, son; I'll try to be a better mother to you hereafter."

I wish you could read the letters I get every day. I can read between the lines in some of them, and I can see that the person who writes me about the dear lost one is, or was, an instrument in the going astray of that person. Young ladies, let me say this to you: You have more power over your brothers than any body else, and if you start right at home you can redeem your brother, and he will thank God for a good sister.

" Endure afflictions." O, how much we have to endure in this life! I want to tell you, the test of character is how you carry the burdens of life. Sister, how much can you carry for your brother and daughter? How much can you carry for your poor mother? O, daughters, hear me to-day. You will never know the burdens your poor mothers carry; and let none of you do another thing to help break your mother's heart. Say, all of you: " I will unload my mother's heart; I will help carry mother's burdens." When my poor wife is broken down with care and trouble, the proudest attitude my daughters can present towards me is to walk up under her burdens and say: "Mamma, you can't carry them—we'll carry them for you." Give me daughters that will help their mothers carry the burdens of life.

Girls, you want to help your brothers, too; and perhaps a wayward sister. You must do all to help you can. You will never know what mother is until you lose your precious mother, and you carry some of the burdens of your precious mother. O, for daughters that are their mother's best friend! for daughters that will walk under their mother's arm, and say, "Mother, use us for crutches. Be a burden to us instead of letting us be a burden to you." When you go home to-day look your mothers in the face and say: "Forgive me, mother; I will carry your burdens in the future, instead of having you carry mine."

"Watch thou in all things, and endure affliction." Wherever you see care on your mother's face run to her and say: "Mother, give me that care; I will carry it for you." Some young women carry nothing for their mother. They trample on her best wishes and her tenderest graces. When their mother says "Do n't," they do. Of course, none of you here do that; I ain't talking to you— I'm talking to the girl that is n't here. Your mother's the best friend you 've got, and she knows what you ought to do and ought not to do; and, girls, listen to your mother; be guided by her. She cares enough for you to help you out of all trouble.

"Do the work of an evangelist." Suppose the Lord had every noble girl in this town at work for him. If you would consecrate the rose on your cheek and the brightness of your eye, and the sweetness of your voice and the helpfulness of your hand, and make it the effort of your life to live well and love God and keep his commandments—I wish thousands of times we had millions of daughters in this land who would do that. I heard once of a young woman whose father and mother were infidels and unbelievers, and when she was sent to college she had n't been there long before she was converted to God, and she wrote back home how sweetly Christ had forgiven her, and how she had turned her back on her previous life, and had turned her face to God and righteousness. The parents read this, and they said: " Why, daughter has taken up with that foolish thing, but we 'll soon wean her from it;" and when she was about to return to her home they prepared all sorts of amusements, and balls, and dances, and parties, in order to distract her from her religion, and make her forget her God in the excitement of the worldly things about her. When she returned they tried to make her renounce her religion, but it was in vain ; so, at last, in their exasperation, they bade her go to her room and put on a poor sun-bonnet and a calico dress and march out of the gate, an outcast forever and disinherited, unless she would say she would renounce her religion. She turned about, and put on her sun-bonnet and calico dress, and walked down and kissed her mother and father, and walked away with this sweet song on her voice :

> " Jesus, I my cross have taken,
>   All to leave and follow thee;
>   Naked, poor, despised, forsaken,
>   Thou from hence my all shalt be."

If we had Christian girls like that we could take this world and redeem it. Girls, consecrate your charms, your voice, your all, to redeeming the race and bringing the world to God ; act as the evangelist going out into the West, and do your duty to the last.

"Make full proof of your ministry." Girls, it is generally understood that almost all young ladies will sooner or later find a beau, and marry. Let me tell you this right along here: In Georgia there were four or five girls pitched in and married the same number of young fellows, who were drunkards. They made it up: "We'll marry these fellows and redeem them." They did marry the boys, and about three years after that, when I was down in that section, I saw more little saddened whippoorwill widows in that town than I ever saw in my life before. They were the palest, saddest widows I ever saw.

Girls, do n't marry drunkards. Better be led to the stake and burned to death by the inch than do that. Whenever a young man comes into your parlor with liquor on his breath, you turn him right around, and say: "Off these premises, sir; I would n't countenance you, sir, any more than I would a rattlesnake." A girl who will sit in a parlor and talk to a man with whisky on his breath will, may be, some day marry a man like that—and the finest specimen of a fool in this world is a woman that marries a man when she knows he has been drinking.

Across this river below here, in Henry County, seventeen years ago, I married a girl, and when she married me she knew I drank, and it was against the wishes of her parents; but she married me, though, and in three short years that woman's heart suffered more than angel's tongue could tell, and she says she will never get through praising God for saving her husband; that it was a miracle. Nothing but a miracle can save a drinking man, girls.

Girls, be careful. Do n't let a man come into your presence with his breath smelling of beer or whisky. I 'd rather be five hundred old maids shut up in one room than be the wife of one drunkard. There are thousands of things worse than old maidhood, and if you can never have company except drunken boys you 'd better die an old maid. That 's what I say. I know what it is.

"Make full proof of your ministry." Map out a line of conduct and follow it until results shall show for themselves what can be done.

What more could I have said, girls? I could have taken a text that would have led me out into saying some nice things and some pretty things; but, girls, let me tell you that sort of business is n't the thing. We want solid things for food. We want meat and greens. We want to quit these light things that will give us the dyspepsia. I want to talk plain and practical words to you, and I have talked to you as I would want a preacher to talk to my daughters when they come to hear him. I hope you will pray for me, and when you are grown up and married, and meet me in after years, I hope you will grasp my hand and say: "Mr. Jones, I followed the line of thought you talked on that day at Music Hall, in Cincinnati, and I have endured affliction, and I 'm the better for it."

Sermon XX.

Trouble Machines.—Imaginary and Real.

" He hath delivered my soul in peace from the battle that was against me, for there were many with me. . . . Cast thy burden upon the Lord and he shall sustain thee; he shall never suffer the righteous to be moved."—Psalm lv, 18, 22.

" Cast thy burden upon the Lord." I suppose the greatest curiosity this world could present to mortal gaze would be an unburdened human heart, a heart perfectly free from all care, all anxiety, and all trouble and disappointment. Four thousand years ago a man of God said that man is born unto trouble as the sparks fly upward. Just as naturally as the sparks ascend from the burning wood, so naturally is man born unto trouble.

After all, my brethren, it is not the part of a philosopher to sit down and number and weigh and measure his troubles, but first, to classify them, and then know what to do with each class. Now, there are what we denominate *real* troubles, and then there are what we call *imaginary* troubles. Poor human nature, how weak, how frail it is! We are always looking around for something we are never going to see. We are always expecting something that's never going to happen. We are always going out to meet something that isn't coming. Poor human nature! Now, it is wise for us to stop

and consider the two classes. That is all-important.
All troubles and all burdens may be classified under
these two general heads—imaginary trouble and
real trouble.

I will show what I mean by imaginary trouble
by an illustration. You've seen a mother—one of
those good, kind, careful mothers, indulgent to her
children. Well, belonging to a family where there
was just such a mother, there was a noble, gentle
horse; he was widely known in the community for
his gentleness, and was called "Old John." The
old horse fairly loved the children in his equine
way. Why, they could go down in the lot and
fairly climb all over him without a fear of being
hurt. They could play about on the green sward
about him, and old John would walk around them,
and it seemed as if when he put his hoof down he
shook it as though to make sure that none of the
little fellows were under it. Really, old John loved
the children. He was a sensible old horse. He
was more sensible in some things than was this
mother I refer to.

One day the mother, in answer to the children's
desire, said: "You may hitch up old John and
drive out to Mrs. So-and-so's; but, children, be
sure and come back by four o'clock." The children
assented to the proposition, hitched up old John
and drove away. By-and-by the clock struck four.
The mother listened to the clock, and when she
saw the hands point to four she went to the door
and looked, and when she did n't see the children
she said: "Why, those children were to be back by

four o'clock, and they never deceived me before. I wonder what's the matter with them. I'm satisfied something has happened." She waits five minutes, and then she looks out of the window and says: "O, how foolish I was for letting those children drive that horse off. I remember now that the other day when I drove old John down the road he took a fearful fright, and I said then, 'Those children shall never drive that horse again.' Then again it hasn't been more than two weeks since I had that terrible presentiment that that horse was going to run away and kill every child I had."

She then began to walk up and down the floor, towards the door first and then back to the fireplace, and she kept this up until directly her husband came in, and he said: "Why, wife, you seem to be in another stew about something. What's the matter?" "Why," said she, "I let those children drive old John off, and they were to be back by four o'clock, and you know, husband, those children never told me a story in their life. They never did, and now here it is fifteen minutes after four and they haven't come in yet. Husband, the last time I drove old John he took a fearful fright, and I said then I'd never let those children drive that horse off." The husband said: "O, wife, hush. You're in one of your stews. The children will be here directly." "No, I ain't in a stew, and it was no longer ago than last week that I had that terrible presentiment as clear as the sun that that horse was going to run away and kill every child I had." "O, wife," said the husband, "that

was something you ate. There is nothing in pre-
sentiments." She then said: "I want you to get
your hat right away and go and look after those
children. I know every one of them is killed by
this time." "O, hush," said her husband, "they'll
be here directly." "Husband," she says, "if you
don't go right away I'll go myself," and he knows
what that means, and he moves out, and he just
about gets to the bottom step of the front porch,
and about the time his foot strikes the pavement
here comes old John jogging up, with all the children safe, and mother looks out the door and she
sees the children, with their faces all alight with joy
at their visit, and old John standing there, as faithful as life, and she walks off into her room, and as
she sits down in her chair she buries her face in
her hands, and says: "O, what a goose I've been."
Brethren, she was, too.

Sister, you aren't by yourself in this matter—I
wish you were. There's that brother yonder. Many
a night he's gone home tired with the labor of the
day, and instead of going to bed and sleeping like
an honest laboring man, or like a thinking man, he
goes to bed and rolls and tumbles all night, to the
annoyance to every body in the house. He's trying to make the buckle and tongue meet! You've
heard about that, haven't you? "Many a time,"
says he, "I've been in a tight place, but this is the
tightest place I ever was in in my life. The fact
of the business is, I believe I'll be sold out by the
sheriff and will be driven off to the pauper-house,
and I and my family will just have to die there.

There's no use in talking, I can't live now. The wolf's at the door, and starvation's at hand."

This man, brethren, runs his trouble machine "most principally," as the darkey says, at night when he ought to be asleep. He starts his machine, and it just runs the whole night. Look here, brethren, I've had about as much trouble in my life as any of you ever had, but I never took any more trouble to bed with me than I could kick off at one lick and go to sleep. I go to bed to sleep, and when I go to bed at night I want to wake up refreshed and be able to run my machine in the daytime. I'm never going to lay my head down on a pillow and lie there in the dark trying to work out the problems of life. I'll take the great issues of my life in the daytime when my mind is clear, and at night when I go to bed I want to sleep.

The worried brain, the fevered look, and nervous tread of many a man in this town tell too plainly that there's a man who has been working out the problems of life up to one, two, and three o'clock, instead of being asleep. I like the idea of that fellow, who, when a man was walking about in the room overhead at the hotel, and he could n't go to sleep until about two o'clock, got up and went up stairs and said to the occupant of the room, " Look here, my friend, I can't get to sleep with you pacing up and down the floor all night. What's the matter with you ?" " Why," said the fellow, " I owe $10,000, and it's due to-morrow, and I have done my best, but I can't get the money." " Have you done your best ?" inquired the fellow from below.

"Yes, I've done my very best," replied the man. "Well, then, you go and get into that bed and go to sleep, and let the other fellow do the walking. He's the one to be troubled now."

That's my doctrine, brethren; when I've done my best, the other fellow can do the walking from that time on! When I've done my best, I'm going to be like the fellow I heard of in Chicago, who went bankrupt for $300,000, and another fellow stopped him on the street and wanted to condole with him, and the man said: "Friend, you need n't sympathize with me; it's my creditors that need your sympathy." I'm going to be scrupulous and do my best, but at the same time, when I've done my best, I am going to bed at night and I'm going to sleep then.

A home-made trouble machine! Did you ever see one? It is something like the old-fashioned loom the sisters used to work in the old times. I've seen the old sisters many a time weaving with one; they had a shuttle in both hands, a broche in their mouth, and they were everlastingly treading with their feet; why, they had to work all over, through and through! And I've seen many an old sister start her trouble machine and work it from head to foot as hard as she could go it. What's the use of doing that?

Look here, brethren, there's but one remedy in the universe of God for borrowed trouble, home-made trouble. I do n't like this home-made trouble on this account. It's just like the old-fashioned home-made cloth and the old-fashioned home-made shoes—they outwear any thing you ever saw. But, O me, how we stick to it, and run this old trouble machine. I've said this much only that you might see the point I am driving at. Listen, friends, there's but one remedy in the universe of God for home-made trouble, and that's the exercise of your good hard sense, and if you have any, use it for yourself! What do you say? You need n't go to the Lord with your borrowed trouble. Just think of the mother asking the Lord to head off old John before he ran away. The Lord won't do it while John is n't running off.

·Just think of a sister asking the Lord to put out the fire in her house, and the house is n't even on fire yet! The Lord is n't going to bother about putting out a fire when the fire has n't started yet. It's all tomfoolery to go to the Lord with borrowed troubles and ask him to relieve you. If the wolf is at the door, shut the door in his face; and if the calf is going to eat up the grindstone, why let him eat it. You can get a new one! This everlasting ding-dong and worry over nothing! looking for something that's never going to happen; expecting something that'll never come about, everlastingly going out to meet something that is not coming! Brethren, let's quit that!

My brethren, it's this borrowed trouble that harasses us in this life. I've been traveling about in the last few years a good deal, and I've read of people that starved to death, but I never yet saw the body of a man that died of starvation. Did any body in this house ever see the body of a man that died of starvation in this country? Why, if the low-down vagabonds of this country can live, and look fat and sleek, I know for certain a gentleman like you and me can get along! Let's quit bothering about those things, brethren. It's a good idea, too! Why, you take these old tramps out on the road, and they carry about one hundred and sixty pounds of avoirdupois flesh around with 'em, and they look fat and sleek, and if these old vagabonds can do this, a decent fellow had better hush up and go along, and do the best he can and say nothing.

This everlasting worry! I've seen the time myself when the meal in my house got pretty low, and coal gave out, and things did look like starvation, but I went on doing my duty, and I said, " If I do starve to death in this country, I'll make out as if I died of typhoid fever." Sister, brother, quit that worry! Why, some good wives are the laughing stock of their husbands, and some mothers are the laughing stock of their children! Sisters, play the woman and use good hard sense, and quit this foolishness. Yes, you need n't be nudging your wife, brother, out there. I suspect when she gets home you'll hear from her.

Now you've got, brethren, the general idea of what I mean by borrowed trouble. Bring your good hard sense to bear and let these things go, and do n't worry about 'em, and do n't you go out to meet any thing that is n't pleasant. You just sit still and wait till it comes, and then fight it until you die.

But, brethren, there are real troubles and real burdens in this life, as well as imaginary ones. There is enough real and genuine trouble in this life without your sitting down and manufacturing more. The real burdens of life! O, how many there are here to-night whose hearts ache. O, how many suffering hearts in this house to-night are carrying more than angel's strength could bear. O, sister and brother, but with that burden comes a sweet message from God, "Bring it back to me." See that Newfoundland dog swimming in the lake out yonder. His master calls him, but he won't come; his master beckons him, but he won't come; his master rebukes him, but he swims around at will; but his master picks up a little block of wood and pitches it out into the lake toward the dog, and the dog swims up to it, and gathers it in his mouth, and swims ashore and lays the block at his master's feet. If there is a burden on your heart, it was pitched there by a hand divine; God called you, but you wouldn't come; God beckoned to you, but you wouldn't come. You're swimming at will out yonder in the lake of sin and death, and he pitches this burden on your heart, and he says, "Bring it back and lay it down at my feet. I am the great burden-bearer."

The burdens of life! There's a burden of guilt that weighs upon the human soul! Who has not felt it? O, guilty before God. How many men are standing here to-night, and their very soul echoes it out, "Guilty, guilty before God! I have sinned against God with a high hand!" The burden of guilt! I have felt it; I have had my soul pressed down with the load of guilt. Brother, I trust to-night your burden may brush down upon your heart and break it into ten thousand pieces! God will not despise a broken heart. "A broken and a contrite heart, O, God, thou wilt not despise!" Guilt! I have sinned! I have sinned!

This burden of guilt in the case of Judas Iscariot caused him to rush out to the brink of a fearful precipice to make a hangman's noose, and in his despair and agony, to kill himself! O, how many men have committed suicide from this one cause— a burden of guilt! "Guilty when I look at the past; crushed with the present, hopeless for the future!" and then the bright blade enters the bared left breast, and the life-blood comes gushing out in a dark red stream from the heart! Guilty! Guilty! The burden of guilt! O, brother, there is a remedy for you. There is a place of refuge for you to go. Thank God that in this old world, loaded with the burdens of guilt, there is a place where you may go and cast your burden down, and come away singing, and rejoice and rest in God our Savior.

There is no such thing there as exchanging burdens. I reckon I have had trouble nobody else has had; but I would n't swap it off. If I have to bear burdens and troubles, God has fitted them to me, so that I can carry them better than any body else can. I remember well the old legend, where a mythological goddess is represented as calling all the inhabitants of the world together, that they might throw their burdens, or troubles, or infirmities, into a pile. Well, they all gathered round and commenced pitching into the pile their difficulties. One fellow had an evil conscience, another had a burden of guilt, another had a crook in his nose, another had a broken arm, another had a bad eye, and every man that had an ailment of any kind he cast it into the common pile; and when they had all thrown in their troubles, and defects, and infirmities, it made a pile mountains high. The goddess then told them that each one could pick something out of the pile that would suit him better than the trouble or burden he had pitched in, and each one then made his selection. The man with the evil conscience took the crooked nose; the man with an aching heart took a broken arm, and each of them changed and got something that they thought he would rather have instead of the one he had pitched into the pile. But the next morning before sun-up the whole concern from bottom to top was back there telling the goddess to call another day of celebration, and give them an opportunity to swap back, and give them what they had before. Well, that's some consolation for a fellow—I would rather have what I have than what you have. We are rich in that sense. Well, we can swap those things off. What will we do with them? I carry this burden of guilt to my Savior's feet and throw it down. " Cast thy burdens on the Lord."

There's a burden of anxiety. O, who knows what that mother's heart bears? If any man, woman or child were to overhaul the letters I have received since I have been in this city, and were to read the letters, and messages, and requests I have read—O, brother, you would know then what burdens of anxiety rest on the hearts of many people in Cincinnati. You would know then what it is to ache from head to foot because of the fearful falsehood of another.

Boys, let me talk to you a minute. Mother has got enough to care for you, my boy. But a precious mother can not stand every thing; a precious wife can not stand every thing. I was visiting the asylum in my State a year or two ago, and I went through the different wards. I met mothers; I met wives; and I looked into the face of what was once a lovely, sweet mother; and I saw the distorted look of the countenance and the wild glare of her eye, and I asked mentally the question: "What brought that mother here—what tore her from her children and her home?" And the wild glare of the eye, as it looked back to me, spoke with more force than any tongue, and said: "Trouble did this; trouble did this; trouble did it."

I know a wife in the State of Georgia, in the asylum of that State, and the besotted, drunken, beastly conduct of her husband first broke her heart, and then broke her mind, and she is to-day a poor distorted maniac. What did it, wives? It was a husband's brutal treatment. God pity a man that mistreats his wife. Brother, she has left father and mother, and home and all, to be yours. She is yours in all the simplicity and sincerity of her heart—yours to love, and cherish, and to keep, so

long as you both shall live; but never yours to
abuse and mistreat, and to crush her precious, loving heart. O, brother, God help us. I love to
throw my arm around my precious wife's neck occasionally, and say: "Wife, I must ask you one more
time to forgive me for the way I used to do in my
wayward life." And before the angels of God in
heaven I want the privilege at least of begging her
pardon for the wayward life I led the first three
years of our married life. Brother, listen. You owe
your precious wife a debt you can never pay until
you pay it at the mercy-seat of God. Boys, you
owe your mother a debt, and you can never pay it
until you pay it on your knees, crying out: " God
be merciful to me a sinner." Won't you cry out
to-night?

A burdened heart! I do n't intend to burden
any body's heart. Every body has as much as he
can carry, has as much as he can go with. I won't
be a burden upon any body's heart. I would n't
inflict a burden upon any human heart. Why,
wives have written to me about their husbands:
"Mr. Jones, intimate from the pulpit that husbands
ought not to be unkind to their wives. Mr. Jones,
say something from the pulpit to touch a boy's
heart that has already broken a poor mother's
heart." O, boys, let us stop to-night! Let us stop
to-night! And let us say: "God being my helper,
I will never burden my loved one's hearts any
longer."

There are the burdens of grief. O, how they
press upon us! Who of us have made a pilgrim-

age to the grave? The black crape in this house
every day tells in burning letters of pilgrimages to
the graveyard. Husband gone! wife gone! child
gone! O, those loved ones who are gone! I buried
one of my sweet loved ones, and she was the only
one we had at our home. My house was never so
dark before. O, how I walked to her little bed-
room, and how I would take up her little doll and
her little playthings, and handle them with all the
sacredness of my nature. And how I have taken
up her little shoes and stockings in my hand, and
I have regarded them as worth all the world to my
home. A precious one gone! gone! gone! O,
what a burden!

I know not what it is to give a wife up. I hope
I shall never know. I hope I shall never know.
I know not what it is to give up a grown child.
But, brother, these burdens come in life; and O,
what burdens! O, what burdens! And then,
brother, there are thousands of burdens rushing in
upon us. The burden of grief, the burden of disappointment, the burden of anxiety, the burden of
losses—O, how they press down upon us! O, this
burden-laden world! What can you do? What
ought you to do? That's the question.

I was reading this incident some days ago, where
a dozen women were sitting in a parlor rehearsing
their troubles: One after another told her troubles,
until eleven had spoken, and a pale, sad face present had not spoken a word. They turned to her
and said: "Tell us what your troubles are?" And
she said: "I have listened to you all, and you

know nothing of what troubles are. I will tell you mine, since you have asked for them : I was raised in affluence and wealth; so was my husband. After we were married he bought a beautiful place on the Savannah River, and there we lived in our beautiful home, and in the course of years God blessed us with four children. One night I awoke in my room, and I dropped my hand out of the bed, and it dropped into water. I awoke my husband, and he arose. The water was already a foot deep above the floor, and my husband gathered myself and the children, and carried us to a small raft near by; and the water rose very rapidly. And my husband said : ' I will take you and the baby first to the hillside, and then come back for the other children.' My husband carried us over, and then went back; and, as the moon was shining upon the flood, the raft was carried away, and my husband sank out of sight, and I have never seen him since. But," she said, "that was n't trouble. I saw the waters rise and carry my three-year-old child out of sight, and I have never seen it since; but that was n't trouble." And she said: "I saw the water rise above the head of the next, and it struggled and passed out of sight. And then I sat there until the water had risen above the head of my first born, and I saw him swept away. But," she said, "that was n't trouble. I was left a widow with just one little boy in my arms. I spent my whole life trying to rear him right. I sent him off to college. There he learned to dissipate ; and when he was sent home he was fearfully dissipated.

He spent all my means, and went from bad to worse; and I've just received letters and papers from Texas announcing the fact that my poor boy was hung upon the gallows, and died a criminal's death, and went to a criminal's grave and to a criminal's hell." And she said: "O, ladies, there is trouble that no human heart can bear."

Boys, if you are going to the bad, remember that you are breaking a poor mother's heart; and, while you dissipate, think of a precious sister at home, a precious mother at home, and quit forever. Boys, let's be a comfort to our mother at home; let's be a consolation to our mother. Husbands, be the pride of your wives' hearts and a consolation to them all the day long. Won't you? If there were nothing else in religion than just something to take a burden off a wife's heart, I would want it for that. I bless God for the other ten thousand things, but for this particularly, because he has been such a blessing to me in saving me to my precious wife. God bless you, brother. He will do the same to you. He will! He will!

"Cast your burden upon the Lord." O, these troubles; they come upon us. You see that little frail bark yonder starting across the ocean. It reaches mid-ocean, and the wind blows, and the waves beat, and the storm tosses this little frail bark, and it is about to go down forever. It is overloaded, and it can't carry its cargo. And just at that time the *Great Eastern*, the grandest vessel that ever plowed the Atlantic—that grand ocean steamer that looks like a little floating city—that grand old vessel comes right up to the side of the little frail bark, and the captain walks up to the bulwark and looks over and says: "You are over-loaded; cast your cargo on me. I will carry it safely through for you." With rope and tackle they toss their cargo up on the deck of the *Great Eastern*, and it does n't make any more impression on it than a fly on an elephant.

Brothers, young men, you are out on the sea of life, poor humanity overloaded, and the wind and the waves and the storm dip and toss your frail little bark, overloaded with sin, and sinking and going down. But just about that time the old ship of Zion, with Jesus Christ as its captain, plows right alongside, and he says: "You are overloaded; cast your burden on me." And with all our power we cast our burden on the grand old ship of Zion. It does n't sink her. It is out on mid-ocean all the time, hunting these frail little barks. God bless you as you to-night feel you may go down forever! Look out, and you can feel the impulse of the grand old ship plowing up to your side to-night. And if she does, then cast your burden on her. Blessed be God! He will not only carry our burden, but carry us, too.

Thank God for the cross. I have shouldered my cross, sometimes, when I thought it the biggest bur-den I had to carry, and I have carried that cross until it was more than I could carry, and I fell down; but as soon as I fell down God put legs to the cross, and he put me on it, and he said, It shall carry you now. Blessed be God for the cross that

was a burden once, and yet carries you safely into
the haven of God.

Now, brother, what are you going to do? Cast
your burden on the Lord? Mother, there is where
you put your burden to-night. Wife, put yours
there. Young lady, put your burden there. Whatever our burdens are let's cast them on the Lord
to-night. Let us go away from here with our burden cast upon the Lord. He will hold you fast;
and, when the last storm is sweeping over you, he
will keep you secure. I do n't care what your burden of troubles is to-night. God says: "Cast it
upon me, and I will sustain you."

And now a word or two on this verse and I am
done. "He hath delivered my soul in peace from
the battle that was against me." Did you ever
think about that expression? "For there were many
with me." Ah, me! I have seen this illustrated
so many times. I have seen the precious old heart-
broken mother, when her boys had gone to the
bad, and patiently she came up to me and said, "I
will have to give my boys up forever; I have
prayed for them every day from their birth to the
present time; I have followed them with my prayers; and at night when they were asleep I have
bathed them in my tears; and yet one of my boys
to-day said to me, 'Mother, do n't you never mention religion to me again,' and scoffed me away
from his presence." And she said, "I will just
have to give up and quit." And the very next
night I saw the two boys of that precious mother
walk up to the altar and give their hearts to God

join the Church and say, "Glory to God, I am a
saved man!" And then I saw the old mother jump
up and clap her hands together, and say, "Glory to
God, he has delivered my soul in peace from the
battle that was against me. I thought my boys
were gone forever; and, blessed be God, they are
saved, when I thought they were lost forever."

I have seen a wife pray for her husband, while
he went to the bad. And I have heard my own
precious wife say, "I am broken down with the
burden; I will have to give it up." She was about
to give it all up in despair when God swept me into
the kingdom of Christ, and I said, "Glory to God!
He has delivered my soul in peace from the battle
that was against me." I thought I had to give up
in despair, but about that time he brought me into
victory, and now I shout over victories unknown to
men. Many a man has been ready to give up and
has been on the verge of despair, but about that
time some providential influence came along and
swept him into the Church, which he thought he
would never reach. Many a time the old brethren
have gathered together and thought the Church had
about reached its end; thought they were not doing
any good, and about the time they were ready to
give up along came some influence and swept
hundreds and hundreds into the Church, and the
old brethren clapped their hands and cried out,
"Glory to God! He hath delivered our souls from
the battle that was against us."

There are thousands of Christian people that
have cried out about Cincinnati, "O this city has

gone to the bad. She has three thousand bar-rooms. Wickedness exists on nearly every block. O, how she is steeped in guilt and wickedness, and communism and dormant riot," and the good men of the city have looked on and said, "O, Cincinnati is gone. With all our prayers and all our efforts and all our preaching, Cincinnati is going to the bad." And just about the time you were all about to give up along comes some influence and starts the whole city to God, and I hope before this time next week we can clap our hands together and say, "Glory to God! This city is restored to Christ. They're flocking home to Christ by the hundreds and thousands."

I'll never desert this grand old ship of Zion; I'm aboard, and I'm going to stay. Many a man has given up and despaired of ever being a good member, and has asked me, when I was pastor, to take his name off the book; but, brother, I'd never let you take your name off. I never felt sadder in my life than when a man came to me and wanted me to take his name off the Church books. Many a man has wanted his name stricken off, but he was rescued at the last moment. Many a time have I gone to a town and worked and worked, but all seemed against me; the preachers would not sympathize with me, and even my wife, I thought, was against me, and my children seemed to be against me; but I fought, and fought, and fought, and I thought I fell, and I said, "I am conquered forever," but blessed be God, when I opened my eyes the din and the smoke of the terrible battle had been wafted away, and angels and good men were all about me, and I said, "Glory to God! I am not alone." I thought I was alone in the fight.

Sister, brother, men, listen to-night. You can't go out alone to fight the battle of right—God won't let you. He will make angels pitch their tents around you, and make the good men of earth stand by you, and God himself will be your friend. Glory to God, you do n't go by yourself! If the devil says you are too weak to walk or start, tell him God is with you.

Brethren, let us all start that way to-night. Let's start a better life, and if you do start to-night God will be with you. He will help you fight the battle.

SAYINGS.

I WISH some of these pastors could see that men never can be saved by pastoral visits. I do n't want my pastor to go fooling around my house two or three times a week in my wife's way, and in my children's way. I want him to study the source of life and truth, and then on Sunday preach a sermon that will set their souls on fire for the week. Then I do n't care whether he calls around or not. If shoeleather will ever save this world, the Lord knows the visiting pastors have worn out enough already to save the whole world. Give us a Gospel of truth and sense. Give us a Gospel that means the conquest of the world by bringing men into contact with truth.

Sermon XXI.

THE CALLS OF GOD.

"Because I have called, and ye refused; I have stretched out my hand, and no man regarded; but ye have set at nought all my counsel and would none of my reproof; I also will laugh at your calamity; I will mock when your fear cometh."—Prov. i, 24–26.

THESE are the words of God our Father, our Benefactor, and the God who will be our final Judge.

If we were wise men and wise women in the best sense, I might stop the pulpit part of these services now, and instead of inviting penitents into the inquiry rooms, we might turn this whole audience-room into an inquiry-room, and the best of us would start out to be better, and the medium class, morally speaking, would make an immense movement forward, and religious altogether seek and obtain the pardon and blessing of God to-night.

"Because I have called." Whatever else we may say of the representations of God's relation toward us, we all must admit—all Bible readers must admit—that this world of men are in danger of something, and that the Lord is doing his best to save men from the danger and death that threatens them; and now we propose, practically, with your prayers, and with the help of God, to go into the question before us. Give us your attention if you are not a Christian, and give us your prayers if you are a Christian.

430

First, we notice the numerous calls given of God to men. The first great influence or agency in calling men to a better life is the third person of the adorable Trinity, which is the blessed Spirit of all grace. Sometimes I think we magnify the work of the Holy Ghost too little in the great work of redemption. Jesus Christ, the Savior of man, came, and suffered, and died, but the suffering and death of Christ would have been of no effect but for the divine agency and power of the Holy Ghost.

Really, brethren, when we think lightly on this question we can never understand the cross, we can never see the cross in its beauty and outlines until it is bathed in the light of the Divine Spirit. I have walked out in the mountainous regions of my own State, an hour before daybreak; I have stood on the porch of some country home and looked at the hills and valleys around me; they presented but the dim outline of something that I could not appreciate, that I could not fully see. I go back into that dwelling, and in three hours more I walk out again on the front porch. The sun has risen on the scene, and bathed the mountains and valleys in a sea of light, and now I look, and beauties and splendors that never met my eye before face me on every side. The light of the sun shows me the beauties of the world, and helps me to understand largely its mysteries. Brethren, I see the cross erected, God's only begotten Son, the victim, suspended; he suffers, he dies, and now I see but the dim outlines of something—I can not catch it in its fullness, I can not take it in in all its beauty, but now the Divine Spirit rises on the scene, and bathes the cross in a sea of light, and I see my Savior in a beauty and power I have never seen before.

Blessed Spirit, live in our world and draw all men to Christ. This Holy Spirit is working in the world, and is touching and moving the hearts and consciences of men. I am so glad of the divine agency of the blessed Spirit! It was so good in God to love me in my wayward life. It was so good for Christ to die for me, and spend thirty-three years among those that lived before me. It was so good in Christ to ascend to the Father, for he said: " It is expedient for you that I go away;" and when he entered the shining courts above the blessed Spirit poised himself a moment, and listened as his lips uttered: "The work is finished among men in sacrificial atonement," and then he flew to earth to sprinkle the nations, and make them meet for the Master's use in heaven. O, brother, this divine agency is in our world to-night. This would indeed be a fatherless, a comfortless, and a starless world without the ever-abiding God manifesting his presence and his power.

It was glorious to Mary and Martha to have Christ their guest. When Christ was with them he was not out in the street unstopping the ear of the deaf and giving eyes to the blind. When he was in the home of Mary and Martha they had him all to themselves. But here is this Divine Spirit. When I bid wife and children good-bye, and walk out of my home, I leave the Divine Spirit with them, and when I board the train for some distant

point, the blessed Spirit rides over these railways
with me; and wherever I come I find that same
Spirit abiding in the hearts of the people. Blessed
be God for this Spirit of grace that dwells not only
in the world, but in the hearts of men.

This divine Spirit is here to-night, and his business here is to woo and beseech and implore every
man to give his heart to God and lead a good life.
Brethren, can you say as you look over the past and
as you survey the present, "No good spirit has
touched my heart; no divine power has moved my
conscience?" This light and this power lighteth
every man that cometh into the world. We are
warned at this point, brethren, to grieve not the
Holy Spirit of God, whereby we are sealed to the day
of redemption. We are taught that this sin, if we
commit it persistently, is a sin for which there is no
forgiveness in this world or in the world to come.

It is that Spirit touching your heart yesterday,
to-day, and to-night, and have you not in your soul
a desire to be a better man? Every good desire
and ever hungering for better things, is implanted
and touched into life in the hearts of men by this
Spirit of grace. O, how fearful and guilty we are
to trifle with this blessed Spirit, this Spirit that
comes back and implores us to lead a better life.
God not only gave us his Son to die for us, but he
let this divine Spirit abide among men to lead them
to a better life.

I have seen the Spirit of God, it seemed to me,
as it touched the hearts and conscience of men; I
have seen them in the face of the call of the Spirit

and the influence of grace reject and reject and reject the call, until I could almost hear the rustling wings of the divine Spirit as it carried away the blessed influence of God to come back no more forever. O, what a fearful sin it is to drive out of your heart the influence of God.

You may trifle with the preacher and laugh at the Church, but, O, brother, I warn you not to trifle with the Spirit of God.

"There is a time, we know not when,
A point, we know not where,
That marks the destiny of men,
For glory or despair."

God forbid that any man in this service to-night should cross the line from beyond which no man ever came back. O, sir, while the good Spirit touches your heart, yield, yield, yield instantly, and yield forever! If God had given his Son to die for us, and we had refused to look at the scene, then we would have died without excuse; but when God not only gives a sacrifice, and points you to the sacrifice by the divine Spirit, we are still more without excuse; he comes closer to us, and calls by his Word, by his blessed Book. On every page of this Book there is a divine call. O, sir, if I begin with Genesis and end with Revelation, I yet have to acknowledge the truth. I have received ten thousand calls from a life of sin to a life of holiness in the sight of God. This Book is full of calls, and every call is plain and easy of understanding. This Book lies on the table in your home, this neglected Book, and you throw it aside as a thing of no moment. If this little bundle of paper I hold in my hand is true, it outweighs all this world; if this Book is true, it outweighs the stars; if this Book is true, then let us read it, and heed its calls, and be guided by its divinely given precepts. O, sir, this Book is yours. God sent it to your home. May be it was a present under God from a good mother to you; may be a precious Christian wife gave this Book to you the day of your marriage; may be some good man dropped this Book in your hands and said: "There is a Holy Bible, Book divine!" Clasp it to your heart and say, "Precious treasure, thou art mine." Take this Book, brother, be guided by it.

Not only does God call us by his Spirit and by his Word, but he calls us also by his ministry. O, how many consecrated preachers there are in the world to-day. Look at this city. It has a thousand pulpits calling men to a better life. O, sir, while you hear me now, I look you in the face and say your criticisms of a preacher, your criticisms upon the pulpit do not lessen your responsibility to God. I do n't care who may be your preacher; I care not whether he is educated or uneducated. This much I can say and tell the truth— I never heard an old African preach or an American preach anywhere that there was not truth enough in his sermon to save a thousand souls like mine. I know that, and whatever you may say about your preacher, you can not say that in any single sermon you have ever listened to there was not truth enough in it to make you a good man, and

carry you home to God. They are doing their duty
the best they can, and I say to you to-night, there are
preachers within hearing of my voice that have spent
restless nights on their knees praying for your husband or your son, when you are sleeping, as if there
were nothing for you to be interested in. No one
who has not filled the relations of pastor to a people
can tell the hours of agony we spend before God in
wrestling at the throne, that God may revive his
work and save the husbands of our good women,
and save the children of our precious mothers, and
bring the world to Christ.

Thank God for the preachers. They have been
worth all the world to me. And I tell you, brother,
as long as sin is in the world, may God let the
preachers stay in the world. There is not a preacher
in any pulpit in this town that is not worth more
to your city than any ten policemen in your city,
when it comes to good order, morals, and civilization; and if you will multiply your churches, you
can minify your police force. If you will make
churches thicker, the bar-rooms will give way before
them, and may God grant to the preachers of this
city power with their congregations and power with
sinners such as they have never had before. Thank
God for the faithful ministry, doing it's best toward
bringing the world to God. Thank God for the
preachers that have not only preached to us, but
have met us on the sidewalk and taken our hands
and said, "I am interested for you; I am praying
for you." They have not only done that; they
have come under our roof and prayed with our

loved ones, when we were away, and careless and thoughtless, and not only that, but they have fallen down on their knees in their studies, and called upon God to bless them. And I venture the assertion, there is not a person in this house to-night whose name has not been registered at the mercy seat, and put there by the prayers of a faithful preacher, and God helps to show that others are interested, and may it interest us now and forever.

God calls men by his ministry. Now we are not perfect; I know we are not perfect, and we have been troubled about that. There is not a preacher in this city who does not, in his heart, wish that he were a better preacher and a more efficient preacher. Brethren, if you want to set your preachers on fire, baptize their efforts with tears and prayers, and God will give force to his Word.

God calls you likewise by his providences. And how closely those providences come to us. How sad they make our hearts, and how they show the hollowness of time or sense. What man or woman is there here to-night who never made a pilgrimage to a grave? Who has not gone and laid away some loved one? Which man here has never, never, had his home circle touched by the hand of death? Where is my father? Where is my mother? Where is my wife? Where are my children? O! these questions bring tears of sadness to many eyes. And I want to tell you men, your precious mothers will not stay much longer. Many have already gone. I was sitting in a train some weeks ago with a commercial traveler. He introduced himself and commenced talking to me. He said: "Mr. Jones, I have been reading your sermons, and I was very much affected. But," said he, "I will tell you something that affected me a great deal more than that." I said, "What, sir?" He pulled out a letter, and he says, "You see this? It is from my precious, good old mother, now seventy years old. Read those sentiments." And they were like the sentiments of an angel of God. Said he: "Mr. Jones, mother has been writing that way to me all my life since I have been away from home, and it is not what mother said that touches the heart, but it is that nervous hand she holds that pen with. She is not going to write to me much longer." And he said: "When I answered the letter I said, 'Precious mother, your boy surrenders to God, and he will never give you any more trouble.'"

Providence touches us on all sides. When I was preaching at Nashville I got on the train Friday evening and started home, and I sat on the engine with the engineer. He said to me, "Mr. Jones, you touched me and got very close to me last night at meeting." Said I, "How is that?" He said, "When you told about your old schoolmate, Virginia." The incident which I related was this: One morning I walked down to an old schoolmate's home, and when I walked in there was the wife and mother, an old schoolmate of mine. I talked to her kindly and took my seat by the side of her child, which was sick. There was a little two-year-old fellow on his mother's lap, looking

like a little angel chiseled out of marble. When I
walked in I spoke to her and sat there a moment.
Said I: "Virginia, I believe God is going to take
this sweet child too." "Yes, yes," she said, "and
this will be the fifth precious one God has taken."
"Well," said I, "Virginia, did it ever occur to you
that God was doing his best to save your poor
husband?" "O," she said, "do you recognize what
it means?" Said I, "I believe it so." "O, well,"
she said, "if God can save my husband by taking
these precious children I will give all my children
up to God without a murmur." And she sat there,
and the tears just rained out of her eyes on the face
of the little sick child. I got up and walked down
town, and I found her husband, a kind-hearted,
good fellow, that had drunk himself to the verge
of perdition. I stopped him on the walk and laid
my hand on his shoulder, and I said, "John, I am
just from your house, old fellow. God is going to
take that other sweet child. Now, John, your wife
is bathing that child this moment in her tears. You
have got as good a wife as a man ever had. Did
it ever occur to you that God is doing his best to
save you from a drunkard's grave?" I saw the
tears start in his eyes; and I want to tell you to-day
that that man is one of the best men in our city,
and an official member of the Church that my wife
belongs to. Thank God, thank God for the means
by which he reaches the children of men and leads
them to a better life.

God came to our home thirteen years ago. And
if you had asked me: "What is the worst thing that

can happen to you?" I would have thought in my heart, "The loss of my father." And I have scarcely seen a day since my father died—he is not dead; he is not dead; I never think of him as being dead; I just think of him as a father in heaven—I have not seen a day since he told me good-bye that I would not have given any thing in the world if I could just have my father back one hour, and just lean my head on his bosom, and have him talk to me like he once did. But he is gone. O, when my Father in heaven took my earthly father, then it was that I realized that he would be a father to me, and bless me beyond all that, that my earthly father could have done. When God came to my home and took our little nineteen-months-old Beulah to that bright world up yonder, I was a poor, cheerless, miserable sinner. I looked in the face of that sweet child, and I am a great deal better father to my other children than I ever would have been if I did not have one in heaven. Gone! and O, how dark and cheerless was my home! I could not pray; I could not look to God. I looked down into the grave, and it was dark, so dark! She is gone! That is the only one of my children that ever saw her father when he was not a Christian. That is the only one that ever saw her father when he was dissipated! She is in heaven. Thank God I have not a living child that ever looked in my face when I was not a Christian trying to set a good example, and trying to lead my children to a better world.

Fathers, you owe your children a debt. God has

come very close to you. If taking your property away from you will save you, God will do that. If taking your wife, and nothing else but taking your wife from you will save you, God will take your wife. If taking your children, and nothing but that will save you, God will take your children. The engineer, sitting on that engine, said: "Mr. Jones, last night, when you told about Virginia, you got mighty close to me;" and the tears started down his cheeks. Said he: "This last year God came to my home and took the sweetest child I had." Then he said: "Mr. Jones, since that I have not cursed an oath and I have not taken a drink. I want you to pray for me. I have got a good wife; I have happy children. Pray for me. I want to be a good man." O, brethren, God gets very close to us when he comes to our homes, and touches our hearts and makes us wish for a better life. O, will you hear?

He calls us by his providences to-night, and by those precious promises he gives us in his book. But God does not stop there. He calls me in every way. I believe it was Mr. Spurgeon who said that, if we but had ears to hear, we should know that God calls us in ten thousand ways. Brother, when you walk out in the morning you see the sun climbing the slippery steeps of the eastern horizon, and God speaks through the sun, and the sun looks down and smiles upon you and says: "O, man, I am climbing up higher, and my pathway grows brighter. Is your pathway upward and brighter, like mine?" When the sun reaches the meridian and looks down again it says: "O, man, I have reached the meridian height! Have you reached the meridian of your life? Will you soon begin to decline as I now do?" And when he sinks behind the western horizon and paints a scene of beauty across it, he whispers back and says: "O, man, suns have their setting. Suns will set, and we shall die. Will you paint the beauties of a happy, well-spent life upon the faces and lives of those around you? or will you die like the sun, going down in gloom and darkness?" O, sir, when I enter my home at night, then God speaks to me. The supper bell rings, and I call my children around the table. They gather, and I help their plates. God looks at the picture and says: "My child, I will feed you on heaven's bread and angel's food if you come to me. You are the father, and these are children. I am a Father; be thou my child and come to me, and I will clothe you and feed you with the bread and raiment of heaven." And then, when I sit down at my gas-jet and begin to read, the little candle fly flits around the light, and I dash it away. "Out, poor, foolish thing; do n't burn yourself to death." It flits around and into the light, and burns itself to death. And God says: "Poor man, you are doing the very same thing yourself. You are dazzled by the pleasures of life, and flitting around them, and you will drop into the heat of despair and be burned up forever." Then, when I retire at night and close my door, God says: "Man, some day heaven's door will be closed. Will you be with the damned, cast out, or will you be shut in forever

with God." When some sudden noise wakes you
at night, God says: "Ye know not the day nor
the hour when the Son of Man cometh. Be ye also
ready." When you walk down town to business,
God says to you as you measure off your yard of
cloth, "Man, I will measure off your days to you."
And when you take the scissors and clip the cloth,
God says: "When I measure off your days the scissors of death shall clip you from time and pass you
into eternity." And when you take the sugar or
coffee and throw it into the scales and weigh it, God
says: "O, man, mene, mene, tekel: thy days are
numbered; thou art weighed in the balance and
found wanting." There you are, a blacksmith, and
as you pound the iron God says: "O, man, I have
pounded upon your heart with the hammer of
truth; yet I have never shaped you unto God."
Here is a school-teacher. Christ comes to you and
says: "Learn of me; I will teach you things that
no other teacher ever knew." Are you a lawyer?
God says to you: "As you represent your clients
there, let my Son be your advocate, for you shall be
tried up yonder by and by." Are you a farmer?
With every seed you drop from your hand God
says: "Man, I have been sowing the seed of God in
your heart. Have they come up?" And, when you
take the sickle in to reap the harvest, God says:
"Man, some of these days the sickle of death will
cut you down, and the wheat shall be separated
from the chaff." As you see that river flowing
through your city, God tells you: "O, man, as you
look upon its waters, will you ever stand redeemed

on the banks of the river of life, and be with God forever?" These beautiful shade trees that mark your streets, God says, as you pass each one: "O, man, will you ever eat of the fruit of the tree of life that grows in the city of God?" Every cracking, burning fire that meets your gaze God says: "Will you be cast out where the worm never dies and the fire shall never be quenched?" And here, as we ride up and down the streets, each house tells me: "There is a house not made with hands eternal in the heavens. Will you live and abide there with God forever, or will you be houseless and homeless in eternity?" Wherever I turn, wherever I go, God is calling me to a better life.

Now, brother, God is not only calling us in a thousand ways, but there is another fact: We have heard those calls, every one of them; those calls have been so loud that all men have heard them. Blessed be God, you have not only heard them with your ears, but they have rung down through the chambers of your souls; and not only have you heard these calls, and heard them a thousand times, but you have understood every one of them. You knew what they meant; you knew their purpose; you knew the desire of God in making those calls. Now, because I have been called in ten thousand ways, and God has made me hear those calls, and God has made me understand those calls, and I have refused them all, God says himself: "I, also, will laugh at your calamities. I will mock when your fear cometh." I do n't know what that means. I read in that Book: "What measure ye mete shall be measured to you again." Hear me, brother; listen: O, men, to-night you scoff and laugh at God. Now, 'as God pleads with you, you laugh and scoff at him, and so, by and by, when you plead and beg, God will laugh and scoff at you. As you treat God to-night he will treat you by and by. You say, " O, that is so unreasonable. It is so wicked to talk that way." It is God's own utterance. Hear it, brother. You laugh and scoff now, and God says, when you plead by and by, as I plead to-night: " I will laugh at your calamities. I will mock when your fear cometh."

O, what a thought! I do n't understand it, I say. I can 't understand it. One minute: I will illustrate, and then leave this awful question with you. One of our old preachers told me the only incident I have ever heard in all my experience that can at all illustrate what this thought is or what it can mean. He said in the village where he then lived, out in the country about two miles, there lived a gentleman of culture and refinement— a Christian gentleman. The man was wealthy, and he had only one child, a boy. Upon this boy he lavished all the love of his heart; he gave him every thing that love could suggest and money could buy. This boy went off to college, and came back home dissipated, and the father exhausted all the infinite sympathy and love of his heart upon him. Yet the boy went from bad to worse. It was the comment of the community that such a father could love, that such a father could bestow such kindness upon such a degraded boy. The father loved him on, and clung to him through it all; but the boy got deeper in his guilt. The father, said the preacher, drove into town one day, and hitched his horse on the square, and started down to a store to procure some things. He met this drunken boy of his staggering along the street. The boy met him, and took his father by the collar and shook him rudely, and cursed him to his face. The father pulled loose from the boy, and with a countenance that meant more than a biography, stepped into his buggy and drove off home. The servant took his horse, and he was seen to walk away to a beautiful grove of a hundred acres in front of the house, and walked down to the furthest corner. Some of them watched him. When he reached the further corner he put his hands to his head, gave the most unearthly shriek that human lips ever gave utterance to, and then took down his hands a moment; then threw up his hands again with a scream that startled all who have heard it, and then walked deliberately back to his house. Just as he reached the porch this boy came walking up behind him on the porch. His father turned around; the boy staggered in. The father caught him and straightened him up in his presence, turned his face toward the road, and said: "Off of these premises forever. You are no longer my son or kin of mine. You vagabond, leave forever." And ten days later that boy died in the gutter in that town, and his father never saw his corpse or attended his funeral. "Mercy knows the appointed bounds and terms of vengeance there."

O, sir, this alone can [illustrate the feelings of the Son of God when he walked upon the hill, near the city of Jerusalem, and looked down upon it in its guilt and said: "O, Jerusalem." It was the wail of a God. "O, Jerusalem, Jerusalem, how often would I have gathered thy children together, even as a hen gathereth her chickens under her wings, but ye would not. Behold, your house is left unto you desolate." Off of my heart forever. Off of my heart forever. God pity the man that pushes divine love to extremities like that.

"I have called and ye have refused." God help us to-night, if we have never done so before, to yield our hearts to God, and be religious from this blessed hour out. Won't you, friends? Won't you? But, thank God, in conclusion, just one sentence:

> "But they who turn to God shall live,
>   Through his abounding grace;
> His mercy will the guilt forgive
>   Of those who seek his face."

God is not implacable towards you. He loves you. He calls you. He seeks you. Come to God and live to-night. Won't you, friend? I beg you come. We are going to invite into the inquiry room every man that does not want to slight another offer of grace and scoff at the Bible, and means to yield to God. We beg you come now. Let us settle the question to-night. It has been the dilly-dally of the past that has been the curse of those here. Now, men of sense and men of souls, hear me to-night. Let us make an eternal decision before we leave this house. If it is right to serve God and live right, let us decide it to-night, and act upon that decision. If it is not right, let us decide, "I won't yield to God," and let that decision be final and eternal. As for one, I utter it from the depths of my heart, if I never surrendered fully to God until now, by the grace of God I make the unconditional eternal surrender to-night. God shall be my portion for ever.

Will you decide that way? If you do n't, then decide the other way, and walk out of this house with destiny fixed and doom settled for all worlds. God help you to say, "This night I surrender to God and make my peace with him through Jesus Christ."

———•———

SAYINGS.

I NEVER did believe in this way of sticking a religious hymn into a fellow and calling him converted. But if you get a sensible man and have him see that is the way to Christ, and get him on that way, that is the way to grace.

SOME fellow is fool enough to say he does n't believe in any thing he never saw. Well, then, he does n't believe- he has a backbone. Another says he does n't believe any thing he can't understand. Well, do you believe that some cows have horns and others are muley-headed?

O! FOR pure society, and pure homes, and pure Churches where all things are pure,. and then it would never be necessary for such things to be discussed. The religion that comes from above is, first, pure, for you get that sort in the pure, undefiled religion of the Bible. Have you, brethren, got the religion that makes you pure in your heart, and pure in your life, and pure in all manner of conversation? Have you got that? That is the first thing to see to, and that is the grandest thing of all—a pure heart, and that heart the sovereign of all your life and actions. Have that, and it indeed shall make your life pure.

WORKS AND FAITH.—The good Book says that faith without works is dead; but it does not say that works without faith are dead. Did you ever think of that? Whenever you see a fellow plowing in some field you will find that the best reason he has for plowing is that he believes that he is going to make grain out of it. Don't you see? He would not plow a lick if he did not think that he was going to make something out of it. So, whenever you see a man going around and doing and acting like God tells him to do and act, he is giving the best test that he has belief in what God says. And, after all, I don't judge a man by his faith, but by his works; and if you do that you will hit a man every time.

38

Sermon XXII.

Whosoever Will.

"And the Spirit and the Bride say, Come ; and let him that heareth say, Come; and let him that is athirst come; and whosoever will, let him take the water of life freely."— Rev. xxii, 17.

YOU see I get this text from the last page of this blessed Book. This is God's last message to man. And for fear that something might be added to, or that something might be taken from, the Scripture, God puts this fearful admonition: "For I testify unto every man that heareth the words of the prophecy of this Book: If any man shall add unto these things God shall add unto him the plagues that are written in this Book. And if any man shall take away from the words of the Book of this prophecy, God shall take away his part out of the Book of Life, and from the things that are written in this Book."

If I have been corresponding with a friend on any given subject, and he has written me a dozen or a hundred letters upon that subject—if I want to find his mind now concerning that, I will turn to the last letter received from him, the one bearing the most recent date. And now, if I want to know God's will concerning the race of man, I do n't run back over Genesis, or Deuteronomy, or the prophecies of Isaiah, or the Epistle to the Romans by St. Paul—I run through the Book, and I turn to God's last words to man, and I see

450

the fearful warning added: "Do n't any man take away these words. If he does, I will take away his part out of the Book of Life. And if any man shall add any thing to this Book, then I will add unto him the plagues that are written in the Book." And after all the fearful warnings, and judgments, and denunciations of the Scripture, thanks be to God, this is his last message: "And the Spirit and the Bride say, Come; and let him that heareth say, Come; and whosoever will, let him take of the water of life freely."

It was a grand day in the world's history when the evening and the morning were the seventh day, and the sons of God and angels shouted over a finished world. It was a grand day in the world's history when Adam and Eve, the first pair, stood before God, with their reason clear and perfect, unruffled by passion, unclouded by prejudice, and unimpaired by disease. It was a grand conception to them as they looked out over a finished world, and said that the flowers were God's thought in bloom; that the rivers were God's thought imbedded; that the mountains were God's thought piled up, and that the dewdrops were his thoughts in pearl as they mingle in loving tenderness and join together on the leaf of the rose. And wherever man looked about him, all nature, in its beauty and freshness, whispered back: "The hand that made me is divine." It was a grand, though sad, day in the world's history when it was announced through the moral universe of God that man had violated the law of God, and had brought misery and woe upon himself and upon his progeny forever. It was a grand day in the world's history when God met the fallen and degenerate pair, and said to Eve: "The seed of the woman shall bruise the serpent's head." It was a grand day in the world's history when the last strong swimmer sank beneath the flood, and left Noah in his ark with his three sons and their wives, and two of every beast and bird to perpetuate the race upon the face of the earth. It was a grand day in this world's history when Pharoah and his hosts, and all of his chariots and men, were swallowed up and engulfed in the Red Sea. It was a grand day in this world's history when a burning hail fell on Sodom and Gomorrah and all the plains thereof and destroyed the cities of the plain. It was a grand day in this world's history when 185,000 soldiers under the blast of an angel's wing were wrapt in their winding sheets. It was a grand day in this world's history when Korah, and Dathan, and Abiram, and their wicked company were swallowed up out of the sight of men.

It was a grander day in the world's history when the old prophet of God stood on the hills of Judea with his spark in hand and let its beneficent rays shine down through seven centuries, and his voice was heard through the seven centuries, saying, "Simeon and Anna, prepare the cradle to rock the babe of Bethlehem." It was a grand day in this world's history when the star poised itself over the manger, and the wise men gathered about the babe of Bethlehem. There they looked upon an everlasting God

lying asleep in Mary's arms, and the King of angels
and God over all blessed for evermore as he was
carried about in a virgin's arms, as they looked upon
the King of angels as the carpenter's despised boy.
It was a grand day in this world's history when, at
twelve years of age, this God-man surprised all the
wisdom of Jerusalem by his forethought and his
intelligence. It was a grand day in this world's
history when the Son of God notified his disciples,
to whom he had been sent from the Father, that he
must be crucified and buried, and that he would arise
on the third day from the dead. It was a grand day
in the world's history when he hung on a cross
suspended between two thieves and cried out with
a loud voice, "My God! My God! Why hast thou
forsaken me?" It was a grand day in the world's
history when they buried this sacrifice in the grave
of Joseph, and put the seal of the Roman government upon it, and put sturdy Roman soldiers around
it to guard it.

It was a grand day in the world's history when
on the morning of the third day God summoned
an angel to his side, because Christ himself had announced the fact, "I am the sacrifice. I go to die
for the world." And now the only question with
his disciples and with all humanity is, "Will God
accept the sacrifice?" He has suffered and died.
He is buried. Will he ever rise again? Will God
accept the sacrifice? God told the angel to go to
earth as swift as morning light and roll away the
stone from the grave, and when he made his appearance at the grave and rolled away the stone,

the Son of God stood up in the sepulcher and took the napkins from his face and the grave clothes from his body, and folded them up and laid them to one side, and walked forth from the tomb, the first fruits of the resurrection. Then God accepted the sacrifice, and grasped the stylus in his own hand and signed the magna charta of man's salvation. And ever since that God-blessed moment it has been written : " Whosoever liveth and believeth in me, shall never die."

It was a grand day in the world's history when the Savior of men stood yonder, surrounded by a company of five hundred, and a chariot descended from the skies, and he stepped into the chariot, and above moon and star he disappeared, until it overvaulted the very throne of God itself. And as they stood gazing up into heaven, an angel flew back to earth and shouted aloud to them, " Why stand ye here gazing up into heaven ? As ye have seen the Son of Man ascending, so he shall descend at the last day to judge the world in righteousness."

That was a grand day in this world's history when the one hundred and twenty gathered in an upper room in Jerusalem, and they had prayed the first day and the second day and the third day, and until the tenth day. They were praying for the enduement of power from on high. Christ had told them : " Tarry ye here at Jerusalem until ye be endued with power from on high. It is expedient for you that I go away."

I have often thought of that expression which Jesus used, " It is expedient. The best thing I can do for you is to leave the world and go home to the Father, and then the Spirit will come." Master, can there be any thing better than thy presence? Thou art the bread of life to us. Thou art the water of life to us. Thou art the door by which, if any man enter, he shall go in and out and find pasture. Thou art the truth and the way and the life. Master, is it expedient, is it best that thou go away? He said: "It is expedient that I go to the Father." And on the morning of the tenth day, when that company gathered and prayed in that upper chamber, the Holy Spirit, the third person of the adorable trinity, flew down to earth, and rushed in upon that company like a rushing mighty, wind; and Peter opened the door, and the company followed him down upon the streets of Jerusalem, and there, on the morning of the tenth day, he preached that memorable sermon in Jerusalem that won three thousand souls to Christ—more conversions through Peter in that one sermon than Christ had in all his ministry. And Christ knew what he was talking about when he said: "It is expedient for you that I should go away."

God gave the Son, and the Son came to suffer, die, and to arise again. And now the Spirit comes to woo and beseech and implore and enlighten and convict and convert the world to God. It seems as if, after God had loved the race and called them to him and they had wandered off, that they would have died without remedy, but God sent his Son to live among us and to die for us and to preach to us and to instruct us, and if he had stopped at that man would have died without the benefit of his

Savior's death. But he did n't stop there. And now the Holy Ghost comes into the world—the third person of the adorable Trinity, and every good resolution we ever have, and every good that ever inspired us, and every good deed ever done, we owe to the inspiration and influence of the Holy Spirit of God.

Thank God! we have an ever present, omniscient, omnipresent God with us to-night. When I bid wife and children "good-bye" at home, God boards the train with me, and he is with me all the weary miles of my road from home. And then I am conscious God is at home with my family, and when I come into the Christian homes of this city there I find God present, and God is with the missionary in China, and God is with thousands and millions of pulpits on earth. No wonder the blessed Christ said: "It is expedient for you that I go away. I will send the Comforter."

O, brother, sister, hear me to-night. Is there in your soul the desire to be good? Is there a purpose to be good? Is there a resolution to be good? It was born under the touch of the divine Spirit upon these cold, dead hearts of ours. And the Spirit comes to woo. He comes to teach. He comes to implore. For when he shall come he will reprove the world of sin and of righteousness and of judgment to come.

> "Come, Holy Spirit, heavenly Dove,
>   With all thy quickening powers,
> Kindle a flame of sacred love
>   In these cold hearts of ours."

Help us to walk close with God! Help us, divine Spirit, ever to be tender and impressible! Help us ever to hear and heed the Gospel of the Son of God! The divine Spirit broods over the congregation to-night. He touched your heart to-day. He touched your heart last night and day before yesterday. He has touched a thousand hearts or more, and called them to a better life in the last few days in this city. And the most fearful sin that you may commit is to wound the Spirit of God, to drive him out of your heart and drive him away from your presence. The book says: "Grieve not the Holy Spirit of God, whereby ye are sealed unto the day of redemption."

You may laugh at me. You may deride me. You may scoff at the Church. You may defy God and you may crucify my Savior afresh and put him to open shame, but I warn you to-night: take heed how you trifle with the Spirit of all grace! I have seen men reject and insult the divine Spirit, until I could almost hear the Spirit of God as he closed the gates of heaven forever in an immortal spirit's face. My friend, to-night, if there is in your soul the desire to be a Christian, nurse it, foster it, shield it. Keep it there and pray God to fan the spark into a living flame, that shall burn on and on when the stars have gone and when the moon shall turn to blood. Let you and I pray for this, and whatever others may do, God help us to be impressible and movable under the divine Spirit of grace.

"The Spirit says, Come." The third person of

the ever adorable Trinity is the active agency in the world to-day to teach men, to move men, to stir men and use men, and but for his divine presence with me as I preach the Gospel, I declare to you the fact, that I would never have the heart to take another text in this world. O, how many struggles the earnest preacher may have in the world! God only knows the burdens that I have carried on my own poor head since I landed in your city. God only knows the wakeful hours, the tears and the prayers that have gone up from my poor heart, and I say: "God save the city! God arouse the city! God save our young men! God save our young women! God save the fathers and mothers in this city!" And I can almost hear God as he whispers back: "I'll be with you, I'll stand by you." God arouse you! And God help his Church to heed the wooing of the Spirit and come to the help of the Lord, to the help of the Lord against the mighty.

"The Spirit says, Come." Well, if God had stopped at the point—given his Son and sent his Spirit to woo men—we would have died without excuse. But God pushes his work on and on and on, until he shall say to a guilty world: "What more could I have done to my vineyard that I have not already done?" God will never leave a stone unturned, God will never leave an effort unput-forth as long as a man is out of hell and out of the grave. And I tell you, my congregation, to-night, I know God is in earnest about the salvation of man, and I have felt thousands of times that the worst of sinners

would rejoice if they were to see his face. God
help men to look up to-night and see their Father's
face with all the love of his heart as it beams forth,
and hear his voice as he calls them to the better
life. God loves you, and he has given you every
manifestation of his love. He tells you in his
blessed Book: "When my father and my mother
forsake me, then the Lord will take me up."

I have seen a mother as she followed a wayward
boy on, and on, and on, to the very brink of hell,
and when the son made his final leap from his
mother's arms, she took his poor body and buried
it, and would go to his grave and water it with her
tears day after day. O, how that mother's heart
clung to that wayward boy! I have seen the wife
when every friend in the world had forsaken her
husband, and all mankind scoffed him away from
their presence—when he would come home drunken
and debauched and ruined, his precious wife would
meet him at the front gate and help him up the
steps, and help him into the room and carry him
to the bed and pull off his muddy shoes and bathe
his fevered face, and imprint the kiss of love and
fidelity upon his dissipated cheek. O, why did wife
do that? Why does mother do that? It is just a
little of the nature of God poured into that mother's heart and that wife's heart that makes her love
and cling to that son and to that husband as
she does.

The sweetest thought in God's Word to me is
the place where we are taught the motherhood of
God. God is not only my father, but God is my

mother, too, in all his loving kindnesses and tender mercies to us. O, my Father! my Father! with the rod of correction, and with the stern words of advice, I look to thee in admiration and love; and O, God, my precious mother, I run to thy arms! Thou art my mother, I love thee with all my heart.

"And the Spirit says, Come." But God did not stop with that. "The Spirit and the bride say, Come." The Church of God is the bride of the lamb. I wish we were wrapped in white waiting for the Bridegroom. O, how I wish we had always lived, and always been faithful to our Bridegroom! He said, "I go to prepare a place for you." You see that young man yonder. He has plighted his vows to a young lady, and he bids her good-bye for a short time—"I am going West to prepare our fortune and build our house and have every thing ready." Brethren, that young lady instead of being faithful to that earnest, laborious young man preparing good things for her, is flirting with her betrothed husband's enemies, and associating with those that despise her husband. God forgive the unfaithful girl. And while Christ is by his divine power and infinite wisdom exhausting all the riches and glories of heaven preparing for us, his bride, here we are consorting with his enemies and flirting with the gay and giddy godless ones of the world. Precious Savior! forgive us, forgive us! We will not associate with the godless any longer.

"The bride says, Come!" I wish we lived better. But there is one thing I have found out—we know we have been unfaithful; we know we have

not been what we ought to have been. But one
thing I can say and tell the truth—the Church of
God Almighty has not lost her interest in sinners
and in the world. For over one thousand years
the Church has been on her knees and praying for
sinners, and the message of the Church of God is a
God-given message. You have cursed the Church
and abused the Church, and degraded the Church
and called them hypocrites, but do you want to see
whether the Church loves you or not? If the worst
old sinner in this city would come with streaming
eyes and say to the Church of God, "Men and
brethren, pray for me; I want to join your company and go with you to heaven," I see the
Church in a minute, as her tears come flowing
down to the earth and she lifts her hand to God,
and she says, "Blessed be God! Another sinner
repenting and coming to life." The old Church of
God does love the world, and she has been praying
for the world in all its ages; and while we have
forgotten a thousand things and neglected a thousand things, thanks be unto God, we have never
neglected to pray for you, my fellow-citizens. There
is not a day or a night that in the Church of God
her best men and women are not on their knees
praying, "God save the wicked of the city and
save the fallen of humanity;" and the cry of the
Church and the song of the Church is, "Rescue the
perishing and save the fallen."

Thank God for the old Church. She has been
worth all the world to me. I know not I should
have wandered a poor motherless orphan if it

had not been for the Church of Jesus Christ. She has been so good to me. She has been a mother in the best sense! I never joined the Church because I thought I could help it along, but I joined the Church that she might take me, a poor babe, in her arms and nurture me, and feed me, and take care of me; and whatever the Church has been to others, I can say of God's people to-night, they have given me my meat and my drink, and they have been friends and brothers to me.

O, friend, you will never know what you have missed by staying out of the pale of the Church of God, and I beg you to hear the voice of the Church of God as it cries to-night: "Come thou and go with us, and we will do thee good." Won't you come? The Church of God, with her Bibles, and missionaries, and preachers, and consecrated ministry, and good women and men on earth, with her Churches and Sabbath-schools, and her prayer-meetings and family altars—they all cry aloud and say: "Come thou and go with us, and we will do thee good."

"The Spirit and the Bride say, Come." It looks as if, had God stopped there, we should have died without help. It goes further: "And the Spirit and the bride say, Come; and let him that heareth say, Come." O, blessed thought! A man need not wait until he comes into the Church before he says to those around him: "Come thou and go with us. . . . Let him that heareth say, Come."

We get this figure from the caravan crossing the desert. When the water is all given out on the desert, and man and beast are famishing for water, then they hold a counsel, and they start one on ahead, hurriedly, and in about five minutes they start another, just so as to keep him in sound of the front one's voice, and in five minutes more they start another, and on and on, until they are stretched out on the plains for miles, and finally the head man finds the oasis, and he halloes back: "Water, I have found it!" to the next man, and the next man voices it on down the line, and on and on until the caravan hears the cry: "We have found it! Water! Water! We have found it!" And they hear the welcome news, and press on with all their might, that they may slake their thirst, and preserve their lives. And all the way from heaven to earth God has strung out a line, and he shouts it from his own lips in heaven, and we catch it up and pass it on and on until we shout at the very gates of hell: "Come! Come! Come! and let him that heareth say, Come!" If you ever heard the Gospel, preach it to somebody else, and say: "Come on! Let's go and live right, and do right, and get to heaven."

"Let him that heareth say, Come!" Let each man be a power that will echo the call, and on and on down the line. Once one of our little boys ran up a stairway calling his little brother, and as he said: "Buddie Paul!" something up-stairs echoed it back, "Buddie Paul!" He ran down to his mother, and said: "Mamma, what is that up-stairs that said 'Buddie Paul' every time I said 'Buddie Paul?'" and his mother explained it by telling him it was the echo of his voice—the walls of the room above echoing his voice back. And brother, when God shouts from heaven, let every man be the sounding-board that will pass it on and on until this whole universe shall hear the glad word: "Let whosever heareth say, Come; and whosoever will, let him take the water of life freely."

"Let him that heareth say, Come." Why, I have often known men to go to work before the word got to them. They have gone around among their friends, saying: "Boys, look here. We have not done right. Suppose we go to Church, and give our hearts to God, and live religious;" and how many men have been brought to Christ by men who were not religious? When I was in Jackson, Tennessee, I was met by the mayor of the city and other gentlemen, and they said to me: "We were going to your room to see you. We have a friend in this town that we want you to talk to. We want him to be saved." Said I: "Gentlemen, I am glad to find you interested; but, gentlemen, are you Christians, members of the Church?" "No, Mr. Jones, we are sorry we are not. We are not Christians, but we feel an interest in our friend." "Well," said I, "God says that when a kingdom is divided against itself it can not stand. And Satan's kingdom is divided in this very town. His very servants are going to the ministers of God and asking them to go and see their friends." When a man is interested, and says: "Boys, let's do better," that man is not very far from the kingdom of God. He has just put his foot over the line, and all he has got to do is to put it down, and one other step, and he is in the kingdom of God.

"Let him that heareth say, Come." There are five hundred men and women here to-night that are just putting their foot over the dividing line, and all you've got to do is to put that foot down and bring the other foot even with it, and you are in the kingdom of God, a saved man—saved forever and forever. Will you put your foot down to-night and say, " God helping me, I will give myself to God? I won't stand here any longer." "Let him that heareth say, Come."

And then he said, "And let him that is athirst come." Whether you have heard any thing or not, God bless you, the call is to you. If there is down in your soul a thirst, a hunger for a better life, God stands with one hand and touches your heart and makes it hunger and thirst, and then he stands with the other hand loaded with the bread and with the water of life, and he quenches the soul's thirst forever. Blessed be God! He stands ready to quench thirst and to appease hunger to-night, and he is going all over this city with one hand laden with the bread of life, and the other with the water of life, and the hungriest man will be the first man to get it; and I tell you, hungry man, to-night, when God rings the dinner bell of grace, throw down your hearts and come in; dinner is ready to eat; and satisfy your longing needs forever.

"Let him that is athirst come." If down in your soul there is a desire to be a good man, start to-night—start to-night. If there is a hungering for a better life, God says: "Blessed are they that hunger and thirst after righteousness." Then he says again: O, how far down the line God brings this to us. He brings it right down to where he throws heaven and hell at every man's feet, and tells him to take his choice.

Now he says: "Whosoever will, let him take of the water of life freely." I like that grand "whosoever" there. I have read a great deal about election, but I think I have found out from God's Word what you mean by election. The "elect" are the "whosoever-wills," and the "non-elect" are the "whosoever-won'ts." Now, which side will you take—the elect or the whosoever-wills, or the non-elect or the whosoever-won'ts? "Elect," whosoever will. Thank God for that grand old word, and thank God that as the ages wear away, men see God in nature, and see God in all his goodness, and see God in his books. Preachers are coming closer to that grand old word every day, and I verily believe that I shall live to see the day when every pulpit in this world will be bottomed on that grand old "whosoever will," and there they will stand and preach the Gospel of the Son of God.

This reminds me of the penitent down in Georgia at the altar. He was agonizing, praying. The preacher went up to him trying to encourage him, "Well," he said, "I am not one of the elect. I am one of the reprobates; I feel it all over"—and I do n't reckon a poor soul ever did try to seek God that the devil did n't slip up with something of that sort—"You are one of the reprobates; God never died to save you"—and there he was in agony, and the preacher said to him: "Well, my brother, listen to me a minute." "Now," said he, "if you could see your name, 'James B. Green,' written upon the Lamb's book this minute, would you believe then Christ died for you and you were one of the elect?" The poor fellow thought a moment and he said, "No, sir. There are other people in this world of my name." "Well," said the preacher, "if you could see it, 'James B. Green, Scriven County, Ga.,' would you believe it was you then?" "Well," he says, "there may have been other people of my name in this county before I was born. I don't know." "Well," said he, "if you could see it 'James B. Green, Scriven County, Ga.,' and the year '1867,' would you believe it was you?" "Well," he said, "it may be there is somebody in this county now of my name." "Well," said he, "if you could see it 'James B. Green, of Scriven County, and the Nineteenth District, and the year '67,' would you believe it was you?" "Well," he said, "I could not know definitely." "Now," said he, "my friend, God Almighty saw all that trouble, and he just put it into one word, and he said, 'Whosoever will, let him take the water of life freely.' And the poor fellow jumped up and clapped his hands and said, 'Thank God! I know that means me.' "

"And whosoever will, let him take the water of life freely." Blessed be God! It is for all of us. It is for all of us. "Whosoever will." Listen, brother. It isn't "Whosoever feels;" it is n't "Whosoever is fit;" it is n't "Whosoever has repented;" it is n't "Whosoever has got faith;" it is n't "Whosoever does this or that or the other," but it is, "Whosoever will—will— will." God throws it all on the will, and I am glad he does. I know God traverses my emotional nature, and runs through hope and fear and desire and anxiety and dread and affection. God runs all through my emotional nature and my sensibilities. God goes as he pleases through my sensibilities. When God reaches intellect, he goes up through perception and conception and judgment and memory and reason, and all the faculties of the mind. God goes through them all, and asks me no questions. But when God goes to the door of the human will, he stands on tiptoe and knocks and says: "Behold I stand at the door and knock, and if any man will open unto me I will come in and sup with him and he with me." Thank God it is "whosoever will." And I like the conclusion: "Let him take the water of life freely." Blessed be God, ye thirsty men can drink; and there is enough for to-day, enough for all of us, enough forever and evermore. Come and drink freely.

And there is another little word in there I like, that little word "let." "Let him take the water of life freely." Six thousand years ago God said, "Let there be light," and there was light. It was a word of command, and God looks out upon a famishing race with the water of life in reach, and he says, "Let him come;" and when God says, "Let him come," he says, "Go behind him, powers and principalities, and clear the way. Let him take the water of life freely." God has taken down the mountains and filled up the valleys, and made you a straight and even and smooth way, so that you can drink and live forever, and if you perish, you perish because you will not live. God never suffered a soul to be captured and carried away by the enemy of souls, and will never suffer you to die—as long as you look to Christ, or lean to Christ, or pray to Christ. God never suffered the devil to take possession of an immortal soul and drag it down to hell until that soul walked up to the feet of the devil and stacked its arms and said, " I surrender forever." Then God's own power and arm can never rescue you. God help you to-night to say, " God's goodness leadeth me to repentance, and I intend to lead a better life."

SAYINGS.

THE LOST SOUL!—Lost! lost! lost! lost! Brother, can you meet your dying minutes without making your peace with God? If you can, you are a braver man than ever I want to be in time or eternity.

WHEN I was pastor, some fellows would growl because I did n't go to see them. What do I want to go to see you for? The Book tells me to keep out of bad company. I suppose if we would visit our pastor when we are well and let him visit us when we are sick, the world would move along better. Be to him a helpmate, and not a drawback. You ought to cultivate your pastor's acquaintance, because it is likely to be broken up some of these days.

WHAT ARE YOU DOING!—Whenever a man gets up before a community and proclaims his infidelity, then I have just one question to ask another party, and one to ask him. I say: "Infidel, what are you doing in this world?" And the infidel steps up and says: "I'm fighting Christianity; that's what I'm doing." "Christianity, what are you doing?" And Christianity says: "I am rescuing the perishing and saving the fallen; I am building almshouses; I am founding Churches; I am speaking words of cheer to the race; I am lifting up the fallen; I am blessing the world; I am saving men from hell; I am saving them in heaven." Why, infidel, are you fighting alms-houses, and orphans' homes, and Churches, and happy death-beds, and pardon, and peace, and heaven? O, get out of my presence, thou great beast! Don't you tell me you are fighting such things as that! You ask me: "Mr. Jones, what's your business in Chicago?" I answer, It's to throw my arms around every poor lost man, and bring him to peace, and happiness, and heaven. And now, opposers, what is your business? What are you doing?

Sermon XXIII.

"What, then, shall I do when God riseth up? And when he visiteth what shall I answer him?"—JOB XXXI, 14.

ALL gospel-taught men believe that there is a great day in the future of this world's history when God will examine every spiritual fig tree to see if there be figs thereon. We all believe that there is to be a great day in the future when God will call upon every man for usury upon the talent intrusted to his care. In other words, we all believe who lean upon that Book that "God hath appointed a day in the which he will judge the world in righteousness." It is spoken of in the Scripture as the day of the final restitution of all things. It is spoken of as the great day of God's wrath, when the question of all shall be: "Who will be able to stand?" Will you, will I, be able to stand in that great day? To stand then means to stand forever. O, the great day of his wrath—the judgment day—the great day in the future when God shall summon men and angels alike to the great white throne, and when every man shall give account of himself unto God!

Now, some think that the judgment is past, and some think that the judgment is going on now; but I believe the Scripture when it says: "God hath appointed a day in the which he will judge the world in righteousness." It is spoken of in the

471

Scripture as a "day." I do n't think we are, by any means, to understand that God will judge this world in a period of twenty-four hours. This term, "day," is used indiscriminately in Scripture. For instance, it is written our Savior said: "Abraham rejoiced to see my day, and he saw it and was glad." Not any particular twenty-four hours of his life, but the whole thirty-three years of his existence on earth was comprehended in that term, "day." Again, our Savior said to the Jews: "O, that thou hadst known even in this, thy day, the things that belong to thy peace!" Here he referred to no particular twenty-four hours he spent in Jerusalem, or upon the bosom of the Lake of Gennesaret, or on the hills of Jerusalem; but the whole three years of his ministry was embraced in this term, "day." And now "God hath appointed a day in the which he will judge the world in righteousness."

And I dare assert this fact: The issues of that day are eternal. When once God says: "Depart, ye cursed, into everlasting fire!" there will be no after jurisdiction; there will be no revisionary control. When God says "Depart," the sentence is written, and shall sparkle forever upon the tablets of eternity. And the issues being eternal, and there being no after jurisdiction or revisionary control, no higher court to which we can appeal, we say God will not hurry matters on that occasion. God will give every soul ample time and opportunity to bring out all the "pros" and "cons" on that occasion. And of this much I rest assured, that up there it will not be as it is in our courts here. We grow tired of long trials here; we grow tired and hungry and homesick, but up yonder we will be spiritual beings; we'll know nothing of hunger or weariness, and I believe that an aggregated world can stand before God's great white throne a thousand years and listen to the issues being sifted between God and each human soul. God will give every man justice, no matter what time may be necessary to hear all of his case. God will never say to you with final emphasis, "Depart, ye accursed," as long as there is hope of your acquittal.

I may say, again, that I am glad there is such a day in the great future, and I am glad there is such a day appointed. Without such a day as that there would be a great many things in eternity that we never could understand. I have fondled the thought for thirty years that I would meet my precious mother in heaven; but, if I walked the Elysian fields from shore to shore along the banks of the river of life, and I could nowhere find my mother, I would wander through all eternity, and demand, "O, where is my mother, and why is she not here?" But, with a day like this, when the whole universe shall stand before God, and God shall individualize my mother, and she shall press her way out of that multitude and stand alone before God, and all that may be said for and against shall be brought out; if, after a fair investigation and just sentence, God shall say to my mother: "Depart, ye cursed, into everlasting fire!" then I will understand it.

This little company gathered here to-night will

be but a drop in the great ocean that shall be gathered before the great white throne; and when on a day like that, after all the issues have been brought out and all the questions solved and justice done and God says to my mother: "Depart, ye accursed," I shall say "Amen," to my mother's damnation; I will say: "My mother is condemned, but God is just."

Without such a day as this in the great future before us we might meet parties in heaven that would astonish us. We have known many a knotty, gnarly, hard-to-be-understood Christian in this world, and we have thought: "Well, if this man gets to heaven we would be surprised," and without such a day as that if we should meet such a man in heaven we would wonder through all eternity, "how could this man have got there;" but with a day like that before us, when God shall bring this brother before the great white throne and shall strip him of all his idiosyncrasies and shall show us all the pure gold of his character, and shall say to him: "Come ye blessed," a universe will stand around and say "Amen" to this brother's commendation.

There are persons in this world that might fail to meet their faithful preacher in heaven. The Book says: "Many will say to me in that day: Lord, Lord! have we not prophesied in thy name and in thy name cast out devils, and in thy name done many wonderful works, and then will I profess unto them, I never knew you." And if, after roaming through heaven I could never find the

faithful preacher that won me to Christ, I should
wonder, through all eternity, where was the preacher
that was so earnest and brought me to Christ, and
I never could understand it without a day like
this. But when the whole universe shall appear
around the great white throne, and God shall individualize the preacher, and he shall stand before
God alone, and God shall strip him of his hypoc-
risy or his unfaithfulness, and show you what he
was and say to him: "Depart, ye cursed into everlasting fire," we will all say "Amen" to that
preacher's condemnation.

Judgment! Judgment! We will look to the
final judgment. Well, now, with that day squarely
before us, let us antedate that day. Let us see
what it is in all its outlines. Let us imagine this
world already standing before God just as you are
standing before me to-night and God shall individualize a soul, and that soul shall walk out into the
presence of God unprepared for the judgment.
Now the question comes up. What shall I say
when God riseth up in judgment? What shall I
say? Now let us run over this question practically
for a minute or two, and may God impress upon
your consciences this question and these answers:
"What will I do? What will I do?" Well, one
man may answer: "I tell you what I will do. I
shall fly away from the presence of God; I won't
come up to be judged."

Brother, listen! If you take the wings of the
morning and fly into the uttermost parts of the
earth, God is there. If you make your bed in hell,

lo! God is there; and no wonder the man of God in ancient times said: "Whither shall I go from thy presence? Whither shall I fly from thy Spirit?"

There is but one way of getting out of the way of God, and that is to run up to God. I can not get out of the way of justice. What will I do? I am unprepared, and I can not fly justice and get away. Well, what will I do? Will I defy the authority of God and say, "I won't be tried by this court?" Here is the court and here I am a prisoner. Men have sometimes defied the authority of courts on earth, and said: "I won't be tried by this court." But shall I do that up yonder? poor, puny, defenseless worm that I am; shall I defy the great judge of all the earth, who in his omnipotent power laid the flaming mass upon the anvil of his eternal purpose and pounded it with his powerful arm, and every spark that flew from it made a world? Shall I resist such an omnipotent God as that? Why, I can not do that. I can not get out of the way of God. I can not defy him to his face.

What shall I do? Shall I plead "not guilty," with every angel of heaven and the record of earth against me? What will I do? I can not get away. I can not defy God's authority; I can not plead "not guilty." What will I do?

Brother, that is the question which some of these days will wake you up. Mark what I tell you. Mothers, hear me a moment. In my town I saw a mother sit for a solid week in court while her boy was on trial for murder. He was a schoolmate of mine, and they tried him for murder, with his mother sitting pale and anxious a whole week in that Court House. She heard every witness testify, and listened to every word, and at times her lips would quiver, and at times tears ran down her cheeks, and at other times you could almost see her heart literally leap into her mouth. And when the trial was over and the jury had gone out to consider the case, and the court summoned the jury after they had found a verdict, that mother took her seat. And the foreman of the jury walked up with the bill of indictment in his hands and handed it to the clerk. The clerk took the verdict out of his hand and read: "We the jury find the defendant——." And it looked as if the mother would die before the remainder of the verdict could be read; and there, the next word, what will it be? O, that mother's heart is bleeding! What will that verdict be? "We the jury find the defendant——." What? what? what? what? All a mother's life and a mother's heart's blood depends upon what the next word shall be! When it was read: "——Not guilty," this mother jumped up and clapped her hands, and said: "My son shall live."

Mother, these children you are neglecting shall stand before that great tribunal up yonder. You are not interested now. You do not care now. O, mark the expression! The time will come when the interest of your children will wake you up. You will be wide awake some time. Father, you fathers that won't pray and talk with your children, mark you, you may not care to-night, but

you are going to care about these children, and God
help you to say to-night: "Whatever else I 'll do,
I 'll train my children to meet God in peace."
What shall I do when wife and children and myself
shall stand before God? What will I do? What
will I do? O, brother, in that hour your mind
will work rapidly, and all the thought of the universe will be bent upon the question: "What will
I do? What will I do?"

Now I want to say this to you: You can not do
any thing. This is the world for doing, down here,
and that is the world up there for receiving judgment for what you have done. Do you get the
idea? You can not do any thing there, but you
can do something here.

 · What will I say? Suppose some of you were
summoned to judgment to-night, at twelve o'clock,
and went up before God unprepared, what would
you say? Will you say that you never heard a
sermon in your life? Will you say you heard a
thousand, but never understood them? Will you
say that you think that you are as good as half the
people in the Church? Will you say that you
never saw any necessity of giving your heart to God
and becoming religious? Will you say that the
reason you did not try to do right was because
about half the people in the Church were hypocrites? What will you say?

I once approached a man—he was a sensible
man—and I said to him: "Hear me! I want you
to join the Church to-night, and give your heart to
God." He said: "I can not do it." I then said:

" I 'll tell you what I 'll do. If you 'll go home to-
night and sit down and write out a reason why
you won't, that you think will stand the final judgment, then I will never mention it to you again."
The next day I met that man, and he said: " Jones,
what you said to me impressed me very deeply.
Talk about writing out a reason that will do up
yonder! It can't be done." And friends, you
may have a thousand reasons here, but if not one of
them will stand the test, you had better not risk
your soul on them. I tell you, every man of you,
to-night, if you have no reason that you think will
answer at the judgment bar, you had better surrender to-night, for your little talk that you make
down here is not going to be worth a cent there.
I do not expect that any man will say up yonder
that he does not believe there is a God, or that he
does not believe there is any thing in religion, or
that he had n't heard a Gospel sermon to suit him,
or that there was no Church to suit him, I wonder what people will say who go to the judgment unprepared. What will they say? O, wonder
of wonders! What will they say? I have thrown
away all my time, and I have thrown away all my
privilege, and I stand before God condemned to-
night! What will I say? What will I say?

Now, I might go on at length here, and call up
the reasons that you may give; but, brethren, if
you ask me what I am going to do at the final day,
I am going to say to the Judge of all the earth:
" I have nothing to do but stand and trust in the
blessed Savior, just as I stood and trusted in yonder

world with him;" and, if you will ask me what I am going to say, I will tell you it will be about this:

> "Jesus, lover of my soul,
>   Let me to thy bosom fly;
> While the nearer waters roll,
>   While the tempest still is high!
> Other refuge have I none;
>   Hangs my helpless soul on thee;
> Leave, O leave me not alone,
>   Still support and comfort me!"

O, blessed Christ, help us to do to-night just what we will wish we had all done when we stand at thy judgment seat! Help us to say to-night just what we can say up yonder, and God will help us and bless us because we do say it.

Fathers, listen! Do not go another step wrong. Mothers, come to God to-night! Sons and daughters, let us live for the final judgment day, when God shall call us into account for our lives and actions in this world below, and then we will be prepared.

If I can get by that day safely I am safe forever; but, O God, help me to live in reference to that day, in every word of my mouth, by every act of my life, by every thing that I do! God help me to live in reference to that final day when I shall stand before him. As I stand before this great multitude, you and I will have to stand up yonder, and I trust that no man that ever heard me preach the Gospel will ever hear God say to me: "Depart, ye cursed, into everlasting fire."

I am going to do my best to live up to what I preach, and shun the evils I denounce. I intend to try to live a pure and upright life, and trust in Jesus Christ, and I know that, if religion is a sham and the Bible a fable, I have the best that this world can give. Call me a fool for believing it, but, thank God, I am a happy fool—I am a happy fool! And if it turns out to be true, my friends, you will be miserable philosophers in eternity forever. God help us to decide to-night that religion is the best thing on earth, and that heaven itself can give us nothing better than religion. And, if this is true, let us have it in time, and have it in eternity, and have it forever.

God bless you all and save you all! I wish I had strength to talk to you longer, and you were comfortable, so you could hear it. I might say many things on this text, but I want to say this, and let it be my parting words: As a poor sinner fourteen years ago saved by the cross, it was the language of my heart then, and when I would get to heaven the language of my heart shall still be: "Worthy is the lamb that was slain to receive all honor, and riches, and power, and dominion, forever and ever."

God bless you all, and God keep you all, and God save you all.

———•———

SAYINGS.

THE thing that keeps me from buying God and doing his works is the price that a man puts on his soul. That is the thing he is selling it for. Whatever keeps us from being baptized with the Holy

41

Ghost, and with power to do his bidding—I do n't care what that is—that is the price we have not only put upon our own soul, but upon every soul that comes under the radius of our influence.

A Revival Wanted.—We want in this town a revival of unity. We want all of your denominations to step into line together. And I tell you, my brethren, we want a revival of earnestness. We want a revival of mercy. We want a revival of charitableness, and we want a revival of that brotherhood that God blesses among men. O, for a revival that shall be as broad as the universe, as high as the shoulders of God, and as deep as human depravity. And when we get that opened upon this city we are going to have a salvation stream that shall flow like a river, and shall cleanse this city. Let us have this kind of a revival, and lay aside all small questions of denominational pride. Let us have a revival like that, and the revival will not pause here in Chicago, but it will spread from our own city. It will go across this river like the great fire which went along in its course as if it did not know that there was any river at all in this town. Let this revival be like that fire. Let it be such that it will pass over rivers as if there were no rivers, and blend all the divisions of Chicago into one Chicago, and God Almighty shall reign in this town.

SAM W. SMALL

DELIVERANCE FROM BONDAGE.

A Temperance Sermon

BY

SAMUEL W. SMALL.

I HOPE you will give me your prayerful attention to-night. What I shall say shall be based
on the sixteenth verse of the third chapter of Acts:
" And his name, through faith in his name, hath
made this man strong, whom ye see and know; yea,
the faith which is by him hath given him this perfect soundness in the presence of you all."

On one occasion there came into the market-
place of a far Eastern city an aged, decrepit, and
travel-stained man, who was a stranger to them all.
He wandered through the vast bazaar without seeming to regard or take notice of the vast stores of
merchandise, wealth, and accumulated wondrous
handicraft of the people. Aimlessly he threaded
his way about in that multitude until he attracted
the attention of the people. Suddenly he stopped
before one of the booths, where hung gilded cages,
in which had been imprisoned birds of precious
plumage and sweetest song. They were fluttering
their little wings against the bars of their prison,
and he listened intently that he might haply catch
some note of their song; but they, thus imprisoned,
refused to give forth any of the melody of their

483

throats, but struggled and struggled impatiently and ineffectually against their imprisonment.

Suddenly the old man put his hands in the folds of his garment, and drew therefrom coin of a strange realm. He asked the price of a cage. He bought it, and, opening the door, he turned the feathered songster loose, and it fluttered its wings, so long untried, and for a little while balanced its slight body in mid-air, until nature restored its powers of equilibrium, and then it mounted up, and up, and up, and with a glad song of joy circled above the heads of the multitude, until it caught sight of the distant cloud-capped mountain, where its home had been, and then, with its precious melody flowing from its soul, it winged its way into the far and ethereal distance, and was lost to sight. Thus one by one he bought these little birds, and thus one by one he loosed them, and they repeated the glad notes of surprise, and took the same course back to their native mountain fastnesses. He seemed to take a greater pleasure and a sweeter joy as each little prisoner regained its liberty, and the tears streamed down his travel-stained and dust-covered face.

Those who stood by said to him, " Why dost thou do these strange things?" He said to them in reply, with a look of charity and joy indescribable on his face, " I was once a prisoner myself, and I know something of the sweets of liberty."

I, brethren, was once a prisoner myself, and now I have tasted something of the sweets of liberty in Christ, and with the precious coinage òf his mercies and his promises I would stand before this multitude to-night and purchase from the willing hearts of men the liberty of their souls from a bondage more despicable and deadly, and more repressive of the natural melody of men's souls, than were these gilded cages to the birds of this far Eastern mart.

I have been under the bondage of sin, a bondage that was galling every moment almost; a bondage from which there was eliminated every element of joy, and from which there seemed to be at times no avenue of escape.

If you will pardon me, I will refer to myself. I will tell you something of my experience, because I would have my young compatriots know it, and know it to the good of their souls. I would have my fellow-men who are in middle life, with families, hear it. I would have these veteran fathers of this community hear it.

I was well born. I was given by kindly parents all the true and the religious culture that a boy could have in a loving home. I was instructed in right speaking; I was encouraged in right doing; I was inspirited at times to consider myself a child of God, and to recognize in my youth my responsibility to him.

And when I had left my mother's side, and had left my father's counsel, and left the old hearth tree and the family altar, and gone out into the avenues of the world, seeking, first, an education, and afterward position and prosperity, I fell into evil ways. With the strong and lusty passions of youth, with

those whom I mingled I found there were courses
and ways, there were allurements and temptations,
that were strange to me ; and I stood reliant only
upon myself, forgetting the prayers and teachings
of mother and father, and I was eager for a place,
eager for the pleasures of this world, eager for the
happiness and the enjoyments that I saw about me.
And thus I easily fell in allurements, thus easily
fell from virtuous thoughts and virtuous acts, and
from the virtuous course of my life.

The great bane, as I look back over my life, and
conjure up the recollections of my past—the great
bane of all my sinfulness, the great moving cause
of all the moral iniquities I committed—was nothing
more nor less than this great gorgon-headed evil
that is devouring so many of the people of this land,
and sowing broadcast sin and sorrow in this chosen
nation of ours—the sin of intemperance.

I thought that it would be manly to do as nearly
every man I saw about me did. I thought there
would be some addition to my pleasure and experience by going with them into their drinking places
and indulging with them. I felt all the time that
I had strength of will enough, that I had force of
character enough, to protect me from the excesses
that I could see other men had fallen into. I believed
that when I reached a dangerous point, if I ever
did, I could put on the brakes of my nature and stop.

I went away to college, and there again fell into
evil courses. I struggled at times with the innate
manhood that was in me, and attempted to throw
off the growing appetite for these things. When I

came away, after I had graduated, and began to enter among men and their pursuits, and endeavored to acquire a profession, I thought still that I must mingle with my fellow-men ; have some participations in their customs and in their habits ; that I must bring myself into some sort of agreement and harmony with their ideas of social enjoyments, and I yielded again and again to the temptations thus presented, and again and again I fell from my rectitude, and away from ideas that lingered with me of what was right and proper. And thus, day after day, these passions grew stronger and stronger within me.

I could feel and see that I was falling, falling, falling all the time. I saw that there would not be left in me strength enough to save me, and I was unconscious at times of the fearful length to which I had fallen ; but I would not look at the picture I knew I was presenting to others. I went on and on. I went until I brought tears from the eyes of my precious mother, until I brought fearful lines to her face, until I brought gray streaks into her beautiful hair, until I had brought the lines of care about her loving eyes ; and until I knew I was dragging, drop by drop the life-blood from her devoted heart. I knew that my strong and manly father was suffering on my account tortures that he would not, in his courage, let the world know were gnawing at his heart and at his soul.

I knew how it went out to me ; how it followed me abroad in other lands, and I knew that the failing of his step, and the silvering of his hair, and the deepening of the lines of grief about his mouth, that had so often spoken golden words of counsel, were due to the course and ways into which I had fallen, and to the apparent hopelessness of my ever coming out of them, and being reformed and being renewed in mind and in body.

O, I shall never feel satisfied short of the ability in heaven to make obeisance at their feet and crave their pardon, which I know has long since been granted me, and which I shall ever see beam on their angelic faces until I am in my grave.

I married a lovable woman. I married one who was proud of disposition; one who had high and noble traits of character; one who had quick and responsive sensibilities; one to whom the very taint of any thing that was disreputable was like a knife-stab to her heart; but I disregarded the love and devotion of that precious wife. I went on and on, unheeding her counsel, disregarding her prayers, and from day to day getting grosser and grosser in my appetites, and getting more brutal in my insensibility to her pleadings and her prayers. And when children came to bless my home, even the sight of them in their little cradles, unconscious in the first moments of their life, and with the smiles of God drawing responsive smiles from them, I found it impossible for me to know that I was doing that which would sooner or later bring shame and sorrow and degradation upon those innocent babes; and as they grew from year to year their voices came, and they prattled about me; it was only at distant intervals that I began to regard the future that was stretching far off in the distance before them, and which I must make either one of peace and pleasure, or one of despair and wretchedness.

And year after year I went on and on in this course of sin and wickedness, and the light of my home went out. The love of my wife gave way, but the process of murder of affection could not last forever; and I saw at last, it seemed to me, that she had returned it to the sepulcher in which she had laid it away in its tear-bedewed cerements forever. I could see that the love and affection of my children were turning from me daily, seemingly by intuition. They saw I was not he who was appointed to be their father in the manifestations of fatherhood that I made to them. I could know, and know with a treble emphasis, that drove unutterable horrors into my soul, but it seemed only to drive me further and further into despair, that they would, at my coming, flee from my presence far away into the darkest and remotest parts of the house, for fear of the consequences of meeting their father.

I had friends, friends in position, friends high in authority, friends who were true and steadfast to me; but they, too, were unable to paint to me any picture that would allure me from the one I was painting with my own hand in the horrible colors of hell itself. They would point me to a goal that my bleared and confused vision would not see. They would endeavor to lift me up on plains of hope and sensibilities of ambition that I had ceased to be sensible of, as being worthy of achievement.

They would endeavor to control my appetite, and find it as useless as to bind with a cotton-woven string the raging lion of the arid and tempest-swept desert.

I had at times my lucid intervals, when there would come memories of mother's prayer, of father's counsel, of wife's tears, and of children's mute and helpless look; and I would say to myself, "I will summon to my aid all the powers of my soul and manhood, and I will put under foot this monster of hideous mien that is dragging me down into degradation, into social ruin, and taking a fast hold upon my soul, and which sooner or later will drag it a trophy into hell. I would summon all my powers, only to find that I was weaker than a babe in the arms of so strong a passion as I had awakened.

I would go to physicians, and ask them in the name of my family and future to do something for me, if indeed there had been found medicines on earth to minister to a mind diseased and an appetite debauched, and they would exhaust their knowledge and their skill, and hundreds and thousands of dollars did I spend in the endeavor to reinforce will, manhood, and my own powers of repression, but all in vain.

There were antidotes that were published abroad in the world, and with the use of which cures are guaranteed, but all, all in vain. I spent hundreds and thousands of dollars, and hours and days of time, and I purchased advertised efficient and warranted cures for drunkenness, and I was as faithful in the application of them as ever human being was; but it was all in vain! in vain!! in vain!!!

There was no medicament in them to cure my aroused passion and appetite.

I went so far that my wife, under the laws then existing in Georgia, had written by the judge of the court in which I was the official short-hand reporter, a legal notice, couched in the language of the law, and had this notice served upon every dealer in liquors in the city of Atlanta, warning them, under penalty of the law, not to let me have their damning fluid over their counters; and yet, outlaws as they were, disregarding my interest, disregarding my wife's pleadings and the tears of my children, and disregarding the very law of the land, they still continued to supply me with the horrible draught for which my inmost nature seemed craving with insatiety.

I even employed attendants and detectives, who followed me as I went about on my business in the streets of my city, and they followed me with the purpose, and were employed for the purpose, of keeping these men who would not keep the law themselves from furnishing me with whisky; and yet I, in conjunction with them, was able to hoodwink and defy detectives and law.

Further and further, deeper and deeper, I was sinking; I was getting hopeless for business; hopeless for all social standing; hopeless for all the temporal interests of this world; hopeless for eternity; and, in the very madness of my disordered brain, and in my very soul, there seemed at times no avenue of escape at all from this self-imposed bondage, except through insanity on the one hand, and through suicide on the other.

I saw that my wife and children had given up all hope ; they did not know, from day to day, how I would come home to them. They had seen me brought there, day after day, time after time, insensible and unable to recognize them, from the influence of this deadly and poisonous drug. They had seen me when I was brought in and laid on my bed covered with blood, and it seemed as though my days were indeed numbered, and that I would soon fall in the midst of my iniquity. They had seen me when I was brought home with the wounds of the knife and pistol on my body, and they had heard the rumors from the streets and dives of the dangers with which I had been constantly surrounded of late. To them it seemed as though there was no avenue, no loophole, of escape for me from a terrible death. There was not the sign of hope or spirit beaming out from their beautiful faces. They knew not, from day to day, whether I would live to greet them another day. They knew not whether, if my life was prolonged, they would be able to procure the very necessities of life from day to day.

They knew not at what hour the very shelter that shielded them from the storm and from the heat would be removed from over their head, and they removed from under its shelter. There were visions of uncertainty, of the sheriff to dispossess, of the heartless landlord to distrain for rent, of the debtor to come and take all. There was no future ahead of them, except a future of impenetrable gloom, through which seemed to come nothing but warnings of deeper woe and agonies yet to come. O, Lord, how good thou wast to me! thou hast given me relief from that bondage at my seeking.

At last there came a time when I seemed to have reached the limit. Something strange impelled me to take my little children, as a loving act, an act, it seemed to me, of reparation for neglects of weeks preceding, and go upon the train to Cartersville, where Brother Jones was preaching to immense audiences, and from which the report had come that there were many and many hundreds, and even thousands, who were coming back into harmony with God. And as I sat upon the platform, endeavoring to take in stenography the words as they fell from his lips, it seemed to me that God had inspired him to preach upon one certain line. He preached it with that faith which is his alone; he preached it with that fidelity which is his distinguishing characteristic; he preached with the earnestness and with the conviction that broke down the casements of my heart and went home to it. When he had finished those words of Conscience! Conscience! Conscience! and of Record! Record! Record! of God, the infinite, the all-seeing and the ever-judging God, came home to me.

I went away from there troubled in mind and soul. I went home, and back into the devious ways, back into the bar-room, back into the open highways, back to the maddening pool, in order to get away from the torments I was suffering from an awakened conscience. But they would not leave me. I could find no solace where I had often found insensibility. I could find no relief in potations where I had often found. indifference and capability to take on a cool exterior. There was nothing there to give me surcease from the sorrow in my bosom; and I went on and on until the second day, on Tuesday, at noon, I went into my library-room, fell upon my knees, buried my face in my hands, and I pleaded with Christ that he would let me cling to his cross, lay down all my burdens and sins there, and be rescued and saved by his compassion; that I might be washed in his blood, and that my sins, though they were scarlet, might be white as snow.

I wrestled for four long hours, in as much agony as I ever suffered. At the end of that time, when I had reached a conclusion, when I had come to understand that there was nothing of earth that could avail me, least of all with Christ, then I gave myself entirely to him, made an unconditional surrender, and that moment he seized my soul. He dipped it in the stream which was white and pure, and the light of heaven shone in upon me.

In my new-found joy, I rushed into the presence ot wife and children. I proclaimed the glad tidings to their astonished ears, and they could hardly believe it, though they saw that some great revolution had taken place. They knew not whether it was a surrender to Christ, or whether it had been a surrender to madness.

But when I went out that evening, I had three thousand circulars printed and distributed all over Atlanta, telling the people I had found my Savior; I had made peace with God, and that I would live a life of righteousness ever after, and desired to make a proclamation for once and irrevocable. They gathered at seven o'clock upon the public streets that night, and there before them I proclaimed the fact, and, blessed be God, I have been proclaiming it ever since with increased joy, and with the certainty that my salvation is complete.

Returning home, I could see that Jesus had knocked at the tomb of my wife's life, as it did at that of Lazarus, and had called it forth in all its pristine strength and beauty, and its bloom and blossom has been my pathway ever since. I could see that my children had found tongue to sing the joy and praise, and their hearts had been set attuned, as they never had been before, to the melody of childhood, singing to the ears of fatherhood. I could see that there was gladness, wherever I went, upon the faces of friends and acquaintances; and, when the news had gone abroad in the land, they who had known me abroad sent me their glad congratulations and their encouragement.

Blessed be God that, from the day he reached down and lifted me up from the horrible pit and the miry clay, and established my feet upon the rock of Christ that is higher than we, I have been going on from joy to joy, a bird of liberty, singing the praises of my Redeemer.

And so, having been thus saved and thus healed,

I would call you who are in that terrible bondage to seek relief of the same great Physician, and to draw your medicine from the same infallible spring.

What are we doing with ourselves? O, how, when we look abroad in this land, we can see how intemperance is becoming the great national vice, and how it is becoming the fell destroyer of so many thousands and thousands of our loved ones. What are we doing with these bodies of ours? "What, know ye not that your body is the temple of the Holy Ghost which is in you, which ye have of God, and ye are not your own?" Fellow-men, fellow-men, let me bring you to the contemplation of the fact that these bodies of ours are the temples of the Holy Ghost, and that they were fashioned after the architecture of his great brains, by the great Being who is the architect of the universe.

These bodies he made of the dust of the earth, and these bones of his rock; he made us with veins and with arteries, and filled them with the blood from the seas of his providence; he gave us breath, which, like the wind, cometh and goeth and scattereth; which cometh we know not whence, goeth we know not where; he gave us sight for all the beauties and grandeurs of the world, and inflamed it with fire from the center of his storehouse of fire; he gave us thoughts, like the clouds, for, like them, they move, and as they play in the sunlight of righteousness, are transformed into beauty, whether it be the beauty of the dawn, presaging what is to come, or the beauty of the sunset, presaging the glorious death toward which we tend.

And we can make these minds of ours reflect the light of heaven, or they can have the light of heaven withdrawn, and be dark and dismal and foreboding as the storm-clouds, from which the mutterings of heaven come and roll the thunders of agony that spread destruction and death upon us. And in these temples he has placed the Holy Ghost in spirit for us, and we are its custodians, the priests of these temples; and when we degrade and defile them, we are degrading and defiling the architecture of God and his chosen resting-place in us.

O, what a touching instance it was when the favorite son of Tertullian died! His companions were bearing his corpse to the cemetery upon their shoulders, and as they went along, occupied with their thoughts of sorrow and grief, they stumbled by the way, when the grief-stricken father, noticing it, called out to them: "Young men, beware how you walk; you bear upon your shoulders the temple of the Holy Ghost."

So with us. We go about bearing with us the temple of the Holy Ghost, and we are recreant to our own creation, recreant to our own destiny, recreant to the great God who fashioned us, recreant to the great God who made us his temples, when we defile these bodies of ours, and ruin them with the licenses of our baser natures and our depraved appetites.

One time Diogenes saw a young man going to a place of revelry, where drinking was the custom, and from which men who went in sober and rational beings emerged besotted, and not knowing their way. He seized upon the young man, carried him to his friends, and informed them that he had rescued their precious boy from a great and awful danger. So it would be well if we had friends who would thus rescue us. But there are times when friends, as I told you, can have no influence, and no Diogenes, however wise, however honest, however mindful of his neighbor, could restrain us from going into these places.

But how many Diogeneses it would take to seize upon those that night after night and day after day are going into these places of danger and ultimate death in the city of Cincinnati! O, let us seek to save ourselves through the only influence, the only medicament, and the only Physician that this universe affords us!

What is intemperance doing? It is not necessary to marshal here before you the figures; you can see it all about you.

Young man, you know that you started in your intemperate habits just as I did. You know what influences have led you; you know what ambitions you thought you could cultivate by listening to them; you know how you have run out and gone into these places with like ideas of strength and ability to control yourselves just as I had. And now you are buoyant in the consciousness that you think that at any time you can slap on the brakes of your nature, and save yourselves from degradation that you see upon the planes just below us.

Beware, beware of that fatal cup. There are fathers, middle-aged; they know what intemperance will do. They are listening to me to-night, and they started on that road just as I started; but if they have not reached the same length to which I went, they are on the high road to it. They can already know that they are not received where once they were welcome guests; they know that they are passed every day on the streets of Cincinnati by men who formerly regarded them with esteem and claimed them as friends. They know that avenues were once open to them of usefulness, and which are now closed upon them forever on account of their habits, their companionship, and their places of resort. They know that the happiness of their families, once complete, is now gone, apparently forever. They know that the blanched cheek of that wife, that the constant redness of eye when they enter home, that the fleeing children, are all evidences of the steady growth of the evil; and they have grown just in proportion as they have gone deeper and deeper into this besotted condition.

There are old men here to-night who have led a long life, it seemed, of moderation, and who thought that they were exemplifying the ability of a man to drink and drink and drink, and yet preserve his manhood and his honest position; but they can see that their excesses are not only sapping the foundations of their health; they can feel that they are untimely gray; they can feel that they have diseases in them that they would not have had but for their intemperance; and they can see before them no life that

is leading them on and brightening their way as
they go. But they are seeing, upon the other hand—
and if they are honest with themselves, they will
confess it to their souls—that they are losing the
powers, and that sooner or later they, too, must
sink into the lowest depths of degradation, and be
untimely cut off, and go to hell to everlasting death.

Families and individuals — cities — prostrated.
There is nothing that is so glaring about them as
intemperance, which sweeps over them like the
storm over a forest, day after day and night after
night. Thank God that my city of Atlanta has
redeemed herself under the white banner of temperance, with the cross of Christ on it! Thank God,
she will shine as a city set upon a hill, giving a
light to this nation! Ohio to-day is giving full
liberty to the whisky dealers to debauch and damn
the most precious sons of your loins and your household.

God can not bless a people who are thus recreant to themselves and thus recreant to their duties,
both to humanity and to God. Thank God that
old Georgia is rapidly redeeming herself, and that
after a while she will still be lying in the very
apron of this nation, a redeemed State from the tyr-
any of alcohol, and that she will raise her banner
and commend it in its purity to every State in this
nation, as it blazons with the legend of Wisdom,
Justice, and Moderation, under the broad and glittering arch of the Constitution.

Nearly twenty-five years ago misguided men in
the South fired the first shot upon Fort Sumter that

awakened this entire nation, and led to reform, and led to liberties, and led to the release of slaves from bondage, led to what no man had contemplated as being capable of realization. It marshaled the most impregnable arms of this continent, and that shot reverberated all through civilization. I tell you that whatever were the disasters of war, it struck the shackles from six million slaves; but to-day, in a holier and grander cause, by the approving smile of God, old Georgia has fired a gun upon the Sumters of sin and intemperance in this country that will arouse this whole nation; and we will batter down these forts of intemperance, whether they are in Cincinnati, Chicago, or New York.

The army of God in this nation is on the march. And you may listen here; and if you have not the courage and the Christian zeal, we will come and break down the barriers; we will pound down the forts of the demon of alcohol, and we will release you from this terrible bondage.

In the midst of influences like this, with these facts staring them in the face, statesmen of this country are too cowardly to seize upon this great question, and make it a question of public policy for the Christian people. Politicians go wandering about among the lower classes, and talk and rant about personal liberty and sumptuary laws, as though they had a right to give laws to these people, when these smiling scoundrels are only seeking popularity and applause from the foolish and depraved.

Scientists are disputing and debating, when all history and all true science have demonstrated that no curse is greater upon a people than to have the saloons and the dissemination of these deadly compounds in the community. These whisky dealers are outlaws; they are against the law; they are anomalous creatures, and the anarchists of the nineteenth century. If they would disobey and disregard the laws in my case, they will do it in yours, and they will do it in the case of every precious son you have got, of every living father you have got, of every devoted husband you have got in this country.

Churches meet in conventions, meet in conferences, meet in assemblies, meet in synods, and pass resolutions on the subject of temperance, and yet the very ministers, it seems, in places, are unwilling to enforce the declarations and laws of their own Churches against their own members, notwithstanding that right here in Cincinnati ministers of the Gospel have been disrobed through its influences, and Churches have been debauched.

And thus our very rulers, law-makers, public men, and public teachers are thus indifferent or cowardly in the face of an evil like that, while the red-winged and fiery-eyed Zamael of these distillers and brewers of the country is sweeping over this land and laying low in horrible death the first-born of American homes, as the angel did at the command of God in the land of Pharaoh centuries ago. And every man and every woman, especially in America, has a direct personal interest in seeing the banner of Christ triumph over the sign of the beer barrel and the whisky worm.

Is there any thing needed to arouse the humanity and the patriotism of you people to the iniquities that are being thus committed in your midst, and the sad havoc that is being made in your homes? If I to-night were to call around me a staff of bailiffs and furnish them with subpœnas, I could send them into the streets, and into the back-yards, and into the slums and alleys and tenement districts of Cincinnati, and I could send to Walnut Hills, and to Mount Auburn, and Avondale, and Mount Adams, and other of your respectable and high-toned suburbs of Cincinnati, and from the palaces of your richest down to the humblest huts and dens of your poorest, and examine the widows and the orphans that whisky has made, and array them here in grand mass by the thousands, with their weeping eyes, with their dismal recollection, with their mourning, with their hearts crushed and bleeding, and they would say to you, "If you are men, in the name of God and humanity, rise in your might and drive this monster out before he destroys and ruins your homes too."

If we but heed these witnesses, and are true to ourselves, to our children, to humanity, and to God, we can destroy this flaming monster, and soon be able to sing out to men and angels that our people are redeemed, regenerated, and disenthralled from the fatal powers of the dragon. Then we will be blessed by our Father in heaven with a posterity given to paths of righteousness and lives of Christian endeavor and achievement.

Our sons shall grow up in strength and honor,

and wear the Christian armor. Their feet will be
shod with the preparation of the Gospel, their loins
be girded about with truth, their bodies guarded by
the breast-plate of faith, their shield be righteousness, their manly, sun-lit brows be crowned with
the helmet of salvation, and their good right arms
will wield the trenchant, victorious sword of the
Spirit, which is the Word of God.

Our daughters will grow up in beauty and come-
liness of Christian graces. Their feet will be san-
daled with truth and faith; their limbs be clothed
with robes of purity, on which, in silver and gold
and prismatic hues, will be embroidered the record
of their good deeds; their waists will be encircled with
the golden girdle of strengthening prayer; their
bosoms shielded by the bodice of innocence covering the virtuous heart, on which burn vestal fires
of love; from their shoulders will drop the mantle
of humility, and their hands will dispense the
golden showers of charity upon the one side and of
mercy upon the other; their throats will be wrapped
with the pearls of precious words; their lips will
give forth sweet songs of praise to God; their eyes
will ever turn in trust to the great white throne,
whose radiance will glint in the folds of their
tresses, and presage the crown of immortal life that
shall press their brows in Paradise.

And these two shall dwell in the splendors and
happiness of the palace of purity, that rears its
walls and dome around and over every true and
consecrated Christian heart. They will go up to it
over the broad white flag-stones of perfect desires;

they will climb up its great steps of geometrically and systematically fashioned purposes and ambitions; they will pass between the grand columns of strength and wisdom that stand before the Gate Beautiful, with its golden welcome, "All that is pure may enter in;" and in the hall of consecration they will put on the insignia of their heaven-given prerogatives, and pass on into the rotunda of a righteous life, and up into the throne-seats of honor in the East. From that exalted place, they may contemplate with rapture the idealized tableaux of the virtues of their lives. Here the picture of Truth—a fair maiden drawing from her exhaustless well the waters of sincerity that are poured out for the ennobling and refreshing of all people, and over her the glittering legend: "*Magna est Veritas et prevalebit.*" There is the tableau of Faith, clinging to the rock-rooted cross that towers heavenward, and around which the wild waves of worldliness, woe, and passion surge unavailing, their highest spray not touching even the hem of her garments.

Yonder is seen the fair form of Virtue, her beautiful feet standing amid the treasures of the upturned cornucopia of fortune, her hands folded in peacefulness across her lovely bosom, and her golden hair blown into a halo about her head by the breezes that are born in the hills of happiness. Here again is figured the faultless goddess of Justice, standing upon the uppermost pole of the earth, holding the scales of God's earthly impartiality, and weighing out the dues of men in harmony with eternal truth. Over her the constellations

43

gather and glitter in the edict of Jehovah: *"Fiat justitia, ruat cœlum!"* There again is the sweet face of Charity, swift-paced to carry succor and life to the hovel of the poor, the cots of the sick and cells of the wretched. And next comes the picture of gentle and tender-hearted Mercy, soothing the cares, relieving the burdens, reconciling the hearts, and ministering to the redemption of all the souls of God's children. And here is the grand portrait of the strong, manly apostle of Temperance, the embodiment of health, vigor, energy, and philanthropy; a giant in all good works, and approved servant of heaven.

Over in the West is the grand horologe of Time, counting out the moments of life in a monotone pæan of patience and labor, while its great pendulum swings through an arc that reaches from the cradle to the tomb.

In the center is the Christian's altar, on which praises and prayers turn to worshiping incense and pervade the place with heavenly odors.

Up in the high center of the vast dome blazes the Sun of righteousness, that lightens forever the splendid scene. Looking into it, the eye of faith, strengthened like the young eaglet's, can discern the transfigured cross of Calvary, pointing the soul to its home and rest around the throne of God in heaven.

Who are these that thus reign and rejoice? They are the Prince Christian and Princess Christiana of the kingdom of God on earth. They are the heirs apparent to everlasting life and the imperishable possessions of the King of kings! God direct us with his wisdom to so live and use our lives as to endow our children with these titles and these palaces of purity on earth—these inheritances of the meek, and pure, and temperate, and dutiful, in "the city whose builder and maker is God."

THE END.

CPSIA information can be obtained
at www.ICGtesting.com
Printed in the USA
LVHW081017100219
607023LV00010B/265/P

9 780266 800774